AF606036

Approaches to Teaching the Works of François Rabelais

Approaches to Teaching World Literature

For a complete listing of titles,
see the last pages of this book.

Approaches to Teaching the Works of François Rabelais

Edited by

Todd W. Reeser

and

Floyd Gray

The Modern Language Association of America
New York 2011

Library of Congress Cataloging-in-Publication Data

Approaches to teaching the works of François Rabelais /
edited by Todd W. Reeser and Floyd Gray.
p. cm. — (Approaches to teaching world literature ; 116)
Includes bibliographical references and index.
ISBN 978-1-60329-097-5 (hardcover : alk. paper) —
ISBN 978-1-60329-098-2 (pbk. : alk. paper)
1. Rabelais, François, ca. 1490-1553? — Study and teaching.
2. Rabelais, François, ca. 1490-1553? — Criticism and interpretation.
I. Reeser, Todd W., 1967– II. Gray, Floyd, 1926–
PQ1694.A77 2011
843'.3–dc22 2011010178

Approaches to Teaching World Literature 116
ISSN 1059-1133

Published by The Modern Language Association of America
26 Broadway, New York, New York 10004-1789
www.mla.org

CONTENTS

ACKNOWLEDGMENTS

We thank the outstanding group of teachers and scholars of Rabelais for their involvement with this project. Creating a community of written texts around Rabelais has been a true pleasure. We thank Alison Halasz and the Humanities Center at the University of Pittsburgh. We also thank the MLA Publications Committee for accepting this project and for carrying it through to completion.

PREFACE

There can be no doubt that François Rabelais (1494?–1553?) is one of the most widely read and influential writers of world literature. Embodying the enthusiasm and exuberance inherent in the expression of the Renaissance spirit of adventure and discovery, his work is crucial to the development of early modern prose and, more particularly, to the birth of the novel. As satirist and parodist, he deals with nearly all the major cultural and intellectual issues of the day with elegance and wit. Thus *Gargantua* (1534), *Pantagruel* (1532), the *Tiers livre* (*Third Book* [1546]), and the *Quart livre* (*Fourth Book* [1552]) are excellent pedagogical tools for understanding not only "high" and "low" Renaissance topics but also issues of direct interest to students today, such as alterity, gender, sexuality, feminism, embodiment, humor, nationhood, politics, religion, and war.

The MLA surveys we have conducted, coupled with frequent conversations with colleagues in a number of colleges and universities, have overwhelmingly confirmed that a volume on teaching Rabelais will provide an indispensable aid both for first-time and for more experienced teachers of the author. Because *Gargantua* and *Pantagruel* are by far the two books most commonly studied in undergraduate curricula, this volume deals especially with them, but also discussed are the problems inherent in the presentation of *The Third Book* and *The Fourth Book*. Given its probable status as inauthentic and the fact that hardly any instructors use it in the classroom, we leave the *Cinquième livre* (*Fifth Book* [1564]) aside. The essays in this volume are designed to help instructors understand and teach large issues of Renaissance culture arising in conjunction with specific episodes. The last section of the volume consists of essays on comparative courses in which Rabelais plays a central role. Our volume is intended, then, to serve instructors in a variety of programs (English, comparative literature, great-books, modern languages) as well as in a variety of courses (survey, special topics, undergraduate, graduate).

Following the format of the MLA Approaches to Teaching World Literature series, part 1 of this volume discusses the materials that can be used in teaching Rabelais. It explains which French editions and French translations of Rabelais are possible to use and focuses on how to incorporate them into the classroom. Other sections suggest secondary readings for students and for instructors; Web sites, music, films, and other multimedia materials that can be used in and out of the classroom; and sample assignments. Most of part 1 is based on the responses to a survey graciously filled out by teachers of Rabelais in the United States, Canada, India, and Europe. In our introduction to part 2, we frame the teaching of Rabelais by reviewing the issues that teaching him raises and discuss the background of Rabelais scholarship. The thirty-four essays then address strategies for teaching Rabelais.

A Note on Editions Used in This Volume

Unless otherwise indicated, citations of Rabelais in French refer to Guy Demerson's "bilingual" 1995 *Œuvres complètes* (whose pagination differs from that of his 1973 edition), and citations of Rabelais in English translation refer to J. M. Cohen's *Histories of Gargantua and Pantagruel* (whose pagination has not changed since the 1955 edition). *Histories* contains all five books. What Cohen calls "the First Book" is *Gargantua*; "the Second Book" is *Pantagruel*. These two editions were selected because the survey we conducted indicated that they were the most commonly used in the classroom. When French text and English translation are referred to without quotation, the page number or numbers for each are given in parentheses, in that order and separated by a semicolon.

Part One

MATERIALS

Editions and Translations

Floyd Gray

French Editions

Since there are a number of editions of Rabelais's work available, choosing the right one for teaching depends on the level of the course, the language of instruction, the length of time allotted to the study of Rabelais, the work or works to be covered, the preparation of students, and the instructor's preference for the type and extent of introductory material and critical apparatus. Costs and availability are additional factors. Whereas editions containing all four (or five) books that retain the original sixteenth-century language, syntax, and orthography are appropriate for graduate courses or seminars in French literature, a choice of just one of the books with modernized language and spelling might prove more suitable in undergraduate courses. For courses in world or comparative literature, there are excellent English translations of Rabelais's complete and selected works.

The complete works are available in a number of editions. The Pléiade edition *Œuvres complètes*, edited by Mireille Huchon, with the collaboration of François Moreau, is impressive in its presentation and documentation, but it is too expensive and closely printed to be suitable for instruction and is useful mainly for research. Much more accessible to instructors and students alike is Guy Demerson's *Œuvres complètes*, which gives both the original text and a Modern French translation in parallel columns. Pierre Jourda's Classiques Garnier edition in two volumes tends to waver, in its introduction and notes, between an essentially historical approach and more recent critical perspectives. Marcel Guilbaud's five-volume *Œuvres complètes de Maître François Rabelais* features copious notes, conveniently placed in marginal columns. Jean Céard, Gérard Defaux, and Michel Simonin have provided a compact one-volume edition of *Les cinq livres*. Although Abel Lefranc, Robert Marichal, and others' monumental critical edition, *Œuvres*, is not really complete, readily available, or suitable for classroom use, graduate students should be made aware of it.

It might prove more convenient, especially if only selections are to be studied, to choose one or more of the several editions of individual books, especially *Gargantua* and *Pantagruel*. Less cumbersome, more numerous, and perhaps more satisfactory are the critical editions of individual books. Both *Gargantua* and *Pantagruel* went through several editions during Rabelais's lifetime, and sometimes important modifications and additions were made because of the political and religious circumstances of the day. Instructors will therefore want to base their choice of an edition not only on the degree of critical apparatus and annotations desired but also on autobiographical, cultural, or historical import. If one is interested in presenting *Gargantua* as an example of Christian Erasmian comedy and royalist propaganda directed against Spanish imperialist ambitions, one might adopt the text of the *editio princeps* of 1534 (or 1535) in Ruth Calder and others' edition. Better still, because more recent and more readily available, is Gérard Defaux's 1994 edition. With an important introduction and substantial notes dealing with classical and historical references as well as with linguistic or lexical difficulties on parallel pages, it is probably the most complete and most convenient edition. If one prefers the text of the so-called definitive edition, published in Lyon in 1542 by François Juste, Floyd Gray's edition, in addition to the usual commentary, calls attention to different ways of reading and interpreting Rabelais, certain *constantes d'analyse*, especially those that relate to or seem determined by ways in which writing conditions meaning.

Since *Pantagruel* underwent various textual, semantic, and ideological changes from edition to edition, choosing which one to teach may prove difficult. Should one prefer the original, an intermediate, or the final version given by the author? All three are available: Verdun L. Saulnier retains the original 1532 text, Defaux the 1534 text, and Gray the 1542 text. The Saulnier edition is outdated, but both Defaux and Gray offer an alternative. Defaux's edition is more convenient in format and presentation, whereas Gray's reproduces the orthography, orthographic signs, paragraphing, and punctuation of the original text. Both provide substantial introductions, bibliographies, and notes, but Defaux's includes variants as well. Two critical editions of the *Tiers livre* are available: M. A. Screech's and, more recently, Céard's. For the *Quart livre*, see Marichal's edition.

Notwithstanding the large selection of editions available today, none may prove completely satisfactory. Ultimately, the best choice may depend on readability rather than on the version chosen, and by readability I mean the tools, historical, linguistic, and critical, offered by the editor to facilitate the reader's comprehension of an elusive text. Thus, some instructors and students might find Demerson's modern French translation a useful adjunct to the original text. Others might prefer to grapple with the text on their own, without the intervention of a translation that, in some ways, is a distortion or recasting of the original.

English Translations and Anthologies

Although Rabelais is generally taught in French and in French departments, often at the graduate level, his works are also taught in English in a wide variety of contexts and courses: undergraduate great-books courses or graduate English and comparative literature courses; interdisciplinary studies in the humanities; women's studies, for his perceived antifeminist stance; and courses on special topics.

Readable and readily available translations include Screech's one-volume paperback translation, *Gargantua and Pantagruel*, and Andrew Brown's *Gar-*

gantua and his *Pantagruel.* In addition, Donald M. Frame's paperback, *The Complete Works of François Rabelais*, has the advantage of containing all Rabelais's writings. Previous English translations of Rabelais, which are less readable or available, have serious weaknesses, some (*Gargantua and Pantagruel* [trans. Urquhart and Le Motteux; Le Clercq]) because their language is too urgent and some (*Rabelais* [trans. Smith]) because it is not sufficiently so. Samuel Putnam's *Portable Rabelais*, although good, is no longer readily available. Burton Raffel's *Gargantua and Pantagruel*, a translation of all five books, has gone largely unnoticed by teachers and scholars. This leaves J. M. Cohen's Penguin translation of 1955 (*Histories*), which remains the most commonly used translation among the instructors surveyed. While Thomas Urquhart and Peter Le Motteux capture much of the tone and some of the texture of the original, their version is a brilliant recasting and expansion rather than a faithful translation. Putnam, Jacques Le Clercq, and Cohen adhere more closely to the text (see, however, Geiringer for Cohen's mistranslations of Rabelais's medical terms), but Le Clercq interlards it with parenthetical explanation, while Putnam and Cohen are archaic at times in language as well as in syntax. Brown's translation renders Rabelais into colloquial English, which may appeal to undergraduates. Frame's translation, although somewhat pedestrian at times—but, then, who can hope to reproduce Rabelais's linguistic virtuosity and inimitable verve?—has the advantage of presenting the translated text alone and unencumbered on the page, with notes and glossary relegated to the end of the volume. For instructors for whom price was not an issue, this was the translation of choice.

Anthologies might provide useful introductions to Rabelais in courses that deal with a number of authors or topics. If available, Gray's *Selections from* Gargantua *and* Pantagruel provides a relatively accurate, literal, readable version of substantial portions of *Pantagruel* and *Gargantua*, as well as some of the most significant chapters of *The Third Book* and *The Fourth Book*.

In summary, Frame's translation is the only English rendering of all Rabelais's works. This completeness is at once an asset and a drawback. Researchers may want access to everything, but students rarely do. In fact, they might be discouraged by the fullness of the critical apparatus, which is designed to make Rabelais more comprehensible but which perhaps also makes him less readable. It is most likely for this reason that Cohen's translation remains the most widely used. See Valerie Worth-Stylianou's essay in this volume for further discussion of the English translations.

Recommended Readings for Students and Instructors

Floyd Gray and Todd W. Reeser

Reference Works and Background Studies

Reading sixteenth-century French need not be particularly difficult, but Rabelais's French is, because of the enormous range of his allusions and lexicon. If orthographic or syntactic peculiarities are not a problem, reading Rabelais in the original French—aloud, preferably—can be a great pleasure. Language may prove to be less an obstacle than the ignorance today of certain fundamental cultural norms. Sixteenth-century writers and readers were familiar with the languages and literatures of Greece and Rome as well as with the Bible and Christianity, but most readers today do not have that background, learning, or range of reference. Increasingly, it is the alterity of sixteenth-century religious norms, customs, and classical culture that makes it difficult for students to approach and understand Rabelais and his times. In addition, what Rabelais laughed at is frequently perceived as inappropriate or incorrect, especially his scatology, obscenity, and the role he assigns women in his frequently ribald comedy. Students will need to learn to read Rabelais with different eyes and expectations, to laugh where he laughs, realizing that sixteenth-century cultural and linguistic norms were different from today's.

If sixteenth-century French is the chosen language, useful resources are Edmond Huguet's multiple-volume *Dictionnaire de la langue française du seizième siècle* (also released on CD-ROM and online by Champion Électronique) and, more recently, in one volume, Algirdas Julien Greimas and Teresa Mary Keane's *Dictionnaire du moyen français*. The Greimas-Keane dictionary contains a helpful description of the formation and forms of sixteenth-century French, but students should also be aware of Georges Gougenheim's *Grammaire de la langue française du 16ᵉ siècle*.

For those instructors and students who have time and world enough to work with primary texts, there are a number of basic works to be considered: Plato and Aristotle, Cicero, Vergil and Horace, Erasmus, and, of course, the Bible. In addition, classical and medieval epics, François de Montcorbier Villon, and eventually Clément Marot.

Secondary Works

In addition to such primary sources, a number of secondary works provide historical and cultural background for the period: Lucien Febvre, *Life in Renaissance France*; Gérald Chaix, *La Renaissance des années 1470 aux années 1560*; Jean Delumeau, *La civilisation de la Renaissance*; Arlette Jouanna, Philippe Hamon, Dominique Biloghi, and Guy Le Thiec, *La France de la Renaissance:*

Histoire et dictionnarie; I. D. McFarlane, *A Literary History of France: Renaissance France, 1470–1589*; Mikhail Bakhtin, *Rabelais and His World* or *L'œuvre de François Rabelais et la culture populaire au Moyen Âge et sous la Renaissance*. Bakhtin could be supplemented by Richard M. Berrong, *Rabelais and Bakhtin: Popular Culture in* Gargantua *and* Pantagruel. For a useful background on humanism versus Scholasticism that is accessible to students, see Charles Nauert, "Humanism as Method: Roots of Conflict with the Scholastics."

A particularly useful general teaching aid is *The Rabelais Encyclopedia*, edited by Elizabeth Chesney Zegura, which has short, accessible articles on key aspects of Rabelais and suggested readings for each topic. The dossier "Rabelais" in *Magazine littéraire* can be of general use for undergraduates, and *The Cambridge Companion to Rabelais*, edited by John O'Brien, has ten articles on broad topics around Rabelais. Additional useful tools are J. E. Dixon and J. L. Dawson, *Concordance des œuvres de Rabelais*; Gérard Milhe-Poutingon, *François Rabelais, bilan critique*; Bruno Braunrot, *François Rabelais: A Reference Guide, 1550–1990.*

Three biographies are available: Jean Plattard, *La vie de François Rabelais* (*The Life of François Rabelais*), Donald Frame, *François Rabelais: A Study,* and Mireille Huchon, *Rabelais*. Finally, in comparison with writers such as Michel de Montaigne, Rabelais tends to write outside himself. Despite the temptation to read his life back into his work—Abel Lefranc's approach—every seemingly autobiographical element in his work is immediately distorted, transposed, or translated into another language, that of fancy or fiction.

Critical Studies

As survey responses indicate, most instructors feel that it is necessary to ask students to read primary works but not secondary readings. Secondary readings are generally not assigned in undergraduate courses, and only a few key secondary works are assigned in graduate courses. Choice here is determined by the instructor's interests, the focus of the course, and the preparation and expectations of students. Studies on Rabelais and his world are so varied and numerous that a selection of them is not only desirable but necessary, and the following suggestions reflect and summarize representative survey replies.

Although somewhat heavy on the religious and serious aspects of Rabelais's work, M. A. Screech's *Rabelais* (French translation by Kisch) continues to provide the best overall introduction, even though it is tendentious in its interpretations. Marcel Tetel and Zegura's *Rabelais Revisited* offers a more succinct and topical reading. Similar books are Michael J. Heath, *Rabelais,* and Jerome Schwartz, *Irony and Ideology in Rabelais: Structures of Subversion.* Terence Cave has an excellent chapter on Rabelais in his indispensable *The Cornucopian Text: Problems of Writing in the French Renaissance* (*Cornucopia: Figures de l'abondance au XVIe siècle*).

Since there are a number of ways of reading Rabelais, it is appropriate to mention two works by Alfred Glauser, *Rabelais créateur* and *Fonctions du nombre chez Rabelais*; two by Floyd Gray, *Rabelais et l'écriture* and *Rabelais et le comique du discontinu*; as well as François Rigolot's *Les langages de Rabelais*, all of which focus in varying degrees and different ways on how Rabelais's text conveys meaning. Most of these critical approaches are represented in the essays in Raymond C. La Charité's *Rabelais's Incomparable Book: Essays on His Art* and in Jean-Claude Carron's *François Rabelais: Critical Assessments*.

There are countless studies on the sources and interpretations of what Rabelais means, especially in relation to the political, philosophical, and religious climate of the day. Among these are Gérard Defaux, *Marot, Rabelais, Montaigne: L'écriture comme présence*, and Edwin Duval's three books on the design of Rabelais's *Pantagruel*, *Tiers livre*, and *Quart livre*. The essays in Jean Céard and Jean-Claude Margolin's compendium *Rabelais en son demi-millénaire* deals with almost every conceivable aspect of Rabelais's life and works. A widely read essay is Erich Auerbach's "The World in Pantagruel's Mouth," from *Mimesis*.

Finally, the advent of cultural, women's, and gender studies has introduced new ways of reading Rabelais or, rather, a new dimension to those ways. Some instructors may want to assign contextual readings in theology and gender issues, such as Febvre's *Le problème de l'incroyance au XVI*e *siècle*; Natalie Zemon Davis's *Society and Culture in Early Modern France*; or Margaret W. Ferguson, Maureen Quilligan, and Nancy J. Vickers's edited collection *Rewriting the Renaissance*. If, for one reason or another, only the *Tiers livre* or the *Quart livre* were studied, then the choice of collateral readings would need to be more specific and could include Screech, *The Rabelaisian Marriage* (*Rabelais et le mariage*), and Paul Smith, *Voyage et écriture: Étude sur le* Quart livre *de Rabelais*. Advanced students should also be made aware of the journal *Études rabelaisiennes*, which publishes both articles and book-length studies on Rabelais.

Aids to Teaching

Todd W. Reeser

Visual and Aural Materials

Instructors frequently use Renaissance painting to make links between written and visual culture, especially works by Pieter Brueghel the Elder and Hieronymus Bosch. Elizabeth Chesney Zegura's essay in this volume discusses using painting to teach Rabelais. Michael Camille's *Image on the Edge: The Margins of Medieval Art* was cited as a good source for illustrations of the marketplace and of lust. One instructor uses images from dissection manuals to help students think about how the body is imagined in the Renaissance. Jonathan Sawday's *The Body Emblazoned: Dissection and the Human Body in Renaissance Culture* is appropriate to this project, as are Rembrandt paintings of the first dissections (e.g., *The Anatomy Lesson of Dr. Nicolaes Tulp*) and the frontispiece of Andreas Vesalius's *De Humani Corporis Fabrica*. Some instructors use images from the recently reissued *Les songes drolatiques de Pantagruel*, introduced by Michel Jeanneret, asking students to think how the images relate to the written text. In order to demonstrate the evangelical possibilities of the text, one instructor shows students an image of Christ in a winepress (see Weinberg, *Wine* 91). A foldout image of the Abbey of Thélème can be located in Charles Lenormant, *Rabelais et l'architecture de la Renaissance*. Because of its similarity to Thélème, the Château de Chambord (referred to in *Gargantua*, ch. 52) is often shown to students to give them a sense of the Renaissance architecture that informs the text.

Maps were used by some instructors to teach Rabelais, including maps by Oronce Fine (1495–1555), the cartographer of Francis I. On this topic, see Tom Conley's essay on using cartography to teach Rabelais, in this volume.

One of the most creative approaches to Rabelais is to have students think about his work as a graphic novel. One instructor suggested having students rewrite chapters of the text as a comic book, perhaps using Gustave Doré's illustrations as the visuals. Students could also be given extracts from a modern graphic novel about Rabelais (see Rodrigue and Mitton) and asked to think about similarities and differences between the Renaissance text and modern artistic production.

Some instructors put film in dialogue with Rabelais. One instructor uses the video *Rabelais and His World* to present the texts to undergraduates. Several instructors mentioned using clips from Monty Python to help students get a sense of a modern text that evokes some of the same humorous elements as Rabelais. The "bring out your dead" scene and the attack of the castle from *Monty Python and the Holy Grail* were both cited. Gary Ferguson's essay in this volume explains how he uses Monty Python to teach Rabelais. Jan Miernowski uses *South Park* as a point of comparison (see his essay in this volume). In this vein, clips from modern satiric texts can be used (e.g., *South Park*; films of John Waters). In his survey response, Christopher Martin explained that he begins his presentation of Rabelais with opening segments from the *South Park* Christmas special ("Mr. Hankey's Christmas Classics") or from *Shrek* (in which the romance text literally becomes an ass wipe). A couple of instructors use the charivari scene (the mock serenade for newlyweds) from *The Return of Martin Guerre* to help students get a sense of the carnivalesque. (A similar effect can be achieved through a discussion of Mardi Gras as cultural institution.)

The orality of Rabelais remains an essential teaching point for the numerous instructors who like to give students a sense of what his text sounds like out loud. A number of instructors play recordings of Rabelais in Modern French. Jacques Bonnaffé's recording of *Gargantua* is a popular set of CDs to play for students. There is also a recording of stories from *Gargantua* narrated by Philippe Noiret and others. See also the discussion of online readings in Karen James and Mary McKinley's essay in this volume. To our knowledge, no Middle French recording of Rabelais is in existence.

A few instructors make musical connections to Rabelais, particularly with the Ensemble Clément Janequin's *Une fête chez Rabelais* and the Newberry Consort's *Villon to Rabelais: Sixteenth Century Music of the Streets, Theatres, and Courts*. Elizabeth Chesney Zegura's essay in this volume discusses in more detail how to teach Rabelais with music.

Rabelais Online

Instructors frequently try to give students a sense of what the original printed book looked like and ask them to think about how the medium relates to the message. To this end, students are shown or asked to examine original editions of Rabelais online at Web sites such as the *Gallica* database, hosted by the Bibliothèque Nationale de France; the site *BVH-Epistemon*, from the Université de Tours; *The Renaissance in Print*, hosted by the University of Virginia Gordon Collection.

James and McKinley (in this volume) discuss the use of Web sites, including these. For background information on Rabelais, instructors frequently use the site *Renaissance-France.org: Le portail de la Renaissance Française* and the Renaissance section on *Tennessee Bob's Famous French Links*. A copious bibliography is available on the Web site of the Société Française d'Étude du Seizième Siècle. For dictionaries of the period, students can be sent to *RenTexte*, at the University of Toronto.

Courses and Teaching

Rabelais makes frequent appearances on great-books or comparative syllabi, according to the surveys conducted. His work is frequently paired with Desiderius

Erasmus's *Praise of Folly* or *Adages*, Thomas More's *Utopia*, Miguel de Cervantes's *Don Quixote*, Tommaso Campanella's *City of the Sun*, and Niccolò Machiavelli's *The Prince*. Carl Fisher teaches a course on comic realism in which he assigns Rabelais, Cervantes, Nikolai Gogol ("The Nose" and *Dead Souls*), and Gabriel García Márquez (*One Hundred Years of Solitude*). In his essay in this volume, he discusses how to teach comic realism comparatively. In his survey response, Roy Rosenstein wrote that he found it productive to pair Pleberio's lamentation over his dead daughter at the end of Fernando de Rojas's *Celestina* with Gargantua's mourning over his deceased wife in *Pantagruel*. Anne Lake Prescott teaches Rabelais after More but before Michel de Montaigne's skeptical essay "Apology for Raymond Sebond." Rabelais is contrasted with other writers, such as Petrarch and Christine de Pizan, to provide students two different images of the period. The "walls of Paris" chapter in *Pantagruel* (ch. 15) can be contrasted with Christine de Pizan's *Book of the City of Ladies* (see also Glidden). In great-books courses of large scope, Rabelais is often taken, as Christopher Martin wrote in his survey response, as "a touchstone for our interrogation of the very notion of 'renaissance.'" In Prescott's course on Renaissance humor, which she described in her survey response, Rabelais leads into a later discussion of Thomas Nashe, John Donne, and John Harington ("all three his fans," she writes). Prescott also inserts Rabelais in the comic tradition through writers such as Petronius, Lucian, and Pietro Aretino. Other teachers compared Rabelais's humor with that of later French authors such as Denis Diderot, Gustave Flaubert, and Samuel Beckett and with Laurence Sterne (*Tristam Shandy*). According to survey participants, comparative literature courses in which Rabelais is studied focus on themes such as the carnivalesque, utopia, literature of travel, cartography, the birth of the novel, the trickster figure, madness-folly, the body, the comic, comic realism, Renaissance humanism, satire and humor, eros, and the representation of women and gender.

Although Rabelais is often included in introduction to French literature courses, it is nearly always in short extracts and with little variation in the episodes taken. The most common episodes studied are the Abbey of Thélème (*Gargantua*, chs. 52–58), the prologue to *Gargantua*, and Gargantua's letter to Pantagruel (*Pantagruel,* ch. 8). The sections from *Gargantua* on education (chs. 14–15, 21, 23–24) were also commonly cited for this level. One survey participant wrote that his students "can relate to what Gargantua does under Ponocrates's tutelage (in relation to their own 'unrealistic' course-work demands)." Gargantua's letter is sometimes linked to or compared with Montaigne's ideas on pedagogy and education in "De l'institution des enfants." The famous chapter in Pantagruel's mouth (*Pantagruel*, ch. 32) is also sometimes studied at this level.

For courses on Renaissance literature or culture taught in French, usually at the advanced undergraduate level, instructors tend to take the entirety of one of the first two books (*Gargantua* or *Pantagruel*). The surveys revealed a nearly equal split between the two books in terms of their popularity at this level.

Instructors usually spend two to three weeks in such courses on the author. Chapter 6 of *Gargantua* was cited as a good example of popular comedy for students in such courses, and chapters 32–33 for comic style and characterization. The storm episodes in *The Fourth Book* were sometimes used to illustrate comedic and episodic aspects of Rabelais. In courses on the French Renaissance, Rabelais is often paired with Marguerite de Navarre. The dedication to *The Third Book* can raise the question of how a book so seemingly misogynous can be dedicated "to the spirit of the Queen of Navarre" (280). Montaigne often follows Rabelais in these kinds of courses, as issues of paradox and skepticism link them. In his survey response, Edwin Duval pairs Gargantua's letter (*Pantagruel*, ch. 8) with Joachim du Bellay's *Défense et illustration de la langue française*. Duval asks his students to focus on the following chapters: prologue, 1–2, 6, 8, 9, 10–14, 18–20, 29–30 in *Pantagruel*; prologue, 1, 3–4, 6, 11, 13–15, 21–24, 16–20, 25–27, 38–41, 45, 52–58 in *Gargantua*. Rabelais is also taught with Amboise Paré's *Des monstres et prodigues,* since both texts deal with monsters (though in different ways).

Graduate courses taught include single-author seminars on Rabelais and various Renaissance courses (gender and sexuality, Renaissance prose, survey of the period) in which Rabelais figures. Nearly all instructors stated that they use secondary literature, criticism, and theory at this level, and Bakhtin's book on Rabelais is by far the most widely cited text. Cave's chapter on Rabelais in *The Cornucopian Text* and Auerbach's famous article from *Mimesis* were also commonly assigned to graduate students along with the primary texts. It is common, too, for instructors to pair work by critics, such as Duval and Michel Jeanneret, M. A. Screech and André Tournon, or Gérard Defaux and Cave, to give students a sense of differing approaches to the texts. Jeff Persels writes in his survey response that he has used the "haulte dame de Paris" episode (*Pantagruel*, ch. 21) as an interpretive center and asked students to read criticism on the episode by François Rigolot ("Three Temptations"), Carla Freccero ("Damning Haughty Dames"), and Duval (*Design of Rabelais's* Pantagruel), asking them to think about how and why three readings of the same episode differ. Todd W. Reeser uses a similar technique with the prologue to *Gargantua*, juxtaposing Richard Regosin's and Defaux's articles on this text (resp., "Ins(ides)" and "D'un problème"). As indicated in the graduate syllabus submitted with his survey response, Duval pairs select chapters of Rabelais with biblical passages: for instance, chapters 1–2 of *Pantagruel* are paired with Genesis 2.4–4.26, 6.1–8; Matthew 1 and 23.29–39; Psalms 22.1–2; Matthew 22.34–40; Mark 12.28–34; Luke 10.25–27; 1 John 3.

Although *The Third Book* and *The Fourth Book* are rarely taught at the undergraduate level, they appear with some frequency in graduate seminars in French programs, but *The Fifth Book* and the minor texts are almost never taught. One survey participant reads only the very end of *The Fifth Book* with his students. The assumed inauthenticity of the text is the reason that most instructors do not teach this book (see Glauser, *Faux Rabelais*; Huchon, *Rabelais grammairien* and *Œuvres* 1598–1600).

At all levels, instructors read aloud to students, or they have students read passages to one another. A sample reading activity is provided by John Parkin's contribution to this volume. James Palmer immediately confronts the problem of Rabelais's obscenity by reading the "walls of Paris" episode (*Pantagruel*, ch. 15) to the students, using the classroom event and student reactions as a springboard for discussion about comedy and the use of the body in the text in a larger sense (see his essay in this volume). Other instructors have students act out carefully selected scenes. For comic effect, Martine Sauret suggested in her survey response the dialogue among the councilors and Picrochole in the war sequence (*Gargantua*, ch. 33). David LaGuardia discusses teaching through drama in his essay in this volume. Christopher Martin wrote in his survey response that he has hired professional actors to perform the debate between Panurge and Thaumaste in chapter 19 of *Pantagruel* to help students get a sense of the visuality of the comedy. Other instructors prefer to have students listen to a recording of Rabelais's text to get a feeling for its orality (using esp. Bonnaffé's recording). A discussion can ensue on the role and influence of the printing press in the development of textuality.

The issue of the language in which Rabelais should be taught is divisive. There appears to be no consensus. Many instructors avoided the question by using Guy Demerson's bilingual edition (the most commonly cited edition), asking students to read mostly in Modern French translation but referring to the Middle French when necessary. Other instructors said that they do not teach in Modern French and that if they go slowly and explicitly help students learn some basic elements of Middle French, students can successfully face Rabelais's original text. Kirsten A. Fudeman's essay in this volume treats the topic of teaching the linguistic aspects of the text. Some instructors ask students not to focus on all the words that are unknown to them but to locate three to four such words and look them up in a dictionary of Renaissance French such as Edmond Huguet's. Another approach is to focus on the concept of the text as difficult as part of the very meaning of Rabelais's text. Reeser's contribution gives an example of how this issue can be taught by using Panurge's linguistic play as metonymic for the student's experience with Rabelais.

Sample Assignments

The most common topics for papers revolve around questions such as whether the Abbey of Thélème is really ideal, to what extent the text is serious, and how orality plays a role in the text. Below are three sets of sample paper topics submitted by survey participants. Bruce Hayes has students work specifically on Gargantua's education. In his survey response, he wrote:

> Of the different activities I do in class, probably the most popular is a group project in which [students] must identify specific differences in Gargantua's two educations and then try to identify why the author draws

> attention to these particular changes, as well as identifying the change in behavior of the giant before and after his second education. I then tie this into a discussion concerning modern humanistic studies and whether Rabelais's optimism about the salutary effects of such an education has any credence. It is typically both an amusing and instructive exercise.

A few instructors use creative writing assignments to help students learn to produce the flavor of the text. In this volume, Palmer discusses an assignment in which he asks students to reproduce the carnivalesque aspect of Rabelais.

Bernd Renner gives the following assignments on *Pantagruel* to students in an undergraduate French course:

> *Pantagruel* est un ouvrage à forte tendance satirique. Choisissez une des cibles de la satire rabelaisienne et montrez comment le sujet est traité à travers le texte. De quels moyens différents la satire se sert-elle? De quelle(s) façon(s) l'intention satirique se manifeste-t-elle? L'approche rabelaisienne est-elle couronnée de succès? Pourquoi ou pourquoi pas?
>
> Panurge est un personnage plein de contradictions. Il est trickster, fou du roi, larron et "meilleur fils du monde" à la fois. Dressez son portrait et montrez comment ces contradictions se manifestent. Quelle est sa fonction principale dans le texte? Est-il indispensable?
>
> L'ouvrage de Rabelais est un exemple du "réalisme grotesque" en littérature. Expliquez ce terme et montrez son impact dans le texte. Quel est l'objectif de ce style?
>
> *Pantagruel* consiste d'un curieux mélange entre le comique et le sérieux, voir par exemple le contraste établi dans le dizain introductoire d'Hugues Salel et le prologue. Quels sont les avantages et les inconvénients de ce style? Pourquoi Rabelais a-t-il décidé de s'en servir? Le trouvez-vous approprié en vue des intentions de l'ouvrage? Justifiez votre opinion!
>
> *Pantagruel* is a highly satirical work. Select one of the targets of Rabelais's satire and explain how the subject is treated throughout the text. What kind(s) of techniques does his satire employ? In what ways(s) is satirical intention presented? Is Rabelais's approach successful? Why or why not?
>
> Panurge is a character full of contradictions. He is trickster, court jester, thief, and "the best fellow in the world" all at once. Construct a character study of Panurge and explain how his contradictions in character operate. What is his main function in the text? Is he indispensable to the text?
>
> The work of Rabelais is an example of "grotesque realism" in the literary arena. Explain the sense of this term and discuss its impact on the text. What is the goal of this kind of style?

> *Pantagruel* is composed of a strange mix of comic and serious, as exemplified for instance by the contrast between Hugues Salel's introductory poem and the prologue. What are the advantages and disadvantages of this style? Why did Rabelais decide to use it? Justify your opinion.

Other examples of essay topics on *Pantagruel* assigned in an undergraduate French course were provided by Virginia Krause in her survey response:

> Le personnage de Panurge dans *Pantagruel*. Basé en partie sur le personnage folklorique du filou (du *trickster*), Panurge, toujours provocateur, devient l'agent principal de la parodie dans *Pantagruel*. Étudiez ce personnage en tenant compte de la définition suivante de la parodie: "imitation consciente et volontaire, soit du fond, soit de la forme, dans une intention moqueuse ou simplement comique" (Dupriez 331).
>
> La liste est l'un des procédés qui caractérisent le plus le style rabelaisien. Étudiez de près ce procédé en vous basant sur l'analyse nuancée d'au moins trois passages de *Pantagruel*. Comment les listes rabelaisiennes fonctionnent-elles? À quel type de logique obéissent-elles? (Une logique phonétique? rationnelle? graphique? thématique?)
>
> L'esthétique rabelaisienne: du mot à l'image. Montrez comment *Les songes drolatiques* et *Pantagruel* appartiennent au même univers esthétique. Consultez l'édition des *Songes* et en particulier l'introduction par M. Jeanneret.

> The character of Panurge in *Pantagruel*. Based in part on the popular character of the trickster or rogue, the always provocative Panurge becomes the main agent for parody in *Pantagruel*. Discuss this character while keeping in mind the following definition of parody: "conscious and voluntary imitation of content or of form, with the intention to mock or simply to be humorous" (Dupriez).
>
> Lists are one of the most common elements of Rabelais's style. Discuss this aspect of the text, closely analyzing at least three passages from *Pantagruel*. Explain the functioning of Rabelais's lists. What kind of logic do they obey? (Phonetic? rational? graphic? thematic?)
>
> Rabelais's aesthetics: from word to image. Discuss how *Les songes drolatiques* and *Pantagruel* belong to the same aesthetic universe. Use the 2004 edition of the *Songes* and Jeanneret's introduction.

The following topics were provided in the survey response by Christopher Martin, who teaches Rabelais's four books in English translation:

> Rabelais claims flatly that he doesn't care about women. How adequately does such a stated outlook account for the absence of primary female characters in his books?

Chance and justice are two abstractions that seem to get a great deal of attention in our authors this semester; the concepts joining most fascinatingly are in Rabelais's Bridlegoose episode (*Third Book*, chs. 39–43). Using the kind of perceptions offered by Rabelais's character, comment on the way any of our authors fashion a calculus of reward and punishment.

The Panurge described in the storm episode of Rabelais's *Fourth Book* (chs. 18–24) seems radically different from the character we have known up to this point in the story. Or does he? In an essay, discuss this apparent inconsistency. If he is different, how do you account for this narrative disjunction? If, on the other hand, you disagree, specify exactly how the portrayal during the storm scene remains consistent with the earlier characterization.

In her survey response, Chloé Hogg outlined an activity that she conducts to teach the Abbey of Thélème episode in *Gargantua*, chapter 53, in a course on prerevolutionary French civilization taught in French:

> Students had read the excerpt on the Abbey of Thélème as homework. I began the activity with a discussion of "utopia," eliciting definitions and associations from students and working with them to identify the function of utopia—a means of imagining alternatives (social, political, gender, etc.). By presenting the etymology of the word, I was able to emphasize the two parts that structure this activity: "imaginary/ideal" and "space." I briefly mentioned Thomas More's *Utopia*, which allowed us to consider utopia as a literary genre and a popular genre in the Renaissance. I then introduced the Abbey of Thélème by positing it as a kind of utopia—our goal was to figure out what kind of utopia it was through the analysis of its space and ideals.
>
> Students were divided in groups and provided with a diagram of the abbey (sketched by me) that shows the outlines of the structure and the river, with the towers, the river, and the *basse-cour* labeled (for the purposes of the exercise, I put the *basse-cour* in the middle of the abbey). Students worked together to fill in the map with information gleaned from the text (library, picture gallery, fountain, men's and women's quarters, garden and labyrinth, etc.). It is very convenient—with the towers and river labeled, students can map out the entire description. At this point, the activity functioned as action—that is, something concrete to do when faced with a daunting text—and as a guide to reading comprehension; my goal here was to have students feel more control over the text so that they would not become frustrated and "turn off" before the discussion began.
>
> Once the groups had completed the maps, the class came together by guiding me as I filled in the diagram on the chalkboard using their in-

formation. (I drew a very large version of their diagram for this.) I asked students to consider what activities took place in the spaces, what was in the spaces (the books in classical and modern languages in the library, the paintings in the gallery ["antiques prouesses, histories et descriptions de la terre"]; jousting and tournaments in "les lices"; tennis in the "jeux de paume", etc.). Students may need some encouragement in "working" the information, so some modeling is helpful. Taking "le grand parc foisonnant de gibier" as my example, I asked them what would be done there; with the easy response, "hunt," I informed them that indeed the hunt was an important activity for nobles (the contrast between this space and the "verger" with its formal groups of fruit trees can also be noted). . . .

Once the space and activities had been identified, I . . . asked students to generate a list of Renaissance values and ideals based on the information they had produced. In reality, the labeling of activities mentioned above moves organically into discussion of their significance. I drew students' attention to aspects they might have overlooked; for example, I ask them to trace out the men's and women's quarters on the diagram, and we noted that they were granted equal space, noting too that the abbey houses both women and men.

This work can be done as a class discussion, with the instructor noting student responses on the board, or students can come to the board to list their "values." As we discuss their responses, I guide the class in synthesizing the material; I also step in to provide necessary historical and cultural background. Students can be prompted by a simple question ("Why all the sports facilities at Thélème?"), which produces a response ("they want to stay in shape") that the instructor can help shape into a statement about Renaissance ideals or cultural values (new and positive interest in the body). Since the class had already had a general introduction to the Renaissance, students were able to reactivate and apply their knowledge—thus the library elicited the mention of humanism from a student, which I reinforced with a discussion of the different languages mentioned in the text.

I end the class with a brief discussion of Rabelais's vision of life at Thélème (ch. 57). . . . I think it is important to consider this passage in order to acknowledge more troublesome aspects of this "utopia" that are not present in the first selection (the abbey's uniformity, questions of who's included or excluded, etc.).

Part Two

APPROACHES

Introduction

Floyd Gray and Todd W. Reeser

Reading Rabelais: A History

In the main, the long history of readings of Rabelais can be placed into four categories and four periods: contemporary readers—that is, how Rabelais was read originally, by his sixteenth-century public; disaffected or uninformed readers, especially in the seventeenth, eighteenth, and nineteenth centuries, who remembered and usually appreciated the fantastic, popular, or mythical Rabelais; the early-twentieth-century historical revival promoted by Abel Lefranc and cohorts, who were interested especially in Rabelais's realism and religion; and structuralist, Marxist, interpretive, feminist, poststructuralist readers, each of whom has added new dimensions to the ways in which Rabelais can be read and understood.

If we begin our history with Rabelais's first readers, especially as they have been cataloged by Marcel de Grève, who, in his *L'interprétation de Rabelais au XVIe siècle*, divides them into those who considered his work heretical, Calvinist, Erasmian, libertine, jovial, and finally a witness and judge of his age, we are impressed by the range of their responses. Much of this variety can be explained by the troubled times in which Rabelais wrote. Dissension and diversity were already disrupting the religious and political structures that had prevailed for centuries, making it difficult to write freely and to be read innocently. The advent of the age of potential heresy produced a time of rampant suspicion, and, as a correlative, censorship, imprisonment, burnings of authors and their books. Rabelais, in a word, needed to write carefully and walk gingerly. That he did neither made his work all the more notorious and therefore successful, and his life all the more adventuresome, punctuated by periods of prudent travel, occasional persecution, and eventually, as evidenced by the prologue of the *Tiers livre*, disappointment at how readers misunderstood him.

Mystified by his linguistic and allusive hybridity, some of Rabelais's original readers were convinced that his characters could be identified with real people—that, for instance, Grandgousier was Louis XII; Gargantua, Francis I; Pantagruel, Henri II; and so on. Perplexed by a work that seemed now historical, now allegorical, and now esoteric, other readers were intent on finding a way to decipher its abundant clues and allusions, to peer behind or through the words Rabelais chose both to veil and reveal his true meaning.

At the close of the sixteenth century, Montaigne classified Rabelais's work as "simplement plaisans" (*Essais*; "simply pleasant" [our trans.]), a judgment shared by many seventeenth-century readers, including Molière. Mme de Sévigné wrote that Charles, her son, read to her chapters of Rabelais "à mourir de rire" (1: 325; "that made me laugh to death" [our trans.]). For Jean de La Bruyère, a defender of good taste, Rabelais's work is an enigma, a

> monstrueux assemblage d'une morale fine et ingénieuse, et d'une sale corruption. Où il est mauvais, il passe bien loin au delà du pire, c'est le charme de la canaille; où il est bon, il va jusques à l'exquis et à l'excellent, il peut être le mets des plus délicats. (*Caractères* 43)

> monstruous jumble of delicate and ingenious morality and of filthy deprivation. Where it is bad, it excels by far the worst, and is fit only to delight the rabble; and where it is good, it is exquisite and excellent, and may entertain the most delicate. (*Characters* 23)

Readers in the age of Romanticism, as exemplified by Victor Hugo or Charles Augustin Sainte-Beuve, admired Rabelais for depth ("un des gouffres de l'esprit!" for Hugo [784; "one of the abysses of the mind!"]) and breadth ("un bouffon, mais un bouffon unique, un bouffon homérique" for Sainte-Beuve, incomparable as to "la forme du langage, l'ampleur et la richesse des tours, le jet abondant et intarissable de la parole" [41; "a buffoon, but an exceptional buffoon, a Homeric buffoon . . . the form of his language, the fullness and richness of his expressions, the abundant and inexhaustible flow of his speech"]). Literary historians at the close of the nineteenth century, such as Emile Faguet or Paul Stapfer, considered his work essentially incomprehensible, whereas at the beginning of the twentieth century, Gustave Lanson, in his landmark *Histoire de la littérature française*, described Rabelais's "doctrine" and the "source profonde de son génie" (Lanson and Tuffrau 117; "deep inner source of his genius") as "l'amour de la vie sous toutes ses formes" ("the love of life in all its forms" [our trans.]).

Abel Lefranc was probably the most compelling and influential of Rabelais's early-twentieth-century readers. He set out to prove scientifically that Rabelais was an atheist, that his secret thought, as evidenced by *Gargantua* and *Pantagruel*, is nothing other than the revolt of a freethinker against Christianity, the oppressor of mankind. Insisting on the "réalisme" of Rabelais's work in his edition of Rabelais, he meant to demonstrate, at times convincingly, that it was "un miroir tout ensemble du temps et de l'existence de son auteur" (*Rabelais* 70; "a mirror both of the time and of the existence of the author" [our trans.]). Despite Lucien Febvre's equally erudite and more temperate study of the orthodoxy of Rabelais's religion in *Le problème de l'incroyance au XVI siècle* (translated as *The Problem of Unbelief in the Sixteenth Century*), the suspicion of his atheism, especially in anticlerical France, remained widespread.

In their wake, Michael Screech (*Rabelais*) and Mikhail Bakhtin (*Rabelais and His World* [*L'œuvre de François Rabelais et la culture populaire au Moyen Âge et sous la Renaissance*]) provided different but equally seminal studies. Screech stressed high humanist culture and Erasmian religious aspects (what is often called Rabelais's Christian humanism), commenting on key episodes of the corpus. Bakhtin concentrated on the influence of medieval and Renaissance popular and comic cultures, together with their Greco-Roman antecedents. The influence of Bakhtin's reading in the American academy has been substantial, and many would say that no other theorist has had the same impact on Rabelais studies. His discussions of the carnivalesque and of the grotesque body, in particular, remain immensely influential (if criticized) concepts in studies of Rabelais and of the Renaissance in a larger sense. For Bakhtin, Renaissance feasts or festivals, parodic literature, and the language of the marketplace create possibilities for subversion of official power structures (especially those of the church and the king). The idea of Rabelais's subversiveness may say more about Bakhtin's relation to Russian power structures than about Rabelais (see Holquist, "Bakhtin"), but the concept was well received by some in the American academy, where questions of ideology, power, and resistance were already of interest.

That the English translation of Bakhtin's text came out in 1968 (though the Russian version was published in 1965) suggests an intellectual climate receptive to studies of subversion. Julia Kristeva is often credited with introducing Bakhtin to the French academy in a 1967 article ("Bakhtine, le mot, le dialogue, et le roman" ["Word, Dialogue, and Novel"]), three years before the French translation came out, perhaps helping create a climate receptive to the Russian theorist. Also appealing was undoubtedly his critique of the academy, the official culture of which Rabelais was part. As Bakhtin himself put it:

> The main failure of contemporary West-European Rabelaisiana consists in the fact that it ignores folk culture and tries to fit François Rabelais' novel into the framework of official culture, to conceive it as following the stream of "great" French literature. (*Rabelais* 473)

Bakhtin's approach has had a lasting influence on Rabelais studies, as evidenced by works such as Michel Beaujour's *Le jeu de Rabelais*, Jean Paris's *Rabelais au futur*, and Samuel Kinser's *Rabelais's Carnival*. John Parkin provides an extended discussion of the lengthy and complicated history of the reception of Bakhtin in chapter 5 of *Interpretations of Rabelais*.

At the same time, Bakhtin was reevaluated and criticized for seeing subversion in the carnivalesque when it was not there and for dehistoricizing Rabelais. Richard M. Berrong's *Rabelais and Bakhtin* repositions Bakhtin's study, especially by examining how his notion of popular culture does not sufficiently take into account learned culture and how pop culture increasingly disappears over the course of the four books. Berrong writes:

> Bakhtin may well have misrepresented the role of popular culture in *Pantagruel* by refusing to acknowledge the equal presence and significance of learned culture in the text, but he was certainly correct in claiming that popular culture played an important part in Rabelais's first narrative. . . . [I]n *Gargantua*, though Bakhtin seems never to have noticed it, there begins a systematic and radical exclusion of popular culture. (21)

In a 1987 review of Berrong's book, Mary McKinley pointed out that the marketplace was not an alien culture to those in positions of power and that popular culture also functioned as universal. Many felt (and many still feel) that the opposition between official culture and popular culture was not as binarized as Bakhtin had made it out to be and that this bias on his part spoke to his Russian or Soviet readers more than to students and scholars of Rabelais who took context seriously. Jerome Schwartz's *Irony and Ideology in Rabelais* can be taken as a critique of a pure Bakhtinian focus on ideology and as an attempt to study irony in a way that "avoids the danger of reducing the text either to a single ideological reading, or to a reading that posits an author having at all times recoverable intentions and meanings to convey" (2).

A further common criticism of Bakhtin's approach, influenced by anthropological work on rites and ceremonies of reversal, is that the carnival functioned not as subversion but as a kind of release or safety valve. In this view, people were in fact more effectively contained through the subversion that occurred during carnival than they would have been without it, and power is paradoxically reasserted through the carnivalesque (e.g., see Stallybrass and White; Davis, *Society*). Others have concluded that the possibilities of subversion are more complicated than an either-or approach suggests. As Natalie Zemon Davis writes in a historically based study of misrule, "[T]he structure of the carnival form can evolve so that it can act both to reinforce order and to suggest alternatives to the existing order" (*Society* 123).

The influence of Bakhtinian analysis also pertains to grotesque realism, particularly in the realm of the body. Rabelais's abundant references to corporeal elements not frequently depicted in Renaissance culture, including what Bakhtin famously calls "the material bodily lower stratum," suggest a rebirth or a symbolic regeneration of the body. The body that is reborn is not the individual biological body; it is "precisely the historic, progressing body of mankind [that] stands at the center of this system of images" (*Rabelais* 367). Thus urine and dung function as carnivalesque images, lending

> a bodily character to matter, to the world, to the cosmic elements, which become closer, more intimate, more easily grasped, for this is the matter, the elemental force, born from the body itself. It transforms cosmic terror into a gay carnival monster. (335)

In this vein, Rabelais's obscenity or vulgarity has remained a central issue in making sense of the texts, and Bakhtin's idea that popular rhetoric of the body overturns established hierarchies is one way to approach the question.

While Berrong nuances this idea with respect to scatology (23–32), critics have considered Rabelaisian vulgarity in other ways. In her 1983 *The Vulgar Rabelais*, Carol Clark follows in Bakhtin's footsteps (along with what she calls "the whole younger generation of Rabelais critics") in order "to explore the popular background to Rabelais's enterprise" while "avoid[ing] the suggestion that one seems to find in certain recent critics that Rabelais's writings are the product of nature, or of 'social praxis' alone." For Clark, ideology is not the determining aspect of what she refers to as vulgarity, for the text is "the product of the acute intelligence of a man who had lived in a wide variety of social milieux, and who was the master of a wide range of prose styles." Clark thus aims to put the author back into the study of popular culture: "If Rabelais expresses popular modes of feeling, or adopts popular stylistic forms, it is because he has chosen to do so" (3).

What Norman Brown discusses as "the excremental vision" of Jonathan Swift (179–201) is also a key approach to textuality for Rabelais. While Bakhtin does discuss scatology in *Rabelais and His World*, recent work has expanded on this aspect of corporality in Rabelais (e.g., Persels, "'Straightened'"; LaGuardia, "Doctor Rabelais"). Jan Miernowski's and Jeff Persels's essays in this volume also provide two ways of thinking about the vulgar or scandalous Rabelais both in the text and in the classroom. The question of the representation of the body and of corporality, a hot topic in literary and cultural studies in the late twentieth century, has also been enlarged from Bakhtin's focus on the lower body and his assumption of a neutral or nongendered body to incorporate other ways of considering corporality. Polly Bromilow, for instance, contextualizes the Rabelaisian body by studying the instabilities of the gendered one-sex body, as made famous by Thomas Laqueur in *Making Sex*.

In a vein more literary or linguistic than historical or formalist were studies by Alfred Glauser (*Rabelais créateur* and *Fonctions*), François Rigolot (*Langages*), and Floyd Gray (*Rabelais et l'écriture* and *Rabelais et le comique*). In response to these readings came a flurry of articles and books of a more traditional bent, centered especially on Rabelais's ideas. Consonant with Screech's reaction to purely literary, structuralist, or deconstructionist readings of Rabelais's writing, Gérard Defaux (*Marot*), seconded by Edwin Duval and his three volumes on the coherence of Rabelais's books (*The Design of Rabelais's* Pantagruel, *The Design of Rabelais's* Tiers livre de Pantagruel, and *The Design of Rabelais's* Quart livre de Pantagruel), argued that every episode in Rabelais is indispensable to the meaning of the whole and that the books' cohesive structure points to a consistent Christian humanism. As Duval writes, "each of Rabelais's books is a complete, whole, and meticulously ordered *work* in the fullest sense of the word." He articulates a notion of design that has been highly influential in Rabelais studies:

> By design I mean not the kind of thematic unity or general coherence of vision that might be inferred from the sum of a work's several parts, but rather a master plan that appears to have preceded and governed the composition of each of Rabelais's books, that is meant to be discerned by the reader even before he has arrived at an understanding of any single episode, and that functions as a guide toward a proper understanding of not only the whole work but also its constituent parts.
>
> (*Design of Rabelais's* Pantagruel xiv)

Concern that the integrity and seriousness of meaning in Rabelais's work were being compromised by those less interested in what it said than how it said prompted what was described as a new quarrel between ancient and modern ways of reading literature. Symptomatic of this quarrel in criticism is the debate that took place over the prologue to *Gargantua*, often taken to establish Rabelais's approach to hermeneutics in a larger sense and to respond to the question whether a higher meaning could be established. Gray first raised this question in 1965 ("Ambiguity"). There ensued a protracted debate between critics who saw a stable or intended meaning in Rabelais on the one hand—including especially Duval and Defaux—and those who considered the text unstable and polysemic on the other (Cave, Jeanneret, and Rigolot, among others). In "Sur la prétendue transparence de Rabelais" (a response to Defaux's "Sur la prétendue pluralité"), Terence Cave, Michel Jeanneret, and Rigolot challenged Defaux's "transparent" reading of the prologue of *Garagantua*, which they claimed assumes that "la duplicité consciente ou inconsciente du texte rabelaisien n'est qu'une fiction inventée par la critique moderne" (709; "the conscious or unconscious double nature of Rabelais's text is nothing but a fiction invented by modern criticism" [our trans.]).

This debate about interpretation could itself be seen as a larger disagreement in the 1980s over whether poststructuralist ideas of stability and meaning could (or should) be brought to bear on the study of Rabelais. Or this issue could be cast as a debate or conflict over the role of critical and literary theory in general. Critics reading French theoretical texts in the wake of poststructuralism began to ask how they related to Rabelais or how the Renaissance writer could be seen to prefigure their ideas. Is Rabelais, for instance, doing something textually akin to what Jacques Derrida centuries later calls *différance*? Despite analogies or correspondences, Rabelais is strikingly absent from the work of French poststructuralist thinkers such as Derrida, Michel Foucault, and Jacques Lacan. Kristeva does include a brief discussion of Rabelais in *Étrangers à nous-mêmes* (162–68; *Strangers to Ourselves*).

One of the most influential critical works inflected with poststructuralism is Cave's 1979 *The Cornucopian Text*. Taking an approach influenced by what he calls "*la nouvelle critique*" (xvi), Cave examines how representations of *copia* or cornucopia in the text (Rabelais's codpiece being one example) are emptied out, how semantic fullness turns into an emptiness or how stable meaning cannot ultimately be established. For Cave, Rabelais exemplifies "hermeneutic displacement," by which "the desire to conserve some original sense . . . initiates an endless series of rewritings . . . and an infinite regression of meaning" (79). Instead of directly applying a specific theoretician to Renaissance texts, Cave elected "to borrow *topoi*, figures, and devices from various forms of *nouvelle critique*, and to juxtapose them with those of more traditional methods, and with themes and figures drawn from sixteenth-century texts" (xvi–xvii). His book puts into practice the critical idea that elements of Renaissance texts prefigure poststructuralist thought, that twentieth-century ideas are already influenced by, in this case, Rabelaisian ones.

Jeanneret's work could also be factored into this side of the quarrel, especially the essays collected in *Le défi des signes*, which articulates Rabelais's hermeneutic position as a Renaissance "crisis of interpretation," in which hermeneutics is necessarily indeterminate, neither purely allegorical nor philological. In a key article on the topic of interpretation and meaning in the prologue to *Gargantua*, Richard Regosin considers the issue one not so much of ambiguity as of "discursive multiplicity" ("Ins(ides)"). For him, the prologue is indicative of a way of thinking about Rabelais aligned with what Bakhtin calls heteroglossia in "Discourse in the Novel." As Regosin writes, the narrator's "speech is never absolutely or unequivocally his own, a unique and personal language distinct from that of others but a composite of utterances drawn from others, outsides which are constantly introduced inside" (64). It is not instability per se, then, but the inevitable and constant input of speech acts coming in from outside the text that creates and constitutes Rabelais's unstable text. From another theoretical perspective, Ellie Ragland-Sullivan (*Rabelais and Panurge*) and Lawrence Kritzman (*Rhetoric of Sexuality*) examine Rabelais psychologically or psychoanalytically, placing him in dialogue with thinkers such as Sigmund Freud, Lacan, and Luce Irigaray.

These kinds of critical divergences of the 1970s, 1980s, and 1990s still take place in the twenty-first century, particularly in the wake of new theoretical orientations and schools. David LaGuardia sums up the polemic as

> the passion for the painstaking work of philology . . . versus the passion for rereading five-hundred-year-old works from the perspectives of modern, postmodern, and "cutting-edge" theories ranging from poststructuralism to queer theory, gender studies, performance theory, postcolonialism, and beyond. ("French Renaissance Literature" 5)

Attempting to realign the traditional debates or assumptions over the role of theory in understanding Rabelais, LaGuardia proposes a moderate or synthetic reading of this critical divide and explains how philology and theory do not have to be taken as antithetical. He reflects the view of a recent generation of scholars who combine or are comfortable with the coexistence of these two traditionally binarized approaches.

The issues of gender and sexuality loomed large in the critical apparatus over the past few decades as critics sought to understand the extent of Rabelais's misogyny, gender relations, same-sex sexuality, and masculinity—all unavoidable topics in the corpus. Early work on gender focused on Rabelais's involvement in the Renaissance configuration of the *querelle des femmes*, the debate over the nature and status of women (Lefranc, *Rabelais*; Screech, *Rabelaisian Marriage*). Much of the later work on gender has taken into account questions of hermeneutics as well as the extent of Rabelais's humor, particularly as feminist critics in the 1980s began to rethink the representation of women in his text. A seminal (and teachable) study on women in Rabelais was provided in 1985 by Elisabeth Chesney Zegura ("Toward a Feminist Reading of Rabelais"), who sought to think beyond a Rabelais-as-misogynist approach. How, she asks, can the unflattering views of women in the corpus be reconciled with the Abbey of Thélème episode, in which gender equality is the order of the day? For Zegura, women function as signs of the unfaithful reader and as tools to satirize men and phallocentric culture, meaning that gender equality is not off Rabelais's radar screen. Rigolot also studies misogyny ("Rabelais") and the question of charity and temptation ("Three Temptations"). A pioneer in early modern gender studies, Carla Freccero destabilized the assumption of father-son lineage in Rabelais in *Father Figures* (1991) and examined representations of women and gender in a sophisticated way, in articles such as "Damning Haughty Dames," "Feminism," and "The 'Instance' of the Letter." In "The Other and the Same," Freccero discussed the queerness of the androgyne device in the description of Gargantua's costume in chapter 8 of *Gargantua*. The "walls of Paris" episode (*Pantagruel*, ch. 15), whose assumed misogynistic representation still shocks many, was studied by Hope Glidden. Gray's *Gender, Rhetoric, and Print Culture in French Renaissance Writing* focused on a wide range of discourses of gender issues and how they reflect literary practices rather than social reality.

Because the *Tiers livre* treats issues of gender more directly than the first two books, critics have discussed it at length, in terms both of the representation of women (e.g., Weinberg, "Written"; Jordan, *Renaissance Feminism* 191–99) and of hysterical or immoderate masculinity (e.g., ch. 2 in Kritzman, *Rhetoric*; ch. 3 in Reeser; ch. 3 in LaGuardia, *Intertextual Masculinity*). The issue of masculinity has also been treated through the Rabelaisian image of the *braguette* ("codpiece"), as for instance in Persels's "Bragueta Humanística; or, Humanism's Codpiece." The fluidity of masculinity in the *Quart livre* has been treated by Alice Berry (*Charm*) and Reeser. In much of this recent work, gender constructs in the Rabelaisian corpus are considered as dialogic or relational, thus about a gender system more than about women or men per se.

With the postmodern interest in space and in the role of travel in Renaissance culture, critical work on the relation between Rabelais and geography has been of great interest. Lefranc's 1905 exploration of the relation between *Pantagruel* and Jacques Cartier in *Navigations de Pantagruel* is a classic on the topic, and Bakhtin's discussion of the "chronotope" famously treats the relation between time and space in Rabelais ("Forms of Time and the Chronotope in the Novel"). Paul Smith's reading of the *Quart livre* considers the issue of travel in a sense more metaphoric than cultural (*Voyage*). Known as a scholar of early modern travel narratives, Frank Lestringant links Renaissance geographic notions with Rabelais in some of his essays in *Écrire le monde à la Renaissance* ("Writing the World in the Renaissance"; e.g., "Rabelais et le récit toponymique" and "L'insulaire de Rabelais, ou la fiction en archipel" ["Rabelais and Toponymic Narrative" and "The Insular in Rabelais; or, Archipelago Fiction"]). Maps and cartographic discourse became important cultural artifacts in the sixteenth century. Their role in shaping Rabelais's text has been studied in depth by Tom Conley in *The Self-Made Map*.

Scholars interested in politics and the nation have published important work on the topic in the twenty-first century, although earlier work brings politics and sovereignty into the discussion (e.g., Screech's *Rabelais*; Hermann Ligier's *La politique de Rabelais* [1880]). In his groundbreaking *Literature and Nation in the Sixteenth Century*, Timothy Hampton examines how the literariness of Rabelais relates to national community and political topics in the period, including the Turkish question in chapter 14 of *Pantagruel*. Sections of Michael Randall's *The Gargantuan Polity* focus on the issue of the individual versus the polity in Rabelais.

This history of reading is without end; its course will and should continue as long as there are readers of goodwill. The present volume is designed to offer additional proof that there are still new ways of reading, rereading, and understanding Rabelais. This is all to the good, for if only one reading were possible, if a definitive interpretation could be arrived at, there would be little left to interest future readers. After so many centuries, Rabelais's work still surprises, still engages us in dialogue. This vitality is the sign of a true polyphonic text.

Teaching Rabelais: An Overview

Although highly appealing at first reading, Rabelais's work presents innumerable interpretive difficulties for students and, consequently, pedagogical difficulties for instructors. With their episodic and discontinuous structure, his books are not plot-driven, which makes the selection of chapters for classroom study all the more important. Instructors may wish to assign sections that provide case studies of major interpretive issues. In the light of the critical debate about design or stable authorial intent, some instructors may wish to present or discuss theories of coherence of the texts, perhaps using the textual mappings in Duval's work as a base to show students how they can be taken as a unified whole and what that wholeness signifies. Other instructors may prefer to follow the side of the critical divide that does not assume a key to understanding the texts but views meaning as never fully present or always out of reach. Still others may ask students whether the two approaches are mutually exclusive or whether there is wiggle room in one model for the presence of the other.

Because certain chapters have become canonical in Western literary and cultural traditions, instructors may wish to privilege them in their courses (see part 1 for the most commonly taught episodes).

If student expectations about the nature of literature make premodern episodic narrative difficult to teach, the chronological gap between the Renaissance and the twenty-first century is also difficult for them to bridge in terms of content. Without a grasp on issues contemporary to Rabelais, students will experience difficulty in understanding how and why the text is satirical, who or what is being criticized, or even what satire means in a Renaissance context. For example, an episode such as the encounter with the Limousin student who butchers the French language (*Pantagruel*, ch. 6) requires that students understand both the cultural context of French humanism and the role of language in the early sixteenth century. Replete with references to other texts (ancient, medieval, biblical, and contemporary) and to high and low culture (in the areas of religion, humanism, education, politics, language, and gender), Rabelais's work requires constant interpretation and explanation, especially for readers lacking the requisite literary and historical background. Students will also need to gain a sense of the orality of Rabelais's text in the context of print culture in the sixteenth century. Because some students are easily paralyzed by an excess of information about the period and by heavily annotated editions of Rabelais, it helps to focus on key episodes and critical questions, and to provide an appropriate amount of context.

Rabelais's frequent use of popular culture and of scatology presents similar hermeneutic problems as students try to make sense of his vulgar allusions and obscene language, perhaps experiencing discomfort or shock with the text. Rarely trained to think about such questions in college or university settings, they may not automatically take an intellectual or interpretive approach or consider how low images may have a higher meaning. Students thus frequently need guidance in articulating how and why Rabelais includes such language in his work. Episodes such as Gargantua's invention of the ass wipe (*Gargantua*, ch. 13) are difficult—if not impossible—to interpret without appropriate background information on the cultural and intellectual context of Renaissance humanism. Bakhtin's thesis, along with its various critiques, can be helpful in discussing corporality because it provides a stimulating theoretical model, or starting point, for instructors to encourage students to begin to imagine and describe what the text is doing beyond the obvious. Students may have difficulty leaving their personal lives and cultural context and thinking about a text that is so different. Openly discussing their responses to the text and processing whether those responses would have been similar to those of Renaissance readers, thus whether Rabelais meant for his work to be shocking or not, can lead to fruitful discussion of diachronic differences. Because students may not consider the body, and its various excretions, it may be necessary to help them think about specific cultural constructs of the body and of vulgarity in a larger sense. Living in a world in which religion may be seen as antithetical to the grotesque body, North American students may ask whether Rabelais's works can be taken as anti-Catholic, antireligious, or atheistic.

Content questions cannot be disassociated from the complications arising from Rabelais's peculiar use of language. Without proper guidance, students risk missing allusions and multiple levels of meaning in a text that is essentially polymorphic and linguistically difficult. Teaching Rabelais in the original requires careful preparation on the instructor's part. Key linguistic issues have to be addressed in a way that allows students to grapple with a different French language. But beyond the actual orthographic, syntactic, and semantic issues raised by language, they will need to deal with the concept of language, to consider how the text reflects on language and comments on a number of specific languages, including Latin and even French. Finally, because much of Rabelais's impact is linguistically based, students who read in translation will lose much of the sense of the original, and instructors who teach in English may want to present select examples of language play to students who have little or no French.

Language is only one side of an even greater problem posed by Rabelais's text: its ultimate intent and meaning. To what extent and in what ways does comedy acquire a serious, more substantial meaning? Since scholarly debate on the topic has focused on the prologues or basic structure or design that would account for the various, frequently contradictory, stances and strands that permeate the work, teachers of Rabelais might want to introduce students to an abridged version of this debate. In the same way that the prologue to *Gargantua* has served as a focal point in the history of Rabelais criticism, it can serve also as a jumping-off point for discussing hermeneutics. A question for students might be, What does the image of the Silenus box tell us about how to read the rest of Rabelais's text? Thinking about a Renaissance text as a statement on the nature of meaning and interpretation will challenge students who are often more comfortable thinking about cultural context or character motivation. Students who come to Rabelais with the idea that they should be able to interpret every episode (as they might with a nineteenth-century novel) are often frustrated when a single or stable meaning escapes them or when one idea is juxtaposed with an opposite idea. The concept that Rabelais is commenting on the nature of reading and writing, or on textuality and meaning itself, may not be in their critical apparatus. Students need to be taught to move away from focusing only on cultural context or on character and to consider as well the self-reflexive aspects of the texts. Hopefully, they will be led to discover the modern or postmodern aspects of the four books and to reconceive their previous image of the Renaissance as outdated or irrelevant. Indeed, students can be invited to make connections between Rabelais and their own media-obsessed cultural context (movies, television shows, Internet videos).

The issue of ultimate intent or seriousness often reaches a head in the classroom during discussions of expressions of alterity in the four books. Students may have no difficulty teasing out ways in which Rabelais's representation of the Turks in *Pantagruel*, chapter 14, for instance, is hegemonic, demeaning, Christian-centered, or orientalist, but they may have more difficulty—or even be unable—to take analysis a step further and consider the extent to which he is playing with ethnic clichés and mocking the non-Turk. Similarly, a frequently recurring pedagogical issue concerns the depiction of women. Students' shock at the "walls of Paris" episode (*Pantagruel*, ch. 15) and at a number of misogynist-seeming episodes in the *Tiers livre* can serve as an incentive for reflecting more deeply on the nature of gender representation. Is a misogynist representation necessarily misogynist? How should we understand gender in Renaissance humanism, the *querelle des femmes*, or marriage and medical discourse? The change of emphasis in gender studies has resulted in a focus in the classroom on questions of masculinity and on how images of women relate to constructions of masculinity, thus allowing for students to question which gender is being mocked and why.

The Essays: An Introduction

All the basic pedagogical issues with teaching Rabelais are addressed in the essays in this volume. The essays are arranged into six sections that deal with important aspects of teaching Rabelais. The first section, "Literary and Textual Approaches to Rabelais," presents the main issues raised by reading Rabelais and suggests strategies for teaching them. Contributors refer to specific episodes, but the focus is on assisting instructors with promoting an understanding of the large-scale issues in the literary and linguistic aspects of the corpus. The first quartet of essays treats the four most major textual issues in Rabelais: hybridity, reading/writing, intertextuality, and satire. Rigolot's opening essay presents a basic element of Rabelais that recurs in other essays in this volume—hybridity (e.g., by Renner and by O'Brien). Regosin's essay discusses how to teach questions of meaning in the all-important prologues, bringing the major issues debated by critics into the classroom. Duval looks at intertextuality, using the Bible as his pedagogical case study. Bernd Renner focuses on teaching satire and parody. A cluster of essays then deals with techniques to help students approach the issue that they confront immediately on starting to read Rabelais in French—namely, language. These essays provide four ways of thinking about teaching the concept and the specifics of language. John O'Brien provides coverage of key critical approaches to language in Rabelais while also guiding instructors toward an important reading of language play. Todd W. Reeser and Kirsten A. Fudeman have contributed sister essays on dealing with Rabelais's French in specific ways, the first on teaching students to deal with anxiety around language through the text itself, the second on practical ways to teach language from a linguistics perspective. These two essays respond directly to the pedagogical problem most often cited in the MLA surveys: student perception that Rabelais's French is difficult or impossible. The section concludes with Valerie Worth-Stylianou's essay on issues around English translation, a question central to this volume, given the large number of instructors who teach Rabelais in translation.

The next section, "Cultural Contexts," provides instructors with cultural and sociohistorical background for Rabelais, discusses its relation to his oeuvre, and suggests techniques for teaching this background. The first two essays treat what (after language) was most commonly cited in the surveys as a teaching problem—the unavoidable question of the obscene or scandalous Rabelais. Miernowski and Persels's essays are complementary since each provides a different approach to some of the more scandalous aspects of Rabelais: Miernowski helps students see how Rabelais meant his work to be shocking in his time, whereas Persels wants to desensitize students by placing Rabelais's scatology in historical context and sensitize them to the historical fertility of scatological humor. The remaining pieces focus on various aspects of culture and context: politics (Timothy Hampton), religion (Deborah N. Losse), individualism (Michael Randall), utopia (Scott D. Juall), cartography (Tom Conley), food (Timothy J. Tomasik), and giants (Walter Stephens).

The next set of essays, "Teaching Gender and Sexuality," is designed to show how instructors can help students think about gender in cultural and literary context as well as place it in dialogue with familiar constructs of gender. Elisabeth Hodges discusses how one might treat the misogynist episodes of *Pantagruel* in the classroom, in particular the infamous "walls of Paris" episode that rarely fails to shock undergraduates and graduates alike. Carla Freccero's and Lawrence D. Kritzman's essays focus on teaching other aspects related to gender that are of interest to many students—namely, masculinity and queer sexuality.

In the following section, "Specific Episodes," contributors examine some of the best-known episodes of the Rabelaisian corpus and explain how to make sense of their polyvalence and how to provide students a focus, or a hook, for understanding them (Marcus Keller, Cynthia Skenazi, Andrea Frisch) or, conversely, how to use a specific episode to introduce students to a larger topic, such as humanism (Virginia Krause) or textuality (Floyd Gray). Survey participants identified the Abbey of Thélème (*Gargantua*, chs. 52–58), Gargantua's letter to Pantagruel (*Pantagruel*, ch. 8), and the prologues to *Gargantua* and *Pantagruel* as the most commonly taught episodes. Cynthia Skenazi's essay discusses teaching the famous letter from Gargantua to his son. See also Juall's essay on Thélème and utopia and Regosin's on the prologues, in this volume.

In "Classroom Contexts," contributors place Rabelais's work in dialogue with modern approaches to teaching, focusing on the use of visual materials (painting, film, the Web, and digital images of printed books) to help students gain a better understanding of text and context. Elizabeth Chesney Zegura discusses how she uses aural recordings and paintings in the classroom, while Gary Ferguson provides a specific lesson using Monty Python to introduce Rabelais. Karen James and Mary McKinley explain how to locate and use online rare book images. Pedagogical discussions of student-centered teaching through in-class reading aloud and student performance of certain episodes are also included (John Parkin, David LaGuardia). James M. Palmer details how creative writing exercises can be used in the classroom and includes sample assignments. This section aims to specify how instructors have gone beyond classic textual analysis or discussion to make Rabelais appealing to both undergraduates and graduates. The essays are particularly useful for making this difficult writer accessible to media-centered students, and most of them are applicable to courses taught in French as well as in English.

Because Rabelais is frequently taught in English translation and outside French programs, the final section of the volume, "Comparative Approaches to Rabelais," concerns how three instructors have integrated Rabelais into their syllabi in comparative contexts and how they relate the writer to other works in a given course. The first essay focuses on a great-books course, the second on a comparative course on comedy, the third on a comparative course on monstrosity. Jerry Root discusses Rabelais's role in the great-books course he has taught for many years at the University of Utah and how the theme of allegory can be used to put Rabelais in dialogue with other premodern writers. Carl Fisher, whose essay recalls Rigolot's essay in the first section, explains how to teach comedy and comic realism in comparative literature courses. While the first two essays focus on literature courses, Kathleen Long discusses ways to put Rabelais in dialogue with very diverse kinds of texts, including the television series *The X-Files*. She describes a survey course on monstrosity, but many of her teaching techniques can be fruitfully applied to other comparative courses as well as suggest ways to put Rabelais in dialogue with pop-cultural texts.

Rabelais and Hybridity

François Rigolot

In his keynote address delivered at the 2006 Montréal international symposium on Rabelais, Edwin M. Duval, the noted Yale Renaissance scholar, remarked:

> Nous vivons aujourd'hui dans un monde hybride, et dans un monde obsédé par l'hybridité. . . . Même nos voitures deviennent hybrides. Alors pourquoi pas la littérature? Pourquoi pas Rabelais? ("En quoi" 1)
>
> We live nowadays in a hybrid world, a world obsessed by hybridity. . . . Even our cars are becoming hybrid. Then why not literature? Why not Rabelais? (my trans.)

To be sure, critical categories used in literary theory often reflect prevailing ethical, aesthetic, and ideological notions at the moment when they are conceived. Whether we are aware of it or not, our reading of the past is influenced by the conceptual framework of the present. This was a key factor, for instance, in the elaboration of Hans Robert Jauss's concept of the "horizon of expectation" (270), and in performative genres the very combination of hybridity and dialogism is a response to the ever-changing "displacing space of cultural transactions," which characterizes our postcolonial world, as opposed to essentialist paradigms imposed by so-called monolithic and monolinguistic discourses (Bhabha 227). Strange as it may seem, Renaissance writers lived in a world that went, mutatis mutandis, through similar sets of cultural transformations, from medieval Scholastic certainties to the unresolved ambiguities of humanism, especially in the northern Renaissance as the Old World was groping toward the new paradigms of the Reformation.

Let us look for a moment at the seemingly anachronistic notion of hybridity. The Latin word *ibrida*, often spelled *hybrida* by contamination from the Greek *hubris* ("exaggerated pride" or "self-confidence"), can be found not only in Pliny's *Natural History* (8.213) but also in Horace (*Satires* 1.7.2), Martial (*Epigrams* 6.39.2), and Suetonius (*Life of Augustus* 19). In his *Dictionarium latinogallicum* (1552), Robert Estienne calls "hybrid" a man who had a German father and a French mother (632 r°). Etymological dictionaries trace the origin of the French adjective *hibride* back to the end of the sixteenth century (1596); it then meant "bastard, or of mixed blood" ("bâtard, de sang mêlé"). The seventeenth-century usage shifted to linguistic grounds to speak of "words formed with elements taken from two different languages, notably Latin and Greek" ("Hibride").

From a taxonomic point of view, a distinction might be made between hybridity and compositionality (Duval, "En quoi"). Compositional objects proceed from mechanical assembling of different parts, whereas hybrid ones are the result of an organic fusion of heterogeneous elements. For instance, the griffin is a mythical animal typically having the head, forepart, and wings of an eagle and the body, hind legs, and tail of a lion. His figure is compositional as opposed to the mule's, which is natural since it results from the physical crossing of a male donkey and a mare. In his book *La grottesque*, André Chastel refers to hybridity as an ambiguous and monstrous form, which is used more widely than generally expected in the Renaissance (40–50). Chastel lists a number of those *bizarreries*, some of them mentioned by Leonardo da Vinci, like winged lizards or horse-headed lyres, which demonstrated to the artist the oddities of nature. The Renaissance held several parallel discourses on what were then called errors of nature and what we would treat today in teratology, the study of malformations, monstrosity, or serious deviations from the norm (Rigolot, *Erreur* 133–64). While some thinkers tried to create a typology of monstrous forms, others thought about the problem of their cause and endeavored to find an esoteric significance or to place them in the category of the unusual, thus explaining our failure to understand these abnormal phenomena by attributing it to our ignorance of the laws of nature (Céard 87–158). More positively, hybridity was interpreted as part of a vast cosmic phenomenon, often presented as *natura naturans*—namely, nature's untamed fertility and unstoppable vitality in the animal, vegetal, and even mineral realms (Jeanneret, *Perpetuum mobile* 123–60).

Much critical thinking has been given to the theory of dialogism as an early modern discursive form, especially in Neo-Latin and vernacular treatises (Burke; Cox; Girardi; Heitsch and Vallée; Hempfer; Kushner; Marsh; Pugliese; Snyder). Yet it may be useful to turn to Mikhail Bakhtin's own handling of the concepts of dialogism and hybridity before exploring Rabelais's version of this intriguing phenomenon. In *The Dialogic Imagination*, Bakhtin gave a definition of what he paradoxically called linguistic "hybrid construction":

> What we are calling *hybrid construction* is an utterance that belongs, by its grammatical (syntactic) and compositional markers, to a single speaker, but that actually contains mixed within it two utterances, two speech manners, two styles, "two languages," two semantic and axiological belief systems. It is the fusion of two opposite semantic and compositional elements, the boundaries of which are effaced. ("Discourse" 304)

Bakhtin's definition blends two heterogeneous orders: on the one hand, construction and composition belong to a mechanical and therefore artificial process; on the other, the word "fusion" refers to an organic blending with obvious natural connotations. Although organicity and mechanicity are clearly distinguished in theory, they become often conjoined in practice, as demonstrated not only in the Bakhtinian oxymoron but also, interestingly, in the way Rabelais advertised his conception of dialogic interlocution.

It is noteworthy that Rabelais borrowed a similar notion from Lucian of Samosata (c. AD 125–after AD 180), the Assyrian satirist who wrote in the Greek language and was rediscovered and translated by Rabelais's contemporaries (Mayer; Lauvergnat-Gagnière 235–61; Duval, *Design of Rabelais's* Tiers livre 216). Although other sixteenth-century texts, like Desiderius Erasmus's *Colloquia* and Thomas More's *Utopia*, enact the Lucian claim to dialogic ambiguity, a particularly clear theoretical assessment of Lucian's key concepts takes shape in Rabelais's *Third Book*, published in 1546 and for the first time under his own name: "François Rabelais, doctor of medicine." It stages philosophical dialogues and comic conversations about a topic dear to Erasmian humanists: matrimonial commitment. In 1506, Erasmus and More had cooperated in translating three of Lucian's dialogues, *Menippus, The Lover of Lies*, and *The Cynic*. The two friends were obviously fascinated by the balance of moral utility and satirical wit they had found in these works.

As a specialist of mock encomiums and absurd dialogues, Rabelais was dubbed the French Lucian in his own time, though mostly by his enemies. Like his Greek, Dutch, and English models, he constantly worried about his readers' responses to the imaginative thrust brought about by his disquieting creativity. By producing hybrid works that mixed genres, levels of style, and rhetorical modes, he displayed remarkable control over a daunting verbal cornucopia (Cave, *Cornucopian Text* 3–34). At the same time, he was afraid that any Lucian-like blending of forms, modes, and registers might trigger a dangerous negative reaction. Highly conscious of his vulnerability, Rabelais placed his narrator under Lucian's protection, having no hesitation to create a strange and ambiguous world where, at every moment, the mixing of literary forms, serious dialogue, and comic elements established a puzzling mode of reading that evaded clear, univocal interpretive resolution (Robinson 130–33, 165–97).

From the start of the prologue, the narrator identifies with Diogenes, the Cynic philosopher who, in Lucian's "How to Write History," ridiculed the historiographers of his time, and speaks ironically about his own situation as a French writer in a country obsessed with the prospect of war with the imperial armies. Toward the end, however, Rabelais switches to a different model, a brief dialogue known for its Latin title as *Prometheus es in verbis* (*You're a Prometheus in Words*), in which Lucian responded to an anonymous friend who compared his work with Prometheus, the mythical hero who fashioned man from clay and stole fire from the gods to ignite him with life (*Works* 6: 417–27). Indeed this is a major text for the development of the notion of dialogicity and hybridity in Western literature. The central episode is the story of Ptolemy, king of Egypt, who thought that, by exhibiting a black camel and a bicolored man, he would please his people, only to realize that he achieved the opposite. This exemplum serves as a parable, showing how difficult it is for a writer to please his readers by producing an impure work, one that does not conform to traditional genres or discursive forms—in this case, a fusion of philosophical dialogue and comedy. In other words, to return to Bakhtin's language, the great challenge for the writer is to generate a "hybrid construction" that blends genres to make a greater work of art.

"So you say I am a Prometheus?" Lucian's narrator asks his interlocutor.

> If by this, my friend, you mean that my works are of clay, I accept the comparison . . . for they are little better than dirty mud. But if you are over-praising my dialogues, implying that they are similar to Prometheus, the wisest of the Titans, you may find that people will detect irony and an Attic sniff in your praise. Someone might console me by saying: "He was praising your originality in following no exemplar, just as Prometheus, at a time when no men existed, fashioned them from his imagination, when he gave shape and form to such living creatures that they might move easily and be graceful to see. He was the master-craftsman, though Athena helped by breathing into the mud and making the models alive." . . . I am telling you, I do not want to be considered an innovator. The originality is no help when you produce an ugly thing. (419, 421, 423; trans. modified)

To make his point, Lucian's narrator tells the story of Ptolemy's mistake with the black camel and the bicolored man and draws the following conclusion:

> Well, I am afraid that I in my turn may seem to have acted something like your Prometheus in mixing female with male, and may be charged with that; or rather that I may seem a Prometheus in another respect—in deceiving my listeners perhaps by giving them bones covered in fat, comic jests under philosophic solemnity. For as to theft (he is the god of theft), away with

> that charge! This alone you could not say was in my words. Whom could I steal from? Unless someone has invented such fish-horses and goat-stags independently without my knowing. But what could I do? I must abide by what I chose once and for all. To change one's plan is the work of Epi-metheus [Afterthought], not Pro-metheus [Forethought]. (427)

To be sure, ever since Plato's and Plutarch's masterpieces, the use of dialogue had been associated with philosophical works, but comic characters and situations belonged to a popular and lower register. In *The Double Indictment*, Lucian already claimed that he had altered the form of the philosophical dialogue by blending other elements into it (*Works* 3: 144–47). Therefore the fusion between two very different genres might appear as a monstrosity: a fantastic creature combining the elegance of a horse with the vulgarity of a centaur. This hybrid figure was used again in the ekphrastic story of Zeuxis, who dared to paint a female hippocentaur, as a symbol for the hybrid novelties of his literary creations (6: 157). To traditional academic circles, philosophy and buffoonery cannot tolerate mixing ugliness and beauty. Lucian's narrator might fall into the same trap by assembling highs and lows in his discourse, an audacious innovation that might turn his audience against him:

> [Philosophical] dialogue and comedy were not entirely friendly and compatible from the beginning. . . . Dialogue's companions she [Comedy] mocked as "heavy-thinkers," "high-talkers," and suchlike. She had one delight—to deride them and drown them in Dionysiac liberties. She showed them now walking on air and mixing with the clouds, now measuring sandals for fleas [a reference to Aristophanes's *The Clouds*]—her notion of heavenly subtleties, I suppose! Dialogue however took his conversations very seriously, philosophizing about nature and virtue. So, in musical terms, there were two octaves between them, from highest to lowest. Nevertheless I have dared to combine them as they are into a harmony, though they are not in the least docile and do not easily tolerate partnership. (425–27)

Lucian's profound reflections on aesthetic responses to literary novelties struck a chord in the imagination of Rabelais as he was writing his *Third Book*. First, he borrowed the story of Diogenes at the siege of Corinth from Lucian's "How to Write History." His narrative persona shared his misgivings with potential readers like the Cynic philosopher: "Je pareillement quoy que soys hors d'effroy, ne suis hors d'esmoy" (522; "In the same way, although I have nothing to fear, I am nonetheless not free from care" [283]). Second, he borrowed the Ptolemy exemplum from *A Prometheus in Words* and remodeled it as follows:

> Me souvient toutesfois avoir leu, que Ptolemé, filz de Lagus, quelque jour entre autres despouilles et butins de ses conquestes, præsentant aux

> Ægyptiens en plain theatre un chameau Bactrian tout noir, et un esclave bigarré . . . , choses non encores veues en Ægypte, esperoit par offre de ces nouveaultez l'amour du peuple envers soy augmenter. Qu'en advient il? À la production du Chameau tous feurent effroyez et indignez: à la veue de l'home bigurré aulcuns se mocquerent, autres le abhominerent comme monstre infame, créé par erreur de nature. Somme, l'experience qu'il avoit de complaire à ses Ægyptiens, et par ce moyen extendre l'affection qu'ilz luy pourtoient naturellement, luy decoulla des mains. Et entendit plus à plaisir et delices leur estre choses belles, eleguantes et perfaictes que ridicules et monstrueuses.
>
> However, I remember reading how one day Ptolemy, the son of Lagus, in the crowded theatre, among other spoils and booty from his conquests, presented the Egyptians with a completely black Bactrian camel, and a slave parti-colored . . . , things never yet seen in Egypt, hoping by these novelties to increase their love for himself. But what was the result? At the appearance of the camel they were all frightened and indignant; at the sight of the parti-colored man, some mocked and others were shocked by what they considered a loathsome monster, created by an error of Nature. In short, his hopes of pleasing the Egyptians, and in this way increasing their natural affection for him, slipped through his fingers. He discovered that they took more pleasure and delight in the handsome, the elegant, and the perfect than in ridiculous and monstrous objects.

Although the narrator remains largely faithful to the Greek text, Rabelais changes a few details, particularly transforming Lucian's "bicolored man" ("hominem bicolorem" in Micyllus's contemporary Latin translation [Lucian, *Opera*]) into a motley-colored slave ("esclave bigarré"), with a much longer and more precise description than in the Greek and Latin sixteenth-century editions of the original (see Duval, *Design of Rabelais's* Tiers livre 226–27):

> un esclave bigarré (tellement que de son corps l'une part estoit noire, l'autre blanche, non en compartiment de latitude par le diaphragme, comme feut cette femme sacrée à Venus Indicque, laquelle feut recongnue du philosophe Tyanien entre le fleuve Hydaspes, et le mont Caucase, mais en dimension perpendiculaire: choses non encores veues en Ægypte). (526–28)
>
> a slave parti-colored (in such a way that half of his body was black and the other white, not divided horizontally at the diaphragm like that female votary of the Indian Venus, who was seen by the philosopher of Tyana somewhere between the river Hydaspes and Mount Caucasus, but perpendicularly. Such phenomena had never yet been seen in Egypt). (285)

Rabelais's slave is described as a strange monster whose body is neatly divided vertically by colors. Unlike a mulatto's, his hybridity shows no fusion of racial features. Similarly, comedy and dialogue are oddly juxtaposed in the writer's discourse. As a result, his readers may be unhappy not to find the pure canonical form of philosophical dialogues in the *Tiers livre*. Interestingly, contrary to Philostratus's picture of the Indian woman, Rabelais's description rejects any hierarchical division—that is, white above and black below: the slave's colors coexist equally, just as discursive seriousness will share textual space with comical exuberance. To speak again like Bakhtin, the promise of organic hybridization is frustrated by a "hybrid construction"—that is, a compositional montage meant to deconstruct artificiality in the name of a hypothetical naturalness.

In the first complete translation of Lucian's works into French, Filbert Bretin added a commentary to explain at length what separates dialogue from comedy, insisting on the radically innovative way in which the ancient satirist decided to bridge their antagonistic nature by adapting them and conjoining them fruitfully:

> Car à vray dire, le dialogue et la comédie n'ont esté familiers et amis de tout temps: veu que celuy là [le dialogue] avoit jadis ses diputes à la maison, et à part soy aux promenoirs, avec peu de compagnie: mais ceste cy [la comédie] se dediant à Baccus soy mesme, frequentoit les teatres, jouoit quant et quant, et faisoit des risées, et donnoit des brocards, et cheminoit à la cadence du hautbois. . . . Et neanmoins nous avons bien osé, ces choses estant de telle sorte, *les conjoindre l'une à l'autre, et les adapter ensemble*: encor qu'elles ne soient flechissantes, et ne souffrent facilement aucune communion. (Lucian, *Œuvres* 7; qtd. in Zaercher 10)

> For, to tell the truth, dialogue and comedy have not been intimate friends forever; in fact, in the days of yore, the first [dialogue] held its disputes at home, and privately during promenades with a few companions; but the second [comedy], consecrating itself to Bacchus, took place in theaters, indulged in playful mockery, loved to gibe and lampoon, accompanied by light musical scores. . . . And yet, these things being what they are, we have dared to conjoin them and adapt them together, even though they are unbending and hardly put up with coalescing. (my trans.)

Such a new companionship may shock the unprepared audience, although it fits perfectly with Erasmus's idea of bringing together heterogeneous discursive paradigms in the form of apparently oppositional terms, motivated by a profound understanding of *serio ludere* ("playful seriousness"):

> Nothing is so trivial as treating serious subjects in a trivial manner; and similarly, nothing is more entertaining than treating trivialities in such a

> way as to make it clear you are doing anything but trifle with them. The world will pass its own judgment on me, but unless my self-love entirely deceives me, my praise of folly has not been altogether foolish.
> (*Praise* 6–7 ["Letter to More"])

Thus Rabelais's readers should not only accept but embrace these bold linkages: first, because Rabelais was not the first to advocate them; second, because they were much praised, translated, and imitated by great fellow humanists. Such enlightened readers will then deserve to become Pantagruel's disciples:

> Je recongnois en eulx tous une forme specificque et proprieté individuale, laquelle nos majeurs nommoient Pantagruelisme, moiennant laquelle jamais en maulvaise partie ne prendront choses quelconques ilz congnoistront sourdre de bon, franc et loyal couraige. Je les ay ordinairement veuz bon vouloir en payement prendre et en icelluy acquiescer, quand debilité de puissance y a esté associée. (528)

> In every one of them I detect that specific and individual quality which our ancestors used to call Pantagruelism; which assures me that they will never take in bad part anything that they know to spring from a good, honest, and loyal heart. I have so often seen them take the will for the payment, and be content with it, when that was all the debtor had. (286)

By bringing hybrid construction and Pantagruelism together Rabelais clearly intends to convince his readers that his own "esclave bigarré"—namely, his new book—no matter how bizarre it may look, is worth perusing. Yet as I have already noted, Lucian did not talk about a slave but simply about a man half-white and half-black ("hominem bicolorem" and, later, "semialbum hominem"). Rabelais gives Lucian's man a new identity; he turns him into a person held in servitude, subservient to a dominating other and negatively affected by "debilité de puissance" (528; literally, "lack of potency"). Yet this bondage is praised, as if, against all expectations, it was endowed with a redeeming value. Debility and hybridity are weaknesses that the Rabelaisian narrator turns into strength as part of his paradoxical strategy, his rhetorical *captatio benevolentiae*.

If Rabelais's rehabilitated bicolored slave stands as an emblem for his work, a case might be made for interpreting the writer's propensity for hybridity in an evangelical perspective. After all, *The Third Book* was dedicated to Marguerite de Navarre, the king's sister and a religious, liberal mind; her patronage was sought actively by the group of reform-minded Catholics to which Rabelais belonged. By warmly welcoming not only a slave but a cross-bred slave, the Erasmian humanist displayed a form of *caritas*, a charitable disposition rooted in the Good Samaritan parable and associated with the patristic notion of *synkatabasis* (Greek for "friendly reception and welcome") (Rigolot, "Quand le géant"). Rabelais owned a copy of Suidas's Greek-Latin *Lexicon*, where he had found many terms, including *panourgos*, from which he derived Panurge's name (Suidas 935; Schrader 80–89; Schwartz, "Panurge's Impact" 7; Defaux, *Curieux* 134). Under the entry *synkatabasis* he had read excerpts from John Chrysostom's homilies, as well as from Origen's *Contra celsum*, which comments on God's decision to engage human beings in dialogue through the mystery of the Incarnation: "Out of his disproportionate love, God *condescends* [*syykatabainonta*] to come to the rescue of ignorant men, poor women, *slaves*, in short all those who receive help from no one. . . ." (1480 cd).

In a similar fashion, Rabelais's giant kings consent to lower themselves and hybridize their forms to reach out to their most humble subjects. Thus Pantagruel enters in conversation with Panurge, the lecherous fool, and shows how much he cares for him (*Pantagruel* 562; 201; ch. 4). Similarly, the composite image on Gargantua's medallion (*Gargantua* 88–90; 56; ch. 8) is designed to emblematize the physical, intellectual, and spiritual values of peace and harmony (Gray, *Gender* 152). Thus for humanist writers with evangelical leanings in the time of the Reformation, hybridity was not limited to a question of aesthetics; it had to be squarely positioned at the center of the renovated biblical message. God's willingness to become man constituted the most extraordinary act of racial cross-breedings. Saint John's "Et verbum caro factum est" ("And the Word became flesh") was no artificial montage; it had become the only possible form of dialogue, established through a total fusion between body and soul, the human and the divine.

Strangely enough, when Rabelais imitates Lucian, he repeats God's philanthropic gesture by presenting his work as the most outrageous and potentially most offensive type of *métissage*. We can understand why the Jews were shocked by the theological implications of this new brand of Christian hybridity: how could they possibly imagine all-powerful Yaweh's lowering himself to the level of human weaknesses? In the rabbinical tradition this was more than nonsense; it amounted to blasphemy.

Just as the Egyptians were furious at Ptolemy's monstrous display, just as the Greeks criticized Lucian's mixing of philosophy and comedy, just as the Jews condemned the Christian God-made-man scheme, some of Rabelais's readers were likely to object to his recasting of hybridity. After all, Rabelais did mix Pantagruel's serious dialogue on Christian ethics with preposterous jesting, bawdy tales, and unabashed banter (Hayes). This doubling also underlies Rabelais's mixed theory of language, which gives equal time to Cratylus and Hermogenes, his opponent (Rigolot, *Poétique* 102–04; Reeser 156–58). Although the narrator may defiantly rule out a possible defeat ("Non fera, Hercules!" [528; "I swear by Hercules that it won't happen!" (285)]), Rabelais seems to have remained uncertain as to how his "bicolored book" might be received by his readers. How would the king's sensualistic court and his sister's evangelical circle respond? What would his fellow humanists make of his strange setup of Pantagruelic philosophy and Panurgic comedy? Would they remain as blind as Ptolemy's Egyptians?

If Egypt remains a land of oppressors, Rabelais becomes a new Moses whose mission is to bring forth the slaves out of bondage (Exod. 3.7–8) and establish a new genre of dialogue based on a cross-breeding of literary forms. Let us not forget that the adjective "biguarré" (528; "motley-colored" [285]) described a jester's costume. As an inspired buffoon, the writer himself dons the motley. Yet this is obviously meant to force us, readers, out of our Egyptian blindness. Lucian and Rabelais share a common tradition, largely based on a rhetoric of exemplarity. At the same time, their common use of hybridity as a literary metaphor allows for a different type of intentionality rooted in a hermeneutical shift that reflects the epistemic changes in the discursive field of their times.

The Prologues: Rabelais on Reading and Writing

Richard Regosin

The prologues, where Rabelais addresses his practice of writing and the anticipated reading and reception of his work, offer engaging material for us as teachers of literature, because they mirror our activity as critical writers and readers and point to the very concerns and practices we address with our students. Each of the prologues provides a different slant on the self-conscious act of writing and draws our attention in different ways to questions of language, narration, tradition, influence, and intertextuality; to issues of style, genre, and literary mode; and to problems about how to read and who is reading. As Rabelais's writing involves us in what we might call its inside dynamic, each prologue also invents, reacts to, and speaks with a historical and cultural outside that asks us to consider as well forces that shape both the content and form of the writing. The study of the prologues causes us to reflect on what we ourselves are doing as writers and readers; invites us to think about our understanding of text and context; opens up consideration of the role of the liminary text; and serves, by what it reveals of the prologues and by what it reminds us that the prologues conceal, as an important prolegomenon to the reading of the books that follow.

Students encounter what is perhaps the most interesting and perplexing element of the prologues, the figure of the narrator, from the first words they read. Where they might have expected to hear the measured words of the authorial and authoritative Rabelais that reflect sensibly on the work to follow, in the prologues to *Gargantua* and *Pantagruel* they find themselves in the presence of the disorienting Alcofribas, the boisterous, eccentric, digressive, excessive, and aggressive "author" of the text. Although this raucous and disconcerting author-narrator is replaced in the prologues to the *Tiers* and *Quart livres* by the more welcoming but equally excessive M. François Rabelais, *Docteur en Medicine*, the student can begin to appreciate that we have not come much closer to the real author Rabelais, who shares his name and profession, that this too is a mask that mediates and thus transforms authorial discourse. It is important—and not only for the study of Rabelais—to turn students' puzzlement to pedagogical advantage, to reacquaint students with the complex relation between author and narrator, and between narrator and narration, that must inform our critical reading and writing. Because Alcofribas and M. Rabelais are both outrageous authors, they put into question authorial voice; because they both are not and at the same time are the voice of Rabelais himself, they pointedly raise the issue of the status and function of the narrator. My experience has been that undergraduate students have difficulty understanding or accepting the narrator as a fictional persona and struggle with the distinction between what should be attributed to that persona and what might properly be attributed to the author. Narrators as literary characters have defining characteristics and attitudes, and reading with students to draw the portrait of Alcofribas, for example, and to determine his point of view can lead to a better understanding of how literary discourses function at multiple levels.

Rabelais's narrators also help us address the question of authorial intention, which so often preoccupies beginning student readers looking for the meaning or message of a literary work. Students frequently conflate narrator and author as a way of determining and confirming intention, as if the narrator speaks the mind of the author directly and as if intention were in fact recoverable in a simple way. Intention is of course a complex literary issue. It may be that what we identify as the motivating force of the writing can be determined only after the fact, can be articulated only in retrospect. Thus intention becomes less the cause of the writing than its effect.

We can underscore the problematic nature of intention by sharing with our students the narrator's own concern with the issue in the prologue to *Gargantua*. Referring to the allegorical readings of Homer and Ovid, the narrator denies that the authors intentionally hide the meanings of their texts and claims that he has not done so either. At the same time, he compares his book to a bone to be broken open to reach its "sustantificque mouelle" (52; "substantial marrow" [38]). Most critics have interpreted the convoluted and contradictory prose in which Alcofribas entangles himself as challenging the status of intention and of replacing certainty in the work of reading and interpretation with ambiguity (Gray, "Ambiguity"; La Charité, "Lectures"). But these passages also produce a competing reading, one that seeks both to affirm the integrity of intention and to restore confidence in the search for hidden meaning. According to this view, Alcofribas is questioning not the existence or accessibility of meaning but rather its source (Duval, "Interpretation"). What has led him to the good company of "Pantagruelistes" is that he doesn't work at writing, doesn't try to be allegorical, doesn't secrete meanings in his text. Instead he writes enraptured by the celestial inspiration induced by wine. Hidden or deeper meaning is therefore not a product of authorial will but a content that emanates from the gods or truth itself, from a higher source, a greater authority, and a more exalted intention than the individual writer could ever represent.

In this reading, hidden meaning does not disappear; it is merely displaced from the writer to a remote origin, one whose transcendence consecrates the importance of what is hidden and guarantees its authenticity. We might argue that this reading complicates rather than resolves the issue of intention, because transcendent intention is no easier to determine or grasp than its earthly counterpart, as the exegetical practice in the early sixteenth century dramatically illustrates. Alcofribas's way of arguing does not lend clarity. His case for the presence of hidden meaning—when for example Alcofribas suggests that books and writing resemble containers (boxes, faces, bones with outsides and insides)—only compounds the problem of what is intended. His own book, he claims, is a variation on the theme of these conventional topoi, a form of Silenus box, an avatar of Socrates's face, a bone enveloping precious marrow, another serious book belied by its cover, where the inside is always privileged as the real or the true intention of the text. But Alcofribas also insists that reading is not just a matter of ferreting out hidden truth, that one does not move in any simple way from outside to inside. The outside of Rabelais's writing—according to his model, all that is not hidden or abstruse, all that lies on the surface as the mirror reflection of the boisterous, raucous, excessive, verbose, earthy, physical narrator—Alcofribas and M. François Rabelais invite us to accept in its own right. Both affirm that this outside is intended to provoke laughter, to entertain, to nourish body and spirit, and to contribute to the reader's good health.

Is the intention hidden or on the surface? transcendent or of this world? What does Rabelais as author intend as the meaning of his text? Or is it his narrators who intend? Or is it both author and narrators? And what precisely does each intend? Juxtaposing author and narrators in this way points to the prologues as meeting places of complex and multiple discourses and intentions. It brings us face to face with the imbricated nature of the writing, composed not in layers to be separated (and subordinated) in order to reach an essential core, as some readers imagine (Defaux, "D'un problème"; Screech, *Rabelais*), but of overlapping elements that bear on one another in many ways. Authorial voices are mixed with narrative voices and references to Socrates, Diogenes, and passages from scripture; they are encased in bodily, scatological, and humorous discourses, from which they cannot be isolated without the distortion of their integrity.

In the prologue to the *Tiers livre*, M. Rabelais refers to his book as "un vray Cornucopie de joyeuseté et de raillerie" (530; "a true cornucopia of ridicule and fun" [286]), an image that underscores the book's comedic, parodic, and joyful dimensions and calls us to include in this horn of plenty its more serious content as well. Like the earlier Alcofribas, M. Rabelais writes with wine goblet in hand; his book, he claims, is itself a wine cask from which the reader is invited to drink. For the writer, drinking might be a source of spiritual inspiration, but it is also a source of joviality and inebriation, of bodily pleasure, as the performances of these narrators demonstrate. For the reader, drinking can be a trope for the pleasure and enjoyment derived from books, but it might also be a metaphor for the thirst-quenching acquisition of knowledge or insight. In the Rabelaisian text the serious and the comic, the real and the fantastic, the secular and the religious, the spiritual and the bodily coexist; they contaminate each other, overlap, intersect, and interact in a cacophony of competing discourses that Mikhail Bakhtin called the dialogic orientation of discourse or heteroglossia and that he considered not only characteristic of the novel but proper to the nature of language itself ("Discourse"). In working with our students, who in their search for univocal meaning often reduce or oversimplify complexity, we can use Rabelais's prologues to help them listen for and appreciate polysemy and its multiple and often paradoxical voices (Regosin, "Ins(ides)").

The cornucopian prologues also provide an entertaining introduction to the important issue of intertextuality by vividly illustrating that they (like all writing) are both generated and inhabited by a diversity of cultural discourses and other writings. We can challenge our students' often held conviction that literature imitates life or communicates singular meaning, by suggesting that writing is rewriting, the absorption and transformation of many other voices. Imitation of nature is an important tenet of Renaissance aesthetics, but it is telling that the primary model for writers of the sixteenth century is nature mediated by art—by the works of Homer and Vergil, for example. Not that our students would mistake Rabelais's narrators for real-life figures, but by their very unreality the prologues help shift the focus from the subject of the imitation of life to the relation of particular texts to other texts and to how writing takes place in connection with and against other writing.

This dialogic relation also informs the way we read and allows us to see how texts are structured by their subtexts. The prologue to *Pantagruel* opens as if it were about the "*Grandes et inestimables Chronicques de l'énorme géant Gargantua*" ("the great and inestimable chronicles of the enormous giant Gargantua"); it extols the entertainment and therapeutic values of this incomparable book, then creates it as its antecedent, offering itself as "un autre livre de mesme billon" (302; "another book of the same stamp" [168]), a book that assimilates, builds on, and exceeds the one that preceded it but continues to traverse it (Gray, "Rabelais' First Readers"). The prologue to *Gargantua* reprises both Plato's *Symposium* and Erasmus's "Sileni of Alcibiadis" (which is itself a striking example of intertextuality), playing with (or playing off) their resemblances and differences to rewrite the metaphor of the Silenus figure and the face of Socrates (La Charité, "Rabelais"). The prologue to the *Tiers livre* gains in significance and intelligibility when it is read in relation to the prologue to Lucian's "How to Write History." Rabelais ironizes the already ironic Lucianic text; he appropriates and transforms Lucian's Diogenes and Lucian as Diogenes as models of his activity; and he subverts the principles for writing good (i.e., ordered) history to write his own disordered text (Gray, "Structure"; Duval, "History"). In the *Quart livre* the prologue performs the same dialogic relation when it takes Lucian's retelling of Aesop's tale of the woodcutter and the ax as a point of departure that continually reverberates in the writing. In addition to the major subtexts that I have identified in each of Rabelais's prologues, there are throughout his texts citations, allusions, references, echoes of other writing, and traces of discourses that are historical, social, religious, political, and philosophical and represent the voices of both high and popular culture.

Questions of writing are always questions of reading as well, and if the prologues are scenes of writing, they are also scenes of reading in which the narrator inscribes his readers in the text, in which he could be said to invent them. Much has been made of the oral nature of the prologues, the performance of Alcofribas as a carnival hawker or chapbook salesman, addressing and entertaining the crowd that he draws to him in the environment of what Bakhtin characterized as the marketplace (*Rabelais and His World*), the informal meeting place where popular culture explodes in raucous laughter; in references to eating, drinking, and the body; in verbal jest and abuse; and in grotesque imagery and coarse jokes. Roughly a century after the invention of printing, Rabelais's texts enact the continuing transition from oral culture, and it is useful to have students identify the elements of form, style, and content with which written language creates the impression of speech and constitutes the fiction of an oral presentation.

Operating on two levels, the first two prologues evoke the listening audience that calls for and sustains the narrator's oral performances; at the same time, they bring into being the necessary readers of the book the narrator is hawking. In the prologue to *Pantagruel* (the first to be written), Alcofribas is preoccupied with selling the book—that is, with creating readers by extolling its virtues to entice them to read (Gray, "Rabelais' First Readers"). With *Gargantua* he instructs his readers how to read, invites them to look for hidden meaning (or not) and to enjoy the experience ("guayement lisez le reste" [54]). Here Alcofribas welcomes generous readers, those who would belong to the company of "Pantagruelistes," and dismisses and insults those who would mistake and misread his intentions or not drink to his health, eliminating them as readers.

In the third prologue, where M. François Rabelais explains and performs his Diogenic activity, he constitutes his initial readership of familiar and receptive people ("Bonnes gens)" to ensure a sympathetic reading; at the same time, he is haunted by those who would refuse or scorn the gift he offers, the service he renders, or the praises he sings. These negative readers also inhabit the writing, and to alleviate his anxiety M. François hopes that they have the quality of Pantagruelism: the unwillingness to take amiss anything that they know to spring from a good, honest, and loyal heart. But even as he guarantees that the wine will not run out, that the pleasure of the text is inexhaustible, the writing is invaded by uninvited readers whom he cannot eliminate, by dangerous enemies, by powerful forces and institutions, and by hypocritical adversaries who like the hounds of hell attack this Diogenes the dog.

The prologue to the unfinished 1548 edition is filled with "gens de bien" ("good people") who profited from the *Tiers livre* and provide the opening for the writing of a sequel by inviting the author to continue his Pantagrueline story. But it is also populated by what the author calls "les calumniateurs de mes escripts" (1134; "the calumniators of my writings" [*Complete Works* 418]), the devils from hell who slandered some of his books and, if allowed, will slander them all so that those who need them will not be able to read them. These "caphards," "cagotz," and "matagotz" ("hypocrites, dissemblers, imposters" [*Complete Works* 418]) are of the same ilk as those vicious and hateful characters who, in *Gargantua*, were denied entry to the Abbey of Thélème. The fictional world of the 1548 prologue, however, cannot be idealized as the abbey was and safeguarded by a portal inscription. Here the inscription of the enemies in the writing reveals that they have already crashed the gates. Four years later, in the new prologue to the completed *Quart livre*, these malevolent readers are excluded by the address "Aux lecteurs benevoles" (826; "To my Kindly Readers" [439]) and by their absence from the writing. From the earlier prologue, M. François reprises and develops the trope of the writer-physician solicitous of the good health of his patients: the book is intended to restore the physical and moral health of the reader, and the readers are only those "gens de bien" who will appreciate and profit from his efforts.

The inscription of or call for the listener or reader is also the call for the speaker-writer. Our students can appreciate from the prologues' concern with their readers and from their appeal to those endowed with Pantagruelism that the writer does not exercise absolute control over the reception of the writing and the meanings attributed to it. The books might be invested with meanings that readers are encouraged to uncover, or they might possess restorative qualities from which readers can profit, but once presented to the world, like the gift represented by the Bactrian camel in the prologue to the *Tiers livre*, the writing is no longer the property of the author. The prologues bring into contact, but also into conflict, the textual object and the reading subject and raise issues of their relation. Because of their explicit concern with their readers and with the reception of the books they introduce, they provide a valuable opportunity to introduce students to questions of reader response and to engage them in discussion about authors' attitudes toward readers, about the readers that different texts seem to imply, about the roles that actual readers play in the constitution of meaning, about the place of reading conventions, and so on. A selection of essays drawn from reader-response criticism (Tomkins) can provide a valuable theoretical supplement to students' practical experience of reading Rabelais.

However and whatever the readers of the prologues read, they are always reading the languages of Alcofribas and M. François Rabelais, so the source and nature of those languages must be acknowledged (Rigolot, *Langages*). Although it is Rabelais who endows his speaker-writers with speech, the words they utter and the forms those words take belong to them, reflecting who they are and how they express themselves. The degree to which those words also represent Rabelais is never obvious but always mediated and often hidden or effaced by the language itself. Rabelais may create Alcofribas in the prologue to *Gargantua* and literally put words in his mouth, but they are Alcofribas's words, and the confusion they reveal, the intoxication they communicate, the contradictions and digressions they enact are also and most profoundly Alcofribas's. The narrator's engagement with language, and his entanglement in it, is Rabelais's design; it amuses and entertains but also draws our attention to the problematic nature and working of language itself. An important function of the prologues is to foreshadow the structure of the books to follow—to suggest, for example, through the image of Diogenes rolling his tub, how the *Tiers livre* turns endlessly on its own axis. But an equally important function is to foreground the performance of the very stuff from which the prologues are made.

Our students do not have to be convinced that Alcofribas's way of speaking makes for difficult reading. Instead of encountering a logical, clearly organized, and developed discourse that allows insight as it works toward a conclusion—in other words, a discourse like the one we expect our students to produce—they become as entangled in his words as the speaker himself. The lurching movement of the prose; the absence of logical transition; the apparently gratuitous accumulation of words; the unsettling mixture of erudite references, coarse humor, puns, and abuse; and the general confusion and contradiction suggest the performance of an intoxicated narrator. Each prologue evokes the life-giving wine barrel and invites readers to imbibe (as the narrator has already done), and each bears these and other marks of inebriation: excess, verbosity, problems of coherence, and raucous laughter punctuated by harsh invective.

But each prologue is also the performance of the wayward inclination of discourse itself and of the problematic nature of signifiers (Rigolot, "Cratylisme"). Each suggests the ways in which language proliferates irresistibly, whether in the description of the decoration of the Silenus boxes or of the precious drugs they contain in the prologue to *Gargantua*, in the multiplication of activities and weapons in the prologue to the *Tiers livre*, or in the infinite regress of stories generating stories in the prologue to the *Quart livre*. Each proceeds in a digressive way, each moves tangentially, diverging, advancing by a process of superficial association, substitution, and displacement that defers and often obfuscates the expression of its object. Each enacts the polysemous quality of language (the narrators' puns are paradigmatic in this regard), and each contributes to the reader's sense of the ambiguity, obscurity, and lack of transparency of the sign. The prologues should make our students aware that, however rambling, obscuring, or excessive these discourses are, and however much they appear to be merely the effect of too much wine, they express what is already in language itself. The errant and erratic nature of discourse is inherent (Regosin, "Opening Discourse").

This awareness should help our students understand that these formal qualities of the Rabelaisian text cannot simply be eliminated or set aside as the frivolous talk of an unstable narrator or as the comic outside of Rabelais's serious and hidden inside. The very language and forms of Alcofribas's discourse, and that of M. François Rabelais, are also the content of the writing, are also what the books are about. If readers find hidden meanings in the text by allegorical or other interpretive means, these meanings too, as a function and reflection of the very discourse we are discussing, because they too are language, are subject to the same ambiguity, obscurity, and lack of transparency as any other meaning. In Rabelais's play with language, the hidden meanings that some might find (Defaux, "D'un problème") become themselves problematic and cannot easily stand as the privileged, univocal expression of Rabelais's truth or of truth itself. Reading the prologues as expressions of Rabelais's explicit interest in reading and writing can also help students understand the larger cultural and historical issues that some critics have identified as a crisis of interpretation in the early decades of sixteenth-century France (Jeanneret, *Défi*).

Intertextuality: The Bible

Edwin M. Duval

A feature of Rabelais's books that makes them especially difficult to read and to teach is the immense learning they display on virtually every page. This erudition is overwhelming to students yet essential to the meaning of the work. Quotations, taglines, allusions, and echoes of classical and biblical texts are frequently intended to draw on the readers' own erudition and refer us to another work, another context, another meaning, which we are expected to know, recognize, and be able to interpret. The problem for us modern readers is that we simply do not possess the literary culture—the *langue* in Roland Barthes's sense—that Rabelais's books presuppose in us and expect from us and that is a prerequisite to understanding Rabelais's work, his *parole*. We often fail even to recognize Rabelais's words *as* quotations or allusions, much less to identify their source and recall their original context. When this happens, we inevitably fail to interpret Rabelais's words correctly—not only their implicit meaning, irony, humor, and satirical bite but often their most basic literal meaning as well.

We teachers are only marginally better equipped in this respect than our students. We too require remedial culture for Renaissance readers. Fortunately, help is available in the footnotes of good editions. Virtually any paperback edition of the original French will suffice. The Demerson edition published by Seuil is adequate but hard to use; the Huchon edition published by the Bibliothèque de la Pléiade is best. In English, only the Donald Frame translation is of any use. For this reason I strongly recommend that teachers of Rabelais in translation consult this edition always, even if their students read the text in the more accessible J. M. Cohen or M. A. Screech translations published by Penguin.

More fortunately still, our cultural deficiency can be turned to good pedagogical advantage. By providing students in advance with the texts to which Rabelais's work alludes, we can help them bring to their reading some of the culture that is presupposed by the work and thus to approximate the experience of a reader for whom this culture was as immediate and spontaneous as a second nature. This simulated experience of Renaissance reading can be extremely rewarding, not only in that it allows access to the meaning of a difficult work but also in that it affords students the intense pleasure of watching significance emerge from apparent insignificance, clear meanings from apparent opacity. At the same time, it develops techniques of reading that are useful well beyond Rabelais, to great works of literature from Vergil to Dante to James Joyce and beyond.

By happy coincidence, the ancient text that Rabelais used most frequently as an intertext is one to which students have easiest access: the Bible. The chief difficulty here is that Rabelais and his readers knew the Bible not in the modern versions familiar to us today but in Saint Jerome's Latin Vulgate version. Not only is the meaning of the Vulgate sometimes quite different from that of more recent translations, but its diction is often entirely different. A word-for-word transposition from the Latin of the Vulgate into the Middle French of *Gargantua* and *Pantagruel*, which would have been immediately recognizable to Rabelais's readers as a direct quotation from the Bible, might have no resonance at all today, even for a reader who knows the same passage by heart in the King James Version. For this reason we sometimes have to provide students not only with the biblical reference and the text in a language they can read but also with the same text in the Latin Vulgate. A similar difficulty arises when Rabelais quotes the Bible in the original Greek or Hebrew texts. He does this, for example, in describing young Gargantua's hat-medallion, which is inscribed with a well-known verse from 1 Corinthians—"Love does not insist on its own way" (or "charity does not seek its own" [13.5])—but quoted in Greek: "'ΑΓΑΠΗ 'ΟΥ ΖΗΤΕΙ ΤΑ 'ΕΑΥΤΗΣ" (90; 56). He also does this in the *Quart livre*, where the islands "Thohu et Bohu" and "Ruach"—misleadingly translated by Cohen as "Vacuum and Void" and "Windy Island" (916, 1018; 487, 514)—are exact transliterations of the Hebrew text of Genesis 1.2: "The earth was *without form and void* [תֹהוּ וָבֹהוּ; tohû wabhohû], and darkness was upon the face of the deep; and the *Spirit* [רוּחַ; rûaḥ] of God was moving over the face of the waters" (Rev. Standard Ver.). Though few students are capable of reading these languages, it is important to dwell on instances where they occur, since recourse to the original text of the Bible was itself a meaningful gesture that carried a strong ideological, even polemical message in this age of Erasmus and the Protestant Reformation.

Three examples will perhaps suffice to suggest the range of meanings and effects Rabelais so often achieves through biblical quotation, allusion, and echo. A relatively simple instance of biblical intertextuality in the service of satire is found in the wonderful harangue delivered by Janotus de Bragmardo in chapter 19 of *Gargantua*. In exhorting Gargantua to return the bells he has removed from the tower of Notre Dame de Paris, Janotus lets fall this Latin phrase: "*Reddite quae sunt Cesaris Cesari, et quae sunt Dei Deo*" (132; 77). He is quoting, from the Vulgate, Jesus's famous ironic retort about paying taxes to Caesar: "Render to Caesar the things that are Caesar's, and to God the things that are God's" (Luke 20.25). What Janotus means by this is clear enough, but there is more to his quotation than meets the eye. Aside from the obvious humor involved in transposing well-known words from great contexts to small (a burlesque technique frequently employed by Rabelais), Janotus reveals a comical misunderstanding of the words he quotes. He apparently takes the verb *reddere* in its most literal sense: to "give back" or "return" something borrowed. This is what Janotus wants Gargantua to do with the bells but is not at all what Jesus had in mind. Janotus has been chosen as the most accomplished of all theologians to represent the most prestigious faculty of theology in all Europe, yet he shows himself to be blithely indifferent to, if not totally ignorant of, the original meaning of Jesus's words in the Bible. Behind Janotus's literal but heedless quotation from the Bible we easily discern Rabelais's satirical invective against the powerful and hated Sorbonne.

The satire goes deeper than this. The implied analogy between the original context of Jesus's words and the present context in which Janotus quotes them raises embarrassing questions to which Janotus is oblivious. Are the bells of Notre Dame analogous to "the things that are Caesar's" or to "the things that are God's"? If the former, then the church is likened in its overweening temporal power to the Roman Empire; if the latter, then the church is likened, in its presumption of omnipotence and omniscience, to God. In either case, Janotus suggests something about his own institution that he surely does not intend but that Rabelais clearly does. If we follow the implications of the analogy even further, we must consider that the bells are either the equivalent of the tribute owed to Caesar—that is, a burden borne by the Jews for the benefit of their heathen oppressor—or the equivalent of the prayers owed to God by good Christians: a brazen material substitute for piety in a degenerate church that has banished all spirituality in favor of formalism. This last possibility is perfectly consistent with what Rabelais says and implies throughout *Gargantua*. From the education of the hero to the consternation of the monks of Seuilly to the founding of the Abbaye de Thélème, Rabelais is merciless in his satire of monastic and liturgical prayers (those prescribed for penance, canonical hours, and masses) recited stupidly, mechanically, and by rote at the sound of a ringing bell. By making the insipid Janotus quote the words of an ironic Jesus here, Rabelais reminds his readers that the bells of Notre Dame serve no good purpose in a world of enlightened, reformed Christianity. The satire of Scholastic theology in the person of Janotus is doubled by a satire of materialism and formalism in the medieval Catholic Church.

Simply by asking students to read Luke 20.19–26 alongside chapter 19 of *Gargantua* and by inviting them to think about the double context (biblical and Rabelaisian) of ten quoted words, I find I can lead them not only to a better understanding of the passage, of the episode, and of an important theme in Rabelais's book but also to a good general sense of Rabelaisian irony and of Renaissance modes of writing. The same technique works for a number of passages in which a biblical tag appears. One great advantage of this technique is that it focuses attention on a small but consequential passage and aspect of the text, thus helping students avoid being overwhelmed by the complexity and difficulty of the work. Another is that it teaches them how to work out the implications of ironic quotations for themselves, both on their own and together in classroom discussions. Students become active and competent readers, prepared and eager to engage in arguments about the meaning of what they have read.

From simple satirical quotations like this one we can direct our students' attention to allusions that are harder to spot and more challenging to interpret.

Sometimes these occur in complex clusters that work together to suggest something more consequential than each considered separately. Often they depend for their meaning on a careful consideration of their double context—that is, the original context in the Bible and their new context in Rabelais. My favorite example occurs at the beginning of the *Tiers livre*, where Panurge suddenly decides to marry. In chapter 7, he appears before Pantagruel dressed in a brown frock with "a flea in his ear." Unlike the modern expression *mettre la puce à l'oreille* ("to arouse suspicions, give ideas"), the sixteenth-century *avoir la puce à l'oreille* meant "to be tormented by sexual desire." Panurge is horny and wants to get married. To publicize this fact, he gives a comically literal, concrete form to a well-known popular expression by having his right ear pierced and sporting a precious gold earring in which an actual flea has been set, then announcing, "J'ay . . . la pulce en l'aureille: je me veulx marier" (566; "I have the flea in my ear. . . . I have a mind to marry" [306]). The meaning is obvious. But the real significance of the passage is to be found in the ear-piercing "à la Judaïque" (566; "in the Jewish fashion" [305]), an allusion to a passage in Deuteronomy concerning the sabbatical manumission of slaves:

> If your brother, a Hebrew man, or a Hebrew woman, is sold to you, he shall serve you six years, and in the seventh year you shall let him go free from you. . . . You shall remember that you were a slave in the land of Egypt, and the Lord your God redeemed you; therefore I command you this today. But if he says to you "I will not go out from you," because he loves you and your household, since he fares well with you, then you shall take an awl, and thrust it through his ear into the door, and he shall be your bondman for ever. (15.12–18)

By piercing his own ear "à la Judaïque," Panurge is expressing his desire to remain a slave forever.

But how are we to understand this gesture? Is Panurge declaring himself a willing vassal to Pantagruel? a slave to his own desire? a candidate for the voluntary servitude of marriage? Yes, yes, yes. But the allusion takes on more significance when it is considered in its double context—the larger fictional context of the *Tiers livre* and the larger scriptural context of Deuteronomy. In the preceding episode of the *Tiers livre*, Pantagruel forgave Panurge the calamitous debts Panurge had incurred as the profligate warden of Salmigondin. Panurge objected strenuously to this gesture, wishing to remain forever indebted so that he might enjoy the eternal solicitude of his creditors, who would care for his well-being and protect him from harm so as not to lose their principal and interest (546; 295–96). The preceding lines of Deuteronomy also deal with the remission of debts:

> At the end of every seven years you shall grant a release. And this is the manner of the release: every creditor shall release what he has lent to his

> neighbor; he shall not exact it of his neighbor, his brother, because the Lord's release has been proclaimed. (15.1–2)

The unwilling beneficiary of precisely this kind of sabbatical remission from debt, Panurge looked around for some other means of guaranteeing his safety and happiness. This he found in "la loy . . . de Moses" ("the law of Moses")—specifically in a law of Deuteronomy, as it happens—according to which "les nouveaulx mariez seroient examptz d'aller en guerre pour la premiere année" (562; "the newly married should be exempted from going to the wars for the first year" [303]; 20.5–8). For Panurge, marriage, like indebtedness, is a means of avoiding responsibility. It is also a form of voluntary servitude and in fact of subservience to the law of Moses.

This last point is made clear through a pair of quotations from the New Testament. As Pantagruel "pardons" Panurge's debts in chapter 5, he conspicuously quotes the "holy Apostle" Saint Paul: "*Rien* (dict le sainct Envoyé) *à personne ne doibvez, fors amour et dilection mutuelle*" (558). His words are a faithful translation of a verse from the Epistle to the Romans in the Vulgate version: "*Nemini quidquam debeatis, nisi ut invicem diligatis*" ("Owe no one anything, except to love one another" [13.8]). (The Cohen translation unfortunately obscures this echo by mistranslating "dilection mutuelle" as "mutual delight" instead of "mutual love" [302]). Context is crucial here. The verse in Romans goes on to say: "for he who loves his neighbor has fulfilled the law;" all the commandments of the Old Testament are "summed up in this sentence, 'You shall love your neighbor as yourself.' Love does no wrong to a neighbor; therefore love is the fulfilling of the law" (13.8–10). By means of this direct quotation and its immediate context in Romans, Rabelais is suggesting that in "pardoning" Panurge and "forgiving his debts," Pantagruel is acting not according to Judaic law, which prescribes sabbatical remission, but according to the single "great commandment" of the New Testament, the new law of love, or "charity" (cf. Matt. 22.36–40), which alone fulfills the entire law of the Old Testament. When Panurge then pierces his ear "à la Judaïcque," he signals his refusal of Pantagruel's evangelical liberation from the constraints of the old law and voluntarily reenslaves himself to the "loy de Moses."

To this unambiguous gesture, Pantagruel responds with a second quotation from the New Testament. Instead of condemning Panurge's earring and new garb, he simply says:

> *Chascun abonde en son sens*: mesmement en choses foraines, externes, et indifferentes, lesquelles de soy ne sont bonnes ne maulvaises: pource qu'elles ne sortent de nos cœurs et pensées, qui est l'officine de tout bien et tout mal: bien, si bonne est, et par le esprit munde reiglée l'affection: mal, si hors æquité par l'esprit maling est l'affection depravée.
> (566–68; emphasis added)

The phrase I italicize here is yet another quotation from Romans, transposed verbatim from the Vulgate version: "*unusquisque in suo sensu abundet*" ("Let every one be fully convinced in his own mind" [Rom. 14.5]). Once again the Cohen translation completely misses the echo, misconstruing the phrase: "Everyone is full of his own ideas" (306). His version should be corrected to read:

> [Let everyone be fully convinced in his own mind,] especially on external, peripheral, and indifferent matters, that are neither good nor bad in themselves because they do not proceed from our hearts and minds, which are the [workshop] of all good and all evil: good if [our hearts and minds are] good and [governed] by the righteous spirit; evil, if they are wickedly depraved by the spirit of evil. (306)

The larger context of the verse quoted from Romans defines Christianity in terms of absolute freedom from the myriad prescriptions and proscriptions of Judaic law, all of which are henceforth inefficacious and "indifferent." But it insists with equal force that the single new commandment of love precludes judgment or condemnation of anyone who nevertheless continues to observe those prescriptions and proscriptions, because "nothing is unclean in itself; but it is unclean for any one who thinks it unclean" (Rom. 14.14). Pantagruel's little speech is in fact a good paraphrase of this whole passage of Romans.

In essence, then, the entire conversation between Panurge and Pantagruel in chapters 5 through 7 is a dialogue between Deuteronomy and the Epistle to the Romans on the subject of the law. Pantagruel begins with Romans 13.8–10 (which he quotes textually). Panurge answers with Deuteronomy 15.16–17, refusing freedom and reenslaving himself to the law. Pantagruel answers in turn with Romans 14 (which he again quotes textually), declaring that Panurge is free under the new law, even to observe the old law if he wishes. In this dramatized scriptural debate, Pantagruel and Panurge do not simply defend opposing positions. They act them out in a kind of contest of liberation and self-enslavement.

Students who begin by reading the biblical passages and their contexts will be able to see this clearly and move on to the next question, What does all this mean? They can discover the pleasures of trying to answer the question for themselves by looking for similar biblical references throughout the *Tiers livre*. With a little guidance and supplemental information—that Panurge's new robe is a Franciscan habit, that holy orders and marriage were (and are) two mutually exclusive sacraments of the Catholic Church, that biblical humanists considered monasticism to be not only incompatible with Pauline Christian freedom but also a new and illegitimate form of Judaism, one far more legalistic than the legitimate Judaism of the Old Testament, and so on—they can grasp on their own some of the major themes of the book, like Panurge's paralysis of the will and irresolvable ambivalence toward marriage.

Yet another function of biblical intertextuality in Rabelais is neither satirical nor ideological but, rather, allegorical. Many quotations and allusions, in *Pantagruel* and the *Quart livre* especially, point to a Christological dimension to the hero. The episode of the debate by signs in *Pantagruel* is an excellent example. Thaumaste says he has come from England to "test" ("esprouver") Pantagruel's legendary knowledge with insoluble problems in the arcane sciences (230; 414), just as the Queen of Sheba came from the faraway East to "test" Solomon's legendary wisdom with "hard questions" in 1 Kings 10.1–10 ("tentare eum in aenigmatibus" in the Vulgate). Like the queen, Thaumaste is satisfied with the answers he receives, all the more in that Pantagruel did not even have to answer for himself but was replaced in this role by a mere "disciple," his companion Panurge. Amazed by what he has seen, Thaumaste exclaims:

> Seigneurs, à ceste heure puis je bien dire le mot evangelicque: *Et ecce plusquam Salomon hic*. . . . Vous avez veu comment son seul disciple me a contenté et m'en a plus dict que n'en demandoys. . . . Dont povez juger ce que eust peu dire le maistre, veu que le disciple a faict telle prouesse, car *Non est discipulus super magistrum.* (428)

> Gentlemen, at this moment I may well pronounce the words of the Gospel: *Et ecce plusquam Salomon hic*. You have seen how his mere pupil has satisfied me and told me more even than I asked of him. . . . You will then have a good idea of what the master could have said, when you read of the pupil's valiant performance. For *non est discipulus super magistrum.* (238)

The two phrases in Latin are direct quotations from the Gospel of Matthew in the Vulgate version: "Behold, something greater than Solomon is here" (12.38–42) and "A disciple is not above his teacher" (10.24). Both are the words of Jesus; both designate Jesus himself as the Messiah. The first is especially significant in that it alludes to the same story of the Queen of Sheba with which Thaumaste had already introduced himself. The context of the quotation is crucial:

> Then some of the scribes and Pharisees said to him, "Teacher, we wish to see a sign from you." But he answered them, "An evil and adulterous generation seeks for *a sign*; but no sign shall be given to it except the sign of the prophet Jonah. . . . The men of Nineveh will arise at the judgment with this generation and condemn it: for they repented at the preaching of Jonah, and behold, something greater than Jonah is here. The queen of the South will arise at the judgment with this generation and condemn it; for she came from the ends of the earth to hear the wisdom of Solomon, and *behold, something greater than Solomon is here*.
> (12.38–42; emphasis added)

Pantagruel has already been compared with Solomon following his miraculous verdict in the hopelessly obscure case of Baisecul versus Humevesne (Kissmyarse vs. Suckfizzle), which the populace compared with Solomon's famous judgment in 1 Kings 3 (384; 213). This parallel episode now establishes Pantagruel in his infinite wisdom as "something more than Solomon"—namely, an analogue of Christ himself. Thaumaste, meanwhile, is shown to be not a sincere seeker of wisdom but an insidious enemy bent on trapping and humiliating the hero just as the wily Queen of Sheba sought to tempt-test Solomon's wisdom and as the wicked scribes and Pharisees sought to tempt-test Jesus with their duplicitous requests for a "sign." The only signs they get are Panurge's obscene gesticulations, while Pantagruel himself emerges as a Christ-like hero.

The clear Christological implications of this episode are consonant with Pantagruel's genealogy in chapter 1, which is modeled exactly on Christ's genealogy in chapter 1 of the Gospel of Matthew; it will be confirmed several times again, intertextually, throughout the book. One particularly neat instance occurs in chapter 24, when Pantagruel prepares to depart for Utopie to accomplish his predestined epic exploit of liberation. A lady he has left in haste sends him a ring inscribed with the words "lamah hazabthani" (446; 247). Editors invariably identify these as Christ's last words on the cross as recorded in Matthew 27.46. But Christ's last words were different: "lama sabachthani?" The difference is crucial, because Christ's words were Aramaic; those of the inscription are Hebrew, as Rabelais explicitly states ("en *Hebrieu* . . . c'estoyent motz *Hebraicques* signifians: 'Pourquoy me as tu laissé?'" ["in *Hebrew* . . . this was the *Hebrew* for, 'Why hast thou forsaken me?'"; emphasis added). Jesus was in fact quoting the first verse of Psalm 22 but in his own native language. Rabelais is quoting the same psalm but directly and in the original language. Christian exegesis invariably interpreted it as the words of the Jewish people soon to be abandoned by God with the advent of the Messiah. The abandoned lady's words are thus not a parody of Christ's dying words on the cross; they establish the lady as a figure of the old covenant and Pantagruel as the messiah of the new.

By examining such recurrent intertextual hints carefully, students will begin to see that Rabelais deliberately establishes a parallel, or an analogy, between the exploits of his hero and the messianic mission of Christ. It is at this point that the real fun of interpretation begins. What justifies this analogy? How are these plots similar and different? What are the similarities and differences trying to tell us about the direction and meaning of the plot and of the book?

The Bible is just one of many classical works exploited intertextually by Rabelais, and intertextuality is of course just one of many means of indirect signification. But biblical intertextuality is sufficiently important in Rabelais's books, and sufficiently variegated in its forms, that by focusing on a few instances a teacher can open students' eyes to essential aspects of Rabelais's meaning, culture, and modes of writing, while at the same time awakening them to the more general skills and pleasures of reading textually, contextually, and intertextually.

NOTE

The quotations in this essay from Rabelais's *Œuvres complètes* are taken from the Huchon edition.

Panurge, Parody, and Perplexity: From Satyr Play to Satire

Bernd Renner

With relatively few exceptions, reading, interpreting, or teaching Rabelais as a satirical author has long been a facet of the overall approach to the Pantagrueline chronicles as comical. This approach is worthy of more intense scrutiny, as the influence of the masters of Greco-Roman satire is present from the very beginning of *Pantagruel*.[1] The Horatian principle of the *utile dulci mixtum* is stressed in the first line of Hugues Salel's opening poem ("Si, pour mesler profit avec doulceur, / On mect en pris un aucteur grandement . . . " (212; "If for combining profit with delight / An author wins great popular renown . . . " [166]). Satirical hyperbole and farcical elements dominate the author's prologue. A reference to Lucian, the model of erudite Menippean satire, closes the book's first chapter. Moreover, satirical writing held a prominent position in sixteenth-century letters, due to political circumstances, moral and aesthetic concerns, and the rediscovery of the ancient masters of the form, in particular Lucilius, Horace, Juvenal, and Lucian, as many studies, especially Pascal Debailly's work, have shown in the last decade. Stylistically and generically, satire underwent major changes in the Renaissance, as the widely translated and imitated ancient texts shared the spotlight with a vernacular satirical tradition, whose main illustrations are farce, sotie, and non sequitur, genres that are recognized as parts of the satiric metagenre in the most important poetic treatises of the time (Du Bellay; for the treatises of Thomas Sébillet, Barthélemy Aneau, and Jacques Peletier du Mans, see Goyet). All these developments change satire from a clearly defined genre, classical Roman *satura*, into an elusive form, attitude, and technique that infiltrate all the traditional genres. These multiple influences also attest to the inherent hybridity of satire, an essential factor in Renaissance letters in general whose considerable influence on the Pantagruelian chronicles is discussed at length in this volume (see Rigolot; Fisher). Hybridity facilitates and illustrates the impact of an aspect that is doubtless instrumental in the recent rise of scholarly interest in satire: polysemy frequently leads to the reader's perplexity and relies on the reader's active contribution to the task of interpretation. As a consequence, it opens a dialogic relation between textual creation and reception, which provides a helpful tool for approaching this difficult work in the modern classroom.

The development of a truly renascent form of satire plays out structurally, in an epistemological division between the two earlier books, *Pantagruel* (1532) and *Gargantua* (1534/5), on the one hand, and the two later books, the *Third* and *Fourth Books* (resp., 1546 and 1552), on the other.[2] The first two books, under the auspices of "Alcofrybas, abstracteur de quinte essence" ("Alcofribas, Abstractor of the Quintessence"), are dominated by farcical satire in a largely medieval (i.e., Scholastic and monological) approach; they are marked by authoritative narrators and easily identifiable targets. The literally and figuratively "bookish" remedy for spiritual and physical ills promoted in the prologue or the exaggerated threats and assertions of the depicted events' authenticity in the tradition of Lucian's *True Story* set the tone for his kind of straightforward satire in the first prologue. The following two books, officially written by the more serious "M. Fran. Rabelais, docteur en medicine" ("doctor of medicine"), feature a more problematic brand of satire, one that usually leaves the reader with a variety of contradictory targets and interpretations—hence the perplexity and need for active contribution to interpretation, for the dialogical approach. Satire seems to have made the transition from a predominantly destructive mode to a constructive one, attempting to heal instead of merely to exterminate, mirroring the opposition between naive parodic humor—limited to the negation of values—and a knavish or devilish variant that aims at inverting values, as John Parkin has recently observed ("Polygelastic Rabelais").

This shift is clearly identifiable in the prologues. In the first two books, they are dominated by Alcofribas's comical yet assertive diatribes, leaving no room for dissent, whereas in books 3 and 4, the unnamed narrator allows the reader's voice to be incorporated in the discourse. Ambiguous examples are presented (Diogenes's behavior, the camel-and-slave anecdote, etc.), which are left to the reader to interpret, creating hermeneutical blanks that are essential to the objectives of the satire. The influence of Lucian's satirical dialogues, two of which are heavily drawn on in each of the two prologues in question ("How to Write History" and *A Prometheus in Words* in *The Third Book*; *Timon* and *Icaromenippus* in *The Fourth Book*), is evident. In *The Third Book*, recently termed the "book of perplexity," the possibility of the "double reading," characteristic of Rabelaisian hermeneutics and aesthetics and introduced explicitly with the two interpretations of the "énigme en prophétie" ("prophetic riddle") at the end of the preceding book, *Gargantua*, imposes itself.[3] The Wardenship of Salmagundia, which had been awarded to Alcofribas for his service in the Dipsodic Wars (*Pantagruel* 32), is given to Panurge, thus erasing the last remnant of the former narrator. It is safe to assume that Panurge also inherits the former narrator's task; he is now in charge of the text's "salmigondis," this eclectic textual ragout that marked the farcical orientation of the first two books. This definite turning point in the narrative responsibilities of the Rabelaisian farce was prepared at various points in *Pantagruel*, particularly in chapter 17, the encounter of Panurge and Alcofribas. Alcofribas, whose satire vacillates between Socratic irony, compatible with the image of the humble servant that he cultivates from the prologue on and the farcical aggressiveness of a diatribist, and the trickster enter into a dialogue that will cement Panurge's dominance.

At the beginning of the chapter, Alcofribas seems firmly in control and, like a parent, is concerned about Panurge's condition:

> Un jour je trouvay Panurge quelque peu escorné et taciturne, et me doubtay bien qu'il n'avoit denare; dont je luy dys: "Panurge, vous estes malade, à ce que je voy à vostre physionomie, et j'entends le mal: vous avez un fluz de bourse; mais ne vous souciez: j'ay encores six solz et maille

> qui ne virent oncq père ni mère, qui ne vous fauldront non plus que la vérolle en vostre nécessité."
>
> A quoy il me respondit: "Et bren pour l'argent! Je n'en auray quelque jour que trop: car j'ay une pierre philosophale, qui me attire l'argent des bourses comme l'aymant attire le fer. Mais voulés-vous venir gaigner les pardons? (dist-il.)
>
> —Et par ma foy (je luy respons), je ne suis grand pardonneur en ce monde icy; je ne sçay si je seray en l'aultre. Bien, allons, au nom de Dieu, pour un denier, ny plus ny moins.
>
> —Mais (dist-il) prestez-moi doncques un denier à l'intérest.
>
> —Rien, rien (dis-je). Je vous le donne de bon cueur.
>
> —*Grates vobis, Dominos*," dist-il. (285)

> One day I found Panurge somewhat woe-begone and taciturn, and I very much suspected that he had not a penny. I said to him therefore: "Panurge, as I can read from your countenance, you are sick, and I understand your disease. You have a flux of the purse. But don't worry, I have still 'six sous and a half that father and mother never saw,' and they shan't fail you in your need, any more than the pox."
>
> "A fart for your money," he replied. "I shall have only too much one day. For I have a philosopher's stone that draws me money out of purses as the magnet attracts iron. But will you come and buy pardons?" he asked.
>
> "Faith," I replied. "I am no great man for pardons in this world of ours, and I don't know whether I shall be in the next. But let's go in, in God's name. There's only a penny in it, more or less."
>
> "Well, lend me the penny, then, at interest," said he.
>
> "Not a bit of it," I replied, "but I'll give it to you with all my heart."
>
> "*Grates vobis dominos*," said he. (226)

The contrast between Panurge's aggressiveness and self-assuredness and Alcofribas's gentleness and modesty, ushers in a more violent satire. We already know about the trickster's numerous dishonest ways of making money but now learn that his alleged "philosopher's stone" is actually his creative use of the Latin language. His idiosyncratic Latin enables him to draw money out of the offertory plates, money put there thanks to the misleading rhetoric (and possibly faulty Latin) of the most powerful and fearsome authority of the time, the Catholic Church. The attack against the sale of indulgences; against the clergy's hypocrisy, debauchery, and intellectual shortcomings; and, in general, against authoritative voices that demand blind obedience could not be more straightforward in Panurge's playful yet scathing parody. Alcofribas's shock and fear at discovering Panurge's new wealth provides the necessary counterpart to the trickster's satirical demonstration:

> A quoy je me seignay, faisant la croix et disant: "Dont avez-vous recouvert tant d'argent en si peu de temps?"

A quoy il me respondit que il l'avoit prins ès bassains des pardons: . . .

Voire mais (dis-je) vous vous dampnez comme une sarpe, et estes larron et sacrilège.

"Ouy bien (dist-il) comme il vous semble; mais il ne me semble quand à moy: car les pardonnaires me le donnent, quand ilz me disent en me présentant les relicques à baiser: *Centuplum accipies*, que pour un denier j'en prene cent: car *accipies* est dict selon la manière des Hébreux, qui usent du futur en lieu de l'impératif, comme vous avez en la loy: *Diliges Dominum* et *dilige*. Ainsi, quand le pardonnigère me dict: *Centuplum accipies*, il vault dire: *Centuplum accipe*." (285–86)

Upon this I blessed myself, making the sign of the cross, and asked him: "Where have you got so much money from, and in so short a time?" To which he answered that he had taken it out of the offertory plates. . . .

"Come now," said I. "You're damning yourself like the serpent. You've been thieving and committing sacrilege."

"Oh yes," said he, "it looks like that to you. But it doesn't look like that to me. For really the pardoners give it to me when they offer me the relics to kiss and pronounce the words: '*Centuplum accipies*,' which is as much as to say that for one penny I am to take a hundred. For *accipies* is said after the manner of the Hebrews, who use the future tense instead of the imperative, as you have it in the Law, where it reads *Diliges Dominum*, for *dilige*. So when the bearer of pardons said to me: '*Centuplum accipies*' he meant *centuplum accipe*." (227)

Such linguistic fireworks are Panurge's trademark in *Pantagruel*. It underlines his prominent position in a farcical universe.

At the end of the chapter Panurge invites Alcofribas to join him, thus assuming the role of the leader and reversing the relationship between the two. He had already done so with his master, Pantagruel, in chapter 15, probably the most shocking display of Rabelaisian farce. At the giant's question of how to construct the walls of Paris cheaply, the trickster replies: "Ne le dictes doncques mie . . . si je vous l'enseigne" (276; "Don't say a word about it . . . and I'll tell you" [219]). Similarly, when the giant wonders how his companion could possibly know that chaste women were extremely scarce in Paris, Panurge asserts, "*Et ubi prenus*? . . . Je vous en diray, non oppinion, mais vraye certitude et asseurance" (279; "*Et ubi prenus*? . . . I will tell you my opinion on this point, and that on certain and assured knowledge" [221]). It is no surprise then that the trickster takes the lead in all the adventures in this farcical universe, sometimes replacing his master outright: the debate with the ridiculous scholar Thaumaste, the punishment of a hypocritical noble Parisian lady, the deciphering of an "encoded" letter from a disappointed lady, the defeat of 660 knights, and the magical resurrection of a beheaded Epistemon are the most striking examples. The noble and awe-inspiring topics of life and literature, such as Scholastic thinking, courtly love, incomprehensible linguistic messages, epic warfare, and miracles, are parodied and unmasked relentlessly in this univocal satire of authority and *exempla*, a satire whose entertainment value clearly overshadows the moral and pedagogical objectives of classical satire. The various amused reactions to the trickster's crude anecdotes and farces underline this purpose. Consider Pantagruel's laughter at the "walls of Paris" story and his final appraisal of the string of obscenities that make up chapter 15: "Vrayement . . . tu es gentil compaignon; je te veulx habiller de ma livrée" (279; "Truly, . . . you're a jolly companion. I should like to put you in my livery" [221]). The cruel punishment of the great Parisian lady—a farcical treatment of destructive satire—is marked as a "mystère" and a "spectacle" and entertains "everyone," including the chambermaids and Pantagruel (307; 244).

Panurge's virtuosity, frankness, and rudeness, all traits that are based on his miraculous codpiece, evoke the Greek satyr play, violent and outspoken verbal attacks on all aspects of society that were staged by actors disguised as the half-human satyrs, demigods from Bacchus's entourage. The satyr play was erroneously considered one of the etymological origins of classical satire in the sixteenth century, and the satyr was hailed as an agent of free speech before his status eroded rather quickly beginning in the 1550s.[4] At any rate, at this point in the chronicles there is a juxtaposition and not yet a Horatian mixture of the *utile* and the *dulce*, the farce thus functioning as a counterpart to the more serious parts of life, as the beginning of chapter 15 states: "Pantagruel, quelque jour, *pour se recréer de son estude*, se pourmenoit vers les faulxbours sainct Marceau, voulant veoir la Folli Goubelin. Panurge estoit avecques luy" (275; my emphasis; "One day, *to refresh himself from his studies*, Pantagruel was walking towards the Saint-Marceau suburb, wishing to visit the Gobelin pleasure-house; and with him was Panurge" [218]).

Panurge's disastrous wardenship of Salmigundia leads directly to his first attempt at reasserting his farcical supremacy in *The Third Book* through another linguistic tour de force. His praise of the "belle saulse verde" ("fine green sauce") made from "Wheat in the Blade" (292) and the subsequent praise of debtors and borrowers (chs. 2–5) falls in the Lucianic tradition of paradoxical praise, which had been reintroduced most famously by Erasmus in his *Praise of Folly*. The trickster tries to justify the irresponsible and wasteful management of his wardenship by showing the absolute necessity of debts for the functioning of the human body, for life on earth, and for harmony in the universe, through a mock encomium that draws heavily on Neoplatonic ideas and language. A major question here is whether Panurge is seriously trying to justify his unjustifiable behavior or whether he is consciously satirizing Neoplatonism, as he already did in a mocking rendering of the language of courtly love in the "great lady of Paris" episode, comparing the lady to Juno, Minerva, and Venus before abruptly concluding:

> O dieux et déesses célestes, que heureux sera celluy à qui ferez celle grâce de ceste-cy accoller, de la baiser, et de *frotter son lard avecques elle*. Par

> Dieu, ce sera moy, je le voy bien, . . . Je . . . suis à ce prédestiné des phées. *Doncques, pour gaigner temps, bouttepoussenjambions*!
> (303, my emphasis)

> O ye celestial gods and goddesses, how happy will be the man to whom you grant the favour of embracing this woman, of kissing her, and *rubbing his bacon with her*. By God, I shall be that man, as well I see . . . I was predestined for this by the fairies. *Therefore, to spare time, let's to and fro and at it*. (240)

Whereas the satirical criticism of hypocritical rhetoric is clear in the earlier book, *The Third Book* offers no such obvious key to Panurge's true intentions. One could ask, however, why Panurge's spontaneous reaction is an abundant expression of gratitude when Pantagruel absolves him of his debts.

Before this deed, the giant voiced his disagreement with his friend's discourse, while still admitting that the trickster has entertained and impressed him with his mastery of Scholastic arguing and rhetoric:

> J'entends . . . et me semblez bon topicqueur et affecté à vostre cause. Mais preschez et patrocinez d'icy à la Pentecoste, enfin vous serez esbahy comment rien ne me aurez persuadé, et par vostre beau parler jà ne me ferez entrer en debtes. Rien (dict le sainct Envoyé) à personne ne doibvez, fors amour et dilection mutuelle.
>
> Vous me usez icy de belles graphides et diatyposes, et me plaisent très bien . . . [Je] suys d'opinion que ne erroient les Perses, estimans le second vice estre mentir, le premier estre debvoir. (389–90)

> I understand. . . . You seem to me good at argument and an enthusiast for your cause. But if you preach and sermonize from now till Whitsun, you'll be astonished to find me finally unconvinced. With all your fine talk you will never make me a debtor. Owe no man anything, says the holy Apostle, save love and mutual delight. You provide me with fine illustrations and figures, which please me greatly. . . . I don't think the Persians were wrong either when they reckoned lying to be the second vice; to owe being the first. (302)

Debts are tied directly to the power of the verb, which hints at Pantagruel's condemnation of the form as well as the content of his companion's speech, a speech that for the first time fails to convince the giant, which marks the decline of the satyr and his influence. The significance of *The Third Book*'s dialogic structure, especially in the context of satire, comes to the fore in this initial episode of the text, as the key question, Panurge's intentionality, seems impossible to answer with certainty, the major trait of what Umberto Eco has called the "open work." The two most plausible readings are diametrically opposed. Did

Panurge, the chronically broke trickster, truly try to praise debtors? In a larger context, was his yet again the voice of liberation from conventional thinking, in the tradition of the satyr (in which case his undertaking appears to have failed)? Or did he intend to perform a satirical dismantling of the abuses made possible by the blinding power of rhetoric? His demonstration would then be even more powerful, as he chose an unjustifiable cause. In this case he succeeded, all the more so as his performance was richly rewarded by Pantagruel. In other words, is Panurge the target of the satire or still its agent?[5]

This episode points to the enormous pedagogical potential of Rabelais's polysemic satire, as it teaches students to read by working closely with the text, without looking for the one and only right answer to the questions that literature poses. Careful interpretation is a personal undertaking, based on reflection, learning, and experience. This approach then translates to life choices—for example, the question of marriage and the role of women, which was widely discussed at the time—and the responsibilities that each person has to accept for them. Pantagruel makes this point many times in *The Third Book*: "Chascun abonde en son sens" (395; "Everyone is full of his own ideas" [306]); "N'estez-vous asceuré de vostre vouloir? Le poinct principal y gist: tout le reste est fortuit et dépendent des fatales dispositions du Ciel" (403; "Aren't you certain of your own wishes? That's the principal point; all the rest is fortuitous and depends on the disposition of the heavenly fates" [313]); "Chascun doibt estre arbitre de ses propres pensées et de soy-mesmes conseil prendre" (476; "Everyone should be his own judge and take counsel with himself" [369]). That the first two of these comments were made before Pantagruel even suggests the series of consultations that constitute the main part of the book appears to invalidate the usefulness of the consultations from the very beginning. Quite unsurprisingly, the learned opinions then lead to no concrete result other than to defend Pantagruel's comments and to illustrate exemplary methods of interpretation, especially in the episode of Trouillogan. More importantly in our perspective, they draw on a strong cynic undercurrent, attacking the traditionally unquestioned supremacy of authoritative voices. It is precisely this blind deference to authority that helps Panurge and the reader shun responsibility (and the hard work of interpretation).

The most interesting comment, however, is made by Panurge, as he elevates the paradox of predicting fate with absolute certainty to a more complex level. When meeting the astrologer Her Trippa, the trickster voices his dissatisfaction as follows:

> Il . . . au demourant glorieux, oultrecuidé, intolérable plus que dix-sept diables . . . Allons, laissons icy ce fol enraigé, mat de cathène, ravasser tout son saoul avecques ses diables privez . . . Il ne sçait le premier traict de philosophie, qui est: *Congnois-toy* et, se glorifiant veoir un festu en l'œil d'aultruy, ne void une grosse souche laquelle luy poche les deux œilz. (462)

> He's more boastful, overbearing, and intolerable than seven devils. . . . Come, let's leave this raving fool, this violent idiot, to drivel his bellyful with his familiar devils. . . . He doesn't know the first point of philosophy, which is: *Know thyself*. He's so proud of seeing the mote in another's eye that he doesn't see a great beam poking out both his own. (357)

This diatribe basically reiterates Pantagruel's comments, but while Panurge is right about Her Trippa, the verdict also applies to him. Panurge's status reflects the evolution of Rabelais's satire as it becomes more and more ambivalent. The passage clearly identifies the trickster as both agent and target of the satire; he is turned into a fine illustration of *coincidentia oppositorum*, a then widespread concept that pushes the concept of the paradox to its limits and defies clear-cut, univocal, and predetermined answers.

That such a complex hermeneutical construct requires careful readers is demonstrated in two of the final episodes of *The Third Book*, the consultation of Trouillogan and the trial of Bridoye. The trial is a scathing satire of the contemporary judicial system. When it comes to passing equitable judgment, all the expertise of a renowned court is worth no more than the naive judge's roll of the dice, by which Bridoye settles all his cases. Nevertheless, the members of the prestigious court in Mirelingues upheld each of the 2309 decisions of Bridoye that were contested. Without approving Bridoye's actions, Pantagruel excuses the judge, but the opposition of fate versus learning is illustrated in an anecdote by Epistemon (which reconnects the paradox to its roots in the realm of the law; see Geonget). The case of a mother who killed her second husband and their son after discovering that the two had killed her son from her first marriage defies a "correct" answer and would therefore justify the use of dice:

> Qui eust décidé le cas au sort des dez, il n'eust erré, advent ce que pourroit: si contre la femme, elle méritoit punition, veu qu'elle avoit faict la vengence de soy, laquelle appartenoit à Justice; si pour la femme, elle sembloit avoir eu cause de douleur atroce.
>
> Mais, en Bridoye, la continuation de tant d'années me estonne. (529)

> If a man had settled that case by a throw of the dice he wouldn't have been far wrong whichever way they had fallen; if it had gone against the woman, she would have deserved her punishment since she had herself taken the revenge which by right belonged to justice; if it had gone in the woman's favour, the terrible grief would have seemed an excuse for her deed. But that [Bridoye] should have been successful for so many years, that does astound me. (410)

Such cases of reversed *coincidentia oppositorum* are extremely rare and justify in no way Bridoye's intellectual capitulation or the court's inadequate learning, which in fact made the judge's prolonged "success" possible.

The far more common case is demonstrated in the Trouillogan episode. The philosopher's paradoxical answers to the marriage question ("both" and "neither") are of no use to Panurge, who is looking for a univocal verdict that will spare him the arduous task of interpretation and reflection as well as absolve him of any personal responsibility for his actions (see Hoffmann; Renner, "'Ni l'un ni l'autre'"). Pantagruel's model reading of Trouillogan's advice is actually the final one of a series of acceptable interpretations offered by Gargantua, Rondibilis, and Hippothadée, a series that underlines each individual's approach—on the basis of their respective backgrounds and learning—to the problem at hand and consequently demonstrates the validity of multiple interpretations:

> Je interprète . . . avoir et n'avoir femme en ceste façon: que femme avoir est l'avoir à usaige tel que Nature la créa, qui est pour l'ayde, esbattement et société de l'homme; n'avoir femme est ne soy apoiltronner autour d'elle, pour elle ne contaminer celle unicque et suprême affection que doibt l'homme à Dieu, ne laisser les offices qu'il doibt naturellement à sa patrie, à la Républicque, à ses amys, ne mettre en nonchaloir ses estudes et négoces, pour continuellement à sa femme complaire. Prenant en ceste matière avoir et n'avoir femme, je ne voids répugnance ne contradiction ès termes. (499)
>
> I interpret having and not having a wife in this way . . . that to have a wife is to have her for the purpose for which Nature created her, that is for the aid, pleasure, and society of man. Not to have her means not to be tied to her apron-strings; not for her sake to debase the unique and supreme love that a man owes to God; not to neglect the duties that a man owes to his country, the community, and his friends; not to abandon his business in order to be continuously waiting on his wife. Taking having and not having a wife in this way I see no conflict or contradiction in terms. (386)

This kind of individual engagement with a text or a problem is one major message that polysemy in general and polysemic satire in particular are meant to convey. Panurge refuses to listen and become what commonly would be referred to as a "sufficient reader" in the early modern period, as his reaction to Pantagruel's reading shows:

> Vous dictes d'orgues . . . Mais je croy que je suis descendu on puiz ténébreux, onquel disoit Héraclytus estre Vérité cachée. Je ne voy goutte, je n'entends rien, je sens mes sens tous hébétez . . . Parlons sans disjunctives . . . Or çà, de par Dieu, me doibz-je marier? (500)

> You talk like a book. . . . But I feel as if I were at the bottom of the dark well where Heraclitus says truth is hidden. I can't see a thing, I hear nothing, I feel my senses all numbed. . . . Let's . . . speak without disjunctives. . . . In God's name, shall I marry? (386)

The "noose of [his] perplexity" (390) retains a firm grip on him, as he is simply waiting for the one predetermined right (and favorable) answer to his question, which is obviously impossible. What renders the situation even more complex and contributes to the full flourishing of the text's ambivalence is that the method itself, the series of consultations, is inappropriate for the problem at hand, as Pantagruel's comments clearly suggested before the series even began. Panurge's stubbornly dissenting voice benefits in two ways from this twist. In the first place, he could be right after all, since the authorities' predictions really have no bearing on his conjugal destiny. In the second place, his resistance to the dominant and very homogeneous interpretations of his companions prevents the dialogue from turning into a monologue, precisely the ill that this satire of authority attempts to heal.

The *Fourth Book* further develops Rabelais's satirical approach by reinserting farce into its increasingly Menippean mix (see the episode of Dindenault [chs. 5–8], of Basché [12–16], and of Homenaz [48–54]). After his marginalization in *The Third Book*, Panurge undeniably regains a more dominant status in those episodes, but the farce is not only more cruel and violent than before, it is also clearly rejected by the trickster's companions—causing, for instance, Friar John's criticism (467), Pantagruel's anger (552), and Epistemon's diarrhea (558). Panurge's exclusion from more serious episodes such as the tempest or the Andouilles war reinforces an antithetical structure that is resolved only at the end of the book—most important, in the final chapter, where the trickster falls prey to a farce and ends up covered in his own excrement, the typical punishment inflicted on victims of the less violent variant of farce that dominates satirical expression in *Pantagruel*. The ensuing symbolic and almost paschal cleansing, illustrated by a fresh white shirt, is immediately contradicted by the trickster's praise of excrement and denial of any fear in the book's final paragraph. The reader is left perplexed yet again. Panurge's ambivalent status—he is both agent and target of the satire—is therefore a promising approach to convey Rabelais's plea for how to read. It helps develop a decision-making skill that extends beyond the realm of literature into real life. It can make the study of such old texts even more interesting and relevant to our students by turning reading into a personal undertaking yet again.

NOTES

The French quotations in this essay are taken from the 1973 Demerson edition of Rabelais's *Œuvres complètes*.

[1] For recent studies of Rabelaisian satire, see my *Difficile*; Duval, "Rabelais"; and Huchon, "Rabelais et les satires."

[2] I leave out *The Fifth Book* (1564) because of the continuing doubts as to its authenticity.

[3] These terms are taken from Stéphan Geonget's study (resp., 425 and 31); translations are mine.

[4] See Lavocat's seminal study on the figure of the satyr in the sixteenth and seventeenth centuries.

[5] See Renner, "Provocation," for a detailed discussion of this episode.

Rabelais and Language: Change, Decay, Transition

John O'Brien

Rabelais is rightly credited with extreme linguistic inventiveness, the ability to spawn proliferating languages that seem to take on a life of their own. Students are immediately aware of this phenomenon when they attempt to read his writings: the dense mass of words on the page constitutes an almost physical obstacle to the process both of reading and of understanding. Interpreters have been correspondingly adept at providing students with intellectual tools for deciphering Rabelais's linguistic exuberance. François Rigolot's *Les langages de Rabelais* is an outstanding instance of such a tool, echoing but differentiating itself from Lazare Sainéan's earlier study, *La langue de Rabelais* of 1922–23, by its emphasis on the polyvocality that heralded Terence Cave's study of *copia* and Michel Jeanneret's interest in Rabelaisian ambivalence and ambiguity (*Défi*). Other critics, such as Michel Beaujour, Alfred Glauser, and Floyd Gray, have similarly given prominence to our author's language play and the comic effects that it produces. Their work is complemented by Mireille Huchon's study of Rabelais the grammarian (*Rabelais grammarien*) and her monumental Pléiade edition (*Œuvres*), both of which provide a copious historical and linguistic basis for understanding our author. Information about what Rabelais's languages are and how to respond to them is plentiful.

A concomitant but not widely studied product of Rabelais's attention to language is the process of change, decay, and transition. Using some of the commonest episodes that are studied in class, we can demonstrate that his work marks moments of cultural or historical change by highlighting and scrutinizing the language in which they occur. Gargantua's letter to his son in *Pantagruel*, chapter 8, is one prime illustration of this phenomenon. It has given rise to diverse critical interpretations. Huchon quotes a representative range of critics who take diametrically opposed views of it (*Œuvres* 1268–69). Some, such as Michael Screech, take the letter as a manifesto of humanism and a humanistically inspired liberal theology (*Rabelais* [1979]); others, such as Gerard Brault, interpret it as a parody of humanism. The perplexities in which the letter has placed critics can be evidenced from the contradictory reactions of Gérard Defaux. He sees the letter as embodying, in a high Ciceronian style, a humanism indebted to Guillaume Budé and Plutarch and creating the myth of Gothic darkness as a description of the Middle Ages. The letter is a "hymne au savoir" ("hymn to learning") containing a "curriculum tout imprégné d'Humanisme" ("curriculum impregnated through and through with humanism"). Yet when Gargantua recommends that his son learn the medieval method of arguing for and against (*pro et contra*)—something specifically condemned by the humanists—even Defaux is driven to ask, "Cette lettre serait-elle ironique à quelque degré?"

(*Cinq livres* 348n39; "Might this letter be ironic to some degree?"). All critics agree nonetheless that this episode marks a transit moment, a moment of change, and that this change has particular linguistic characteristics and identity. This remains true whether one takes the letter to be a portrayal of humanist ideals or their caricature. The letter emblematizes that in-between status of the moment it describes and embodies, a moment when the cultural habits of the past still inflect the incipient discourse of the future, when the complex and often contradictory transition from medieval to early modern makes the tone of parts of the letter particularly hard to judge.

Corresponding episodes act in a more obviously satirical way to stage the decay of language. Janotus de Bragmardo is a striking instance here. This representative of the Sorbonne has come to recover the bells of Notre-Dame, which Gargantua has stolen. His very opening words use macaronic Latin (a mixture of French and Latin) of a particularly incomprehensible variety, which mocks the Latinized speech of the Schoolmen (the Scholastic theologians whom Rabelais makes the butt of his humor): "la substantificque qualité de la complexion élémentaire que est intronificquée en la terrestérité de leur nature quidditative" (91; "the substantific quality of the elementary complexion which is inherent in the terrestiality of their quidditive nature" [77]) was as obtuse to Rabelais's audience as it is to us (although more familiar to them than to us).

The mockery is finely extended to encompass that Scholastic form par excellence, the syllogism, one of the chief methods by which Renaissance students were taught logic: "Omnis clocha clochabilis, in clocherio clochando, clochans clochativo clochare facit clochabiliter clochantes. Parisius habet clochas. Ergo gluc" (92; unchanged in English translation, 78). Rabelais mimes exactly the pattern of the syllogism, with the major premise ("Every bell . . ."), the minor premise ("Paris has bells"), and the conclusion ("Therefore"). But the form is without a content; it is held together solely by play on the word for "bell," bound together by repetition and rhythm; while the putative finale, "Ergo gluc," is in fact a Renaissance formula denoting an absurd conclusion. Similarly at the close of his speech, Janotus makes use of connectors and interjections that standardly occurred in Scholastic (and other) forms of argument: "verum enim vero, quando quidem, dubio procul, edepol, quoniam, ita certe, meus Deus fidius" (92; unchanged in English, 78), but these terms pile up without any proper structure for them to articulate. Indeed, Janotus's speech abounds with the vocabulary and technique of Scholastic argument, yet the dynamic of that argument is lost in the sheer flow of words, far in excess of the logical work they are called on to do and the end to which they are supposedly directed. The theologian's purpose is thrown into disarray by the words that he uses or that, perhaps, in a sense, use him: he becomes a *moulin à paroles* ("windbag," "motor mouth"), churning out words that escape his control.

All the elements of a recognizable Scholastic discourse are in place, but the message slips further and further out of sight. This is language fundamentally unable to carry out its communicative purpose; it is a picture, in fact, of language in chaos and decline. Note that the representation of decline here is not by shrinking or shriveling, as one might expect, but by the opposite—the bloating and swelling of discourse characterized by repetition, redundancy, and confusion, a vast expansion of an empty core; decay is conveyed by a swollen body of language. This is not to say, of course, that the Sorbonne suddenly altered its teaching methods as a result of Rabelais's intervention. Yet his satirical vignette marks such pedagogy with the sign of antiquarianism, as something archaic and outmoded. In that sense, this episode anticipates change, and a historical parallel for Rabelais's intervention might be Peter Ramus's attack on and revision of Aristotelian logic in his *Dialectique* of 1555. It is also worth emphasizing to students that fiction has its own way of participating in debates contemporary with its writing, and its distinctive feature is the plurality of modes in which that historical depiction takes place: comic portrait, linguistic characterization, and critical reflection all combine.

A complementary point emerges in a political context when Picrochole discusses his empire-building plans with his advisers in *Gargantua*, chapter 33. The picture of the local squire with world-conquering ambitions is itself an essay in disproportion, conveying a lesson in hubris. Picrochole is a fantasist who takes language for reality as he reconquers the Roman Empire and then retraces the campaign trail of Alexander the Great, creating afresh his empire in the Chinonais. La Roche Clermaud expands to the dimensions of Asia Minor and Palestine as wishful thinking solidifies into "fact." This change is brought about by the very discourse Picrochole and his advisers use, particularly the switch in tenses between a hypothetical future of conquest and the constraining present that they are seeking to transform. When the future itself melts into the perfect tense and then, more tellingly still, into the past historic, the conquest is complete—in and to their mind. The change in this case is purely mental but carefully, and comically, articulated through subtle manipulation of linguistic signs. Yet the effect does not rest there. Erasmus's adage "Festina lente" (143; "More haste, less speed" [111]), which in its original context conveyed an anti-imperialist lesson, is misappropriated by Picrochole's advisers for their own purposes. It sets up an ironic tone in the text but also points to a further body of writing that was discussing the validity of war and condemning empire building. There is thus a twofold movement in this scene: on the one hand, Picrochole indulges in the greedy land grabbing that annexes countries and builds castles out of thin air, while on the other, the language of Erasmian humanism embedded in the discussion acts like an explosive charge by contesting this feature of monarchical behavior. The episode thus dramatizes in miniature the tensions of the historical and cultural time to which it belongs and the shifts and changes in the understanding and perception of empire that were being debated in the public sphere.

As instructors, we can underline two further implications in these two emblematic instances. The first is that, by deliberate counterpoint, oversize words emerge from a human-size person and swell to giant proportions. The device is a versatile comic weapon in Rabelais, bonding together the monstrous, the fantastical, and the grotesque into a critique of a particular language or outlook. Students can thus be alerted to the fact that the theme of gigantism, at the broadest levels, covers a wider area than just the activities of Grandgousier and Gargamelle, or Gargantua, Badebec, and Pantagruel. The theme can easily be extended so that human beings can also be gigantic, in their own way, and when this occurs, it usually acts as a form of critique of characters who, by their one-dimensionality, are ossified into a particular viewpoint or outlook, unable to move beyond their mode of being or laugh at themselves. Students can thus be encouraged to think about the links among outsize, wrong size, and a text that is itself disproportionate in size.

The second implication is that, in both cases, the idiolect that these figures use and that is coterminous with their character shows serious signs of instability in the face of other emergent discourses plentifully on display in Rabelais's work. This feature can lead to a study of adjacent but contrasting incidents in *Pantagruel*. The ludicrously pompous Latinate French of the Limousin scholar in chapter 6 is a parody of grand Parisian style that is not far removed from the diction of Janotus, though much expanded; and the scholar speaks naturally, in his native dialect, only when Pantagruel takes him by the throat and threatens to skin him alive. This incident, another point on the cultural map, shows that the attempt to graft Latin onto the vernacular is a symptom of decline, not of rejuvenation. By contrast, when Pantagruel meets Panurge a few chapters later, Panurge is just as incomprehensible as the Limousin scholar, but that is because he symbolically takes his interlocutor on a linguistic tour of Europe (not forgetting Greek and Latin) before coming back to his "langue naturelle et maternelle" (255; "natural mother-tongue" [201]), the French of Touraine (geographically close to Limousin, but linguistically distinct from it). In this case, the classical languages have their place here alongside the vernacular, not instead of it or superimposed on it, and that moment when the vernacular stands on a par with its antique predecessors is fully represented in Rabelais's text. These two episodes compose a vignette of a transitional time when an emergent language becomes the match of learned languages. If the Limousin scholar is not unlike Janotus in his inflated jargon, Panurge is, however embryonically, closer to an early modern linguist, with a virtuoso command of language that befits a traveler from foreign parts.

So far, the instances cited have provided a series of individual occurrences of change and decay together with the particular implications that we might wish students to draw out of their study of these examples. But our students can also be shown that such discrete moments, however numerous, fit into a larger pattern; advantageously, by projecting such instances against a broader canvas, one can demonstrate to students that, as often in Rabelais, change and decay are not unambiguous. The example here will be the *Quart livre*, arguably his finest and richest exploration of the notions of decline and transition. This book deploys a rich variety of literary idioms—burlesque, fable, parable, a three-act drama (the storm at sea, with a catastrophe, labeled as such)—but one idiom holds special importance for our purposes: the term *farce tragique*, which describes the marriage of the Seigneur de Basché, is one of the expressions used for "tragicomedy," as Rabelais himself makes clear in the "*Briefve declaration*" (776; not translated by Cohen). This term could, with due reservations, be extended as a focus for the book as a whole, inasmuch as it provides a way of envisioning the link between the comic and the serious—something that begins badly and ends well (or the reverse) can also begin seriously and end comically (or the reverse). Thus the Andouilles look like a replay of the Basché episode, when they receive the drubbing formerly reserved for the Chiquanous. Yet the opposite is true: after the fighting is over, the Andouilles have their wounds cured by an application of mustard, since sausages and mustard go so well together. What seemed fated to end badly has turned out (comically) happily.

Not all such parallel scenes end thus. The Bringuenarilles (Slitnose) episode, for example, is pure slapstick: a giant who swallows pots and pans chokes to death on a pat of butter, with mock-classical authorities drafted in by Rabelais to offer "supporting" instances of absurd deaths, as "proof" of the verisimilitude of the incident. Yet when a similar episode occurs later, its tone is graver. Here the person of heroic stature is not a comic giant but Guillaume du Bellay, Rabelais's patron and protector, and the description of his passing is met with universal mourning amid extensive reference to classical writers, notably Plutarch. The comic death of Bringuenarilles has transmuted into the tragic death of Du Bellay and, with him, the disappearance of the "gloire et protection" ("glory and protection") that France enjoys in the person of this "tant perfaict et nécessaire chevallier" (657; "so perfect and essential knight" [509; trans. modified]). It is worth examining the linguistic features of this scene. Cave has rightly underscored the importance of the Macraeons episode: "Pantagruel and his friends pick their way through a landscape littered with the remains of a lost civilization, with enigmatic inscriptions and pieces of fallen architecture" (*François Rabelais* xxx). Such remnants indicate, he concludes, both the idea of antiquity as the repository of learning, but whose restoration is now compromised, and the shattering of certainties that Du Bellay's death brings in its wake. Antique and foreign languages—hieroglyphics, Ionic, Arabic, Moorish, Slavic—recur in a context where remoteness and strangeness rather than mastery and intelligibility are the keynotes. They combine with the cry of mourning that goes up, "Pan le grand Dieu [est] mort" (659; "the great god Pan [is] dead" [511]), to act as the linguistic signals of decay and unwelcome change, emphasizing the significance of this scene for the book as a whole: the storm the travelers endure is already attributed by Macrobe to the cosmic convulsions brought about by the death of a hero, and the various monsters and prodigies that the Pantagruelists encounter from now on are embodiments of the bloating and swelling that had seemed satirically amusing in earlier works but that can now be portentously threatening or uncomfortably enigmatic.

It is against this background that a figure such as Homenaz (Greatclod) should be viewed, for he offers further evidence of the ambiguities of change. His praise of the Decretals is a tableau of language frozen into a particular mode: static, not dynamic, condemned to mechanical repetition in denial of the difference that change brings. His hyperbolical cries—"O dives Décrétales!", "O séraphicque *Sixieme*!", "O chérubicques *Clémentines*!", "O *Extravaguantes* angélicques" (717; "O divine Decretals," "O seraphic *Sixth*," "O cherubic *Clementines*," "O angelic *Supplementaries*" [557])—cross the ecstatic afflatus of poetry with the rather more earthy flatus and inflation of a Janotus or a Picrochole. They are a reminder that the new does not simply displace the old in Rabelais, that something that seemed outmoded or in decline at one stage in his work may return in another guise and with dangerous implications. Homenaz's exchanges with Pantagruel and his company abound with references to divine vengeance and the punishment of heretics. The bishop, unable and unwilling to break out of his narrow angle of vision, seeks to confine others in the same rigid perspectives—if necessary, by violence. Rabelais does not underestimate the power of the "agelastes" (519; "humorless" [437]).

Sequence is crucial here. It is the ordering of the narrative in this section of the *Quart livre* that establishes and reinforces meaning. The narrative pathway from Bringuenarilles to Du Bellay and then to Homenaz invites us to ponder how quickly laughter can turn into sadness, how comedy is akin to sorrow, how humor can edge into threat. Screech has spoken of laughter at the foot of the cross. In the *Quart livre*, Rabelais opens broader perspectives yet by plunging us into the many-stranded depiction of tumultuous times—everything from monetary inflation to religious strife—with the fragmented voyage a vehicle for the plural, conflicted itineraries that stretch narrative and humanism in different directions. In *Gargantua* and *Pantagruel*, the paths of humanism and history had run together: the developmental scheme of humanism could be accommodated in an encompassing framework. By the time of the *Quart livre*, this is no longer the case, and its narrative offers a reflection on the absurdity of chance and contingency, on the way in which fortune can rapidly change, casting optimism into shadow. An atmosphere of foreboding hangs over all; emblematically, when the frozen words in chapters 55 and 56 unfreeze, what the travelers hear are sounds of battle, groans of the dying, the clash of arms, horses neighing. Where the prologue of *Gargantua* had presented the relation between seriousness and laughter as the problematics of container and contained or appearance and depth, the *Quart livre* establishes a rough continuum between comedy and seriousness in tragicomic mode but one that constantly switches between its constituent poles, taking the reader by surprise with sudden changes in direction, reversals, and disruptions. Will the tragicomedy end well? Will it end badly? Resolution is deferred while localized instances of change and transition are fitted into a larger model that weaves Panurge's personal quest into the upheavals that beset Rabelais and his country in the 1540s and early 1550s.

Clearly, the aforegoing is a small, but one hopes representative, sample of a much larger body of instances of change, decay, and transition. They would all bear out Cave's observation that Rabelais is interested in thematizing the new and the archaic: "the sense of the past, of changing generations, changing styles is central in Rabelais" ("Travelers" 52). Yet equally, as Cave emphasizes, it would be an exaggeration to depict all incidents of change as identical, as if all decay, all change were somehow the same or proceeded at the same speed. On the contrary, Rabelais is supremely sensitive to evolving circumstances and persuasively subtle in his handling of them: the bumbling dialectician Janotus is not viewed in the same way as the maniacal Bishop Homenaz, even though both share some vital characteristics and perform a similar role in their respective narratives. Extending the perspective, we can say that Rabelais gives us a mobile language map on which are plotted specific incidents embodying the tensions and contradictions, but also the linkages, between the forces he sets in motion. If such a map comprises "a discovery structure, a network of experimental connections" (Cave, "Travelers" 55), it does so in ways that are finely attentive to the stop-start, ebb-and-flow processes of change and their linguistic expression.

Wes Williams provides confirmation of this point and offers us another, and concluding, perspective on change and transition. In his analysis of chapter 63 of the *Quart livre*, he highlights in particular the word *transpontin*, a linguistic borrowing that French took from Italian but that was current only for a few decades in the early to mid–sixteenth century before being replaced by the now-standard term *hamac*. We would naturally be tempted to translate both words as "hammock," but in so doing, Williams insists, we are not only being anachronistic with respect to *transpontin*, we are also missing its transient and transitional quality, which Rabelais captures and displays for us. By this and other episodes Rabelais underlines that his work is a particular linguistic and cultural equivalent of Montaigne's statement that "toute humaine nature est tousjours au milieu entre le naistre et le mourir" (*Essais* 601; "human nature is wholly situated for ever between living and dying" [*Complete Essays* (Screech) 680]). It is an in-between hybrid, a series of middles between emergence and decay, a sequence of transitions in no hurry to reach its goal; and one of our purposes, as teachers of Rabelais, is to sensitize our student readers to the ways in which he not only prismatically refracts the history of his transitional moment but also articulates it richly, unexpectedly, and above all comically.

Teaching Rabelais's Language: A Literary Approach

Todd W. Reeser

Nearly all participants of the survey made in preparation for this volume who teach Rabelais in French identified student perception of the extreme difficulty of language as the main problem in teaching the author. The problem was mentioned repeatedly for courses at both the undergraduate and graduate levels. Even when students understand the words, some instructors commented, they feel frustrated because they cannot necessarily construct meaning out of them. This issue was mentioned both by instructors who teach Rabelais's original French and by those who use a modernized version. Students reading Rabelais sometimes believe that there is something wrong with them or their linguistic abilities, unaware that the text presents itself as difficult and as requiring interpretive effort. My essay aims to help teachers in French programs begin to deal with this issue from the first moment of teaching Rabelais and thus to allay student anxiety about language from the start. What pedagogical strategies can help students feel that they can tackle Rabelais's text on their own, that it is not unreadable? To make the issue less of an issue, it should be confronted head-on. My focus here is not so much the actual linguistic difficulties of Renaissance French as how the concept of the difficulty of Rabelais's language and of his text in a larger sense can be dealt with in the classroom. By considering the idea over the actuality of language, my essay is meant to serve as a companion to Kirsten Fudeman's contribution to this volume, which treats ways to teach specific aspects of Rabelais's Middle French.

My first class on Rabelais is entirely devoted to helping students begin the process of thinking through the idea of language and its relation to meaning. In my experience, the importance of this issue for students trumps the difficulties associated with Rabelais's cultural or literary context, which can be presented in subsequent class sessions. Students do not have to begin their study of a literary text by reading its first chapter or section; they may profit more from beginning with a selection from the middle of the text. In the first class, my students read not the prologue to *Gargantua* or *Pantagruel* but an episode that invites them to reflect on the concept of language itself: chapter 9 of *Pantagruel*. Pantagruel meets Panurge for the first time, but before they can communicate in French, Panurge speaks a series of languages, most of which Pantagruel and his friends do not comprehend. My overall pedagogical goal is to help students realize that Rabelais himself is commenting on language difficulty, that he is teaching his readers how to deal with it and thus implicitly with how to read his own difficult text.

I begin class with specific questions about the setting of the encounter in the first sentence: Where is Pantagruel? What is he doing? With whom? Why is he walking with his friends and with students, and why he might be "walking outside the city" (196; "se pourmenant hors la ville" [356])? If students are not familiar with the ancient Peripatetic school, I explain that the group of men here is being compared with the Greek philosophers who talked and philosophized together while walking, often outside the city walls, and I mention Plato, Socrates, and the Academy. Students are then provided lead-in questions to work on so that they can focus on the details of the encounter. I tell them that they will work together in small groups, not unlike the Peripatetics, who worked together on philosophical questions. My goal is for them to consider the communication gap between Panurge on the one hand and Pantagruel and his party on the other. I do not yet tell students that this episode can be taken as metonymic for their own reading process or for their own textual encounter with Rabelais, as I want them first to focus on gathering relevant textual details. I ask them the following questions:

1. Comment est l'apparence physique de Panurge quand Pantagruel le voit pour la première fois? A votre avis, pourquoi a-t-il cette allure?
2. Pantagruel décide que Panurge n'a pas normalement cette apparence. Que peut voir Pantagruel? Comment arrive-t-il à voir le « vrai » Panurge?
3. Quand Pantagruel pose des questions, Panurge répond d'une façon étrange. Que fait-il?
4. Comment Pantagruel et ses amis répondent-ils à ce que dit Panurge?
5. Finalement, Panurge commence à parler en français, sa « langue naturelle et maternelle » (page 363). Est-ce que Pantagruel est fâché contre lui pour son jeu linguistique? Quelle est sa réaction ? A votre avis, pourquoi a-t-il cette réaction?

1. How does Panurge look when Pantagruel sees him for the first time?
2. Pantagruel decides that Panurge does not normally look this way. What does Pantagruel see? How is he able to see the "true" Panurge?
3. When Pantagruel poses a series of questions, Panurge answers strangely. What does he do?
4. How do Pantagruel and his friends respond to what Panurge says?
5. Finally, Panurge starts to speak French, his "natural and maternal language" (201). Is Pantagruel angry at him for his language game? What is his reaction? Why do you think he has this reaction? (my trans.)

After students have finished working, I start the class discussion by asking how Panurge's current appearance is different from his actual identity. Panurge is "un homme beau de stature et elegant en tous lineamens du corps" ("a man of handsome build, elegant in all his features") but "pitoyablement navré en divers lieux et tant mal en ordre qu'il sembloit estre eschappé ès chiens, ou mieulx resembloit un cueilleur de pommes du païs du Perche" (356; "pitifully wounded in various places, and in so sorry a state that he looked as if he had escaped from the dogs, or to be more accurate, like some apple-picker from the Perche country" [196]). The sense of "navré" ("wounded") has to be supplied. At the beginning of the second paragraph, Pantagruel explains to his companions that "il n'est pauvre que par fortune" ("he is only poor in fortune") and assures his friends that "à sa physonomie, nature l'a produict de riche et noble lignée, mais les adventures des gens curieulx le ont reduict en telle penurie et indigence" (356; "His physiognomy tells me for certain that he comes of some rich and noble stock. It must be the misfortunes which always befall the adventurous that have reduced him to his present ragged and penurious state" [197]). For both these juxtapositions, I ask students to explain how the way he looks is different from his physical body and how perceptions of class play a role in the articulation of difference.

I also ask students what "physonomie" is and how it allows Pantagruel to decide that Panurge is "de riche et noble lignée" ("of some rich and noble stock"). I show students sample images from Renaissance treatises on physiognomy in which a body part is shown along with its corresponding meaning, so that they can see why the "lineamens du corps" ("features") are significant. I ask how we informally read the "lines" of the body today and how we ascribe characteristics to people that we do not know, particularly in the area of class. My goal here is for students to understand that Panurge's body functions as a sign to be read, a sign that Pantagruel is able to read because he has trained himself.

We move to the questions about language play (3 and 4 above). Students usually point out that Pantagruel does not give up when Panurge starts speaking, the first time in German: "Mon amy, je n'entens poinct ce barragouin. Pourtant, si voulez qu'on vous entende, parlez aultre langaige" (358; "My friend, I don't understand a word of this gibberish. If you want to be understood you must speak another language" [197]); "Par Dieu, mon ami . . . ce que vous voudriez dire, dites-le-nous dans une langue que nous puissions comprendre" (361; "Really, my friend . . . tell us what you want in some language that we can understand" [199]). Pantagruel also attempts to work with those around him to discern meaning ("'Entendez vous rien là?' dist Pantagruel ès assistans" (358; "'Do you understand any of that?' Pantagruel asked the company" [197]), and Epistémon and Eudémon help him. As the group of companions continues trying to make meaning out of the various languages, they progressively make more sense of what Panurge says. They begin to identify the languages spoken: Carpalim understands his Greek, Pantagruel understands his Utopian, and then Panurge speaks Latin, which the humanists presumably understand. Finally, Pantagruel asks if he does not speak French, which of course he does. Because students tend to come to Rabelais with the expectation of character and psychology, they often wonder why Pantagruel is not angry at Panurge for playing with him when he could speak French all along and why the episode has made the giant feel bonded to his new friend. Pantagruel says, "j'ai déjà pour vous tant d'amitié, que, si vous consentez à mon désir, vous ne me quitterez jamais, et vous et moi, nous ferons une nouvelle paire d'amis comme celle d'Enée et d'Achate" (363; "I've taken such a liking for [you], I swear, that if I have my way you'll never stir from my side. Indeed you and I will make such another pair of friends as Aeneas and Achates" [201]). Their new friendship is founded not on an ability to communicate but on the linguistic game itself. I ask students to hypothesize why Pantagruel might have this response. They sometimes comment that Pantagruel must appreciate linguistic diversity and polyglotism, like a typical Renaissance humanist.

Having gathered details and worked with the literal meaning of the episode, we move to another level and consider how this chapter could be taken as autoreferential, or as a reflection on language, meaning, and comprehension. Because undergraduate students often have difficulty moving outside the plot or surface incidents of certain Renaissance texts, I say outright that this episode can be read as a statement by Rabelais on the nature of language and meaning and that each of the two sections of the chapter that we have examined (Pantagruel's reading of Panurge's body and the series of linguistic utterances) are also making statements about reading in a larger sense. I ask students to reconsider the opening of the chapter and locate similarities between Pantagruel's approach to Panurge and reading or interpreting. They revisit physiognomy as a reading-like practice, in which the body is a kind of text to be interpreted. Clothing and wounds are superfluous signs that have to be disregarded in the search for Panurge's less visible identity. Once students see how Pantagruel is reader-like, I ask them how Panurge is text-like. Perceptive students evoke Rabelais's use of "lineamens" and "lignée," which, because they are rich, noble, and elegant, suggest that Panurge is a text worth reading. Rabelais might be telling us how to read not just the bodies that we will encounter in his work but also the "lines" of the text before us. I ask students how Panurge's language could be described in the episode and how his language could be imagined as similar to Rabelais's own text. We discuss how Rabelais might be taken as variable, changing, in motion, not fixed, incomprehensible, or difficult. I invite students to think, as they read more Rabelais, how there are numerous languages embedded in the text. I then move out of the Renaissance context to ask what kind of encounter between us and Rabelais's text this episode is imagining. What parallels is Rabelais setting up between the text and our experience in the twenty-first century? How is Pantagruel like us? Like the humanist giant, we will have to learn to look beyond certain "wounds" of the Rabelaisian text for the "richer" or "noble" aspects behind them. I ask students what kind of symbolic wounds they imagine that Rabelais will present us with. Those who know or have heard that Rabelais is dirty, racy, or naughty, usually connect Panurge's wounds with this aspect of Rabelais's text.

Finally I bring student attention to the end of the chapter, in which it becomes clear that Panurge has been starving and thirsty throughout the episode. I ask why, if Panurge is so hungry and thirsty and can communicate in French, he does not directly ask for food and drink. Why does he go through all these languages? As students catch on to the kind of autoreferential reading that I am inviting them to perform, they often discuss how language performance or questions related to communication and meaning are more important to Panurge—and by extension, to Rabelais—than more practical questions of communication or storytelling. I conclude by asking students what this way of reading the episode means about how they should approach Rabelais on their own. What is Rabelais telling us today about how to read his text? Students may comment that language play should not make us toss away our book in frustration; it should link us to the text and create a bond with Rabelais, as Pantagruel takes a lifelong liking to his new friend. Rabelais is also showing students that they should work together to make meaning (as the group does in the text) and that, if they keep trying to make meaning, they will move closer to their "natural and native language."

Once students see that Rabelais is modeling how to treat linguistic or hermeneutic difficulties in theory, we move on to deciphering the actual language by closely examining a section of the text. My goal is to help students understand that although they might perceive Rabelais's language as difficult and foreign, they should continue their attempt to make meaning; in time they will be able to interact with or to "communicate" with the text. I often use the first two sentences of the prologue to *Pantagruel*, which will be part of the reading I ask students to do for the following class. I have students read the first two sentences of the prologue to themselves, and then I ask them what differences they can locate between Modern French and the Middle French in the passage. They usually pull out common spelling differences, such as final –*z* for final –*s*, the position of *ne*, the use of *y* instead of *i*, the absence of subject pronouns, the internal –*s*- that is not yet dropped (*vostre*) or the internal –*s*- instead of *accent aigu* (*estiez*, *mestier*). I give students a few minutes to read through the rest of the prologue to locate other differences in spelling and syntax, including the third-person imperfect (*faisoyent*, *estoit*, *donnoyent*), *ouyr* for *entendre*, *oncques* for *jamais*, and common words that are unfamiliar to them (*dudict*). In this group exercise, I let students give the Modern French equivalent themselves (when possible) so that they can build self-confidence in reading Rabelais's language. Once we have finished this part of the class, I point out to students that they can make a difficult language into one that is comprehensible if they invest some time and effort. If we read *Gargantua* in the course, I use the opening of the prologue for this purpose, since the famous Silenus box metaphor can be closely connected to the issues around reading discussed here. Another option is to use the exercises provided in Fudeman's essay, in this volume, on teaching Rabelais's language.

Students have been shown how in Rabelais visible signs hide something for those who know how to read between the lines. I ask them to read a section of the text, find a detail, and determine what sense may be located underneath it. The opening of the prologue to *Pantagruel* evokes *Gargantua* in its opening sentences. We are assumed to have read the first book obsessively, to the point that we ignore our own work ("ne se souciast de son mestier") and forget what we are doing ("et mist ses affaires propres en oubly"), even to have memorized the book ("jusques à ce que l'on les tint par cueur" [300]). I ask students what Rabelais is saying about his previous text and what his statement about the second might mean. I point to the passage later in the prologue in which Rabelais compares *Gargantua* with the Bible:

> Et le monde a bien congneu par experience infallible le grand emolument et utilité qui venoit de ladicte *Chronicque Gargantuine*: car il en a esté plus vendu par les imprimeurs en deux moys, qu'il ne sera acheté de Bibles en neuf ans. (302)

> The world has throughly acknowledged by infallible experience the great returns and benefits proceeding from this *Gargantuine Chronicle*. For more copies of it have been sold by the printers in two months than there will be of the Bible in nine years. (168)

Is Rabelais being sacrilegious, or might there be a richer meaning underneath this ludic comment?

My purpose is not to focus on particular details but to help students think about textual performance and imagine how a statement that appears one way (in this case, comicly sacrilegious) might be performing a very different function. As part of their reading assignment for the next class, I ask students to keep the Panurge-Pantagruel encounter in mind; to find three examples of how visible signs hide another, different meaning; and to find three examples of linguistic play whose function they can explain. As the famous *écolier limousin* episode is usually assigned as part of the reading for the next class, this last part of the assignment serves as a bridge between the two classes.

NOTE

I would like to thank my friend Andrea Frisch for her help with this piece.

Teaching Rabelais's Language: A Linguist's Perspective

Kirsten A. Fudeman

To read Rabelais aloud with an authentic pronunciation, to understand his syntax and plays on words, to profit from the richness of his vocabulary, and to appreciate the close relation between the choices that Rabelais made as a writer and sixteenth-century theories of language, one must devote time to studying his works from a linguistic perspective. On the basis of experience teaching Rabelais's language in both graduate and advanced undergraduate courses on the history of the French language, I present some practical advice for integrating study of Rabelais's language into the study of his texts. I also offer sample exercises.[1]

Phonology

Students not yet trained in Renaissance French are ill equipped to read Rabelais's works aloud, although the delight Rabelais takes in phonological wordplay shows that he certainly intended them to be. A first step in helping students read aloud passages of Rabelais with as authentic a pronunciation as possible is to present to them principal phonological characteristics of Rabelais's French, of which a list can be found in Mireille Huchon's *Œuvres complètes* (xxxv–xxxvii). (See Huchon, *Français* 83–95, on phonological characteristics of Renaissance French more generally.) It is one thing to study these lists and quite another to apply them consistently when reading Rabelais aloud. Some recommendations for the teacher are rehearse the reading aloud of selected passages before going to class, consulting reference works as necessary; model the pronunciation of one of these passages for students, having them imitate the teacher's pronunciation line by line; ask individual students to read the same passage again, correcting them as necessary; and, finally, ask individual students to read new passages out loud, correcting them as necessary. Presenting these class readings as rehearsals leading up to a performance is both fun and motivating. In a class devoted to Rabelais, one could organize a special hour-long performance outside class where students read passages of Rabelais aloud or even recite them from memory. In a performance tied to a course on the history of French, Rabelais might be only one of the writers represented.

Some passages of Rabelais lend themselves particularly well to reading aloud, such as those that repeat sounds (e.g., ". . . tousjours gualante, succulente, resudante, tousjours verdoyante, tousjours fleurissante, tousjours fructifiante, plene d'humeurs, plene de fleurs, plene de fruictz, plene de toutes delices" (86; *Gargantua*, ch. 8) or those that contain plays on words (some are given below).[2]

I offer the following activities to help students internalize rules for pronouncing Rabelais's French, to help them see the importance of studying his pronunciation, and to break their inhibitions about reading French aloud with an archaic pronunciation. A natural follow-up question is, "What is the significance of the wordplay in its context?"

My first objective is to have students apply generalizations about the phonology and spellings of Renaissance French to their recognition and understanding of phonologically based wordplay. They are asked to use each generalization about the pronunciation of Rabelais's French to determine how the underlined word would have been pronounced in his time. Then I ask them to explain the wordplay.

One generalization is that *oi* is pronounced [wɛ]. In certain words, such as *foible*, [wɛ] is reduced to [ɛ].

> A propos (dist le moyne), une femme qui n'est ny belle ny bonne, à quoy vault *toille*?
> ——A mettre en religion, dist Gargantua.
> ——Voyre, dist le moyne, et à faire des chemises!
> (268; *Gargantua*, ch. 52; my emphasis)[3]

The wordplay results from the fact that *toille* ("cloth, linen, canvas") and *telle* (fem. indefinite pronoun) are pronounced alike.

Under the influence of the *r*, many pronounced *er* as *ar.* According to grammarians, some Parisians said *guarre* for *guerre* ("war") and *Piarre* for *Pierre* (Huchon, *Œuvres complètes* xxxvi).

> Maistre Janotus tondu à la Cesarine, vestu de son lyripipion à l'antique, et bien antidoté l'estomac de coudignac de four et eau beniste de cave, se transporta au logis de Gargantua, touchant davant soy troys vedeaulx à rouge muzeau et trainant après cinq ou six *maistres inertes*, bien crottez à profit de mesnaige. (130; ch. 18; my emphasis)[4]

The wordplay is based on the similarity of *maistres inertes* ("passive authorities") and *maistres in [ès] artes* ("master of arts"). Compare Latin *magister in artibus*.

Rabelais plays with word boundaries.

> ——Au reste, vous pry n'y espargner ma peine. Seulement advisez si voulez confesser et jeuner les troys beaulx petitz jours de Dieu.
> ——De cons fesser (respondit Panurge), tresbien nous consentons.
> (1042; *Quart livre*, ch. 49)[5]

The play here is on *confesser* ("confess") and the multivalent *cons fesser* ("spank fools" or "savor/inflict blows on a certain female body part"). According to Demerson (Rabelais, *Œuvres complètes* 1042n23), "Dans ce jeu de mots scabreux, le verbe *fesser* doit être proche de son sens de *consommer*, savourer jusqu'au bout" ("In this risqué play on words, the verb *fesser* ['spank, beat with a stick'] must be close to its meaning of 'drink' ['savor to the end']). Demerson refers to the expression *Un homme fesse bien son vin*, found in many older dictionaries.

Another objective is to have students recognize and understand the homonymy in pairs of selected words and phrases from *Gargantua*, chapter 9 (94).

1. *un espoir* ("hope") ~ *une sphere* ("sphere")
2. *pennes* ("feathers") ~ *poines* ("pains")
3. *un lict sans ciel* ("a bed without a sky," i.e., "canopy") ~ *un licentié* ("graduate")
4. *moustarde* ("mustard") ~ *moult tarde* ("much is long in coming")

The phonological bases of these homonymies are as follows:

1. Word-initial *e*, as in *espoir*, and word-final *e*, as in *une*, are both pronounced as a schwa (Huchon, *Œuvres complètes* xxxvi).
2. The digraph *oi* is pronounced [wɛ] or [ɛ]. In *poines*, it is pronounced [ɛ], making *poines* and *pennes* homophonous (Huchon, *Œuvres complètes* xxxv–xxxvi).
3. The *c* of *lict* is not pronounced; it is an etymological letter (Modern French *lit* < Latin *lectus*). The *l* of *ciel* is not pronounced; final consonants had ceased to be pronounced in popular speech (Huchon, *Œuvres complètes* xxxvi).
4. The *s* of *moustarde* and the *l* of *moult* are both etymological letters no longer pronounced by Rabelais's time.

Vocabulary

As Kurt Baldinger demonstrates, the meaning of no word or expression in Rabelais's works can be taken for granted: "En principe, il n'y a que de faux amis dans un texte d'une époque du passé. Il est indispensable de les mettre à l'épreuve" (37; "As a rule, one finds only 'false friends' in texts from earlier time periods. Putting them to the test is vital"). To reinforce this idea, a teacher might assign Baldinger's "Splendeurs et misères des glossaires" or "Gargantua, nouvelles recherches lexicologiques" (19–38, 39–47) or simply integrate some of Baldinger's examples into a lecture. *Rivières*, for example, is used by Rabelais with the meaning "terrain qui borde un cours d'eau" (28; "lands beside a river or stream"). Discussion of the meaning of forms is most effective when paired with discussion of their context.

Teachers may also assign prereading exercises that prepare students for dealing with Rabelais's rich vocabulary and the presence of etymological, nonpronounced letters. I offer two suggestions.

One objective is to have students identify etymological, nonpronounced letters and to improve their recognition of relations between words of Renaissance and Modern French. They can use a reference work such as *Le nouveau*

Petit Robert or the *Nouveau dictionnaire étymologique et historique* to learn the Latin etymologies of the following words, which are given in both Renaissance and modern spellings. They determine which of the words contains a false etymological letter—that is, one that was not present in the Latin etymon (source word). They try to discover the source of the false etymological letter.

Rabelais	**Modern French**	**Explanation**
aultre	*autre* ("other")	< Latin *alter*, accusative *alterum*
(bancque)roupte	*(banque)route* ("bankruptcy")	< Italian *banca rotta*. The *p* of *roupte* is an etymological letter; Italian *rotta* < Latin *rupta*.
comprins	*compris* ("understood")	Modern French *comprendre* < Latin *comprehendere.*
dict	*dit*, infinitive *dire* ("say")	Modern French *dire* < Latin *dicere*.
doibve	*doive*, infinitive *devoir* ("owe," "have to")	Modern French *devoir* < Latin *debere*.
escripre	*écrire* ("write")	< Latin *scribere*. The *p* is represented in various related forms, including the past participle *scriptus* (m.), *scripta* (f.), *scriptum* (n.).
faict	*fait*, infinitive *faire* ("do," "make")	Modern French *faire* < Latin *facere*.
lict	*lit* ("bed")	< Latin *lectus,* accusative *lectum*.
mieulx	*mieux* ("better," "best")	< Latin *melius*.
oultre	*outre* ("besides")	< Latin *ultra*.
nuict	*nuit* ("night")	< Latin *noctem*.
sçavoir	*savoir* ("know")	< Latin *sapere*, originally "taste, perceive," later "know." The often encountered spelling *sçavoir* (not limited to Rabelais) is based on a false association with *scio*, *sciēre* ("I know," "to know.")

Another objective is to have students develop on their own a sense of the varied sources from which Rabelais drew his vocabulary and to appreciate to what extent his language would have seemed challenging or artificial even in his own time. They are asked to study the *Briefve declaration* and to identify at least six languages or dialects of French from which the words come. I ask them which languages or dialects are best represented. On the basis of their experience with Modern French and English, can they tell which of these words have passed into common usage?

Morphology and Syntax

Students exposed to Renaissance French for the first time may be challenged by many of its features, including the omission of subject pronouns, the use of *ne* on its own to mark negation (as well as the use of archaic reinforcers of negation such as *mie* and *goutte*), relative freedom in word order, and imitations of the Latin ablative absolute construction. For example, "Eulx tenens ces menuz propos de beuverie, Gargamelle commenca se porter mal du bas" (76; *Gargantua*, ch. 6; "While they were having this little chat about drinking, Gargamelle began to feel uncomfortable down below"). Some other morphological and syntactic features do not generally cause comprehension difficulties, even though absent from Modern French—for example, the separation of the subject pronoun from the verb: "Je (dist Panurge) me trouve fort bien du conseil des femmes, et mesmement des vieilles" (618; *Tiers livre*, ch. 16).[6]

One objective is to guide students in translating Rabelaisian sentence structures into Modern French or English. They render the following examples into natural-sounding Modern French. Then they identify particular grammatical structures that are ungrammatical by today's standards. The point is to see in action how Rabelais's syntax and morphology differ from those of Modern French.

> Quelle difference est entre bouteille et flaccon?—Grande, car bouteille est fermée à bouchon et flaccon à viz. (72; *Gargantua*, ch. 5)[7]

> Je me doubte que ne croyez asseurement ceste estrange nativité. Si ne le croyez, je ne m'en soucie, mais un homme de bien, un homme de bon sens croit tousjours ce qu'on luy dict, et qu'il trouve par escript. (80; ch. 6)[8]

> [Two things that Gargantua did when he was young.] Mettoyt la charrette devant les beufz. De cheval donné tousjours reguardoyt en la gueulle. (104; ch. 11)[9]

> Pantagruel, avoir entierement conquesté le pays de Dipsodie, en icelluy transporta une colonie de Utopiens en nombre de 9 876 543 210 hommes, sans les femmes et petitz enfans. . . . (532; *Tiers livre*, ch. 1)[10]

> Ces parolles achevées, feurent aportez les œuvres de Virgile. Avant les ouvrir, Panurge dist à Pantagruel. . . . (588; ch. 11)[11]

NOTES

[1] I recommend Ayres-Bennett's presentation of two short passages from *Gargantua* with detailed commentary on its orthography, morphology, syntax, and vocabulary (142–48).

[2] ". . . always agreeable, succulent, juicy, always green, always flowering, always fruitful, full of sap, full of flowers, full of fruits, full of every kind of delight." This and all other translations are my own.

[3] "Incidentally," said the monk, "a woman who is neither fair nor good, what is such a one good for? [*or* what is linen good for?]" "For making into a nun," said Gargantua. "True," said the monk, "and for making shirts!"

[4] Master Janotus, his hair cut like Cesar's [i.e., he was bald], dressed in his *lyripipion* in the ancient style, and his stomach well fortified with baked cotignac and holy water from a cellar [i.e., wine], took himself to Gargantua's dwelling, driving before him three red-nosed beadles. Lagging behind him were five or six artless Masters of Art, thoroughly covered with mud.

[5] "Moreover, I beg you not to spare me. Only inform me if you want to confess and fast the three lovely little days of God." "We readily consent to *cons fesser*," Panurge answered.

[6] "'I,' said Panurge, 'am happy in the company of *femmes* ["women"], likewise in the company of *vieilles* ["old women"].'" Rabelais takes advantage of the morphological difference, suggesting that *vieilles* are not *femmes*.

[7] "What difference is there between a bottle and a flacon?" "A big one, because a bottle is corked shut and a flacon is screwed." The wordplay is on *flaccon*, which, spoken, can be interpreted as one word or two. Note that both *flacon* and *flagon* entered the English language from French. *Flagon* is used with a wider variety of meanings.

[8] "I suspect that you most certainly do not believe this strange birth. If you do not believe it, I do not care, but a man of worth, a man of good sense always believes what people tell him and what he finds written down."

[9] "He would put the cart before the horse [lit., before the oxen]. He would always look a gift horse in the mouth."

[10] "Pantagruel, having conquered the land of Dipsodie, transported to it a colony of Utopians numbering 9,876,543,210 men, not counting the women and children. . . ."

[11] "When these words were finished, the works of Vergil were brought. Before opening them, Panurge said to Pantagruel. . . ."

Teaching Rabelais in English Translation

Valerie Worth-Stylianou

In an ideal world, all students aspiring to read Rabelais would have the education of the inhabitants of Thélème:

> [I]l n'estoit entre eulx celluy ne celle qui ne sceust lire, escripre, chanter, jouer d'instrumens harmonieux, parler de cinq et six langaiges, et en iceulx composer tant en carme que en oraison solue. (284)
>
> [T]here was not a man or woman among them who could not read, write, sing, play musical instruments, speak five or six languages, and compose in them both verse and prose. (159)

However, few tutors or instructors today offer either musical performance or creative writing in verse as assessment options in their courses on Renaissance texts and culture, and relatively few students (at least in undergraduate programs) confront Rabelais in his sixteenth-century French without some help from a paraphrase or translation. Before we simply fall into a nostalgic regret of times past (the direct opposite of Gargantua's eulogy in *Pantagruel*, chapter 8, of "la lumiere et dignité [qui] a esté de mon eage rendue ès lettres" [350; "learning has been restored in my age to its former dignity and enlightenment" (194)]), we should recall that true multilingualism was the preserve of a very elite minority even in the Renaissance[1] and that Rabelais's text constantly challenged his contemporary monolingual as well as all literally minded readers (and listeners).

My reference to the spectrum of Latin possessed by men and women of the French Renaissance (on a scale from "none" to "very sophisticated native-speaker and -reader equivalent") provides a neat parallel for the French-language skills of the diverse bodies of today's students. In teaching Rabelais to both second-year French undergraduates and a select *agrégation* class in Rennes in the 1980s, I soon learned why Guy Demerson's parallel text (French original and Modern French side by side, in the fashion of Renaissance bilingual editions of the classics)[2] has proved so popular. Demerson is an outstanding scholar of Rabelais, a man of humor and erudition in equal measure, whose footnotes will satisfy rigorous *agrégatifs*. But most educated francophone readers of Rabelais also look—more or less intermittently—at the Modern French translation (or paraphrase) when Rabelais's linguistic inventiveness defeats their normal lexical resources. (Tellingly, with Rabelais it is above all the individual words, the lexical level of the text, that challenges French as much as anglophone readers, whereas with Montaigne, today's French students may recognize most of the lexical items but still stumble awkwardly in their comprehension of the twisting syntax that reflects the sinuous thought patterns.) So, if French students do not shy away from reading Rabelais in an intralingual translation, it would be uncharitable to begrudge anglophone students recourse to a version in their language. It's a pity no publisher has yet produced a bilingual French-English student version of the text, following the layout of the Demerson edition, but students have long been adept at the art of reading simultaneously an original text on top of the desk and a crib underneath it. And that is essentially how most of our undergraduate students in French courses will tackle Rabelais, retaining the French original as their destination text, to be cited in assignments and discussed in seminars, but with the English translation as the guide or interpreter charting their passage.

Another large group of readers of Rabelais do not even ostentatiously place their French text on the table, for many students in comparative literature or general humanities courses cannot read Rabelais other than in English. Once again, in a cohort (as in large groups following such courses at my previous institution in the United Kingdom) students display a vast range of acquaintance with French, some having majored in it at high school, others having an elementary grasp, still others having no knowledge at all. For those completely without French, the English translation simply replaces the original. Yet even some of these students, and certainly students who have some intermediate level of French, frequently ask the lecturer, "Am I missing something by not reading Rabelais in French? If so, what?"

Herein lies the twofold purpose of my contribution to this volume: to provide an honest and nuanced answer to the first question and to suggest, with practical examples, some ways in which teaching Rabelais through an English translation can be made to work. As a Renaissance scholar with a particular interest in the practice of translation in early modern France, I consider that teaching Rabelais through an English translation raises particular challenges because of the extent to which his humor is uniquely dependent on his control of language. For students who cannot access the French at all, how far is the nature and immediacy of the humor preserved by any translation? And how far can the instructor mediate the linguistic humor when the translation alone is insufficient?

The first issue is which of the available translations of the complete works to recommend.[3] What of the potential value of using the early English translation by Thomas Urquhart and by Peter Le Motteux?[4] While agreeing with Michael Heath that "[t]emperamentally and stylistically, Urquhart and Rabelais were made for each other" (123),[5] I recognize that most students prefer to read Rabelais in Modern English, even at the expense of a period flavor (not unlike their French counterparts' welcoming Demerson's Modern French paraphrase).[6] Modern versions of the complete works currently in print are those by J. M. Cohen, by Donald Frame, and by M. A. Screech.[7] It is telling that most respondents to the MLA survey conducted in preparation for this volume opted for the Cohen translation—a choice echoed by students I have taught in comparative literature and humanities courses. The point about Frame and Screech is that, as lifelong and distinguished Renaissance scholars, neither can conceive of Rabelais's text existing without a ghost presence of the French. In Frame's translation, parenthetical citations from Rabelais's French are scattered throughout the English, in square brackets, regularly reminding the student of aspects of the work that in Frame's view defy translation. Frame's comments on the act of translation and interpretation are reserved for long but illuminating endnotes. For Screech, while there is limited paraphrastic citation from French in the English translation, the visual intrusion to smooth reading of the translation as a text in its own right comes in the form of a substantial headnote to each chapter, in which scholarly exegesis is presented.[8] Cohen is not a Rabelais scholar, and therefore his text is untrammeled by such apparatus.[9] Essentially, Frame and Screech are best suited to students of French studies who want to read Rabelais in the original but need some reassurance and guidance; Cohen is better for anglophones who want to be allowed to enjoy Rabelais without continually worrying that this is literature in translation.

I compare some details of their translations below, but suffice it to say that Cohen's is a sound though not always inspired attempt at what the translation theorist Lawrence Venuti would term "domesticating" Rabelais—that is, toning down the foreign elements.[10] Cohen, like Rabelais, does not shy away from calling a spade a spade or a turd a turd. Frame and Screech want the foreigness, the irreducibly French nature of Rabelais's writing to come through their version. Frame describes his aim as "fidelity (which is not always literalness)" (xxvi). His distinction is crucial: the ideal (but impossible) translation would replicate Rabelais's achievement in the target language, but it would do so by relying at least some of the time on different lexical, syntactic, stylistic resources. How far does he succeed? In varying degrees, I think. He is at his best in lists of challenging but discrete lexical items, such as invented names; he can convey Rabelais's shifts of register sure-footedly and has a neat command of vulgar American English.[11] Yet when we read sustained chapters, the sparkle of Rabelais is only intermittent. Screech is even more deferential to a humanist reading of Rabelais—and perhaps temperamentally less inclined to play with the linguistic riches of obscenities. Some of his translations of invented names do work well, but overall his version has the strengths and limitations of a safe translation: it won't let the student miss what Screech believes Rabelais wanted to say, but neither will it risk putting the original in the shade. Perhaps this is as it should be, but when teaching Rabelais to students who are also following English creative writing programs, I can't help wishing a writer like Roald Dahl had turned his hand to the task!

Thus I proceed on the assumption that most students reading Rabelais in English will use Cohen's version but that the tutor or instructor has access to Frame, Screech, and Demerson as well as to the original French. Which linguistic feats of Rabelais's word spinning do we most need to highlight to anglophone students, and how can we compensate for the inevitable translation loss?

I start with individual lexical items. Invented names are a great source of humor throughout Rabelais's work. All modern readers need to be reminded that "[t]he past is a foreign country" (Hartley 5) and, to extend the metaphor, that not all inhabitants of that country would have got all the jokes anyway. If anglophone readers of the early twenty-first century do not see humor in the name "Dr Rondibilis" (*Tiers livre*, ch. 31), they should be reassured that neither will their francophone peers, and probably only Rabelais's inner circle (humanist friends, physicians) would have made a link in 1546 with the venerable Doctor Rondelet of Montpellier. So Cohen, Frame, and Screech sensibly leave Rondibilis's name the same in English. Rabelaisian humor through invented names is, however, language- rather than context-dependent in an episode like Panurge's encounter with Dindenault in *Quart livre*, chapters 6–8. Cohen's version, "Dingdong," epitomizes the humor better than any footnote.[12] We may tell a class that the French name relies on the association with *dinde* ("stupidity"), but if they are reading Cohen's text, this detail is a supplementary afternote, not essential to immediate enjoyment. Linguistic humor is far more obviously foregrounded in the many lists of made-up names, and here all three translators take up the challenge of one-for-one equivalence—for example, in *Quart livre*, chapter 40. Whether in English or French, students appreciate the humor best if they read the lists aloud (in deadpan Monty Python style is one good challenge), and we can invite the more inventive to add a few of their own coinages. Some guided creative response is surely the best tribute to Rabelais's humor; it also ensures that students have actively understood how the chapter functions.

Translation loss is inevitable in most puns; homophones are almost never the same in two languages. But inviting the class to create parallel examples in English can rekindle the humor, even if a contextual explanation has to precede the laughter for an appreciation of the joke. Take Homenaz's gift to Pantagruel of the "poires be bons Christian" (1066; "Good-Christian pears" [565]). Most commentators agree the po-faced dialogue is puzzling, but *chapeau* to Screech for succinctly telling his readers in the headnote to the chapter that part of the humor at least relies on the fact that *poire* means a "booby." If students might not frequently use the term *booby*, invite them to think up a current vernacular insult that can also be applied to a gift! This exercise is in fact a localized (purely lexical) application of the pedagogical principle that students best appreciate Rabelais if from time to time they try to imagine how he might have cast similar episodes in English, referring to contemporary events. Who would be the recognizable modern equivalents of Gargantua and Picrochole? Answers vary depending on international conflicts of the day. What trio of experts would today be assembled to counsel Panurge on marriage? A doctor, but probably no longer a theologian or a philosopher. Perhaps a life coach and a divorce lawyer?

What about Rabelais's many coinages and plays with language that do not make complete sense even to a French reader? Here is the real rub: should a translation strive to be less obscure than the source text? I'd argue that the tutor's or instructor's role is to reassure anglophone readers—no less than their French peers who pour over Demerson's footnotes only to come away still unsure they have got the point—that some puzzlement can be an appropriate response. We can gnaw away at the bone, but sometimes it seems hollow. In

"Fanfreluches antidotées" (58), we sense that in his "Antidoted Bubbles" Screech has relished the task of composing doggerel verse that is semiopaque but not humorless (211–15), whereas Frame's playful poetic strain is a touch too transparent in comparison with the original, unlike Cohen's "Corrective Conundrums," which are followed by a rare (and rather tetchy footnote) commenting that "[t]here is very little sense in this riddle" (45).

Students usually accept that a parody of nonsense verse is meant to defy easy comprehension. Baffling lists are not dissimilar, since they tend to fall midway between poetry and prose and should be read aloud to do justice to their rhythm. Of the twisted metaphors applied to Quaresmeprenant's anatomy in *Quatre livre*, chapter 30, for example, some should be self-evidently funny ("His bladder like a catapult").[13] Others risk becoming less abstruse in translation, something of which we must explicitly warn anglophone readers. How many sixteenth-century French readers, except medical students who had attended dissections, would have known where to locate their *conare*, let alone what it looked like? Isn't Rabelais being deliberately obfuscatory, partly to parody the ease with which doctors lapse into medical jargon? When the comparison is rendered as "His pineal gland like a bagpipe" (513), it gives English students the same deceptive confidence as that enjoyed by their francophone peers who glance across to Demerson's reassuring paraphrase ("la glande pinéale, comme une cornemuse" [968]).

If all three translators already err in the direction of explaining and rationalizing poetry and lists, it is unsurprising to find a general if tacit assumption that other episodes should be made comprehensible. The task is less tricky where Rabelais sets up a single misguided and incomprehensible fool against a rational interlocutor, such as the *écolier limousin*'s encounter with Pantagruel (*Pantagruel*, ch. 6) or Janotus's harangue to Gargantua (ch. 19). Here, the challenge facing the translator is that of capturing the specific idiom of the fool's speech, and pretentious false erudition is obviously fair game. Cohen sets the reader on the right track by an artful gloss in the chapter title: "How Pantagruel met a Limousin who *murdered* the French language" (183; my emphasis; for "Comment Pantagruel rencontra un Limosin qui *contrefaisoit* la langaige Françoys" [332; my emphasis]). He, like Frame and Screech, then produces ridiculously Latinate English, equivalent to Rabelais's ridiculously Latinate French. The only problem for most of our contemporary students (English or French) is that they may not have a sufficient smattering of Latin to realize how clever some of these coinages are! The same problem arises, and cannot be sidestepped in teaching, with Janotus's speech. How can an audience unable to conjugate any Latin verbs appreciate the horrendous howler "et ego habet bon vino" (77)? Grammatical explanations may be offered but are a poor substitute for immediacy, so again we might invite some creative imitation. Suppose Janotus were a learned professor in the French department charged with representing your venerable institution: imagine him delivering a formal speech in English but peppered with French phrases taken quite out of context and ending up with the sort of howlers no first-year student should produce. (Students usually enjoy this chance to turn the tables!)

Less amenable to creative rewriting are episodes in which it is not clear that any character makes sense, but equally we are not sure that Rabelais does not have a serious point somewhere. In chapters 9–11 of *Pantagruel*, students can recognize the principle—satire of legalese—but why does Rabelais indulge at such length in the satire? Are we missing some hidden comic vein? Heath sums up the dilemma neatly: "The difficulty lies, of course, in the fact that the speeches make complete sense grammatically and none at all semantically" (34).[14] Students, whether reading Rabelais in French or in English, need to be aware that the author may just be laughing at our search for meaning—in any language!

Finally, reading Rabelais in translation poses the particular problem of his play with registers.[15] One language's sense of obscenity, erudition, or pomposity does not always map directly onto another's. The task is easier when Rabelais engineers a clear break in register, as in Pantagruel's letter to his father in *Quart livre*, chapter 4. The abrupt shift from hyperformulaic humanist *formules de politesse* to the informal domestic injunctions on care of the exotic pet should lose little in translation. Frame is particularly adroit here; his use of English contractions fits the lower register very neatly.[16] More difficult to capture in a translation are Rabelais's constant shifts between registers within a couple of sentences or even a phrase. In the juxtaposition of crudity and erudition, a literal translation may not carry quite the same resonances in English. For example, Screech makes the point, in his prefatory note on the translation, that "*[s]hit* in English is far more arresting than *merde* in French. . . . *Shit* is by no means always the best translation of *merde*. *Pooh* or some other word may serve better" ("Note" xlv). I am not convinced that attenuation of crudity is always a good solution, but he is right that the immediate affective impact of words varies between linguistic cultures.[17] In the famous "torchecul" episode (*Gargantua*, ch. 13), where Rabelais has Gargantua alternate between erudition way beyond his years and disingenuous vulgarity, his subversive, carnivalesque humor is supported by the sharp exploitation of clashes of register,[18] as in, "Puis, fiantant derriere un buisson, trouvay un chat de Mars; d'iceluy me torchay, mais ses gryphes me exulcererent tout le perinée" (112; "Then, as I was shitting behind a bush, I found a March-born cat; I wiped myself on him, but his claws exulcerated my whole perineum" [67]). Many five-year-olds might have known *fianter*, but I doubt any would have been able to describe their physical suffering with such medical precision! Cohen, Frame, and Screech all get close to Rabelais's achievement, but none quite matches it. Perhaps *fianter* should be "crapping" (rather than "shitting" [Cohen 67 and Frame 34] or "poohing" [Screech 147]). Cohen is probably right to retain "exulcerated" (67; where Frame and Screech "domesticate" the form, using "ulcerated" [34 and 147, resp.]). It's only a small phrase; in the run of the translation, it scarcely matters, and all three versions give anglophone readers a fair flavor of Rabelais's linguistic humor. However, this example provides a salutary reminder that if we want our students to engage in close textual analysis of Rabelais based on an English translation, it is useful for the instructor to check the version against the original.

When teaching Rabelais in translation, the tutor or instructor must guide the English reader toward concealed losses and accretions in translation. This guidance in its turn affords a fine opportunity for students to reflect on what is linguistically or culturally specific, as opposed to what is universal in communication, and thus to test the hypothesis that "[m]ieux est de ris que de larmes escrire, / pour ce que rire est le propre de l'homme" (49; "mirth's my theme and tears are not, / For laughter is man's proper lot" [36]).

NOTES

The quotations in this essay from Rabelais's text are taken from the 1973 Demerson edition.

[1] See Cave's discerning remarks on the large sectors of the population with a limited, purely functional grasp of Latin, as opposed to humanist mastery of it (*Pré-histoires II* 68).

[2] For a discussion of the significance of bilingual formats in sixteenth-century French translations, see Worth-Stylianou.

[3] I do not discuss translations that cover only a single book of Rabelais, since I am addressing the need to furnish a complete text of at least *Pantagruel*, *Gargantua*, *Tiers livre*, and *Quart livre* for anglophone students.

[4] Urquhart's translations of *Pantagruel* and *Gargantua* were published in 1653, that of the *Tiers livre* posthumously in 1693; Le Motteux's versions of the *Quart livre* and the *Cinquiesme livre* followed in 1694. The work of both translators was republished in the Everyman collection in the early twentieth century.

[5] I share Heath's view that the continuation by Le Motteux is unable to match Urquhart's stylistic verve.

[6] English studies students wishing to pursue Rabelais's potential influence on later sixteenth- and seventeenth-century English writers can be referred to the masterly analysis by Prescott.

[7] For a brief survey of English translations between Le Motteux's and Cohen's, see Frame's prefatory "Translator's Note" (xxv).

[8] There are also occasional footnotes on specific references.

[9] The fluency of the version comes—as has been generally acknowledged—at the price of occasional slips in his comprehension of sixteenth-century French.

[10] Students can usefully be directed to read Venuti's essay "Translation, Community, Utopia."

[11] For example, the Americanized "Ass-wiper" in *Gargantua*, chapter 13 (Frame 37), captures the childish obscenity of "torchecul" perfectly (Demerson 77).

[12] Screech and Frame leave the name untranslated.

[13] An instance in which Frame's exegetical zeal ("The bladder, like a stonebow ['crossbow' or 'catapult']") stands in the way of the obvious humor (50). For a review of approaches to the episode, see Schwartz, *Irony* 182–83.

[14] Cf. La Charité's comment that "language is on show, holds centre-stage, and means whatever it means contextually, precisely because it does not mean referentially" (*Recreation* 70).

[15] See Tetel's analysis of the linguistic resources that Rabelais exploits in his comic parodies (35–57).

[16] For example: "You'll like him ["le tarande" (592)]. He's as manageable and easy to train as a lamb. I'm also sending you three young unicorns" (445).

[17] For an illuminating recent general discussion, by a psycholinguist, of the affective connotations of obscenity, see the chapter "The Seven Words You Can't Say on Television" in Pinker (323–72).

[18] Not unlike many of the effects achieved by Queneau in *Zazie dans le métro*, Rabelais's humor is potentially more politically charged, given Gargantua's elevated social status.

The Prologue of *Gargantua*; or, A Lesson in Scandal Management

Jan Miernowski

> Amis lecteurs qui ce livre lisez,
> Despouillez vous de toute affection,
> En le lisant ne vous scandalisez. . . . (49)
>
> Good friends who come to read this book,
> Strip yourselves first of affectation;
> Do not assume a pained, shocked look. . . . (36)

Everyone who has taught Rabelais knows how difficult it is for students to follow Rabelais's advice. "Potty humor," "misogyny," "obscenity"—many initial reactions express disgust, contempt, and sometimes, even more alarmingly, a quite misguided hilarity. Of course, our job as philologists is to put Rabelais's prose in historical perspective. We therefore invest a lot of effort in demonstrating to our students that Rabelais is *not* scandalous, that in fact he only *seems* outrageous to untrained modern and postmodern minds, minds blinded by contemporary culture and unable to notice the contexts that make harmless even the most salacious jokes of Alcofribas and his fellow characters. In doing so, we follow many of our illustrious predecessors, who shed a proper light on Rabelais's obscenities. To name two: Michael Screech, whose erudition made us understand the depth of Rabelais's humanistic humor, which remains largely obscure when isolated from its theological and legal intertexts (*Rabelais* [1979]); Mikhail Bakhtin, whose anthropological perspective, when freed from the Marxist rhetoric imposed by Stalinism, revealed the carnivalesque nature of Rabelais's laughter engaged in a polyphonic dialogue with popular (one may say mass) culture of his time (*Rabelais*).[1] No doubt that armed with such powerful interpretative tools, we can help our students progress beyond their initial shock and help them in effectively disarming the scandalous character of Rabelais's prose.

But what if the discomfort felt by our students is not so anachronistic after all? What if Rabelais's preliminary plea addressed to the readers of *Gargantua*, asking them not to be "scandalized," testified to a quite real anxiety of the author, who did anticipate among his sixteenth-century audience a moral and emotional reaction somewhat similar to the indignation that we often witness nowadays in our classrooms? If such is the case, our efforts to sanitize Rabelais's laughter and disarm the scandalous effect of his fiction may be at least partially misguided. Instead of telling our students how much they overstate Rabelais's vulgarity, we should maybe admit that, indeed, Rabelais foresaw the indignation of his readers and even intended to shock them. Once having conceded the coarseness of Rabelais's humor, we should then point to its specific function in the writer's ideological and artistic project. Such are the two goals of this essay. First, I would like to give back to Rabelais's fiction the scandalous character that I believe it originally had. I intend to achieve this by exploring the moral connotations of the term *scandal* in sixteenth-century French and by reexamining the grammatical structure of the pivotal fragment of the prologue of *Gargantua*. Second, I suggest ways of demonstrating the specificity of Rabelais's scandal in contrast with our students' culture. I end by comparing Rabelais's scatology with the one that our students know from the popular cartoon series *South Park*.

Let's start by giving back to Rabelais's scandals the sharp edge that I believe they originally had, and which were blunted by some of our best interpretative tools.

Screech has rightly pointed out that the verb *scandaliser* used by Rabelais refers to its Greek form in the Gospels. In this sense, *scandale* is an obstacle on the path to one's salvation, and the initial *dizain* of *Gargantua* thus constitutes a warning addressed to the readers not to loose faith (197).[2] Such specific evangelical signification should however not overshadow the broader meaning of *scandaliser*. Even a quick look at corresponding entries in the dictionaries of Du Cange and of Edmond Huguet shows that in Middle French this verb meant in general to blame or to discredit someone, to harm somebody's honor, reputation, or sense of personal dignity. Accordingly, besides its strictly biblical meaning (which no doubt is crucial for Rabelais), *scandale* had a more mundane significance: it designated a moral condemnation or the cause thereof. In the ninth novella of the Marguerite de Navarre's *Heptameron*, a poor but virtuous nobleman is welcomed into the household of a beautiful young girl, where he easily gains respect and sympathy thanks to his spotless behavior and character.

However, some baseless rumors soon force the mother of the girl to ask the gentleman to make his visits less frequent—not without regret, since she has never doubted his honesty,

> dont elle se tenoit aussy asseurée que de nul de ses enfans, fut fort marrye d'entendre que on le prenoit à mauvause part. Tant que, à la fin, craignant le scandalle par la malice des hommes, le pria pour quelque temps de ne hanter pas sa maison. . . . (60)
>
> [having] no less confidence in him than she had in her own children. It was therefore with some distress that she learnt that his visits were being seen in a bad light [literally, "taken in a bad part"]. In the end, afraid lest, human nature being what it is, malicious gossip might lead to some sort of scandal, she decided to ask him not to come to the house for a while. (115)

Clearly, the prudent mother is concerned less about the spiritual well-being of her daughter than about her daughter's reputation. Panurge shares such concern when he proclaims that skipping one's supper, "c'est erreur. C'est scandale en nature" (612; "an error, a scandal in nature" [328]), in other words a great dishonor, opprobrium, and rightful subject of public blame.

In sixteenth-century French, *scandale* implies therefore the judging, condemning gaze of others. *Scandalizer* is to blame someone or dishonor someone's name. In the *Heptameron*, the scandal may result from the fact that the malicious neighbors have taken the virtuous nobleman's behavior "in a bad part." Evidently Rabelais would like to preserve his characters and his chronicles from such negative judgments.[3] It is why Pantagruelism consistently promotes interpretation "in good part" as a way to avoid being "scandalized." Pantagruel is not disturbed by Panurge's dilapidation of Salmagundia, because "toutes choses prenoit en bonne partie, tout acte interpretoit à bien. Jamais ne se tourmentoit, jamais ne se scandalizoit" (540; "he took everything in good part . . . and was never scandalized" [293]). After announcing to Panurge that he will not be a cuckold, "if it please God," Hippothadeus clearly expects the worried candidate for matrimony to display some Pantagruelism: "prenez en bien mes parolles. . . . Est ce condition blaspheme ou scandaleuse?" (696; "take my words in good part. . . . Is that a blasphemous or scandalous proviso?" [371–72]). At the end of the prologue of *Gargantua*, Alcofribas asks his readers to interpret his deeds and words "en la perfectissime partie" (54; "in the most perfect sense" [39]). This final plea echoes the initial call of the preliminary *dizain*, asking the readers "not to be scandalized" by the book. Edwin Duval stresses the theological overtone of Alcofribas's final request of the prologue, which was certainly familiar to the biblical culture of its Renaissance readers ("Interpretation"). Alcofribas asks not merely for a favorable reception of his book, but, as demonstrated by Duval, he also advocates Christian charity. But would the book start so dramatically by warning its readers against being scandalized if Rabelais were not worried that the adventures of his giants may meet with moral disapproval? His commitment to the evangelical cause makes the readers' religious faith his most important concern, but does he not take also into account their indignation?

Let's consider the grammatical and logical structure of the most debated fragment of the prologue, in order to see anew *Gargantua*'s scandal in its genuinely shocking dimension. Alcofribas ends the exposition of the Sylenic structure of his book by a bold claim: the reader should follow the example of Plato's dog, break the bone, and extract from it the substantial marrow, that is a doctrine

> laquelle vous revelera de treshaultz sacremens et mysteres horrificques, tant en ce qui concerne nostre religion, que aussi l'estat politicq et vie oeconomicque. (52)

> which will initate you into certain very high sacraments and dread mysteries, concerning not only our religion, but also our public and private life. (38)

Come then the famous question and two alternative answers: "Croyez-vous . . . ," "Si le croyez . . . ," "Si ne le croyez . . ." Duval convincingly demonstrates that the personal pronoun *le* included at the beginning of both answers designates the entire sentence of the question:

> Croiez vous en vostre foy qu'oncques Homere escrivent l'*Iliade* et *Odyssée*, pensast ès allegories, lesquelles de lui ont calfreté Plutarche, Heraclides Ponticq, etc. (52)

> [D]o you faithfully believe that Homer, in writing his *Iliad* and *Odyssey*, ever had in mind the allegories squeezed out of him by Plutarch, Heraclides Ponticus, etc. (38)

At stake here is not the existence or absence of allegorical meaning in *Gargantua*, as previously thought by some proponents of the self-contradictory meaning of the prologue, but the intention of Alcofribas's allegorical writing. The reader should not think for a moment that Alcofribas forethought the allegorical meanings, which indeed are the substantial marrow to be found in his jolly chronicles, no more than one should suspect Homer of having planned his epic poems as the moral and natural allegories that later ancient and Renaissance exegetes considered them to be. Such lack of conscious intention does not mean that Rabelaisian chronicles are deprived of deeper meaning concerning religion and public and private life, just as it does not mean that the Homeric epos is merely the story of a war and a journey of a Greek warrior. On the contrary, as Duval reminds us, nobody in the Renaissance would doubt the allegorical, and specifically moral and natural, meaning of Homer's epics, even if Homer, as it was believed, was just a blind vagabond. By analogy, no one should doubt the allegorical meaning of *Gargantua*, even if Alcofibas dictated his book while drinking, as his readers should do as well.

Such an analysis of the prologue seems to provide a final solution to the problem of this preliminary text's contradictory meanings. The only scandal that Rabelais may have apprehended was the distrust of a reader who took *Gargantua* for a merely commercial venture, instead of seeing it as it is: a pastiche of the popular stories of folkloric giants, rich with religious and philosophical meanings, which must be extracted from the comic kernel as the moral and philosophical signification of the *Odyssey* must be extracted from the adventures of its titular hero. All the elements of the puzzle fall into place except one: the pronoun "en" in the sentence "Si ne le croiez: quelle cause est, pourquoy autant n'en ferez de ces joyeuses et nouvelles chronicques" (54).[4] What is the antecedent of this pronoun? What should be the model for the reader's understanding of *Gargantua*?

To answer this question, Duval refers us back in the text to Plato's philosophical dog, skipping the controversial question ("Croyez-vous . . .") and the first, affirmative answer ("Si le croyez . . ."). There is however a more economical, although also a more scandalous solution: instead of going back half a page, we can simply look at the paragraph, or, more precisely, at the sentence that directly precedes "pourquoy autant n'en ferez." In this case, the antecedent of "en" is the allegorical reading imposed on Homer's and Ovid's poems by later exegetes. Readers should proceed with *Gargantua* as the exegetes did with these prestigious ancient texts—that is, read allegorically. The problem is that while it is commonly accepted to read Homer's epic poems as allegories of truths in moral and natural philosophy, it is not equally legitimate among Renaissance philologists to read Ovid's tales as religious allegories of the Gospel's teachings. Surprisingly, Alcofribas designates such a spiritual allegorizing of the *Metamorphosis* as the direct antecedent of the pronoun "en" and thus posits it as the model for reading *Gargantua*. At the same time, he clearly brands such exegesis as an intellectual aberration:

> . . . icelles [the allegories] aussi peu avoir esté songées d'Homere, que d'Ovide en ses *Metamorphoses*, les sacremens de l'evangile: lesquelz un frere Lubin vray croquelardon s'est efforcé demonstrer, si d'aventure il rencontroit gens aussi folz que luy et (comme dict le proverbe) couvercle digne du chaudron. (52)

> For I believe them [the allegories] to have been as little dreamed of by Homer as the Gospel mysteries were by Ovid in the *Metamorphoses*; a case which a certain Friar Lubin, a true bacon-picker, has actually tried to prove, in the hope that he may meet others as crazy as himself and—as the proverb says—a lid to fit his kettle. (38–39)

In other words, our controversial sentence—"Si ne le croyez, quelle cause est, pourquoy autant n'en ferez . . ."—should read: If you do not believe that Homer, in writing his *Iliad* and *Odyssey*, ever had in mind the allegories squeezed out of him by later exegetes, allegories no more intended than the Gospel mysteries found in Ovid by the stupid Friar Lubin, what reason is there for you not to read also allegorically my *Gargantua*, although I have not planned ahead its allegorical meaning while composing the book?

Should the reader of *Gargantua* be so crazy as to look in the jolly chronicle for evangelical truth, as the foolish friar tried to do with the *Metamorphosis*? Such is the most direct interpretation of the controversial pronoun in "pourquoy autant n'en ferez." Nonetheless, while it is perfectly understandable that Alcofribas encourages his readers to follow the example of the exegetes of Homer, it is quite scandalous to suggest that they emulate an idiot. First, it is a moral scandal, because Friar Lubin is a known literary embodiment of lechery, heavy drinking, and immoderate eating.[5] Second, it is an intellectual scandal, because Renaissance philologists, who were Rabelais's target audience, rightly saw any attempts to ascribe Christian meaning to pagan authors, and especially to Ovid, who lived before Christ and could not benefit from the Revelation, as an error typical of the medieval lack of historical understanding of ancient literature.[6] In sum, it is quite scandalous for Alcofribas to suggest that the readers of *Gargantua* should look in this comic, grotesque, obscene, scatological fiction for high sacraments and dread mysteries, concerning not only our public and private life but also—and most of all—our religion. His bold claim is more than a parody of some charlatan's sales talk; it is a true scandal—in other words, exactly what the preliminary *dizain* announces it to be.

With one caveat, however. Let's not forget that the encouragement to follow Friar Lubin's example comes not from Rabelais himself—the well-respected physician and philologist—but from his fictional, comic alter ego: Alcofribas.[7] The moral and intellectual scandal of the book is therefore an intentionally planned and well-executed hermeneutic provocation. Unlike the narrator of his book, Rabelais requires his readers *not* to sink unconsciously into Friar Lubin's stupidity and Alcofribas's alcoholic slumber but to commit *intentionally* an intellectual aberration: to look for spiritual truth in the midst of a grotesque story of giants. As scandalous as it is in itself, such a project corresponds exactly to what is ultimately at stake for Rabelais: the charitable interpretation "in the perfect part" of something that deserves no serious consideration or respect. Readers who decide to look with Christian charity on a book so repulsive may attain the religious and ethical perfection called Pantagruelism.

Applying "pourquoy autant n'en ferez" to the ludicrous figure of Friar Lubin is not only grammatically sound and rhetorically economical, it is also historically pertinent and pedagogically stimulating. It is historically pertinent, because the morally and intellectually scandalous character of Rabelais's fiction does not contradict in any way its religious meaning, which has been so masterfully exposed by the work of Screech, Duval, Gérard Defaux, and others.

On the contrary, by asking his fellow humanists to emulate a stupid monk who looks for the Gospel's mysteries in salacious pagan fables, Rabelais proposes a truly challenging exercise in Christian spirituality. Friar Lubin's pious exegetical speculations were of course idiotic. However, when chosen by knowledgeable philologists, they become an exercise in intellectual humility. The most noble boozers called on in the prologue are not convent simpletons but savvy literati who by reading the adventures of Rabelaisian giants should become simple in spirit. They are not idiots, but by considering a popular adventure story as a deeply spiritual and philosophical book they become *idiotae de mente*, so respected in the evangelical milieu. Indeed, to grasp the full extent of Rabelais's artistic and ideological undertaking, we have to realize that Rabelais encourages his readers to seek the mysteries of our religion not *despite* but *because* of the scandalous character of his books. His literary provocation testifies to his interest in seeing his grotesque allegory as a "dissimilar sign" of God's truth—that is, a fiction that does not attempt to resemble the spiritual meaning that is the ultimate goal of its interpretation but deliberately develops the most base and negative imagery in order to give to readers the opportunity to annihilate their "cuyder" and aspire to God's unreachable transcendence (see my *Signes*).[8]

Such a reading is also pedagogically stimulating, because while respecting Rabelais's philological and religious culture, it opens up his difficult books to our contemporary readership, who is so attached to the idea of personal and thus multiple interpretations. The provocative, scandalous character of Rabelaisian fiction is based on a particularly radical interpretation of Augustinian hermeneutics, which was fundamental to the French early Renaissance. Saint Augustine helps us understand that there is no more contradiction between the uniqueness of truth and the multiplicity of readings than there is between the scatology and obscenity of the chronicles and their religious meaning. First, according to the Augustinian hermeneutic tradition, allegory is not the result but the process itself of interpretation. At stake in such an interpretative culture is not some static religious proposition that readers must uncover but the moral and spiritual dynamic transformation that they undergo during the process of reading (see Pépin). In Rabelais's chronicles, the aim is to change the readers into true Pantagruelists, a community of people who interpret in the best way even the most scandalous stories narrated by Alcofribas. Second, what ultimately matters in reading is not the achievements of human intellect but the unique truth that the divinely inspired writer, willingly or not, has inscribed in the text: Christian charity. From this transcendent perspective, the many paths that readers have taken to reach this goal of their spiritual quest are unimportant. Even if some paths are philologically erroneous, the reading is not untrue, provided that we build up Christian charity (Augustine, *De doctrina* 1.xxxv–xxxvi, 39–41; 3.xxvii, 38). Such an approach elaborated by Saint Augustine on the interpretation of the Bible is duplicated by Pantagruel's philosophy of life, since the great good fellow knows very well that nothing on earth should upset our affections (293).

Our students may feel sympathy for Rabelais's acceptance of multiple and diverse interpretations, but they should understand that such a plurality of meanings has nothing to do with the interpretative relativism of their own culture. Similarly, they may share with Rabelais's first readers some sense of shock and uneasiness but should be told that the artistic and ideological function of the scandalous scatology of the chronicles is quite different from the same kind of humor in their own popular culture. To demonstrate these historical differences, it may be pedagogically useful to contrast the story of Gargantua's nativity with an episode of the series *South Park* entitled "More Crap."[9] Both narratives revolve around unbelievable scatological and erotic achievements of their respective characters; however, scatology and eroticism play in both instances diametrically different roles.

Thanks to the classical analysis by Bakhtin, we know that the festive circumstances of Gargantua's birth point to the carnivalesque mixing of cultural values and the polyphonic interplay of ideological discourses. Gargamelle's parturition, associated with the "chewing of dung" (48; i.e., eating tons of freshly prepared tripe), symbolizes the joyful coalescence of new life and the decay of rotting flesh, the newborn child and excrement (ch. 4). On the other hand, thanks to the equally illustrious reading of Gargantua's nativity by Screech (*Rabelais* [1979]), we know that the miraculous delivery through Gargamelle's left ear symbolizes the acceptance of faith *ex auditu* (ch. 6). Both readings effectively corrected the previous, anachronistic image of Rabelais as the founding father of Third Republic *laïcité* ("combative secularism") and anticlericalism. My reading of the prologue adds to these classical interpretations the sharp awareness of the radical character of Rabelais's artistic and ideological project. If readers keep in mind the scandalous model of Friar Lubin's idiotic allegorizing of the *Metamorphosis*, they are reminded that from the intellectual point of view there is no more reason to believe that the Messiah was born to an obscure Jewish virgin than, as Alcofribas tells us at the conclusion of chapter 6, that Bacchus was begotten from Jupiter's thigh or Crochemouche from his nurse's slipper. Nevertheless, when challenged by Alcofribas to find the "Gospel mysteries" among such "delicate maggots" (38, 39), readers should use all their Christian charity, all their Pantagruelism, not *despite* but *because* the fiction they are confronted with is so scandalous.

Finding the Gospel mysteries among the scatology and obscenity is not the task of the viewers of *South Park*. In the Rabelaisian chronicles, the moral and intellectual scandal is meant to be the trigger of the reader's spiritual transformation; in the TV series, scatology and obscenity are used for moralistic social satire.[10] In "More Crap," the dad of Stan, one of the characters, heroicomically competes with the rock star Bono for the title of world champion in producing the biggest turd. The cartoon clearly satirizes the male gender role in American culture. It also constitutes a critique of humanitarian campaigns used as publicity stunts by celebrities. The first target of the satire is seen in the fact that the act of defecating is for the male characters of the episode a substitute for giving birth.

The female characters are unable to understand the passionate interest and the pride that the male characters take in their excrement. This critique of fatherhood in American culture—well known in other series, such as *The Simpsons*—is skillfully associated with a parody of Hollywood movies, where the affection and solidarity of a loving family helps the struggling character overcome even the most challenging obstacles. The challenge here comes from Bono, presented as a selfish man whose every effort, including his activism on behalf of Africa, is dictated by the ambition to be number 1. In the climactic scene of the episode, the gigantic turd that Stan's dad painfully produces is considered the world record. Stan also succeeds in revealing Bono's secret: the pop star is not a human being but a "piece of crap" himself, born years ago from one of the top judges of this excremental competition. In conclusion, with a wordplay known to every preschooler, Bono is exposed as just a number 2.

The *South Park* satire is of course distant from Rabelais's call for Pantagruelism, which, if truly absorbed by readers, should save them from any possible scandal, intellectual, moral, or religious. Note that by comparing Rabelais's chronicles and *South Park*, we stress the cultural differences between the two narratives. The point is to make our students appreciate and enjoy the historical strangeness of Renaissance literature.[11] Despite our students' overwhelming respect for cultural diversity, such a pedagogical project may be an intellectual and moral challenge no less difficult to undertake than was Rabelais's scandal proposed to his readers in the prologue of *Gargantua*.

NOTES

[1] Bakhtin is usefully supplemented by Jeanneret, "Polyphonie."

[2] Screech links the occurrence of *scandaliser* in *Gargantua*'s final enigma (ch. 56) with its source in the Gospels (Matt. 11.6 and Luke 7.23).

[3] One such judgment was Calvin's attack on Rabelais in his *Concerning Scandals*. See Defaux, *Rabelais Agonistes* 471–73.

[4] Cohen's translation is faulty: "If you do not believe those arguments, what reason is there that you should not treat these new and jolly chronicles of mine *with the same reserve* . . .?" (39; emphasis mine). A more accurate translation would be, ". . . what reason is there that you should not treat these new and jolly chronicles of mine in the same way . . . ?" By asking readers to approach Rabelais's book with reservation, Cohen is forced to eliminate the paradoxical transition to the next sentence. Instead of the original concessive "combien que," the translator has to use a consecutive argument ("seeing that . . ."), which effectively neutralizes the paradox of Rabelais's literary and spiritual project.

[5] See, for instance, Marot's "D'ung qu'on appeloit Frère Lubin" (112).

[6] On the criticism of the tradition of the *Ovide moralisé* and its readings of the *Metamorphoses* according to the fourfold sense of the scriptures, see my "Literature and Metaphysics," notes 6 and 7 in particular.

[7] The 1535 edition of *Gargantua* is signed by "l'Abstracteur de quinte essence," referring the reader to "Acofribas Nasier," the anagrammatic pseudonym of François Rabelais, known to his readers from the edition of *Pantagruel*.

[8] "Cuyder" refers to intellectual pretentiousness, a version of the sin of pride that is condemned virtually on every page of Marguerite de Navarre's writings.

[9] I thank my sons, Tomek and Michaś, as well as my graduate students Mary Claypool and Jenny Meyer for initiating me into the subtleties of American popular culture.

[10] For the latest analysis of Rabelaisian satire, see Renner, *Difficile.*

[11] My pedagogical aim is exactly opposite to that of ventures such as Arp's *South Park and Philosophy*. This book tries to familiarize the students with classical philosophical problems by illustrating them with elements taken from the TV series. The problems, moreover, are presented in an intentionally infantile language.

Teaching Rabelais's Backside

Jeff Persels

> He resembles a natural process much more nearly than do most writers . . . and one might as well scold a flower for growing on a manure heap, or a manure heap for producing a flower. (57)

E. M. Forster may have been talking about D. H. Lawrence, but here he unwittingly suggests a useful approach to cultivating student appreciation for the backside of the smelly Pantagrueline chronicles. In my experience, the tendency among many who initially encounter Rabelais's *gros rire gras* ("belly laugh") is to cordon it off as a crude, vestigial curiosity from a more childish, less civilized culture and time. This inclination is all the more marked when, as is increasingly the case, undergraduates first read Rabelais in English translation and are thus deprived of the linguistic filter that more often than not softens the graphic edges of his prose: Baisecul, Humevesne, and Machemerdes are good for a knowing snort; Kissass, Suckfart, and Shiteaters can make nostrils flare. If, as a sophomore once hypothesized to the class at large, *Pantagruel* and *Gargantua* could be purged of their author's sophomoric "bathroom humor," whatever useful lesson or truth they might contain—and her skepticism here was palpable—would be more accessible, just possibly rendering, in her seasoned judgment, the works worth reading. Maintaining that Rabelais's scatological imagery and rhetoric are integral to what others have argued is the chronicles' redemptive design (Duval, *Design of Rabelais's* Pantagruel) and making the most of noteworthy critical efforts to reevaluate and rehabilitate these most troublesome aspects (Bakhtin, *Rabelais*; Bowen; Clark; Gaignebet), I have worked out the following strategy to help students avoid the pitfalls of failing to smell, as it were, the flower for the manure.

Instead of attempting to dodge or explain away the stench, I find it more enriching to rub their noses in it. What seems at first whiff to be a merely juvenile, prurient delight in natural or bodily processes can, if taken seriously, offer one interpretive lead, or scent, among many to guide us through the chronicles. Undergraduate readers are, of course, surprisingly earnest (and gifted) natural bloodhounds. They do want to follow their senses and training to guide them to the prey—in this instance to meanings, especially in a maddeningly enigmatic work that hints broadly from the outset that it has some very important meanings, all the while making manifest by its very form that it is not going to give them away without a fight. Rubbing their noses in it is a destabilizing process that helps move students out of what they thought was both a natural and a settled relation to the body and to what we are trained simply to reject as its waste products. Humble as it sounds, if they end up concluding simply that sometimes a turd is not a turd, I consider that I have done my job as a teacher.

Lesson 1: The Manure Heap

Experience has led me to concentrate, when working with undergraduates, on *Pantagruel* as the first, shortest, and arguably most broadly comical of the corpus. It is of course more fragmented, disjointed, and elliptical than the more expansive, paternal prequel *Gargantua*, qualities that have their disadvantages, but its concise, discrete episodes are both easier to work with and more efficient to cover in a crowded course in early modern French literature and culture.[1] Its beginning, too, which starts with one of the most familiar of all beginnings, the parodic biblical genealogy, is a far less daunting starting point at this level than *Gargantua*'s rodent-gnawed *fanfreluches* ("fripperies"). Before getting there, though, we undertake a close, collective reading of the prologue. We work methodically through its heterogeneous list of cures and consolations, both anecdotal and antidotal, for the inherent sufferings of the post lapsarian human condition: boredom and frustration, the toothache, the pangs of childbirth, the dolorous cost of sexual indulgence. And we consider in all seriousness the prologue's visceral closing curse, should our skepticism lead us to reject authorial claims to healing powers, a curse similarly couched in terms of human suffering and focused significantly on the fundament. Once sensitized to the notion of reading as therapy in and for a fallen world, to the idea of ingesting *Pantagruel* as panacea, students generally find much more manageable the subsequent segue into the mock Genesis and Matthew of chapter 1. Faith in the miraculous powers of the Gospel gives hope of spiritual healing and redemption; faith in the miraculous powers of this comic riff promises physical healing and redemption. May we burn in hell if we do not believe in the former; may our asses burn if we do not believe in the latter. The proof of the former is in the unbroken genealogy from Adam to Christ; the proof of the latter, in the unbroken line from Chalbroth to Pantagruel.

Such a reading assumes at least a passing knowledge of the form and content of the Bible and the basic function of Christian exegetical tradition. Given the difficulty of making head or tail of much early modern literature without reference to those, I have found it increasingly useful to spend a class period on them, working generally from a one-page summary of the Bible I have developed, supplemented by discussion of the four traditional excerpts found in the Books of Hours and the text of the Roman Mass. This introduction covers the gist efficiently and makes for about five or six pages of preparatory reading only. Time and technology permitting, a further supplement in the form of Pieter Brueghel the Elder's sins and virtues serves both to illustrate popular notions of contemporary Christianity and to ease the transition into the earthy landscape of Rabelaisian prose.[2]

Taking note of and discussing the prologue's physical signs of the Fall, my students proceed to catalog others as we work through the text proper. Most prominent among them, they find, are references to urine and excrement, for which they have been prepared by the prologue's vivid closing. The manure, they are quick to point out, is heaped hyperbolically, and thus suspiciously, high. How might it contribute to an overall understanding of the chronicle? In the stream of beshittings and bepissings that punctuate Pantragruel's and his companions' *vitae*, both active and contemplative, I help students discern a pattern. Characters who come into contact with Pantagruel have a marked tendency to lose control of their bowels, including the Limousin schoolboy (ch. 6), the consternated judges in the Baisecul-Humevesne case (chs. 10–13), the foreign scholar Thaumaste (chs. 18–20). Others suffer from constipation, like the enemy giant during the epic *agon* between Pantagruel and Werewolf (ch. 29) and, most tellingly, Pantagruel himself, in an episode rendered all the more significant by its placement at the chronicle's close (ch. 33), though he, unlike Anarche's soldier, is ultimately cured. Once students have detected what seems to be a curious but consistent insistence on excretion and its discontents, they stop laughing (or being offended) at the simple gross ubiquity of bathroom humor and start asking what the pattern might mean. Why does Pantagruel provoke both thirst and diarrhea? Why does he himself fall ill in both bladder and colon, requiring such a comically elaborate enema? How can his urine have healing powers? How can such excremental discourse be meaningful? How can jokes about shit be mingled with talk of salvation in any way not blasphemous?

Lesson 2: The Flower(s)

The final fumet Rabelais drops in the track of my seekers after signs comes logically at the very end, in a seemingly minor scatological insult tossed off by the narrator. We join the epilogue (ch. 34) to the prologue and arrive at answers to our questions through the profit-driven shit sifting of the *coquins de village*.[3] The narrator, Alcofribas, asserts derisively that they paw through children's turds for profit, as, analogically, we have been scavenging the book for meaning. When, then, is a turd not simply a turd? When, as this strategically placed anecdote suggests, it contains an undigested pit precious to the apothecary's art, valued for its curative powers. Having traced the contours of and cracked open an extended excremental metaphor that runs through *Pantagruel* from beginning to end, we consider in open discussion whether it might not be something of a philosopher's stone for unlocking Rabelais's sacred truths. What seemed initially to be his juvenile delight in the manure heap no longer seems so juvenile. In full and natural exegetical fervor, students usually set about making their own interpretive leaps, particularly when brought back to the therapeutic theme established in the prologue. Each of the major excremental episodes advances it, consistently and unerringly. Characters such as the Limousin schoolboy, the judges, and Thaumaste, once physically purged, recognize Pantagruel for who he is, pay homage to his wisdom and greatness, which surpass, in Thaumaste's paean, even those of Solomon (ch. 20). To coin a richly mixed metaphor: once they were constipated, like the enemy giant (ch. 29), but now they can see. The shit has dropped from their asses as scales from their eyes. The Christian humanist (and very human) prince Pantagruel is likewise necessarily subject to bouts of constipation and purging. His body, the fallen but redeemable body politic incarnate, can and must be washed clean before he can lead his people home, as he does both here, in the restoration and expansion of Utopia (ch. 32), and in the ensuing voyages of the *Third*, *Fourth*, and *Fifth Books*.

Not only has the manure heap produced a flower, or flowers, which my students have plucked and woven into a rhetorical chaplet, but also Rabelais has made it plain to those with eyes to see, ears to hear, and noses to smell that without the manure heap there can be no flowers. The cherry pit, to gain its valuable, curative properties, must pass into the mouths of babes and out their backsides, "embroidered with shit," as Rabelais will say of the law books of his day (ch. 5). Nothing more graphically takes the measure of our fallen state than our excrement. It is an extension of the dust from which we were born and to which we will return, the very smell and substance of our shared humanity and our mortality. "Kings and philosophers shit," as Michel de Montaigne will similarly universalize in the *Essays*, "and ladies, too" (*Complete Essays* [Screech] 1231; 3.13). *Inter faeces et urinam nascimur* ("We are born between feces and urine"), long if apocryphally attributed to Augustine, is the baldest statement of essential and inescapable human baseness. To be purged of it when it accumulates—those unable to recognize Pantagruel on first encounter are, to put it indelicately, full of shit—and to maintain regularity, Rabelais seems to be suggesting, are as close to godliness as we can hope to get in this fallen state. Pantagruel and his evangelical humanist rule effect the necessary purge and cure, a physical metaphor appropriate to a corporeal, matter-bound world.

Such a reading owes as much to Edwin Duval's *The Design of Rabelais's* Pantagruel as to Mikhail Bakhtin's *Rabelais and His World*, and with my students I normally parlay the excremental pattern thus traced into post hoc discussions of the central theses of these two seminal critical works. Reconciling the former's argument for reading the chronicle as a Christian humanist epic, an "epic new testament" (1–15), whose hero is Christlike yet very much of this world, with the latter's rehabilitation and celebration of the "material bodily lower stratum" (368–436) that that same hero represents, offers a coherent framework for understanding what, on its surface, seems a model of incoherence. Bakhtin's radical rehabilitation of the role and influence of early modern popular culture, of the subversive carnivalesque, particularly its earthier and more grotesque manifestations, in Rabelais's fiction has proved to be among the most fruitful lines of critical inquiry, involving as it does the first serious (and the most comprehensive, before Claude Gaignebet) treatment of scatology. "We must not forget that urine (as well as dung) is gay matter, which degrades and relieves at the same time, transforming fear into laughter" (335). But it also transforms, as I have just argued, laughter into meaning. Paradoxically, it is elevating as well as degrading and relieving. The world of Rabelais criticism is as fecund a manure heap as one could imagine, and the excremental approach is merely one possible, compelling introduction to the Rabelaisian corpus and to the uses of literary criticism. The excremental approach teases out one pattern among many and brings a couple of sophisticated minds who have worked to crack the Rabelaisian enigma—Duval and Bakhtin—to bear on it.

The ultimate point of approaching Rabelais, or at least approaching the question of design and intent in *Pantagruel*, through his backside is not merely a facile exploitation of one of the author's most notorious features, nor is it merely a quasi-scientific account of my own experimental and experiential readings. The foregoing exercise having been completed and prompting subsequent merry chases back through *Pantagruel*, or on into *Gargantua* or *The Third Book*, to seek other excremental patterns, encourages students to look for other constructs or leitmotifs that may (or may not) help us deduce meaning from a distant work as well as consider how and why the producers and consumers of the work thought to construct that meaning. The manure heap produces many flowers. If a cultural interpreter such as Rabelais thought excrement worth working up into a significant narrative pattern, I ask students how we might also read like references—and they are common enough—in other canonical sixteenth-century works such as Marguerite de Navarre's *Heptameron*, which shares an evangelical humanist matrix with Rabelais's works, and Montaigne's *Essays*. The distance is not so great from Rabelais's backside to Montaigne's, perched precariously on "the loftiest throne in the world" (3.13) and producing "some excrements of an aged mind, now hard, now loose, and always undigested" (9). And none of us, I presume, ever teaches our students that Montaigne's turds, of all early modern turds, did not produce some very fine and fragrant posies indeed.

NOTES

[1] *Pantagruel* has other advantages. One particularly fruitful writing assignment I have given over the years is to compose a "missing" chapter or episode, from either Pantagruel's career or Panurge's. Pastiche, when framed and executed with care, can require more sophisticated understanding and more thoughtful interpretation of a work than does a traditional analytic essay.

[2] To this end, I have also found it useful to view and discuss either Daniel Vigne's *The Return of Martin Guerre* (1982) or Leslie Megahey's *The Advocate* (1994). The former, when combined with Natalie Zemon Davis's short and accessible study of the same name, makes for a worthy preparatory unit on early modern culture in and of itself, again time permitting. If it can be worked in, a preliminary unit on Pauline rhetoric—a class session or two spent on selected epistles, followed by Erasmus's *Praise of Folly*, in whole or in part—has also proved to be time well spent.

[3] The Cohen translation gives "village ragamuffins" (278), whereas Frame's prefers "village scavengers" (245). The modest price of the former makes it the most appealing for a survey course. The latter more fluidly adapts to this approach, but its cost can be prohibitive in a course where only one of the Rabelaisian chronicles is read.

Locating and Teaching Politics in Rabelais

Timothy Hampton

> Even as I was falling asleep, I continued to reflect on what I had just been reading; but my reflections took on a particular cast; it seemed to me that I was, myself, that about which the book spoke: a church, a quartet, the rivalry of Charles V and Francis I.
>
> —Marcel Proust, "Combray"

I try to teach Rabelais every year, in one format or another, in French or in English. Much of my teaching is in graduate seminars, upper-division French courses on the Renaissance, or comparative literature courses on the Renaissance. However, I am also committed to teaching Rabelais in diverse contexts and in dialogue with texts from other traditions and historical periods. So I might teach him in a course on vagabonds; in a course on the invention of Europe; or in a course on tricksters, where his work might be juxtaposed with the Chinese tale *The Monkey* and the Brazilian writer Mario de Andrade's novel *Macunaíma*. To my mind it is crucially important to get Rabelais's work out of the narrow contexts in which it is usually read and into the larger conversation of the humanities.

The topic of politics in Rabelais is broad and involves not merely statecraft or public action but also the intersection of different forms of behavior and belief in the public world—not to mention the literary project of representing those forms. In the prologue to *Gargantua* (1534), the second book he wrote but the first in the sequence of adventures, the narrator, Alcofribas, tells us what the book is about. He states that it will reveal "de tres haultz sacremens et mystères horrificques, tant en ce qui concerne nostre religion que aussi l'estat politicq et vie oeconomicque" (40; "very high sacraments and dread mysteries, concerning not only our religion, but also our public and private life" [38]). This statement seems quite clear: we may debate what is meant by "sacremens" and "mystères," but there should be no mistaking this description of the subject of the book. What we are about to read involves religion, politics, and what the translation calls "private life." By the phrase "vie oeconomique" Rabelais probably means what we would today call "domestic life," the art of running a household.

The narrator's description, suggesting that to speak of politics in Rabelais is also to speak of religion and social organization, raises two issues. The first is how we contextualize Rabelais: how we find a way to read his text that accounts for the shifting intersection between the three elements of politics (in the modern sense of the word), religion, and domestic life. The second, which offers a perfect entry into a classroom discussion of rhetoric and form, is how a particular literary text signifies to refer to and evoke these three different areas of action. The second question involves not merely the thematic content of the work but also its form, its ability to signify in particular ways. In other words, the political in Rabelais must be read both as a theme and as a topic that encompasses genre, rhetoric, and eventually our own position as readers.[1]

We know that Rabelais was one of a group of Catholic thinkers influenced by humanism, critical of the church but committed to reforming it from within instead of breaking with it altogether, as was advocated by Luther and later Calvin. This reform involved a return to the text of the New Testament (to be studied in the original Greek, following the precepts of humanism) and a privileging of the Gospel narratives and the letters of Saint Paul as guides for comportment. The most influential figure in this group was Erasmus of Rotterdam. Erasmus's many writings on politics stress the notion that all political action should be conducted under the influence of New Testament theology. Princes should not act selfishly or in ways to promote their national interest but rather according to the dictates of Christian and classical moral philosophy. That is, political action should be good action, moral action, just action.

When I teach *Gargantua*, I set the context by looking at Erasmus's most systematic discussion of statecraft, his 1516 treatise *The Education of a Christian Prince*, written to the young Charles of Burgundy, who would come to be the king of Spain, Holy Roman emperor, and the most powerful monarch in the world. In the section of that work "The Arts of Peace," Erasmus urges the prince to cultivate virtue in order to maintain peace in his kingdom. To do otherwise, he notes, imposes on the prince the necessity of somehow flattering the people into submission:

> And by this means the same things tend to happen to the prince among his people as happens to foolish husbands who wheedle from their wives, with flattery, presents, and subservience the love which they ought to win by their good qualities and upright behavior. (66)

There follows a brief digression on the importance of love in the conjugal relationship and the home. Husbands must win their wives' obedience by demonstrating virtue. Wives must learn to appreciate the lovable qualities in their husbands. "In the same way, let the people get a taste for the best and let the prince show that he is of the best. They love long whose love was well judged to begin with" (67). Erasmus goes on to affirm that it is essential for the prince to "show himself to be someone who deserves to be beloved" before pursuing policies that will solidify his place in the hearts of his people (67).

Erasmus's discussion illustrates the proximity of the Christian moral philosophy, husbandry, and politics in the Christian humanist thinking that was so important for Rabelais. Indeed, so imbued is the account of statecraft with images of domestic life that it is difficult to determine whether marriage is to be understood as a figure for the political life of the kingdom or vice versa. In this image of a Christian politics ("la religion," "l'estat politicq") that is also a politics of the household ("la vie oeconomicque"), we seem to be close to Rabelais's description of his book in the prologue to *Gargantua*. Here, at least, the political is the domestic and domesticity is political.

When teaching this text, I ask students to consider the limitations, both practical and theoretical, of the comforting analogies set up by Erasmus for discussing the public world. Erasmus assumed a unified community in which all members were more or less the same. It was precisely such a unified image of community that was being tested by political events as Rabelais was writing his books. The reign of Francis I was marked by a series of largely unsuccessful forays into the Italian peninsula, in an attempt to gain control of Milan, leading to a bitter and protracted struggle on several fronts with Charles V. Presumably impervious to the exhortations of humanists like Erasmus to study peace instead of war, Charles repeatedly outmaneuvered and defeated Francis, most notably at the Battle of Pavia in 1525 where Francis was taken captive and then dumped into prison in Madrid.[2]

Needless to say, these secular political struggles challenged the ideals of a renovated Christian community espoused by Erasmus and others. How can one speak of a harmonious Christianity if one is fighting one's brother in Christ? When I teach *Gargantua* and *Pantagruel*, I focus on the contrast between the ideologies of Christian universalism and charity promoted by writers such as Erasmus (using the selections from his political writings) and the various scenes in which Rabelais depicts violence against those who are not aristocratic French males—that is, Turks, women, peasants, and so on. For it is at these moments that the tension between literary representation and Christian humanist ideology is made legible. I ask students to think about how these violent episodes might be linked to the deployment of different generic registers—epic, colloquy, romance. Politics in literature is most frequently a politics of genre, since genres define convention and thus collective expectation. It is through a shifting deployment of narratives about community that Rabelais inscribes the great political struggles of the 1520s into the very fabric of his books.

Since my own pedagogy assumes that much of the modernity of Rabelais comes from the way in which he asks us to reflect on power, it is important to track how the relation among subject, community, and power mutate as we move through the books. The key moment in the text for studying this mutation comes in the prologue to the *Tiers livre*.

The *Tiers livre* appeared in 1543. Much had changed in Europe and in France since the publication of *Pantagruel* and *Gargantua*, in relatively quick succession (1532–34). Francis's long and frustrating struggles with Charles V led to increasing tensions between France and Spain, which was itself becoming increasingly invested in its wars with the Low Countries, to France's north. Francis's relatively tolerant approach toward the new religious ideas coming from Germany had hardened following the Affaire des Placards in 1534. Intellectual positions began to solidify into dogma, and major figures were pursued by political or ecclesiastical authorities and silenced. Some, such as Rabelais's friend Étienne Dolet, were burned for heresy.[3]

Rabelais responds to this situation by shifting the focus—and the political dimension—of his writing. The topic of *The Third Book* is no longer the education of a prince or a war for the preservation of community, the great collective themes of the first two books; it is the problem of desire and individual destiny. Pantagruel's friend Panurge desires to take a wife but fears that he will be made a cuckold. His quest to learn whether his fears will be realized is a quest to know the future, to transcend time, not through procreation but through an act of the will. Scholars have often stressed the sacramental dimension of the theme of marriage, presenting it as a kind of figure or allegory of larger issues of human concord and political harmony, much in the sense that marriage was evoked in Erasmus.[4] It is worth noting, however, that at issue in the quest of Panurge is not how to have a good marriage or how to establish the rules for a happy domestic life; it is whether to marry at all—a much more fundamental problem, as it involves the individual subject's struggles with his own fear and uncertainty.

Readers of modern literature are familiar with dramas of personal will, which form the raw material of the literary genre most obviously associated with Western modernity—the novel. Yet in contrast to the conventional novelistic heroes of later narratives, who pursue the objects of their desire in an attempt to combine worldly success and personal happiness, Rabelais shows little interest in Panurge's quest for a woman or for personal glory. The problem, rather, is the difficulty of knowing whether and when to act. Like Shakespeare in *Hamlet*, Rabelais places the problem of heroic action on the side of the action itself. The difference between the two characters is that instead of interrogating himself, as Hamlet does, Panurge interrogates the authorities around him. The *Tiers livre* thus becomes a story not about community but about knowledge and will.

The crucial moment of transition from the epic tales of war and conquest in the first two books to Panurge's very modern drama of individual will comes in the prologue to the *Tiers livre*. This is, in my view, one of the key moments in understanding the politics of Rabelais's text. It is also a passage on which I spend considerable time when I teach Rabelais in any context. The narrative of *Pantagruel* ends with a scene in which the narrator journeys into his character's mouth. He is thus literally swallowed by his own narrative. Whereas *Gargantua* ends with the communitarian episode of the Abbaye de Thélème, the *Tiers livre* begins with an evocation of the distance among narrator, reader, and text. The narrator proclaims that he cannot see us without glasses, then evokes the classical philosopher Diogenes the Cynic, who becomes a figure for the author.

Diogenes replaces the Socrates so famously evoked in the prologue to *Gargantua*. Diogenes is a quite different figure: insolent, acerbic, and, well, cynical. One of the many differences between these two figures lies in their political role, their place in the public sphere. Socrates was both a military hero, having fought bravely in defense of Athens, and a figure for the ideal but lost virtue of the Athenian polis. By contrast, Diogenes was a curmudgeon who mocked everyone he met. Rabelais shows us Diogenes by rewriting a scene from "How to Write History," a text by the Hellenistic writer Lucian. The city of Corinth is about to be attacked. As the citizens all prepare to defend the city, Diogenes, who lives in a barrel, worries that he might not be doing his part. He begins to roll his barrel about so as not to be thought idle. Similarly, says Lucian to his friend Philo, "to avoid being the only mute in such a polyphonic time, pushed about open-mouthed without a word like an extra in a comedy," he will offer a text. Writing is thus compared to barrel rolling.[5]

Rabelais adapts this moment to describe his own situation as a writer. Considering the situation of France ("consyderant par tout ce tresnoble royaulme de France, deça, dela les mons" [365–66; "considering this noble kingdom of France, on both sides of the mountains"]), he notes that everyone is working to fortify the country in order to drive away enemies and establish strong borders: "desormais sera France superbement bournée, seront François en repous asceurez" (366; "the frontiers of France will be superbly fixed, and the French in certain peace").[6] The kingdom of France is thus compared to the city of Corinth. Rabelais feels ashamed that he will be seen by others as useless and merely a "spectator" of the "tragic-comedy" that knightly heroes are playing out before the gaze of all of Europe: "ay imputé honte plus que mediocre estre veu spectateur ocieux de tant de vaillans, disers et chevalereux personnaiges, qui en veu et spectacle de toute Europe jouent ceste insigne faible et tragicque comedie" (366; "I have felt it to be most disgraceful to be seen an idle spectator of these valorous, eloquent, and warlike persons who are performing their noble interlude and tragic-comedy before the watching eyes of all Europe" [283–84]).[7] To help out, he adds, he will rattle his barrel and ask us to drink from it.

Rabelais changes Lucian's text as he borrows it. Lucian's figure of Diogenes longs to be useful, so as not to stand around like an extra in a comedy. Rabelais expands the topos of the theater and applies it to politics, now seen as a "tragic-comedy." Even more important is the way he infuses the description with motifs of spectacle and vision that are absent from Lucian. Indeed, the entire description is marked by repeated references to sight and by repetition of the verb *voir*. Lucian's Diogenes doesn't want to be useless. Rabelais's Diogenes doesn't want to be seen to be useless ("n'estre veu seul cessateur et ocieux"). Similarly, as he "considers" France (the verb *considérer* carried a more powerful visual connotation in the Renaissance than it does today), Rabelais doesn't see himself worthy of public action ("me voyant n'estre fait aulcun pris digne d'œuvre"). For, he notes, little glory comes to those who only "use their eyes" ("peu de gloire me semble accroistre à ceulx qui seulement y emploictent leurs oeilz" [366]).

The imagery of vision dominates the episode, from the opening moment, when the narrator fumbles for his glasses in order to see us clearly, through the entire passage comparing the narrator with Diogenes. It reaches a climax in the description of Rabelais as the narrator-author fearing "to be seen a spectator" at the play of history. This focus on sight distances the narrator of the book from the public or political world. The issue is not, as it was for Lucian, how to act effectively; it becomes how to be seen acting effectively, which is quite a different thing. This description makes the position of the writer problematic, potentially subject to the gaze of fellow citizens who might judge him. It suggests the risks of writing and separates the author from the community to and for which he presumed to speak in the first two books. Given the political context of the 1540s, when intellectual experimentation and innovation had become dangerous activities, this nuance added to the description of the author suggests Rabelais's awareness of the fragility of the intellectual in the public sphere. The uncertainty of the author mirrors the confusion of his unruly protagonist, Panurge.

The shift at the outset of the *Tiers livre* to a drama of personal will constitutes one element of Rabelais's modernity. The modulation from communitarian narratives of the first two books to the vision of an isolated writer who is hesitant before the crisis of political community, who writes about a single figure (Panurge), and who struggles with his own desire points ahead to paradigms of the emerging novel form. It may be no accident that when Rabelais returns to communitarian themes in the *Quart livre*, he does so through an increasing use of the conventions of allegory. The group of mariners that accompanies Panurge on his quest gives itself over to that quest, yet many of the ports at which their ships drop anchor feature societies that stand as allegories for political actors or groups (the Council of Trent, the papal court, etc.). Once the epic impulse of the first two books is abandoned, political topics resurface in the contrast between a heroic but quite ordinary group of travelers and a series of allegorical representations of the political world.

Thus the political dimension of the text changes as Rabelais's narratives unfold. In the first two books the focus is on the destiny of community and on epic depictions of communal experience. In the *Tiers livre* the focus shifts to the politics of knowledge and desire and the fragility of the writer in the face of political uncertainty. In the *Quart livre* politics becomes intertwined with allegory. By examining the intersection between political themes and modes of representation, students can begin to come to terms with the ways in which literary form redistributes and recasts political tensions and ideological struggles. They can understand how the text works as a kind of grab bag of generic conventions, bits of discourse and fragments of language that both narrator and characters manipulate in various ways. They can see how Rabelais's deployment of different generic registers has a political dimension, even as they begin to reflect on how the unfolding of his works creates a world that becomes progressively more familiar, through its focus on the desiring self, and, through its evocation of allegorical mystery, progressively more strange.

NOTES

The epigraph of this essay is the third sentence of Proust's *Remembrance of Things Past*. The translation is mine.

[1] Saint Paul's dictum in his Epistle to the Ephesians, "One Lord, one faith, one baptism" (4.6 [Rev. Standard Vers.]) was picked up in the middle of the sixteenth century by Rabelais's near contemporary Guillaume Postel and reformulated as "un roy, une foy, une loy" ("one king, one faith, one law"). This secularization of Paul was later reordered by Catholic apologists in the wars of religion as "Foi, loi, roi." Rabelais's text pre-dates these developments, but the narrator's description defines public life in ways that would obviously become a focus of debate two decades later. For background on these developments, see the chapter "National Identity" in Le Roy Ladurie.

[2] For background on the wars with Spain, see Knecht, especially chapter 11. On the relation between political violence and genre in Rabelais, see Hampton, *Literature*, chapters 2 and 3.

[3] The classic account in English of France's descent into political violence during this period is Salmon.

[4] This is the approach taken by Screech in his well-known work *The Rabelaisian Marriage*.

[5] I quote the Loeb Classics edition of "How to Write History" (*Works*). See *Lucian in Eight Volumes* (6.7). My general understanding of the prologue to the *Tiers livre* has benefited from Gray, "Structure"; Cave, *Cornucopian Text* 189–204; and two essays in Carron: Duval, "History," and Regosin, "Opening Discourse."

[6] The translation is mine because Cohen uncharacteristically misses the nuances of the passage.

[7] I have altered the translation, as Cohen misses the visual motifs.

Writing Reform: Evangelical Reform and Religious Controversy in Rabelais's Work

Deborah N. Losse

Rabelais's sustained criticism of Scholasticism and specifically his critique of the training of theologians at the Sorbonne is not immediately apparent to students unfamiliar with the principles of Christian humanism and evangelical reform in the French Renaissance. I propose two steps to providing the tools to decipher Rabelais's criticism of the church. The first is to furnish the principles on which the evangelical reform was based, and the second is to apply these principles to specific episodes where the text is often clothed in enigma and parody.

To introduce students to the basic principles of evangelical humanism, a brief summary of Henry Heller's "The Evangelism of Lefèvre d'Étaples" provides an overview of Erasmian and Fabrist reform. First and foremost, as Mack B. Holt reminds us, Erasmus and Jacques Lefèvre d'Étaples were "both scholars and spiritual writers rather than true reformers in the mold of Luther," and like many of the scholars and writers of Christian humanism who frequented the court of Francis I, they favored "maintaining the unity of the Christian church" (13). This distinction between evangelical humanism and true Protestant reform is essential to understanding Rabelais's works.

Lefèvre, with Erasmus, sought to move away from the Scholastic practice of complicated exigesis based on levels of interpretation in order to focus on the spiritual meaning of the text. Keeping Christ's words and actions in the biblical context ensured that the Christian came closest to the meaning of the text, without layers of interpretations by theologians. The translation of scripture into the vernacular and efforts to raise the literacy of the faithful facilitated the transmission of Christ's words. Within evangelical humanism, as practiced by Lefèvre and followed by others in the Circle of Meaux such as Guillaume Briçonnet, bishop of Meaux, the Christian is dependent on Christ, receives his faith through Christ's sacrifice—faith is a gift of divine grace—a gift from God to man. Scripture is the foundation of doctrine and speaks directly to the Christian rather than through the interpretation of the priest. Finally, justification comes through the grace of faith and not good works. The gift of faith changes the behavior of the Christian and leads to good works. Good works, however, without a faith that brings the will of the believer in line with the will of God, are without merit (Heller 55–59).

Some episodes are accessible to students because of their ludic nature. The episode of the *écolier limousin* (*Pantagruel*, ch. 6), in which the young student speaks a corrupted mixture of French and Latin-French syntax and Latin lexicon, illustrates both the lack of rigor as well as the lax moral instruction in the formation of clerics at the Sorbonne but also the evangelical emphasis upon plain speech in the vernacular. A second equally playful episode concerns

Panurge's play on Christ's words: "And every one who has left houses or brothers or sisters or father or mother or children or lands, for my name's sake, will receive a hundredfold and inherit eternal life" (Matt. 19.29 [English Standard Vers.]). Interpreting a figurative passage literally, Panurge places one coin in the basket of the clerics selling pardons for every one hundred he removes: "Ainsi, quand le pardonnigere me dist: *Centuplum accipies*, il veut dire *Centuplum accipe* . . ." (286; "So when the bearer of the pardons said to me: '*Centuplum accipies*' [Thou shalt receive one hundred fold] he meant *centuplum accipe* [Receive one hundredfold]" [227]). Behind this play on words lies a vigorous attack on the practice of selling pardons or indulgences. For the reformers, salvation could not be bought with money or good works—it was a question of divine grace given to some and not others.

A further example whose humor conveys reform content is the episode between Grandgousier and the pilgrims (*Gargantua*, ch. 45), in which Grandgousier rails against the practice of pilgrimages aimed at holding the saints responsible for human disease and natural disasters. Asking the lead pilgram, Lasdaller ("Wearybones"), where he is going, the pilgrim responds that he is going to Saint Sebastian.

> —Nous allions (dist Lasdaller) luy offrir noz votes contre la peste.
> —O (dist Grandgousier), pauvres gens, estimez vous que la peste vienne de sainct Sebastian?
> —Ouy vrayment (respondit Lasdaler) noz prescheurs nous l'afferment.
> —Ouy (dist Grandgousier), les faulx prophetes vous annoncent ilz de tez abus?. . . . (174)

> We went, said Wearybones, to offer up our vows to that saint against the plague.
> Oh, said Grandgousier, you poor creatures. Do you imagine that the plague comes from Saint Sebastian?
> Yes, of course, replied Wearybones, our preachers assure us that it does.
> Indeed? said Grandgousier. Do the false prophets tell you such lies then? (136)

Grandgousier denounces the blasphemous teachings of the clergy who attribute evil to God and to his faithful following: "La peste ne tue que le corps, mais telz imposteurs empoisonnent les ames" (175; "Pestilence only kills but the body, but these impostors poison the soul" [137]).

Reform ideology is more subtly embedded in two other sequences, the Abbey of Thélème and Panurge's marriage quest. By approaching these episodes in the light of Christian humanism as filtered through the teaching of Saint Augustine and Erasmus, students gain a better understanding of how the concept of free will exists within the context of grace and divine will. Students also come to terms with principles that separate the evangelical reform and orthodox Catholic thought taught at the Sorbonne. In regards to the Abbey of Thélème, we begin by pointing out that the entire episode of the founding of the abbey by Frère Jan is introduced by a discussion of self-mastery: "Car, comment . . . pourray je gouverner aultruy, qui moymesmes gouverner ne scaurois" (3190; "'For . . . how should I be able to govern others,' he said, 'when I don't know how to govern myself'" [149–50]). It is at this time that the concept of bringing one's own will into harmony with God's will—an evangelical concept, with its roots in the work of Saint Augustine, will be introduced to the students. In fact, we might heed Michael A. Screech's advice to search for the "echoes" of Augustinian thought in Rabelais ("Echoes"). The reform view of free will is not constrained by God's grace or divine will. The faithful are free to choose or refuse the path leading to God. Conventional monastic life is ruled by clocks, punishment, and even withdrawal *in pace*—all tools that constrain rather than encourage the exercise of free will. Self-mastery is closely linked to the notion of grace—a gratuitous gift within evangelical doctrine. The echo rhyme, "Or donné par don / Ordonne pardon" ("Gold freely given, / A man's freely shriven") at the end of *Gargantua* (365; 155), a poem that could be interpreted as a nod to the *grands rhétoriqueurs*, serves to illustrate that grace is a gift that cannot be bought or earned by good works—a basic tenet of evangelical theology.

With the knowledge of the *Confessions* of Saint Augustine, the Epistles of Saint Paul, or the teachings of Erasmus, students can achieve a better understanding of Panurge's dilemma in the *Tiers livre*. Again, self-mastery—bringing one's will in harmony with God's will, would lead Panurge away from inaction. In chapter 10, Pantagruel asks the critical question, "N'estez vous asceuré de vostre vouloir?" (403; "Aren't you certain of your wishes?" [313]). Self-love, subjugation of the will to lust, blinds Panurge to *caritas*, so that he is incapable of achieving the self-mastery necessary for faithful Christians. The inhabitants of Thélème have brought their individual wills into harmony through mutual love of God and respect for others. Strengthened by their faith, they leave Thélème and marry, secure that they will not stray from the path of faithful Christians. Blinded by philautia, Panurge never achieves self-mastery. Pantagruel clearly states Panurge's problem: "et congnois que Philautie et Amour de soy vous deçoit" (476; "and I see that you are misled by philauty—by self-love, that is" [369]).

The single law of Thélème, "Fay ce que vouldras" ("Do what you will") in chapter 57 of *Gargantua* (203; 159) echoes Augustine's "Dilige et fac quod vis" ("Love and do what you will") in his *In Epistolum Ioannis ad Parthos Tractatus Decem*. The omission of the key word *dilige*, evoking the love that Saint John ties so closely to divine love or charity, responsible for the divine grace that pardoned original sin, both masks the Augustinian intertext and leads readers of the nineteenth century and beyond to interpret will as license (Augustine, *Commentaire* 7.8.230). Rabelais's appropriation of a celebrated phrase from Saint

Augustine introduces students to the notion of intertextuality (see Angenot). This is the occasion for students to explore how the displacement of a text from one author to another reshapes the phrase as it inhabits a new context, with distinct sociocultural values and meanings. Awareness that Rabelais has a particular text in mind as he articulates the motto for his abbey: "fay ce que vouldras" gives the students first a tool for making sense of the chapters on the Abbey of Thélème and provides them with an example of how reader response may jump to an erroneous conclusion without a deep understanding of text and context.

Within the Augustinian context, the faithful Christian will bring his or her will in line with God's will. There will be no disjuncture between God and the one who loves him. In the *Confessions*, Augustine says, "For you do what you will and you grant me, as you always will, the grace to follow you gladly" (10.35.243). One interpretation of why the inhabitants of Thélème are so eager to act in concert, whether in the choice of dress or activity, is that their love of God inspires a common willing in harmony with God's will. Within the evangelical context of early Christian reform, willing is antonymous to license and reckless behavior. It emanates from free choice and not coercion.

Let us turn now to Panurge's dilemma in the *Tiers livre*, for students the most complex, since narrative frame takes second place to philosophical dialogue. As Screech has shown, marriage is at the center of the *Tiers livre* (*Rabelaisian Marriage*). Rabelais attacks two trends in the Catholic Church: the privileging of the priesthood over marriage and the intervention of the church in affairs of marriage. At the very end of *Gargantua* (ch. 40), Gargantua attacks idle clergy ("ocieux moynes"), as he compares monkeys to clergy. One defecates wherever it goes, the other eats fecal matter: "ilz mangent la merde du monde, c'est à dire les pechez" (161; "they eat the world's excrement, that is to say, sins" [125–26]). The monk's idleness is in sharp contrast to the work ethic of peasants, warriors, physicians, or even of "le bon docteur evangelicque" (161; "the good gospeller and preceptor" [126]).

Without marriage, society cannot flourish. Marriage is the responsibility of the parents. It is they who approve or reject the union. Through his prince Pantagruel, Rabelais affirms the right of the father to find him a suitable spouse:

> Je n'ay jamais entendu que par loy aulcune, feust sacre, feust prophane et barbare, ayt esté en arbitre des enfans soy marier, non consentans, voulens et promovens leurs peres, meres et parents prochains. (538)

> By no laws, sacred or profane and barbarous, that I have ever heard of have the children ever been free to marry, unless their fathers, mothers, and nearest relatives deign to desire and promote the match. (418)

Gargantua goes further and attacks members of the clergy ("pastophores taulpetiers" ["dreaded molecatchers"]) for sanctioning clandestine marriages arranged without the knowledge of the parents:[1]

> Et ne sçay que plus doibve abhominer: ou la tirannicque praesumption d'iceulx redoubtez taulpetiers, qui ne se contiennent dedans les treillis de leurs mysterieux temples et se entremettent des negoces contraires par Diametre entier à leurs estatz, ou la supersituieuse stupidité des gens mariez, qui ont sanxi et presté obeissance à telle tant malignes et barbaricques loigs. . . . (538)

> Really I don't know which is the more abominable, the tyrannical presumption of these dreaded molecatchers—who do not confine themselves within the bars of their mysterious temples but meddle with matters utterly foreign to their condition—or the superstitious stupidity of the married folk, who have sanctioned and obeyed such perfectly malicious and barbarous laws. (418)

Panurge's problematic marital situation is foregrounded against the more conventional conjugal situation of Pantagruel, who will leave the choice of a spouse to his father without the unwanted intervention of the clergy. Students learn from Panurge's unsuccessful pursuit of the "haulte dame de Paris" (*Pantagruel*, chs. 21 and 22) that his motivation is sexual and that, once thwarted, his anger turns to cruelty in seeking to get even through setting all the dogs in Paris to urinate on her door.

From the start of the *Tiers livre*, a somewhat aging Panurge turns to contemplate marriage. The irony of changing his dress from the braguette—a sartorial piece that prominently displays masculinity—to adopt a robe that looks remarkably similar to a monk's garb is not lost on Pantagruel:

> Mais ce n'est la guise des amoureux ainsi avoir bragues avalades et laissez pendre sa chemise sur les genoilx sans hault de chausses, avecque une robe longue de bureau. . . . (394)

> It isn't the habit of lovers to have their trousers tumbling down like this and their shirts hanging out over their breechless knees, or to wear brown serge. . . . (306)

Furthermore, Panurge's reasons for contemplating marriage are motivated by self-interest. On the one hand, he is burning with sexual desire. He explains the efficacy of his new costume:

> Je ne l'ay prins qu'à ce matin, mais desjà j'endesve, je deguene, je grezille d'estre marié et labourer en diable bur dessus ma femme sans craincte des coups de baston. (395)

> I only put it on this morning, but already I'm raging, itching, and crackling to be married and to work my wife like a brown devil, without fear of a beating. (306)

A second reason for wishing to marry is also grounded in self-interest. He wants to see his name and line carried on:

> Voire mais, dist Panurge, je n'aurois jamais aultrement filz ne filles legitimes ès quelz j'eusse espoir mon nom et armes perpetuer, ès quelz je puisse laisser mes heritaiges et acquestz. . . . (402)

> "But," said Panurge, "there's no other way of getting legitimate sons and daughters, by whom I can hope to perpetuate my name and armorial bearings, and to whom I can leave my inheritances and acquisitions. . . ." (312)

In the chapter on Thélème, those who sought to reform the church returned to the teachings of Saint Augustine to reinforce the connection between grace and free will. Setting one's will in line with God's is an act of choice. However, to commit to any path of action requires that one make a conscious choice. From the outset, Pantagruel perceives Panurge's indecision and inability to commit to a path:

> N'estez vous asceuré de vostre vouloir? Le poinct principal y gist: tout le reste est fortuit et dépendent des fatales dispositions du Ciel. (403)

> Aren't you certain of your own wishes? That's the principal point; all the rest is fortuitous and depends on the disposition of the heavenly fates. (313)

Panurge looks outward for signs instead of turning inward to bring his action in line with his faith. At the beginning of the consultation sequence with professionals (theologian, physician, philosopher, lawyer), the theologian Hippothadée remarks, "Mon amy, vous nous demandez conseil, mais premier fault que vous mesmes vous conseillez" (478; "My friend, you ask us for advice. But first you should so consult with yourself" [371]). Interpreting the words of the dying poet Raminogrobis, Pantagruel sums up Panurge's situation:

> Il veult dire sommairement qu'en l'entreprinse de mariage chascun doibt estre arbitre des ses propres pensées de soy mesmes conseil prendre. (476)

> His meaning is, concisely, that in the matter of marriage everyone should be his own judge and take counsel with himself. (369)

Until his decision to marry is grounded in *caritas*, a higher love that allows the couple to set their conjugal relationship in the broader context of the love of God, Panurge's interest in marriage will be motivated by self-interest: lust and the desire for posterity. Augustine explains that lust blinds the Christian to divine love and enslaves the individual. Speaking of his own experience prior to bringing his will in line with God's will, he states: "The enemy held my will in his power and from it he had made a chain and shackled me. For my will was perverse and lust had grown from it, and when I gave in to lust, habit was born, and when I did not resist the habit it became a necessity" (*Confessions* 8.5.164). Rabelais's theologian, Hippothadée—whose name is eponymous with the bishopric (Hippo) to which Augustine was named—articulates the evangelical view of marriage, where the conjugal relationship does not get in the way of Christian faith and duty:

> Le sainct Envoyé (dist Hippothadée) me semble l'avoir plus apertement declairé quand il dict: "Ceulx qui sont mariez soient comme non mariez; ceulx qui ont femme soient comme non ayans femme." (499)
>
> "The Holy Apostle seems to me to have put it more plainly," said Hippothadeus, "when he said: 'Let those that are married be as if they were not married; those who have wives be as if they had no wives.'" (386)

Here the text paraphrases Saint Paul (1 Cor. 7.29).

A final echo of the prevailing reform in thought and belief to mention is the question of predicting the future. Two forces are at play here: Rabelais's interest in creating an inventory of all kinds of prognostications and the unambiguous message to Panurge from all quarters. Given his character, driven by "les aiguillons de la chair" (470; "pricking of the flesh" [371]) and his distrust of female sexuality, it is very likely that he will be cuckolded, beaten, and robbed by his future wife. Evangelism has a deep distrust of the presumption of human knowledge. The great thinkers of the French Renaissance had a thirst for knowledge but understood the limits of knowledge. Rabelais's Gargantua expresses the awe of the early scholars of the French Renaissance as he writes to his son Pantagruel as he embarks on his studies: "Somme que je voy un abysme de science" (248; "In short, let me find you a veritable abyss of knowledge" [195]). Gargantua ends the famous letter to his son by cautioning him that knowledge comes with responsibility:

> Mais par ce que, selon Saloman, Sapience n'entre point en ame malivole, et science sans conscience n'est que ruine de l'ame. . . . (248)
>
> But because, according to the wise Solomon, Wisdom enters not into the malicious heart, and knowledge without conscience is but the ruin of the soul. . . . (196)

The quest for knowledge without a grounding in faith is misguided and leads to ruin. Here again, Rabelais and his fellow scholars Erasmus and Lefèvre d'Étaples find common ground with Saint Augustine, who cautions us to know the limits of human knowledge: "This futile curiosity masquerades under the name of science and learning, since it derives from our thirst for knowledge and sight is the principal sense by which knowledge is acquired, in the scriptures it is called *gratification of the eye* (I John 2: 16)" (*Confessions* 10.35.241). Panurge's push to see the future, to interrogate the future through signs and a series of fashionable methods of prognostication, represents "futile curiosity." Humankind, without faith and revelation, is stuck in the present. It is folly to head off in pursuit of the golden oracle, the "Dive Bouteille" (535; 422). As Augustine states, "By whatever mysterious means it may be that the future is foreseen, it is only possible to see something which exists; and whatever exists is not future but present" (11.18.268). Panurge will not progress further along the knowledge path until he loops back and takes the time to interrogate himself in his relationship with God.

Seeking knowledge of future events outside the scope of divine revelation is fruitless. Augustine asks, "But how do you reveal the future to us when, for us, the future does not exist? Is it that you only reveal present signs of things that are to come? For it is utterly impossible that things which do not exist should be revealed" (11.19.268). Revelation of future things comes through grace, not through human intelligence:

> The means by which you do this is far beyond our understanding. I have not the strength to comprehend this mystery, and by my power I never shall. But in your strength I shall understand it, when you grant me the grace to see, sweet Light of the eyes of my soul. (268)

Panurge's quest to see into the future runs counter to the narrator's definition of *Pantagruélisme* as defined by the narrator of Rabelais's *Quart livre*: "certaine gayeté d'esprit conficte en mespris de choses fortuites" (568; "a certain lightness of spirit compounded of contempt for the chances of fate" [439]).

Pantagruélisme embodies the core of evangelical Christian values in warning against the censure that closes off the free circulation of knowledge, ideas, and beliefs. The essence of *Pantagruélisme* cautions us not to waste our time in railing against those things that are related to fortune and the future and beyond our capacity to grasp or to command. If the princes embody humanist evangelical values, Panurge wrestles with the individual's desires: for happiness, for physical companionship, for offspring, and ultimately, for control over future things. These desires, if unguided by either faith or revelation, lead the individual on fruitless quests for knowledge that lies outside our reach. It is this very human thirst for what lies beyond our grasp that is embodied in Rabelais's most human character, Panurge.

NOTE

[1] As Guy Demerson points out, Rabelais plays on the similarity between the word for Egyptian priests (*pastophores*) and the word *pasteurs* and the word for mole (*taupe*) to refer to the priests who work in the dark in clandestine ways (Rabelais, *Œuvres* [Demerson] 538n).

On Gargantuan Individualism

Michael Randall

As in all Rabelais's novels, *Gargantua* abounds in passages that place enormous value on the exercise of the individual will. At the same time, *Gargantua* and the other novels also contain many passages that depict the exercise of that will as detrimental to the well-being of the community. What, then, are students to make of individualism in *Gargantua*, where private interest is suppressed in some passages and placed at the novel's ethical heart in others? Are they to understand it as a literary aberration, as a form of authorial confusion, or might there be something of greater importance at stake here? The seeming contradiction regarding individual will found in *Gargantua* can bring Rabelais's text into the world of modern students, since the questions underlying the novel regarding personal freedom and social responsibility are not that different today from what they were in the mid–sixteenth century, even if our answers to them are not the same today. The beauty of Rabelais's text is that its very foreignness can bring these questions to light in ways that more familiar and more recent texts cannot.

An Ethics of the Common Good?

Gargantua, like all Rabelais's novels, is grounded in an ethics of the common good (Langer). In such a moral system, all actions taken to enhance the individual interest will jeopardize the common interest. This is the gist of the message Gargantua's father, Grandgousier, sends to Picrochole, his formerly friendly neighbor, who started an unjust war for spurious reasons. At the end of this war, Grandgousier sends Toucquedillon, one of Picrochole's captains whom he captured, back to Picrochole with a message. Toucquedillon is to tell his ruler that he should not act to better his self-interest, because to do so will lead inevitably to the diminishment of the common good. When the common good is lost, Grandgousier explains, so too, inevitably, is private interest:

> Allez vous en, au nom de Dieu; suyvez bonne entreprinse, remonstrez à vostre roy les erreurs que congnoistrez, et jamais ne le conseillez ayant esgard à vostre profit particulier, car avecques le commun est aussy le propre perdu. (246)

> Go your ways, in God's name, and follow noble aims. Remonstrate with your king when you see him to be in error, and never give him counsel with an eye to your private profit. For when the common interest comes to grief, private interests fail with it. (138; trans. revised)

This lesson is not learned by Picrochole and another of his officers and counselors, Hastiveau, who subsequently has the messenger Toucquedillon torn to bits. Both Hastiveau and Picrochole come to an equally sad end shortly afterward, bearing graphic witness to the wisdom of Grandgousier's advice. Grandgousier, on the other hand, treats the defeated troops with great generosity, giving them many gifts and advantages, and ends up improving his own well-being through the undying affection of his new subjects. Grandgousier's success and Picrochole's defeat and death stand in narrative and ethical opposition to each other; where the one acted charitably and knew great success, the other acted out of individual interest and came to an untimely end.

This passage represents, in many ways, the ethical drift of much of Rabelais's novelistic world. In the *Tiers livre*, for example, Panurge's *Eloge des dettes* (chs. 3–5; "Praise of Debts") is condemned by Pantagruel because it exhibits a love of self that is in complete opposition to Pauline charitable love. In the same way, in the "Tempête en mer" chapters of the *Quart livre* (18–24), Panurge's selfish actions will be contrasted with the selflessness of the other Pantagruelians who come to the aid of others in time of need. The ethical imperative that the individual must love others fixes these novels' moral compass (see Langer).

An Ethics in Praise of Individual Will?

While all the novels place the common good at the center of their ethical universe, they are also filled with fully formed characters performing great acts of individual bravery. Frère Jean, who saves the Abbey of Seuilly in *Gargantua* (ch. 27), is perhaps the most obvious example of an individual exercising his will. His efforts to save his abbey when it is attacked by Picrochole's troops are contrasted with the lack of action on the part of his fellow monks. Where the other monks do not show any individual initiative and continue to pray collectively, Frère Jean fights vigorously to save the abbey. He will be generously rewarded for his services to Gargantua during the war with Picrochole at the end of the novel, when Gargantua offers to build him an abbey (the Abbey of Thélème), which will be unlike any other monastery, and to make him its abbot.

The reward for his acts of heroism, the Abbey of Thélème, is organized around the principle of individual will. The injunction to act according to one's own will in the abbey's maxim—*Fay ce que vouldras* (284; "Do What You Will" [15])—is based on the abbey's antithetical nature: whatever happens in Thélème is the opposite of what happens in a regular abbey or monastery. If women are not allowed in a normal monastery, then women will be allowed at Thélème; if rules govern the daily life of a normal monastery, then the only rule at Thélème is that there are no rules. And just as monks are supposed to give up all ideas of individual will, the monks of Thélème will have as their only rule "Do what you will."

Thélème as a Consensus of Wills

How are students to understand a novel in which the common good is suppressed in some passages and praised in others? How are they to understand a novel that includes both Grandgousier's message to Picrochole and the Abbey of Thélème's maxim? First, it is important to remind students that there are two moments of *thelema* ("will" in Greek) involved in the abbey. If the first act of *thelema* is the recognition of individual will, the second is the subordination of that will to a greater, more general will (Demonet 281; Nykrog). All the Thelemites end up doing what all the others do. For example, if one says, "Let us drink" (159), they all drink ("Si quelqun ou quelcune disoit 'beuvons,' tous buvoient" [284]). This second moment of individual will is the crucial part of Gargantuan individualism. In the abbey, the autonomy of the individual is grounded in an evangelical desire to love the other. As in other sections of the novel—for example, the message Grandgousier sends to Picrochole—there is no room for individual will as we understand it today.

Chapter 9 in *Gargantua* provides a passage that can help students understand how individual will exists in the context of an ethics of common interest. The narrator describes the "colors and devices" (*couleurs et livrée*) of Gargantua's clothes. He objects to the way courtiers have given meaning to colors based on the authority of a work on heraldic devices called the *Blason des couleurs*, which described the meaning of colors (Screech, "Emblems"). The narrator rises in great dudgeon against the effrontery of the author of this work. He states that to impose an arbitrary meaning on colors is to be like a tyrant who imposes his will on his people:

> Mais au reste je ne scay quoy premier en luy je doibve admirer: ou son oultrecuidance ou sa besterie. Son oultrecuidance, qui sans raison, sans cause et sans apparence, a ausé prescripre de son autorité privée quelles choses seroient denotées par les couleurs; ce que est l'usance des tyrans qui voulent leur arbitre tenir lieu de raison, non des saiges et scavans qui par raisons manifestes contentent les lecteurs. Sa besterie, qui a existimé que, sans aultres demonstrations et argumens valables, le monde reigleroit ses devises par ses impositions badaudes. (92)

> For the rest, I do not know which surprises me more, his presumption or his stupidity: his presumption in daring, without reason, cause, or probability, to prescribe by his private authority what things shall be denoted by what colours; which is the custom of tyrants who would have their will take the place of reason, not of the wise and learned, who satisfy their readers with display of evidence; or his stupidity in supposing that without other proofs and valid arguments the world would regulate its practice by his foolish impostures. (57–58)

Imposing individual will on meaning or on political subjects is equally abhorrent. Meaning is understood by convention, by consensus, by an *ius gentium* or the law of the peoples. In the following chapter, speaking of the meaning of white (*joie*) and black (*tristesse*), for example, the narrator says:

> Et n'est ceste signifiance par imposition humaine institué, mais receue par consentement de tout le monde, que les philosophes nomment *jus gentium*, droict universel valable par toutes contrées. (96)

> Nor is this significance based on a mere human interpretation. It is accepted by that common consent which philosophers call *jus gentium*, universal law, valid in all countries. (59)

The meaning of these colors is understood by consensus, because people have always agreed on that meaning and not because one individual has said so.

These passages indicate how power and meaning in Rabelais's novels are decided not by the will of one individual but through the consensus of many. The passages from chapter 9 and 10 regarding the meaning of colors provide a key for understanding how individual will and common good coexist in the Abbey of Thélème at the end of the novel. Individual will might exist in the abbey, but it cannot be exercised as we might in our world today. Just as Pantagruel's criticism of Panurge's *Eloge des dettes*, in which individual interest is understood as the glue holding the world together, flies in the face of the logic of modern capitalism, which is based on the exercise of the individual will, so too the logic of Thélème and the message that Grandgousier sends to Picrochole seem antithetical to the ethos of much modern Western society, in which the common good is seen operating through the protection of individual interest (see Desan on representation of modern capitalism in Renaissance literature). It is important to recognize that no one person tells the Thelemites what to do. The abbey is not, as at least one modern commentator has believed, a precursor of the modern totalitarian state (Glucksmann 11–35).

Filled with clearly defined characters exercising their will for the good of the community, Rabelais's novels offer students a model, if an imperfect one, of a society in which individual will is not related to self-interest. *Gargantua* features a political system typical of the late medieval world, in which the king's power was considered limited and kings themselves were considered imperfect (Tierney; Ullmann). Gargantua, Grandgousier, and Gargamelle are often described in terms of their human imperfection: Grandgousier is referred to as "le bon homme Grandgousier" (70, 116; "good old Grandgousier" [48, 69]), and the narrator notes the "belle matiere fecale que doivoit boursouffler en elle" (70; "fine faecal matter which must have swollen up in her" [48]) in Gargamelle. In these early novels, individuals, whether kings or subjects, because of their imperfection, cannot exert their will in favor of their own interest without imperiling the well-being of the whole society. It is only in the later novels, such as the *Quart livre*, that the monarch has absolute power over his subjects. The ruler Gaster, in the *Quart livre* (chs. 57–62), has no ears and so cannot hear the remonstrations of his subjects. These subjects, the Engastrimythes and the Gastrolatres, act as sycophants and never express any individuality. The Pantagruelians and Gargantua and his followers are all individuals, but they are not modern individuals, in the sense that the fulcrum of society is not based on their individual wills. They are early modern individuals in a society in which the fulcrum is grounded in the common good.

Although few people would want to return to a world of monarchical power, even a limited monarchical power like that found in *Pantagruel* and *Gargantua*, these novels do offer students (and all modern readers) an example of a society in which individual will flourished as a vital part of a greater common good. Passages from *Gargantua* that praise both the virtue of the common good and the need for individual will can prompt discussion of the seemingly intractable dilemma of modern democratic societies. If modern democracies often seem torn by a desire to give full weight to the notion of individual liberty and by a desire to ensure that all individuals are given an equal chance, Gargantua and his companions offer a model of a society that accommodates individual will (liberty) at the same time that it sublimates that will to the greater common good (equality). The individual is defined in terms not of the self but of obligation to others.

Neither a totalitarian community in which individual will would disappear nor a neoliberal society in which solidarity is disdained in favor of individual independence, the Gargantuan polity is one in which the individual will is defined in terms of social obligation. Rabelais's novel can be used as a starting point for a discussion of how modern technology and economics can both connect and alienate members of society, allowing individuals greater mobility and personal freedom but also detaching them from the community and one another. It can encourage students to understand how they can be Gargantuan citizens, exercising their wills for the common good and not turn inward to a virtual subjectivity that risks making them self-absorbed and sycophantic Engastrimythes, worshipping at the altar of a virtual self that sometimes seems to reign over modern society as ruthlessly as Gaster did over his. They can learn to be like Frère Jean, exercising their wills for the greater good of the community.

NOTE

This essay draws on material developed in more depth in my book *The Gargantuan Polity*. I thank the University of Toronto Press for permission to express here some of the ideas developed in that book.

Utopian Dimensions of *Pantagruel*

Scott D. Juall

While the land Utopie is mentioned explicitly in only some seven chapters of *Pantagruel* and solely in the first chapter of the *Tiers livre*, the theme of a utopian society—a topic frequently elaborated in early modern European literary and philosophical works—is an overarching concept in the Pantagruelian cycle, and it plays a central role in the cycle's overall meaning. In the second chapter of *Pantagruel*, we learn that the main character hails from Utopie, the home of his mother, Badebec, "fille du Roy des Amaurotes, en Utopie" (314; "daughter of the king of the Amaurots in Utopia" [174]), and the country where his father, Gargantua, reigns as king. As Pantagruel's homeland and primary source of his thought, Utopie ostensibly serves as a point of reference throughout *Pantagruel*. Since ideology and utopia are intricately connected, Utopie evokes crucial elements of Rabelais's perspectives on the sociocultural and especially political dimensions of early-sixteenth-century France. An analysis of the role of Utopie in *Pantagruel*, as both a visionary place and ideological concept, provides therefore a highly useful pedagogical approach for teaching some of the most provocative elements of Rabelais's subversive political project.

To emphasize the significance of utopia in early modern European thought and its direct relevance to Rabelais's oeuvre, I would encourage teachers to assign the English reformist Thomas More's *Utopia* (1516), an essential literary point of departure for a discussion of many topics that Rabelais addresses in *Pantagruel*. More's work was the first to present a remote—and ostensibly fictional—visionary land, in the reformist manner, as an example of a utopia. In the satirical treatise, Hythlodaeus, having returned from his voyage to Utopia, reports on the land's ideal system of political governance and models of law, economics, morals, and sociocultural practices, which greatly contrast with those in Western Europe. The traveler's lengthiest critique of European society is that of imperialist quests of contemporary monarchies. Targeted in particular are wars that recent French kings waged in order to conquer parts of the continent and territories that they used as part of a strategy to manipulate international relations to their own benefit (58–59). Utopia's pacifist stance against war, on the other hand, permits combat only to defend itself when its territory—or that of its allies—is invaded, save another people ruled by a tyrannical leader (109), or enlarge its domain because of overpopulation (78–80). When the Utopians must engage in battle, they prefer to implement ruse rather than military combat (110). These aspects of Utopia's orderly society, which promote harmony and peace, are important elements of the land's egalitarian and democratic ideology.

One of the most effective elements of the utopian genre is its ability to situate an idealized society in an ambiguous location. As Louis Marin states, the Greek toponym plays on two prefixes that create a pun between "*eu*topia" ("good place") and "*ou*topia" ("nowhere") (*Utopiques* 27). Because of the double meaning of utopia and the genre's ambivalent treatment of space, More's Utopia only pretends to draw attention away from its real target—the ideologies dictated by contemporary European kingdoms and the rule of its sovereigns. Marin asserts that utopia is incapable of escaping from its own realities and is a direct reflection of them: "As a figure in discourse, utopia is written and imagined within the discourse which criticizes it. It is a discourse located within its own truth, giving it power and authority" (*Utopics* xxi; see also Desroches 84, 86). More's new Utopian social order thus represents a satirical critique of the religious, socioeconomic, and political institutions that early modern Western European monarchies and empires imposed on both their own people and those whom they conquered.

In *Pantagruel*, the link between Utopia and Utopie is not only toponymic but also ideological. In his revision of More's satirical treatise, Rabelais draws on numerous sociocultural, political, and religious reforms described in *Utopia* and transforms them to reflect his own subversive concept of a utopian society. While More created his Utopian ideology against the backdrop of Tudor England during the reign of Henry VIII, Rabelais's rewriting of utopia in *Pantagruel* reflects elements of early-sixteenth-century French society under Francis I. As a broadly educated evangelical humanist party to the intricacies of the French court, Rabelais gained myriad experiences in religious, intellectual, and professional spheres, and he possessed a remarkably boisterous spirit and ribald sense of humor. He drew on these diverse qualities in creating the order of Utopie, reflecting what Edwin Duval describes as Rabelais's "Christian humanism . . . an all-encompassing ideology that embraces both content and form, serious and comic, high and low, sacred and profane in a single coherent view," one in which the "low style and coarse, popular humor are in fact crucial to its meaning" (*Design of Rabelais's* Pantagruel xviii). Such a humanism calls into question concrete modes of thought and, by extension, fixed ideological concepts; Utopie thus demonstrates the subversion of general conceptions of the predominant social order. A uniquely Rabelaisian revision of utopian ideology—a *Utopien* counterideology—thus emerges in *Pantagruel* as an alternative to the prevailing imperialist ideology of sixteenth-century French and broader Western European monarchies and empires, which the work repeatedly targets.

Rabelais undertakes an innovative narrative strategy to demonstrate the Utopien ideology in *Pantagruel* by situating his revised ideological program not only in Utopie but also in the traveling Utopiens. During Pantagruel's circular voyage, which begins and ends in Utopie, the hero and his companions stop at a number of *utopoi*—textual commonplaces that are suggested by More's *Utopia* and that Rabelais reconfigures to create a Utopien (in)version of the dominant political and cultural plan. His inventive approach to undertaking a critique of contemporary ideologies thus greatly diverges from that in the intertext. In *Pantagruel*, Rabelais presents the ideology of utopia not in a detailed treatise explaining a visionary society, as does More's *Utopia*, but rather in the series of *utopoi* that arise repeatedly in the work. While pursuing their travels, the Pantagruelians confront characters and events related to the dominant religious, political, and broader sociocultural conventions that serve as obstacles to their progress—physical, intellectual, and ideological. Instead of telling of the stable, orderly political and sociocultural aspects of Utopia's society, as does More's traveler Hythlodaeus, Rabelais shows the ideals of a visionary land in flux and transformation by means of his characters' dynamic engagement in a number of Utopien strategies.

Some of the fundamental elements of the Utopien ideology are initially revealed when Pantagruel leaves Utopie to seek an education in France and begins a peripatetic tour of the principal French universities. There he finds a medieval Scholastic system that proves insufficient for his present intellectual needs. In a letter sent from Utopie to Pantagruel in Paris, Gargantua urges his son to pursue a novel pedagogical program that reflects the contemporary humanist education. This letter, which emphasizes the study of classical languages, liberal arts, civil law, nature, medical treatises, and sacred texts, identifies Utopie as the source of the new educational *cursus*—one that will provide Pantagruel with a means of further cultivating his Utopien thought. In the missive, Gargantua states the primary goal of his son's learning: "je te admoneste que employe ta jeunesse à bien profiter en estude et en vertus" (352; "I beg you to devote your youth to the firm pursuit of your studies and to the attainment of virtue" [195]). He insists that Pantagruel return to Utopie only once he has acquired "tout le scavoir humain de par delà" (354; "all the knowledge to be gained in the parts" [196]). Pantagruel's quest for progress is enacted in both physical and intellectual domains, as traveling allows him to cultivate his Utopien *savoir*. Gargantua requests moreover that his son systematically put his developing knowledge to the test as he advances through France and pursues his education:

> [E]t veux que de brief tu essaye combien tu as proffité, ce que tu ne pourras mieulx faire que tenent conclusions en tout scavoir; publiquement, envers tous et contre tous, en hantant les gens lettrez qui sont tant à Paris comme ailleurs. (354)

> I wish you shortly to show how much you have profited by your studies, which you cannot do better than by publicly defending a thesis in every art against all persons whatsoever, and by keeping the company of learned men, who are as common in Paris as elsewhere. (196)

Immediately after Pantagruel sets out to learn according to the idealized intellectual plan that his father demands he follow, he meets Panurge, who speaks, among many other languages, Utopien. Panurge will of course become Pantagruel's traveling companion and intellectual counterpart, whose ruse, wits, and mischievous ways play an integral role in the work's subversive Utopien ideology. The bawdy, rambunctious humor for which Rabelais is so well known serves as an essential complement to the extremely serious intent of Gargantuan's letter. Pantagruel and Panurge participate in a number of activities that target contemporary French social, religious, and political institutions by putting into practice and testing elements of Utopien thought, just as Gargantua has suggested that his son do. Through a number of rhetorical debates, battles of wits, and ideological clashes that present comical strategies for resolving problems, these series of *utopoi* parody lawyers, law proceedings, and judicial practices; mock Scholastic theologians and their approaches to practicing religion; and call into question conventions of social decorum and interpersonal relations. Rabelais's conception of utopia thus represents a peculiar version of a "critical utopia"—what Michael Gardiner describes as a kind of utopian discourse that functions "in a more oppositional and subversive manner"—one that is "self-ironising and 'internally' deconstructive . . ." (26).

By repeatedly presenting human interactions negotiated through power struggles in linguistic, rhetorical, religious, and social spheres, Rabelais draws attention to conventional means of asserting authority over others. Mikhail Bakhtin's theories of Rabelaisian poetics shed much light on this aspect of the Utopien ideology. Bakhtin maintains that the concept of "carnival" in Rabelais "opposed the protective, timeless stability, the unchanging established order of ideology, and stressed the element of change and renewal" (*Rabelais* 81). The theorist argues that carnivalistic laughter, which is "the laughter of all of the people . . . , is universal in scope," explicitly contests fundamental elements of the prevailing ideology and calls into question hierarchical ordering and all claims to superiority (11–12). In a similar vein, Barbara Goodwin emphasizes the topsy-turvy world in Rabelais's works, which "infer serious criticism of existing society, and the need for change or revolution. [The] subversive effect of inversion can at least provide the impetus for constructing the present" (25). In *Pantagruel*, Rabelais thus addresses the most serious of topics through the humorous, subversive strategies of the Utopien counterideology that his characters promote.

While such episodes reflect many important elements of Rabelais's parody of sociocultural institutions of contemporary French society and questions of power struggles tied to them, the explicitly political and martial dimensions of the Utopien counterideology arise in chapter 23 of *Pantagruel*. During his stay in France, Pantagruel learns that on the death of his father, the imperialist Dipsodes, a neighboring people ruled by their king, Anarche, have transgressed their geopolitical boundaries and invaded the hero's homeland. The enemy's armies then "avoyent gasté un grand pays de Utopie, et tenoyent pour lors la grande ville des Amaurotes" (442; "had devastated a great tract of Utopia, and were just then besieging the great city of the Amaurots" [245]), capital of Utopie, with the aim of conquering its inhabitants and dismantling their Utopien ideology. Such an imperialist war between neighboring kingdoms is precisely the kind of battle that the Utopians in More's work strictly condemn. In his letter, Gargantua asserts a Utopien stance toward war by stating that in order to defend Utopie from such imperialist aggression, Pantagruel should

> apprendre la chevalerie et les armes, pour defendre ma maison et nos amys secourir en tous leurs affaires contre les assaux des mal faisans. (354)

> learn chivalry and warfare to defend my house, and . . . help our friends in every emergency against the attacks of evil-doers. (195)

The Dipsodian invasion of Utopie provides the occasion for Rabelais to depict several battles by undertaking a narrative strategy different from that presented in *Utopia*. More's work merely describes Utopian attitudes toward war without furnishing any concrete depictions of battles between the Utopians and their adversaries, but Rabelais devotes ten successive chapters of *Pantagruel* to the intricacies of warfare between the Utopiens and the Dipsodes (23–32). In these episodes, Rabelais emphasizes the clashes between the two central political opponents—Pantagruel, heir to the throne of Utopie, and Anarche, king of the invading Dipsodes. In order to draw attention to the illegitimacy of Anarche's imperialist rule, Rabelais selects a name for the sovereign that immediately recalls—and contrasts with—that of Ademus, the ideal king of More's Utopia. As Duval points out, Ademus, from the Greek for "without a real people," represents an imaginary prince, while Anarche, the name of Pantagruel's usurping adversary, signifies "an illegitimate prince because he is a ruler 'without sovereignty,' 'without rule,' or 'without the authority to rule' . . . , the antithesis of what a good Utopian Prince should be" (86). Anarche is moreover not only an anti-Utopian but also an anti-Utopien leader—an "antiprince [who] functions as a political antitype to Pantagruel" (87), the ideal prince of Utopie whose approach to war provides an alternative to aggressive imperialist quests.

Rabelais describes the battles between Pantagruel and Anarche to develop More's criticism of imperious battles for territory into a full-blown indictment of empire. Acutely aware of the double meaning of *utopia*, Rabelais places Utopie and its condemnation of empire in an uncertain location that recalls a number of contemporary imperialist conflicts. As More's work reminds us, France attempted to conquer and maintain several regions of Western Europe during the late medieval and early modern periods. By the time that Rabelais wrote *Pantagruel*, France frequently participated in hostile military engagements. The wars that Rabelais portrays recall most immediately the contemporary imperialist quests of Francis I. Under his leadership, the French monarchy became more authoritative and absolute; he also greatly developed the strength and activity of the French military. The French king pursued a very aggressive foreign policy and devoted much of his reign to waging war against his great nemesis, Charles V, one of the principal figures in early modern European imperialism and assuredly another of Rabelais's targets in *Pantagruel*. After defeating Francis I's candidacy for emperor of the Holy Roman Empire in 1519, Charles V, who already possessed the Netherlands, Burgundy, and a multitude of lands under the crown of Castile, inherited the Hapsburg possessions. In the decade preceding the writing of *Pantagruel*, since the immense territory under Charles V's reign surrounded France along nearly all its terrestrial borders, the emperor posed a serious threat to Francis I's domain. Throughout his reign, the French king constantly battled Charles V, not only to regain territories lost to the emperor and defend France from his expanding empire but also to provoke imperialist conflicts of his own. Through his depictions of war in *Pantagruel*, Rabelais thus revisits contemporary imperialist politics through the perspective of his Utopien ideology.

Rabelais develops his parody of contemporary imperialism after Pantagruel and his companions respond to the Dipsodes' invasion of Utopie. The Pantagruelians, enlightened with the moral, intellectual, and philosophical precepts that humanism provided to early-sixteenth-century Western Europe—and armed not with conventional weaponry but with Rabelais's peculiar brand of comical strategies—leave Paris immediately to rescue Utopie from its invaders. During the highly circuitous route from France to Utopie, several digressive moments representative of Utopien counterideology interrupt and delay the physical progression and call into question the conventions of epic battles and the imperialist narratives that recount them. Pantagruel's decision to say good-bye to "une dame de Paris" (444; "a lady of Paris" [246]) before setting out to rescue Utopie privileges personal concerns over *patria* and temporarily halts the advance, thereby subverting one of the essential conventions of imperialist epic, which unequivocally demands that the hero defend his homeland under such circumstances (see Freccero, "'Instance'" 50). A number of lengthy discursive delays also defer the advance of the five heroes. This ragtag group of warriors from diverse lineages stops to discuss elaborately their amazing physical prowess rather than demonstrating their talents (448; 248). They also postpone their advance to the battle by enjoying an immense, extravagant feast, which temporarily causes them to forget the imminent war (452–54; 251–52). With the approach of the immense Dipsodian army led by Loup Garou, captain of the Giants, Panurge is much more preoccupied with how he might "arranger à braquemarder toutes les putains qui y sont en ceste après disnée" (456; "manage to roger all of those whores there this afternoon" [253]) than defeat the enemy. The other Pantagruelians quickly enter the discussion and further delay their arrival at the battlefield.

While the heroes occasionally resort to using combat to defeat the enemy, they much prefer to employ intelligence and cleverness, the ideal approach to battle practiced by More's Utopians. Once Pantagruel and his companions arrive at the port of Utopie, they fight scouts of the Dipsodes' army, whom they conquer through wit and cunning. Panurge, Epistémon, Eusthènes, and Carpalim defeat the assailants effortlessly by luring them into a trap and pretending to surrender (450–52; 249–50). The heroes also undertake a strategy of trickery when they advance to fight Anarche's army. Instead of leading a daring and valiant attack against the Dipsodes, Pantagruel deliberately misleads the enemy by telling a Dipsodian captive that they expect reinforcements of the Utopien army that would greatly surpass the number of Anarche's troops (465; 256–57). Rabelais further transforms More's Utopian strategy of combat by adding comical strategies to his characters' Utopien military pursuits. Pantagruel aims to defeat the Dipsodes "bien estrangement" (464; "very strange[ly]" [256]) by sending the captured Dipsodian prisoner back to the enemy camp with "une boette pleine de Euphorge et de grains de Coccagnide confictz en eau ardente en forme de compouste" (464; "a box full of euphorbium and spurge-laurel grains steeped in brandy, made up into pastilles" [257]), which causes Anarche and his men to consume so much alcohol that they pass out. The wily Panurge then gives a potent drug to Pantagruel that forces him to urinate in huge quantities on the camp of the sleeping Dipsodes, after which Carpalim sets fire to their shelter (464–70; 256–60). Anarche, who survives the raid, is carried away from the danger by a number of surviving giants. The war continues as the protagonists from opposing camps prepare for their final battles.

Such comical dimensions of the Pantagruelians' battles with Anarche's armies mock the serious nature of military campaigns undertaken by contemporary leaders such as the king of France and the Holy Roman emperor, whose advocacy of imperial interests is implicitly equated to that of the king of the Dipsodes. The immediate aftermath of Pantagruel's defeat of additional Dipsodian troops demonstrates Rabelais's subversive Utopien ideological stance most effectively. Having had "la couppe testée" (480; "his chop headed off" [264]) during a duel between Pantagruel and Loup Garou, the injured Epistémon temporarily descends to hell. There he encounters legendary heroes of epic narratives; numerous emperors, monarchs, and generals of some of the most powerful empires; and a series of popes (480–92; 264–70). As Duval states, all these leaders have served "the cause of empire, expanding their dominions beyond legitimate borders to usurp the rule of neighboring or distant lands and extending their personal power beyond legitimate rule to tyranny" (*Design of Rabelais's* Pantagruel 106). Epistémon also reports that in hell an inversion of social, economic, and political status exists among those who were less powerful on earth: "les philosophes et ceulx qui avoient esté indigens en ce monde, de par delà estoient gros seigneurs en leur tour" (488; "the philosophers and those who had been penurious in this world, had their turn at being great lords down below" [268]). Once Anarche's kingdom is defeated, the overthrown leader's plight shows the same inversion of power and hierarchy as that in hell: Anarche becomes "un bon cryeur de saulce vert" (494; "a good crier of green sauce" [272]), and Panurge weds him to an impudent old whore.

Although the numerous leaders in hell represent a long heritage of abusive rulers who promoted imperialist ideologies in the past, the wars that take place up on earth allude to invasions and battles of the kind undertaken by Charles V and Francis I in the present. A certain fate is thereby prescribed to such contemporary sovereigns. Rabelais recounts the manner in which Pantragruel is rewarded for his military accomplishments. After defeating their adversary, the Pantagruelians arrive in the city of the Amaurots, where the inhabitants enthusiastically greet Pantagruel and lead him through the city's gate with much fanfare. The Utopiens then expand their territory by colonizing the whole land of Dipsodia—an action sanctioned by both the Utopian and Utopien concepts of defensive war. The Dipsodes, delivered from their tyrannical leader, are delighted by Pantaguel's arrival; they surrender to him and celebrate his leadership of their land. This scenario promotes Rabelais's Utopien model of an ideal resolution to political confrontation and an ideal outcome of war.

As the work draws to a close, we assume that Pantagruel becomes "roy des Dipsodes" (295, 508; "King of the Dipsodes" [165, 278]), since his new position as leader of Dipsodie is announced twice, on the title page and in the final sentence of the work. However, in the final chapter of the work, Rabelais's narrator, Alcofribas Nasier, states:

> vous avez ouy un commencement de l'histoire horrificque de mon maistre et seigneur Pantagruel. . . . Vous aurez la reste de l'histoire à ces foires de Francfort prochainement venantes. (506)
>
> you have heard a beginning of the horrific history of my lord and master, Pantagruel. . . . You will have the rest of the story at the very next Francfort book-fair. . . . (277)

The moment describing the ultimate outcome of the military conflicts between the Utopiens and the Dipsodes is therefore both at hand and yet to come. The continuation of the war is displaced outside *Pantagruel* and deferred until the *Tiers livre* (1546), a work in which the expanded Utopien state is briefly reintroduced in the first chapter before it is dropped altogether. Rabelais thus composed the conclusion of the Utopien war with the Dipsodes some fourteen years after *Pantagruel*. What he wrote in the interval between *Pantagruel* and the *Tiers livre*—precisely where the land Utopie appears not to be developed—is *Gargantua* (1534). This work provides a diegetic space in which Rabelais elaborates another dimension of the subversive Utopien ideology, although in a different context and under another name, the Abbaye de Thélème.

In the end, we see that More and Rabelais are radically different kinds of ideologues. Instead of presenting plausible solutions to social problems that More elaborates in his traditional utopia, Rabelais creates a society that lacks harmony, identity, and stability. Gardiner argues that such a conception of utopia reflects ironic characteristics of a visionary society "via the incorporation of elements of contradiction, ambiguity, and openness" (26). Rabelais's Utopie reflects thus a form of utopian discourse that leads to a much less conclusive elaboration of utopian ideals than that of More's Utopia. Rabelais understood the unfortunate inevitability of social discord, international conflicts, and imperialist war during his time and the unlikelihood of any infallible solution to them. Therefore, while Marin states that "L'utopie est une critique idéologique de l'idéologie" (*Utopiques* 249; "Utopia is an ideological critique of ideology"), Rabelais takes this conception one step further. In brief, Utopie embodies what Gardiner calls an "anti-utopian utopia" (32)—that is to say, a parody of both the utopian genre and the idealistic solutions to the sociocultural, political, and religious problems that critical utopias traditionally provide. Instead of coherently prescribing elements of a new ideological order, Rabelais is more interested in drawing attention to ideological problems of his time by presenting strategies for change that, being ambiguous and comical, might resist partisan attack and polemical criticism.

This approach to teaching *Pantagruel* establishes a model for analyzing utopian space and ideology in other works of the Pantagruelian cycle, which frequently reflect on idealistic, ambiguous, or topsy-turvy Utopien spaces in order to call into question the manner in which ideology dictates contemporary social, political, and cultural conventions. An analysis of the Utopien ideology therefore encourages readers of Rabelais to reexamine early modern political, religious, and broader sociocultural conventions in other works of the French Renaissance, such as Marguerite de Navarre's *Heptaméron*, Michel de Montaigne's *Essais*, and Jean de Léry's *Histoire d'un voyage fait en la terre du Brésil* ("History of a Voyage to the Land of Brazil"). This pedagogical strategy provides moreover a great deal of insight into methods of assessing the complex relation between utopia and ideology beyond early modernity, and it should inspire students to reconsider the ideological constructs—and the means of portraying them—in their own society.

Rabelais and Cartography

Tom Conley

It is difficult to see how Rabelais could ever be taught outside the context of cartography. The four books were conceived and written on the heels of the Columbian voyages, in the heyday of oceanic voyages to the east and west, and at a moment when maps and mapping were part and parcel of Erasmian humanism. The books were written at a moment when two different modes of representing the world—one through the authority of the manuscript and printed book, the other through the graphic records of voyage over land and on the high seas—converged and informed each other. The new and inventive maps that contained and conveyed much of the information concerning the discoveries found their way into the work and indeed even affected the author's signature. When students see how the books were born and evolved in the context of mapping, the force of their form can be quickly discerned. Students can also grasp how the world found itself being reconfigured as never before.

When Rabelais published *Pantagruel* in 1534, he also traveled to Italy (in February) to prepare a topography of ancient Rome for his protector, Cardinal Jean du Bellay, who had been summoned to argue for the suspension of a papal order to excommunicate Henry VIII of England (Rabelais, *Œuvres complètes* [Huchon] 1743n1). While serving the prelate in the guise of his *médecin ordinaire* ("general physician"), Rabelais studied the *urbs* before discovering that Bartolomeo Marliani (1490?–1560), a Milanese antiquarian of the same generation, had just published a *Topographia antiquae Romae*. Rabelais returned to Lyons to prepare and write a dedicatory letter to Du Bellay for an edition of Marliani. A doctor who had closely examined living bodies and dissected a cadaver during his medical studies at Montpellier, Rabelais took note of what he saw in meticulous detail. The fresh experience of the world as it could be seen within and through the body was translated into the spatial and lexical forms of the writing. The work that we now know is in constant dialogue with anatomical and cartographic material; it evolved and changed no less than did the maps and projections that informed the books as the books developed from 1534 to 1552.

Students ought to be familiar with five or six types of interrelated maps that informed Rabelais's writing. The first belongs to the medieval heritage of the *mappa mundi*, a schematic map of the world contained in a circle whose circumference was often shown to be a *mare oceanum* ("ocean sea") circulating about the three continents bequeathed to the sons of Noah. Called a T-O map because of the vertical bar or architectural trumeau of the consonant representing the Mediterranean (when it is read from bottom to top, the map goes from west to east, not, as in modern maps, from south to north) and the crossing trait (or lintel) at its top joining the Nile and Tanais or Danube Rivers, which separate the landmasses of Europe (given to Jaseth) and Africa (to Cham) from

Asia (belonging to Shem), the schema or memory image appears in its first printed form in an edition of Isidore of Seville's *Etymologiae* in 1473. Recalling the *Orbis terrarum*, the image signals that the habitable world is enclosed by a watery surround. The second type, a variant on the same schema, is the zonal diagram that distinguishes five climates divided by the lines of the equator, two tropics, and arctic and antarctic circles. Frigid worlds are to the north and south of the temperate climes in the northern and southern hemispheres, while a torrid zone stretches across the middle of the earthly sphere. Landmasses tend to be floating islands and not massive continents. The world is shown in thermal flux that in fact invites intrepid travelers, like Vasco da Gama and Columbus, to sail southward (see Wey-Gómez) and through what had been imagined to be seas of boiling water.

Such are two late-medieval schemas that portray not a flat world but a form whose circular enclosure carries the allegory of a great globe whose center is everywhere and circumference is beyond human ken (see Woodward, *History*; Edson). Where these world pictures are circumscribed, Rabelais's is not. His world opens much in the way that the atlases based on the Alexandrian geographer Claudius Ptolemy (c. AD 145) charted the globe for humanists from the fifteenth to the middle of the sixteenth century. The third type, Ptolemy's *Geographia*, found printed editions in Italy, in copperplate, as of 1477 and in the north, in Germany, in woodcut form, from 1482. In it, a world map prefaced twenty-six regional projections of the known world, whose place-names were registered in an appended gazetteer in which degrees of longitude and latitude allowed readers to find the places on the maps. Oceanic discoveries by the Portuguese and Spanish prompted editors not to jettison the old Ptolemy but to juxtapose the inherited projections to their new counterparts, which included, after Martin Waldseemüller's *Cosmographia introductio* (1507) and his subsequent world maps, indications of the places Columbus and Vespucci discovered. Students know well that the exhumation and new editing of Ptolemy figured prominently in the rebirth of the knowledge of antiquity—that is, the process of editing, adjusting, correcting, and establishing a book that confirmed and at once rivaled with and exceeded the biblical world on which it was said to be based.

The fourth type of map that bears on Rabelais is the portolan chart. A navigator's image of the coastline of the Mediterranean, the portolan was drawn on vellum and held in scrolled form in containers on ships that eventually sailed west of the Columns of Hercules at the mouth of Gibraltar. Drawn in differently colored inks and charted according to a marteloio system of rhumb lines or loxodromes and compass roses (see Jacob), it drew on the experience of artists who observed the shorelines that sailors sought whenever possible to keep in view. The portolan chart offered fairly accurate outlines of the Mediterranean coasts, islands, and sea mass where Ptolemy's depiction had been grossly distended along its east-west axis. In France some of the authors of portolan charts, many of whom had been affiliated with Portuguese commerce, found a productive center in Dieppe in the 1520s and 1530s. The style of the charts affected world maps and manuscript atlases. Their rich depictions of landscapes in continental or island masses, along with detailed rendering of information about the new world, made them at once oneiric and realistic views of the state of the world at the very moment Rabelais undertook the writing of *Pantagruel* and *Gargantua*.

Two other types of maps are pertinent. One, the regional or topographic projection, spun off the first paragraph of Ptolemy, who distinguished a *mappa mundi* from a city view or a map of a locale by comparing a portrait of a human face to any of its details (fig. 1). The former was seen as analogous to a world map, while the latter—an eye and an ear—was set in juxtaposition to a city view. The irony of similitude is that the eye and the ear were implied to be the organs with which the reader could see and "read" the maps and their gazetteers. Seeing was taken to be a function of hearing and vice versa. The topographic projection evolved into an estate map or even an image of an area in view of its logistical virtues—that is, how it could defend itself or define a boundary maintainable by a strong military presence. The other, the island map of the *isolario* or book of islands common only to the Renaissance (indeed at its height, in the time of Rabelais's writings from 1534 to 1551), conceived the world as an open-ended aggregate of islands floating in an ocean sea. The style of the *isolario*, although an integral model is not illustrated here, is shown in the three sheets (of a sum of nine) that compose the western third (or left side) of the Olaus Magnus map of Scandia, Iceland, and its neighboring islands (see below, fig. 5). It is a type of map that informs the style and composition of the *Quart livre*.

Above and beyond these types of maps, the production of Oronce Fine (1492–1555, a life span almost identical to that of Rabelais), the greatest French cartographer of the sixteenth century, finds enduring and even graphic presence in Rabelais's four books. The son of a schoolteacher in a hamlet near Briançon, Fine studied with eminent Spanish mathematicians in Paris in the early years of the sixteenth century. A gifted mathematician and cosmographer, he edited an illustrated edition of Georg Peurbach's work on astronomy (1517) at the same time he drew a map of the Holy Land (in a hastily composed reedition of Bertrand von Breidenbach's elegantly illustrated *Voyage à la terre sainte* of 1483), most likely in anticipation of a crusade that the newly crowned Francis I was seeking to undertake. Fine's success as a draftsman led him to compose a (lost) single cordiform projection of the world, which he later redrew and printed in woodcut in 1534 (see below, fig. 4). The celebrity of the woodcut map was such that it was copied in copperplate in 1565. Yet it was in 1531, in preparing a bicordiform projection of the world for Simon Grynaeus's *Novum orbis* (fig. 2), that the cartographer produced an image bearing directly on Rabelais's *Pantagruel*.

When Fine's map is shown in the context of chapter 32, "Comment Pantagruel de sa langue couvrit toute une armée, et de que l'auteur veit dedens sa bouche" (330–33; "How Pantagruel covered a whole Army with his Tongue, and what the Author saw in his Mouth" [272–75]), an anthropology, indeed a will to embrace the other or the foreigner, becomes clear. In his celebrated analysis of

GRAPH. PETRI AP. 2.

ræ imitatio. Et à Cosmographia differt, quia terrā distinguit per montes, fluuios, & maria, aliaque insigniora, nulla adhibita circulorū ratione. Iisque maximè prodest, qui amussim rerum gestarum & fabularum peritiam habere desyderant. Pictura enim seu picturæ imitatio, ordinem sitúmque locorum ad memoriam facillimè ducit. Consummatio itaque & finis Geographiæ, totius orbis terrarum constat intuitu, illorum imitatione, qui integram capitis similitudinem idoneis picturis effingunt.

Geogra. à Cosmogra. differt.

Geogra. qui bus maximè necessaria.

Geogr. finis.

GEOGRAPHIA. EIVS SIMILITVDO.

CHOROGRAPHIA QVID.

CHorographia autem (Vernero dicente) quæ & Topographia dicitur, partialia quædam loca seorsum & absolutè considerat, absque eorum ad se inuicem, & ad vniuersum telluris ambitum comparatione. Omnia siquidem ac ferè minima in eis contenta tradit & prosequitur. Velut portus, villas, populos, riuulorum quoque decursus, & quæcunque alia illis finitima, vt sūt ædificia, domus, turres, mœnia, &c. Finis verò eiusdem in effigienda partilius loci similitudine consummabitur: veluti si pictor aliquis aurem tantùm aut oculum designaret depingerétque.

Chorographia quid cō sideret.

Choro. finis

CHOROGRAPHIA. EIVS SIMILITVDO.

Fig. 1. Peter Apian, similitude of geography and topography in his *Cosmographia* (Paris ed., 1551)

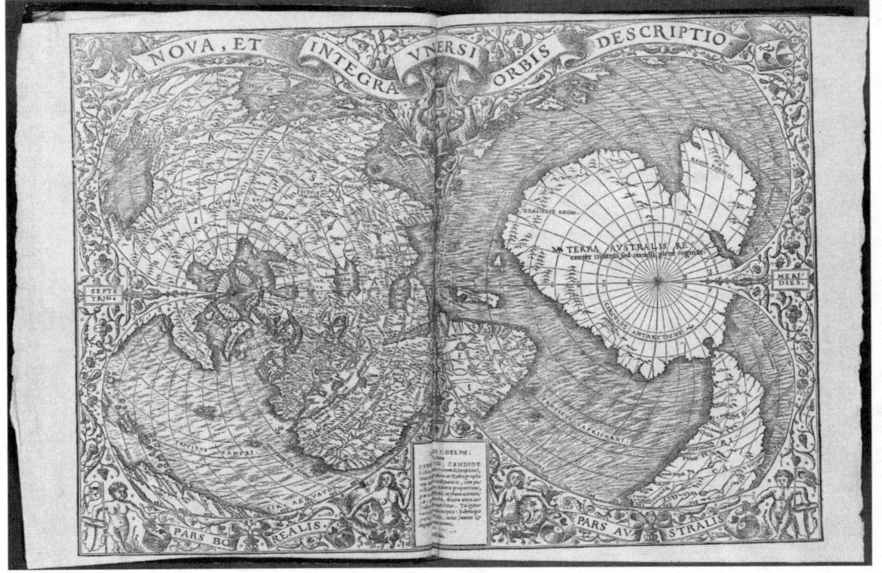

Fig. 2. Oronce Fine's bicordiform projection of the world, from Simon Grynaeus's *Novum orbis* (1531)

the episode, Erich Auerbach notes that the narrator who has climbed into his master's mouth discovers on the landscape of the tongue a strangely familiar cabbage planter who could hail from the author's own Touraine. What Rabelais takes from Teofilo Folengo's macaronic *Merlin Cocai* (*Opus*) or even the biblical tale of Jonah to craft the episode draws a new and foreign hemisphere into its fold. Alcofribas walks along roads that lead him from the mountains of Pantagruel's teeth (*les monts Dannoys*) and down through forests and cities of the size of Lyons or Poitiers. He meets the farmer and, hearing the man's description of his environs, exclaims, "Jesus! (dis je) il y a icy un nouveau monde?" (498; "'Jesus,' I said. 'Is there a new world here?'" [273]). The printed characters conveying the words of the conversation call the site of the encounter into question: is it, as Auerbach's reading would suggest, located in Rabelais's Touraine? Or, in view of the map that the author had probably seen, is it somewhere between worlds known and unknown? The cabbage planter's words are suggestive:

> Certes (dist-il), il n'est mie nouveau, mais l'on dist bien que hors d'icy y a une terre neufve, où ilz ont et Soleil et Lune, et tout plein de belles besoignes. Mais cestuy cy est plus ancien. (330)

> "Of course," said he. "But it isn't in the least new. They do say, indeed, that outside there is a new earth, where they have both Sun and Moon, and that it's packed full of fine things. But this one here is the older." (273)

Key is *où* ("where"), adjacent to the *terre neuve* shown to be "out of here," shown and turned topsy-turvy in *nouveau monde*. The Latin presence of *unde*, behind *où*, is found inverted in a graphic echo embedded in *on* at the center of the word denoting the world. Following the planter's advice, Alcofribas sets off to the nearest city of Aspharage. Along the way he discovers (*trouvay* in the text) a man extending a net to catch homing pigeons that fly into the giant's mouth from the other world as they seek a *colombier* (dovecote) that would gather them. The allusion to Columbus is obvious, and so also is an implicit line of demarcation drawn between one hemisphere and the other. The point is underscored at the end of the chapter, when Alcofribas observes that "la moytié du monde ne scait comment l'aultre vit" (500; "one half of the world doesn't know how the other half lives" [275]). Not unlike his words, Oronce's map shows that an old and inhabited world (to the left), replete with place-names and having at the polar axis an arctic sea and an archipelago, has a new counterpart, where cannibals (in northeastern Brazil) and the fabled Prester John (in southern Africa) are said to live. If, as Rabelais suggests, one world is attached to but separated from the other, the map that was designed to be folded along the central meridian and inserted or bound in the *Novum orbis* causes the narrative to describe the very aspect and condition of the projection. Its two axes offer as many points of view that engage a sense of bipolarity and binocularity implicitly felt needed for the world to be seen in all its depth and changing proportion.

In *Pantagruel* the presence of the cordiform world map finds frequent reference to a topographic counterpart. Teachers of Rabelais often contend with ever-changing scales of proportion and size that seem to lack rhyme or reason: now the giant is huge, now he is of human measure. Allusion to the woodcut image that Pierre Apian drew for his *Cosmographia* (that witnessed twenty-nine editions from 1529 up to the end of the sixteenth century—see fig. 1 above) shows how Rabelaisian measure works by way of supple analogy. Apian illustrates the first sentences of Ptolemy's *Geographia*, in which the Alexandrian cartographer states that the distinction between geography and topography can be understood when a world map and its analogue, the full portrait of a human being, is juxtaposed to its topographic complement, a city view and what would be its corollary, the depiction of an isolated eye or ear. The woodcut image brings the art and anatomy of isolating and of dissecting things small into the image of the world that can never be seen in its entirety. A sliding scale of proportion is such that a world can be found in an ear, or even cut into an eye, if the viewer looks closely to discern the circles of latitude and lines of longitude that define the pupil.

Topography or chorography would amount to the depiction of local spaces and their pertinent traits. In earlier chapters Rabelais describes the giant's institution or education as one that includes geography. In the famous letter that Gargantua sends to Pantagruel (ch. 8), he implores his child to learn the landscape and, literally, to leave no detail unattended. The counsel is nestled in a sequence of careful design. The future hero (ch. 6) meets and thrashes a

Limousin student who does not speak French properly. The moral of the fable, taken from portolan charts, is that a common and national idiom, French, must be used for the sake of the community and that unwieldy and pretentious Latinate diction must be avoided, "en pareille diligence que les patrons des navires evitent les rochiers de mer" (336; "as carefully as ships' pilots avoid the rocks at sea" [185]). The good user of an idiom needs to sail around and about the shoals and unexposed rocks of language. Pantagruel then encounters the contents of a bookshop (ch. 7) presented much like an index or a gazetteer of names and places. He receives the letter from his father before meeting Panurge, the Limousin's counterpart, who utters twelve languages before discovering that his interlocutor also speaks French, a common "langue naturelle, et maternelle . . . au jardin de France" (362; "natural mother-tongue . . . in the garden of France" [201]). The Touraine is the garden of France. In his words Panurge begs for a piece of bread as he draws a polyglot map of the greater world. To the idea of a sum of real and virtual languages he brings a sense of proportion and perspective. He acts out—indeed, he maps out—a variety of idioms that are shown having their own space and place in a greater picture of things, which, when Pantagruel listens to Panurge, he begins to fathom.

In these chapters and, no less, in much of the locale that marks those in *Gargantua* of the hero's childhood and adolescence, the Picrocholine wars, and the establishment of the Abbey of Thélème, awareness of a national topography accrues. The events in the novels can be located on the map of France. They clearly constitute what David Woodward calls a "route-enhancing" map ("Roger Bacon's Terrestrial Coordinate System" 119) or Frank Lestringant a "toponymical tale" ("Rabelais" 110). For these readers, narratives are designed according to itineraries charted and followed according to the vagaries of a line drawn such that it becomes a map. Yet students of Rabelais would wish to know by whom and in what shape and form the map of Pantraguel's or Gargantua's France emerges. Teachers do well to review the maps of *Gallia* that inform the first two books. They should have various editions of Ptolemy's *Geographia*, especially those following the Columbian discoveries that include an old and a new world map and twenty-six regional maps. Students quickly learn how the Italian maps, the first to use copperplate technology (such as the Berlinghieri atlas) differ from their northern counterparts (such as the Strasbourg atlas of 1512), whose maps are in woodcut. Yet all the maps of *Gallia* in Ptolemy, schematically rendered, remain confined to an order that moves from the British Isles to Iberia, Gallia, Germany, and Italy, and then eastward to the Holy Land. In chapter 33 of *Gargantua*, in which Lucian's *Dialogue of the Dead* is refashioned for comic ends, three counselors (the duke de Menuail, Count Spadassin, and Captain Merdaille) offer Picrochole advice about how to conquer the world. In a setting that in our time would be a briefing over a table strewn with maps, the advisers utter volleys of names of countries and toponyms that loosely follow the sequence of maps as they are found in the *Geographia*.

By strong contrast, the topography of France marking *Gargantua* is discerned through comparison of the names and places with those in Oronce Fine's great *Nova Totius Galliae* (1525), which in its woodcut form now survives in a unique copy, dated 1553, published by Jérôme de Gourmont. Oronce's map extends the claims of the nation by having its orography (the depiction of mountains, in the shape of molehills that are more finely drawn than the crude chains of sugar-loaves in Ptolemy) cut into the Spanish Pyrenees and the Alps of Savoy and northern Italy. Correcting Ptolemy's latitudes and tracing a meridian (following the crease in the middle of the map) that runs from Flanders to the Mediterranean south of Narbonne, the projection displays the image of the nation as French humanists would have idealized it. (The map, redrawn by Jean Jolivet, was later printed by Abraham Ortelius in copperplate in his *Orbis theatrum terrarum* of 1570; in 1555, Pirro Ligorio etched the map in copperplate [shown here in fig. 3].) The viewer of Oronce's (or Ligorio's) map quickly notes the keen rendering of rivers, those virtual highways of the nation that irrigate especially the "garden of France," Rabelais's Touraine, to which detailed reference is made throughout the first three books.

The *Tiers Livre* (1546) appears to relegate the presentation of space and place, what cartographers today call locational imaging, to the background of the dialogues about marriage among an aging Panurge, the ever-wise Pantagruel, and the many specialists whom the protagonists consult and query. Movement on and over the map of France is reduced to forays about the Touraine, until the protagonists ultimately decide to take to the high seas. Not far from the middle of the book, Apian's similitude figures in a brief but incisive geography of the aging body. Frère Jean, consoling Panurge over his concern about erectile dysfunction and cuckoldry, reminds his agonistic partner that his face is becoming riddled with the lines of a world map. He asks Panurge to look at himself from near and far:

> Ta barbe, par les distinctions du gris, du blanc, du tanné et du noir, me semble une Mappemonde. Reguarde icy. Voy là Asie. Icy sont Tigris et Euphrates. Voy là Afrique. Icy est la montaigne de la Lune. Voidz tu les Paluz du Nil? Deçà est Europe. Voydz tu Theleme? Ce touppet icy, tout blanc, sont les mons Hyperborées. . . . (682)

> Your beard looks to me like a map of the world with its mixture of greys and whites, of red and blacks. Look here. See this is Asia; here are the Tigris and Euphrates. There's Africa. Here are the Mountains of the Moon. Do you see the Nile marshes? On this side is Europe. Do you see Thélème? This quite white tuft here is the Hyperborean Mountains. (365)

The snowcapped mountains of the great continents are shown high above the cold valleys where Panurge's codpiece lies. The words are drawn exactly as if

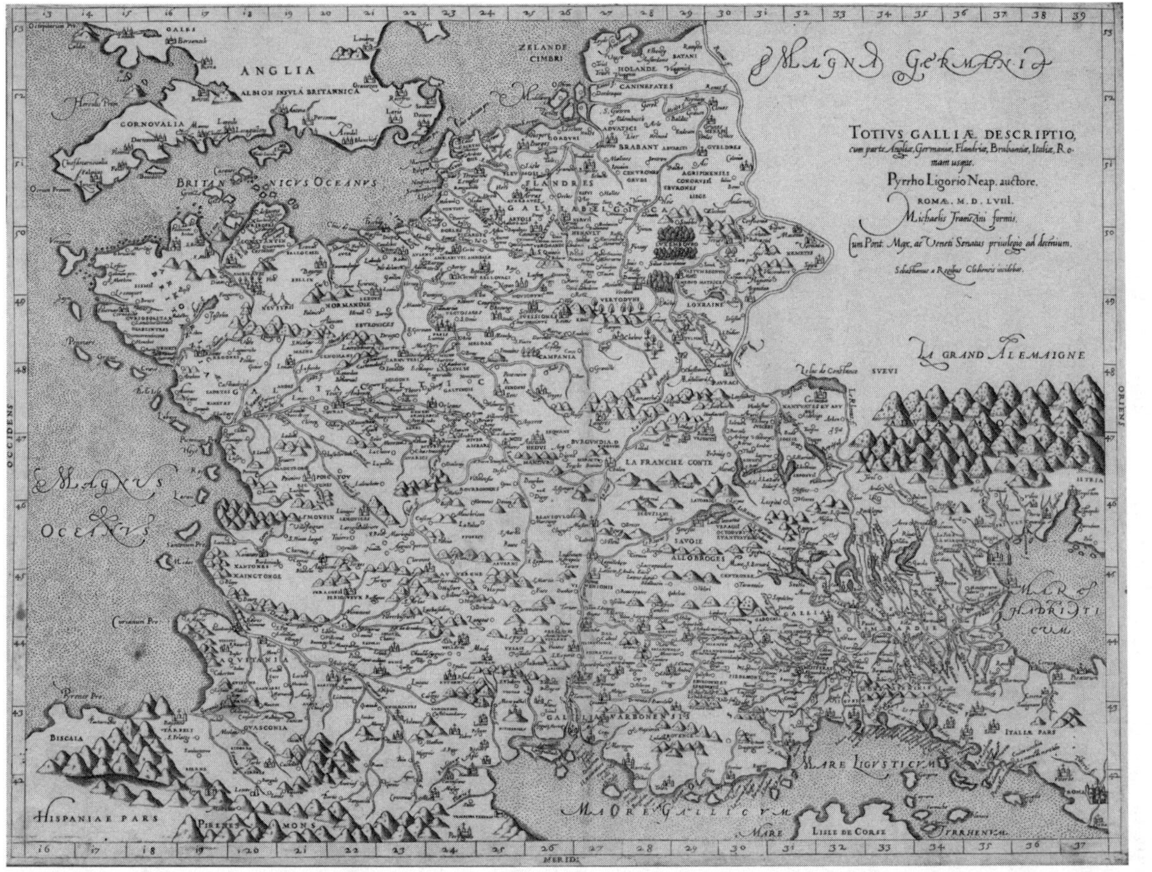

Fig. 3. Pirro Ligorio, "Totius Gallia Descriptio" (1555), after Oronce Fine (1525)

the author were describing, in cartographic ekphrasis, the details of Panurge's face in view at once of the continents and rivers of Asia and Africa that make Thélème (or Chambord, the château in the Touraine that served as its model), the site invented for the ending of *Gargantua*, difficult to find. The undulating landscape on which the characters tread forms a strong contrast to the deep furrows and ridges of the antagonist's face.

The title page of the early editions of the *Tiers livre* offsets the topography and even displaces the ostensible locale and implied intimacy of the dialogues. The teacher does well to remind students that editions from 1546 to 1552 were signed by François Rabelais, *docteur en medicine* (in sharp contrast to the alchemical scribe, Alcofribas Nasier, of the two earlier volumes). Rabelais is also qualified as "Calloier des Isles Hieres" ("the hoister of the Hyère Islands"). Located off the coast of France south and east of Toulon, these islands were refortified in 1549 to defend Provence. Why the toponyms were removed from the editions of 1552 and afterward remains a mystery. In any case their mention alludes to a unique cartographic genre, the *isolario* ("island book"), which witnessed its greatest success from the fifteenth to the end of the sixteenth century, at a moment when the portolan chart of the Mediterranean gave way to sea charts of the Columbian discoveries and when the book of cosmography mutated into the modern atlas. It may be that the author saw the sequel to the *Tiers livre* as an oceanic chronicle, indeed a work in which the Hyères Islands would figure as modern analogues to the islands met in the legend of Jason and the Argonauts. The outcome of the debates would be a departure taking the travelers to the high seas and in and among a variety of strange places.

The *Quart livre* (1552) cannot be taught without copious allusion to the *isolario*. A compendium of maps born of Cristoforo Buondelmonti's widely copied account of the Aegean archipelago (over sixty manuscripts of it were copied in the fifteenth century), the *isolario* found its way into print in Bartolomeo Sonetti's work of 1485, in which woodcut maps of the Greek islands are juxtaposed to sonnets that describe their virtues and tell of the narrator's navigations. They are set in prose and extended to include the islands of the New World in Benedetto Bordone's *Isolario* of 1528 (reprinted often until the 1570s) and then appear in copperplate illustrations, with more emphasis on worldwide navigation, in Tomasso Porcacchi's *Isolario* of 1572. In Bordone and Porcacchi, the world is seen not as a mix of continents and water but as a scatter of islands floating in a *mare oceanum* whose contrasting poles are Venice (a city of a thousand islands) and Temistitan (Mexico City, then an island city surrounded by a great lake). For Rabelais, the open-ended structure of the island book permits the creation of a modular narrative. Events and episodes can be added in the context of isolated places discovered and visited. The voyagers become open-minded travelers, ethnologists who inquire into the strange shapes and forms they find in an expanding world. That the islands are self-enclosed and large makes them ripe for expression, long before Swift's *Gulliver's Travels*, of mordant satire. And each carries a mood or tone such that it becomes, in the prescient words of Alfred

Glauser, a "mental island" or even a space where fantasy meets the hard facts of geography (*Rabelais créateur* 147).

The voyage that Pantagruel and his companions undertake to find the *Dive Bouteille* (*Œuvres complètes* [Huchon] 494) defies tracing on any given map. But replete with maps it is: the ship sails both east and west, at once in the Mediterranean and toward the New World. Students wishing to imagine an itinerary can be encouraged to consult a number of projections. First, Oronce Fine's great single cordiform map of 1534 (Giovanni Cimerlino redrew it in copperplate in 1565 [fig. 4]) takes note of Magellan's voyages at the same time it depicts the peninsula of Baccaclear (Canada, a place to find codfish), reaching, as it were, toward Europe, at a right angle to the eastern coastline of North America, which is indicated as Terra Francesca and runs from present-day Florida northward to Long Island and beyond. It may be, as Samuel Eliot Morison has suggested, that French sailors knew of the New World before Columbus, having fished in the Great Banks. Manuscript maps of the Dieppe School, drawn by sailors and navigators from the 1530s to the end of the sixteenth century—which should be

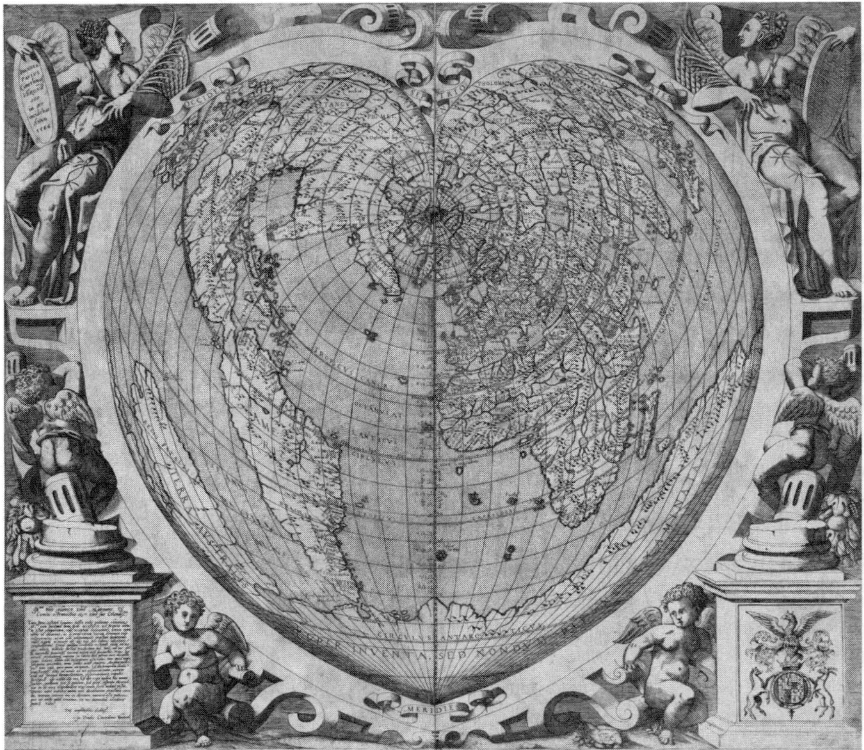

Fig. 4. Cordiform map by Giovanni Cimerlino (1565), after Oronce Fine (1534)

included in any course on the *Quart livre*—now and again indicate that French presence near Canada had preceded both Verrazano's and Cartier's expeditions. Some of the maritime knowledge and the cartographic apparatus known to that school are found on Cimerlino's map.

A woodcut map that definitely bears on the *Quart livre*, published in Venice in 1539 and no doubt known to travelers in Italy, is Olaus Magnus's *Carta marina* (fig. 5). The first accurate image of the northern countries and the islands north and west from the Scandinavian peninsula to Iceland, the map includes, much as in Sebastian Münster's *Cosmographia*, images of sea monsters, which Rabelais inserts into the narrative and describes in the mode of ekphrasis. At chapter 33, the optical and spatial center of the book, Pantagruel takes sight of

> un grand et monstrueux Physetere, venent droict vers nous bruyant, ronflant, enflé, enlevé plus hault que les hunes des naufz et jectant eaulx de la gueule en l'air davant soy, comme si feust une grosse riviere tombante de quelque montaigne. Pantagruel le *monstra* au pilot. . . .
> (982; emphasis added)

> a huge and monstrous spouting whale, making straight towards us. It was snorting and thundering, and so puffed up that it rode high on the waves, above the main-tops of our ships. As it drew near it sent great jets of water from its throat, which looked like mighty rivers tumbling from the mountains before it. Pantagruel pointed it out . . . to the ship's captain. (521)

The sight, as Povl Skarup has shown, comes directly from the area of the map where monsters dwarf the ships they are attacking. One of the beasts, named *physetere*, surges from the sea and, like others in the swell and toss, displays a carapace of thick scales (figs. 6 and 7). Soon brave Pantagruel (in contrast to Panurge, who shrieks and shivers with fear), "considerant l'occasion et necessité, desploye ses braz, et *monstre* ce qu'il sçavoit faire" (984; emphasis added; "saw the urgency of the situation and put out all his strength. Then he showed what he could do" [522]): he rams a lance into the beast's jaws; once it is immobilized, he sinks spears into each of its eyes. He harpoons its caudal fin and plunges three more harpoons into its spine at equal distances between the tail and the head before firing fifty arrows into one side and fifty more into the other. Prostrate and spiked like a porcupine, the dead monster "estoit chose moult plaisante à veoir" (988; "It was a jolly sight to see" [524]).

Allusion to the *Carta marina* becomes especially forceful when we recall (via François de Dainville) that cartographers—especially Oronce Fine—constructed their maps from a point set at the axis of what would become the greater composition. A pivotal axis is designated; then units of longitude and latitude are measured according to Ptolemy (or his correctors') indications; a surrounding frame is drawn; cities are marked before rivers and relief are traced to fill

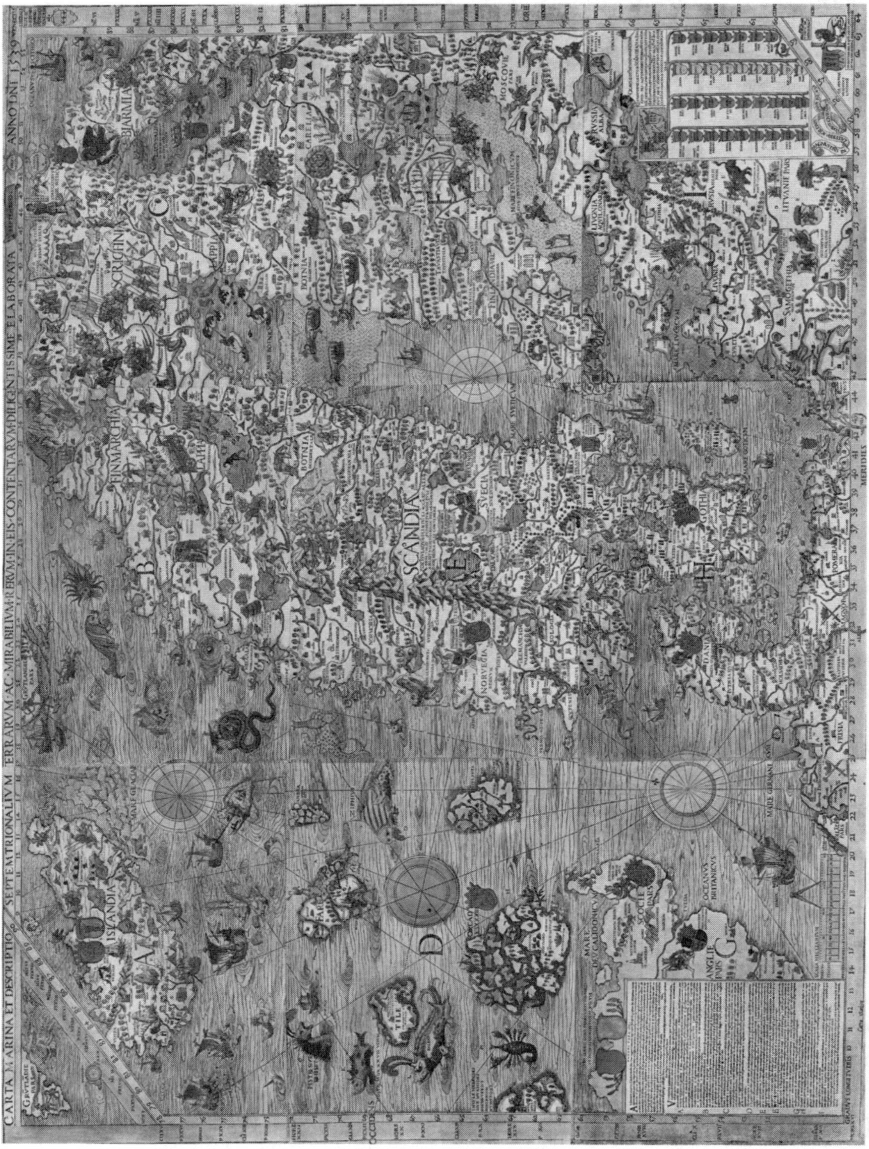

Fig. 5. Olaus Magnus, *Carta marina* (1539)

Figs. 6 and 7. Details from fig. 5

in the composition. In the *Quart livre*, the monstration (as emphasized above, where *monstre* ["monster"] seeps into the verbal texture) of the Christian sailor's defeat of the *monstrueux physetere* is the virtual origin at the center. Chapter 33, whose numerical symmetry is laden with Christian and Pythagorean symbolism, stands at a point between the thirty-two chapters on either side. The book converges on this apical or generating point, not unlike those at the poles of Oronce's two cordiform projections. Its spatial composition resembles Olaus Magnus's map, which is also built about a center and then punctuated with compass roses (of which four are visible on the *Carta marina* and at the central E, seemingly equidistant from the four corners of the map). Like the map, it can be read in view of its surface tensions and along intersecting lines of connection, much as the loxodromes radiating from the roses. Readers thus are encouraged to move about the work along a variety of itineraries.

Here and elsewhere the relation that Rabelais establishes with cartography allows readers to navigate the ocean sea of his words, their letters and spacings; it draws a plethora of images into the verbal matter in ways that transform them into hieroglyphs or enigmatic and composite forms fashioned from words spoken and words printed and from images and graphic devices embedded in the text itself. When studied through cartography, new dimensions of the work and its history become manifest. The visual pleasures afforded to student and teacher alike are many. The digital revolution has further enhanced the pedagogy, insofar as many of the maps that bear on Rabelais and his time are now easily available through search engines of the order of *Google Images*. Although their quality cannot rival the objects themselves, many of the digitial resources at the major libraries where maps are held allow viewers to study their digitized reproduction in extraordinary detail. Students are encouraged to consult *Gallica* of the Bibliothèque Nationale, the digital images on hand at the Newberry Library of Chicago, the Houghton and Pusey Libraries of Harvard (whence are drawn some of the images in this essay), and many others. Teachers can scan or photograph the text of facsimile editions and transfer them, like maps and their details, to a *Powerpoint* presentation.

Any study of cartography and the literature of Rabelais and his age should begin with Woodward's *History of Cartography 3: The European Renaissance*. Students seeking an introduction to the joy of cartographic readings will find in Christian Jacob's *Sovereign Map* a variety of approaches, drawn from history and theory alike, that build on the great work of Michel de Certeau, J. Brian Harley, Helen Wallis, Frank Lestringant, Monique Pelletier, and others. In addition to the books and articles to which Mireille Huchon draws our attention in her critical edition of Rabelais (*Œuvres*), Père François de Dainville's *Le langage des géographes* and Numa Broc's *La géographie de la Renaissance* remain baseline texts. With maps, teachers and students of Rabelais find before their eyes many new horizons and itineraries of inquiry.

The World in Pantagruel's Mouth: Alimentary Aesthetics and Culinary Consciousness

Timothy J. Tomasik

Rabelais and food: like peas in a pod, or *pois au lard* (*cum commento*), the two seem to form an inevitable pair. Food references pervade the chronicles of Pantagruel, and like many of the discourses that traverse the Rabelaisian text, it is polyvalent and polyglot. Unlike many of the humanistic discourses and references that challenge beginning readers of Rabelais (undergraduate and graduate alike), food offers a less distanced frame of reference. Beginning readers often struggle through allusions to Alcibiades in the prologue to *Gargantua*, but they will quickly grasp the irony of a major war's breaking out over grapes and *fouaces* in the Picrocholine war episode in the same volume. Rather than just a marker of excess or realism, food in Rabelais's work is a discourse that in fact filters humanistic debates in such a way as to make them more savory and thus more assimilable.

Several scholars have made productive use of alimentary perceptions to elucidate a wide variety of critical issues in Rabelais's work: grotesque realism and the carnivalesque (Bakhtin, *Rabelais*; Kinser), spirituality and corporality (Gaignebet), the symposium tradition (Jeanneret, *Des mets* and "Parler"), the power of poetic language (Rigolot, *Langages*), religious parody (Duval, "Messe"), humanist satire (Renner, "From the 'Bien Yvres'"), humor and farce (Bowen). I would argue that most of this critical work gravitates between two main poles. On the one hand, food is regarded as a popular upwelling of carnivalesque spirit à la Bakhtin. According to the author of *Rabelais and His World*, the triumph over the natural world finds expression in the excesses of carnival during which social and religious constraints, like natural constraints, are temporarily cast off by an ideological, class-based society. Food in excess thus becomes a space of reversal, renewal, and rebirth. On the other hand, food is but another erudite humanist discourse whose primary motivation is satiric. Michel Jeanneret's *Des mets et des mots* (*A Feast of Words*) forms the center of gravity of this approach in focusing on food symbolism in the context of the ancient symposium tradition. Here, banquets are of words, and the dishes served remain secondary to the rhetoric of conviviality and Renaissance humanism.

Food in Rabelais's work is thus either popular or erudite in orientation; it is either excessive or satiric. There are no third terms. Yet what stakes would be raised if Rabelaisian food were analyzed from a culinary angle? What would practical knowledge of the period's cuisine imply for literary studies of Rabelais? Furthermore, how would a practical approach to food references in Rabelais provide students with a compelling and ultimately more digestible point of departure for reading and understanding a work of such complexity and historical distance?

Not since Lazare Sainéan's 1921 *Histoire naturelle et les branches connexes dans l'œuvre de Rabelais* ("Natural History and Related Branches in the Work of Rabelais") has any scholar attempted a systematic analysis of Rabelais's mobilization of food in light of contemporary practical culinary discourses such as cookbooks, dietetic treatises, and natural histories. As late as 1998, Barbara Bowen puts forth the call that studies of Rabelais and food "need to be based on knowledge of what the period actually ate, and in what terms it was accustomed to discuss food, cooking, eating, and diet" (158–59). Recent research in Renaissance culinary history now makes possible such an innovative approach to the chronicles of Pantagruel.[1] By bringing to bear the practical language of food on studies of Rabelais, we may bridge the two poles of popular and erudite conceptions of food in the Rabelaisian oeuvre. This bridge in turn will provide an approachable gateway for beginning readers who can see food as a familiar frame of reference. While drawing such readers in, this gateway also reveals that food in Rabelais is not necessarily that of the twenty-first century.

In terms of the overall structure of Rabelais's complete works, modern criticism generally recognizes a change in tenor between the first two books and the second two: an exuberant and playful tone gives way to a more sober and pessimistic outlook. On the surface, the role of food follows a similar pattern. *Pantagruel* (1532) and *Gargantua* (1534) are most relevant to Bakhtin's conception of food and excess. The giants in both works are represented with appropriately gigantic appetites. Even as a child, Pantagruel in the eponymous volume "humoit le laict de quatre mille six cens vaches" (322; "swigged off the milk of four thousand six hundred cows" [179]). But even in the jubilant, life-affirming excess of food lists in the first two books, examples of other food discourses abound.

In *Gargantua*, just after the chapters detailing the excessive birth and education of the title character, we come to the episode of the Pichrocholine war, which involves Gargantua's father, Grandgousier. The episode begins with an angry encounter between Grandgousier's shepherds and the neighboring *fouaciers* or cake bakers of Lerné. As the cake bakers are heading to market, the shepherds offer to buy some of the cakes to savor with the local grapes. The *fouaciers* refuse this reasonable request and in fact insult the shepherds, injuring one of them. The shepherds react in defense of their injured comrade and beat the retreating *fouaciers*. In the bargain, the shepherds take the cakes for themselves but not without paying a more than fair price.

Once returned to their own lands, the cake bakers complain of their treatment to their king, Pichrochole. True to the angry, choleric humoral complexion implied by his name, Pichrochole becomes enraged by the "attack" on his people and launches an all-out war against his neighbor, Grandgousier. After a number of skirmishes between the combatants and Grandgousier's attempt to buy off Pichrochole by offering exorbitant amounts of *fouaces* and funds, Gargantua enters the fray and aids his father in finally defeating the attacking army.

The Pichrocholine war is the central episode in *Gargantua*. In Rabelaisian criticism, the main thrust of interpretation places the war in a general and specific context. The specific context refers to the author's native land in that much of the action takes place in and around La Devinière and Chinon, and the main conflict echoes a dispute between Rabelais's father and a local lord from Lerné. This local dispute is used to evoke the larger French context of territorial conflicts between Francis I and Charles V, which serve as a backdrop to the traditional antiwar ideology of early humanists. To return to the two poles of Rabelaisian criticism with which we started, the popular approach relates the episode to Rabelais's hometown rural life; the erudite approach connects it to feuding kings of Europe and the ideology of warfare.

Although these interpretations provide essential contexts for our students, I wonder if this traditional *entrée en matière* is the most effective introduction to Rabelais's text. I would suggest another path for an episode that is so clearly framed by food. The conflict begins with *fouaces* and ends with a festive banquet. Why does Rabelais place such a particular foodstuff, the *fouace*, at the center of this episode? It is clearly a regional delicacy and so of course contributes to the realism of the events. Yet his strategy goes beyond realism. While the *fouace* is the cause for the war, it is also figured as a potential solution.

When Grandgousier realizes how serious Pichrochole's attacks have become, he attempts to forestall further hostilities. Learning that four or five dozen of the pastries were taken, he sends a delegation to Pichrochole to offer five cartloads of *fouaces* along with additional money and land. But Grandgousier does not want to send any old *fouaces*. One wagon will contain *fouaces* made according to his own recipe—that is, "faictes à beau beurre, beau moyeux d'eufz, beau saffron et belles espices" (194; "made from fresh butter, good yolk of egg, fine saffron, and choice spices" [107]).

To my knowledge, no recipe for *fouaces* appears in French cookbooks of the time. The addition of saffron to Grandgousier's pastry recipe stands out. Saffron was not a traditional spice used in early modern pastry making. In the Middle Ages, it was prized more for the color it added to a white dish such as blancmange than for its taste. Dishes enhanced with saffron would turn golden, a worthy color for the tables of the nobility. The spice also had a medical use.

In the humoral medical theory of the time, the ideal human complexion was slightly warm and slightly moist.[2] Since saffron shares those qualities, it was often thought to temper one's humor, to bring one's complexion closer to the ideal. If we look at contemporary dietetic treatises, we can see that saffron was thought to contain other qualities at the time of Rabelais. According to Nicolas de La Chesnaye's 1507 *Nef de santé* ("The Ship of Health"), saffron "donne force a lesperit et entendement de soy esiouyr" (ch. 18; "gives strength to the spirit and intellect for the purpose of enjoying oneself"). It is also useful for dispersing the vital spirits from the heart to all parts of the body "avecque ioyeusete" ("joyfully"). The author concludes his article on saffron by saying "pour ceste cause ont dit aucuns acteurs que manger demye once de saffron induist la mort en ryant et faisant ioyeuse chere" ("for this reason some authors have said that eating half an ounce of saffron brings about death from laughter and joyful eating"). Taken in excess, saffron may be deadly, but the emphasis in this treatise is on its joyful qualities. Indeed, it provokes laughter. In offering his recipe for *fouaces* to Pichrochole and his men, Grangousier is trying not only to avert a war but also to correct the humoral imbalance that is the source of his enemy's ire. While the warm and moist qualities of the saffron compensate for Pichrochole's excess of cold and dry black bile, the joy-inducing qualities of the spice counteract his bellicose nature.

Perhaps in response to the positive élan and exuberance of food and cuisine in the first two books, the tenor of the *Tiers livre* (1546) and the *Quart livre* (1548, 1552) tends more toward the failure of knowledge and communication. The joyful overabundance of culinary images in the first two books engenders a *crise de foie* ("indigestion") that in the last two books might be more aptly expressed as a *crise de foi* ("crisis of faith").

The *Tiers livre* enacts the failure of communication and knowledge, figured in Panurge's inability to decide whether to marry. This failure is reproduced in one of the notable meals of the book. At the beginning of a series of chapters (29–36), Pantagruel has assembled a number of scholars at a dinner to aid Panurge in his quest for understanding marriage. Among these scholars are a theologian (Hippothadée), a doctor (Rondibilis), a lawyer (Bridoye), and a philosopher (Trouillogan). The discussion over food is marked by failure on the philosophical level, expressed as indigestion on the alimentary level.

Jeanneret shows to what extent Panurge's philosophical banquet is a failure. It is a parody of the conviviality found in models such as Plato's *Symposium*. One of the guests at dinner (Bridoye) does not show up; the discussion fails to produce a consensus; the proposed topic of discussion eventually leads to insults ("Parler" 276). Throughout the table talk, there are brief references to the food being consumed, but these references are more to digestive aids than to the dishes themselves.[3]

During the second course, Panuge listens to the advice of Hippothadée. Unsatisfied with the answer, Panurge offers him some digestive foods:

> Mangez ce taillon de massepain. Il vous aydera à faire digestion, puys boirez une couppe de Hippocras clairet: il est salubre et stomachal. (698)
>
> Eat this piece of marzipan; it will help you with your digestion. Then drink a cup of red hippocras: it is healthy and good for the stomach. (373)

If at this point in the discussion, the diners have passed from the second course to dessert, the reference to marzipan seems logical, since sweets and pastries were often served at the end of the meal. But the "red hippocras" gives pause as to its place in the meal. Hippocras made with white wine was generally considered an aperitif, while that made with red wine was most often served as a digestif (Sainéan, *Histoire* 439). Therefore Panurge is offering a digestif just after the second course instead of at the end of the banquet. In any event, the reference to sweet foods implies the presence of sugar, which was thought to cure a number of digestive ills. Panurge thus seems to suggest that Hippothadée's education has not yet been fully assimilated or digested. A few sweets are needed after his lengthy and unhelpful discourse on marriage.

The use of digestive foods reappears during the course of Panurge's consultation with the doctor, Rondibilis. In chapter 31, Rondibilis enumerates remedies one can use to curb carnal desire. Among them are excess consumption of wine, various drugs and plants, hard physical labor, fervent study, and—paradoxically—having copious sex. Since Panurge is endowed with a fair amount of sexual desire, Rondibilis advises him to marry. Panurge greets this solution with enthusiasm. In the following chapter, however, the specter of cuckoldry is evoked by Panurge as a threat to the salubrious view of marriage. Rondibilis provides yet another lengthy discourse, this time on the inconstancy of women and the eternal threat of cuckoldry. Having endured this lecture and expecting yet another, Panurge interrupts with another significant offering of food from the banquet table:

> Mangez un peu de ce pasté de Coins ilz ferment proprement l'orifice du ventricule, à cause de quelque stypticité joyeuse qui est en eulx, et aydent à la concoction premiere. Mais quoy? Je parle Latin davant les clercs. . . . Voulez vous encores un traict de Hippocras blanc? Ne ayez paour de l'Esquinance, non. Il n'y a dedans ne Squinanthi, ne Zinzembre, ne graine de Paradis. Il n'y a que la belle cinamome triée et le beau sucre fin, avecques le bon vin blanc du cru de la Deviniere, en la plante du grand Cormier, au dessus du Noyer groslier. (710)

> Eat a little of this quince cheese: quinces are good for closing the orifice of the ventricle on account of some astringent that is in them; and they are helpful in the initial digestion too. But come! I'm speaking Latin before clerks! . . . Would you like another draught of white hippocras? Don't be afraid of the quinsy, no. There's no squinancy in it, or ginger, or cardamom-seed. There's nothing but choice sifted cinnamon and the best refined sugar, with good white wine from the vintage of La Devinière, grown in the vineyard with the great sorb-apple above the rooky walnut tree. (379)

This rich passage abounds in references, both explicit and implicit, to foods renowned for their digestive qualities. Panurge himself explains the medical qualities of the quince as something that in effect stops up the stomach, thereby preventing noxious vapors from rising to the diner's head. The references to sorb apple and walnuts regarding the provenance of the wine also reflect foods thought to aid digestion at the end of a meal.[4]

By offering these items to Rondibilis, Panurge is attempting, on one level, to ensure the doctor's efficient digestion of the meal. Given the length of Rondibilis's speech, a veritable diarrhea of the mouth, Panurge may wish to stop up something else. Rondibilis's discourse on cuckoldry is not to Panurge's taste, hence this culinary solution to the doctor's discursive malady. The reference to hippocras is problematic. Panurge specifically offers white hippocras, although the other foods are expressly to be used at the end of a meal, where red hippocras would be the traditional accompaniment. He has inverted the proper ordering of the banquet by serving an aperitif as a digestif. The failure of the four guests to assuage his concerns about marriage is thus mirrored in the inverted banquet that he serves to them.

Moving from *fouace* to hippocras, we can see that Rabelaisian food references are complex. Rabelais does not simply allude to food; he invests himself in culinary discourses as a privileged space from which to draw both linguistic and literary inspiration. In addition to providing fodder for satire, parody, carnival, and Renaissance humanism, food serves as a powerful locus for the celebration of the culinary, linguistic, and cultural inventiveness of Renaissance France. A greater understanding of Rabelais's culinary realm, the world in Pantagruel's mouth, will not only make his texts easier to swallow, both for beginning and advanced students, but further aid students in savoring and digesting them as Rabelais and his contemporaries would have done.

NOTES

[1] See in particular Flandrin and Montanari; Hyman and Hyman, "Imprimer," "Livres de cuisine et le commerce," and "Livres de cuisine imprimés." The inspiration for this essay comes from my thesis work, in which I attempt to read Rabelais through the prism of contemporary culinary discourses.

[2] For a cogent summary of humoral physiology in early modern Europe, see Albala.

[3] Bernd Renner has also made productive use of the culinary reference in this episode by way of his work on satire and farce (*Difficile* and "From the 'Bien Yvres'").

[4] Nuts of all kinds, as well as hard cheeses, were thought to provide a plug at the top of the stomach so that unhealthy humors produced by digestion would not rise to the person's head. Regarding the sorb apple, Jean Bruyérin-Champier, in his 1560 *De re cibaria*, affirms that this fruit has constipating qualities similar to those of quinces. He adds a personal note that a large quantity of raw sorb apples saved him, in his youth, from a near-fatal attack of dysentery (*Alimentation* 365–66 [bk. 11, ch. 22]).

Rabelais's Giants

Walter Stephens

Rabelais and giants go together, even for people who have never read his work. The names Gargantua and Pantagruel are by now shorthand for exaggeration and outsized appetites. However, ideas about giants in early modern culture and Rabelais's treatment of giants were both far richer than modern readers are likely to suspect, involving important questions of history, politics, and interpretation of the Bible.

Clearly, some resonances of giants are timeless. Giants symbolize excess and are intimidating in all cultures. The giant represents the other in many guises: the foreigner seen as actual or potential enemy, the natural world of vast heights, depths, and extents threatening to engulf and annihilate the individual or an entire society (Stewart 70–103; Stephens, *Giants* 1–97). The giant can also embody the menace of our own excessive appetites, even a dangerously egoistic nostalgia for a state of undifferentiated being, "the abandoned pleasures of the presocial" (Cohen xv). As symbol of both self and other, Rabelais's giants will appeal to undergraduates' affection for story and very likely stimulate positive childhood recollections of fairy tales and animated cartoons. "Jack and the Beanstalk" will rank high among such memories.

Certainly the *Grandes chroniques* and other popular tales of Gargantua, to which Rabelais alludes frequently from the very first lines of *Pantagruel* (300–01; 167), are amenable to the kind of discussion that begins from students' previous experiences with narratives of giants, as are Rabelais's portrayals of his protagonists' childhood exploits in chapters 11–15 of *Gargantua* and chapter 4 of *Pantagruel*. The giant is an appropriate symbol for the hyperbole that marks Rabelaisian style: enormous lists, interminable strings of adjectives, references to inconceivable numbers and quantities—the 17,913 cows required to produce the young Gargantua's milk (82–83; 53) or the 9,876,543,210 colonists transported into Dipsodia by the triumphant Pantagruel (532–33; 289). Yet it will be important for students, particularly for undergraduates, that they not see the subject of giants as somehow foreign to or discordant with Rabelais's enthusiasm for the world of learning. Giants in 1532 were neither children's entertainment nor a timeless symbol of polarities in human psychology; they were the protagonists of learned discourse in several related fields, in all of which Rabelais was conversant.

Students should also be made aware that although the analogical mode of the gigantic (Stewart 74) informs much of Rabelais's style and although his narratives mention a number of giants, there is no uniform representation of giants in his work. In the first place, as Donald Frame noted, Rabelais's protagonists are not consistently or reliably gigantic (*François Rabelais* 144–47). After *Gargantua*, references to their enormous stature and appetites recur only at scattered moments. Second, Rabelaisian giants demonstrate a range of character traits. Grandgousier, Gargantua, and Pantagruel are pious, ethical, and learned to varying (and variable) degrees, but Loup-Garou ("Werewolf") and his horde are uniformly and defiantly evil. To the extent that a middle ground of giants' behavior exists, it seems limited to the grotesque, as in the case of Bringuenarilles ("Slitnose"), the swallower of windmills and cooking vessels (916–21; 487–90), or the monstrous Caresmeprenant ("King Lent" [964–81; 512–20]).

With the exception of these two examples, the anthropology of Rabelais's giants does not follow folklore and medieval romance. Unlike Rabelaisian giants, those in older traditions are usually loners who "in their anonymous singularity always seem to be the last of their race" (Stewart 74). In folkloric tales, hagiography, and medieval romance, such solitary figures are defeated and occasionally converted (e.g., Saint Christopher in the *Golden Legend* [Stephens, *Giants* 43–50], Pulci's Morgante) by smaller, smarter heroes representing organized cultures or triumphant religions. Rabelaisian giants are not monstrous singletons or genetic freaks but constitute distinct races of hominids, capable of reproduction and even societal organization. In this respect, they resemble giants in Greco-Roman and biblical literature, such as the Cyclopes (*Odyssey*, bk. 9) or the Anakim (Num. 13). Rabelais's protagonists surpass even these figures by having a distinct and extensive recorded genealogy, as if they are not giants but the epic heroes or Old Testament patriarchs who overcame giants. In fact, the lineage of Grandgousier represents civilization and eventually high culture.

Since literary scholars first turned serious attention to Rabelais in the eighteenth century, they have sought sources and analogues for all aspects of his tales, including the giants. His most obvious inspiration came from the series of chapbooks known as the *Chroniques gargantuines* ("Gargantuan Chronicles"), published in the same years as *Pantagruel* and *Gargantua*, between 1532 and 1535 (Desrosiers-Bonin; Huchon, *Œuvres* 153–207, 1171–210). In these grotesque comic tales, which Rabelais mentions explicitly, the possibly folkloric figure of Gargantua performs horrific feats against evildoers, including other giants, in the service of King Arthur. Aside from the *Chroniques*, the grotesque comic romances of the Italian authors Luigi Pulci (*Morgante* [1478]) and Teofilo Folengo (*Baldus* [1521]) have long been seen as sources of Rabelais's inspiration. Rabelais mentions the two works and their personages in *Pantagruel* and *Gargantua* and appears to model aspects of his narratives on them: Panurge resembles Pulci's half-giant trickster Margutte (cantos 18–19), while the band-of-brothers retainers of both Pantagruel and Gargantua resemble those of Folengo's hero Baldus. During the early nineteenth century, at about the same time that copies of the "Gargantuan Chronicles" were first rediscovered and published (Huchon, *Œuvres* 1174), French antiquarians encountered illiterate peasants who told tales of a giant named Gargantua to explain the topography of their countryside. The antiquarians hypothesized that both the "Gargantuan Chronicles" and Rabelais took their inspiration from ancient Celtic folklore that possibly pre-dated the Roman conquest of Gaul. In the same period, antiquarians and scholars of folklore uncovered documentary evidence that some late medieval towns had enormous anthropomorphic puppets in their pageantry—for example, Antwerp's Antigonus. Both kinds of evidence were interpreted to argue that the medieval, folkloric figure of the giant was a benign symbol of the people who celebrated him (Stephens, *Giants* 9–23).

With the translation of Mikhail Bakhtin's *Rabelais and His World* into French and English in the 1960s, a new explanation gained currency, according to which Rabelais's giants, those of the "Gargantuan Chronicles," and the ancient and medieval figures discovered by folklorists all symbolized the indomitable vitality and humor of the common people in their struggle against the oppression of their masters, particularly the medieval church. The giant became for Bakhtin the symbol of a carnivalesque culture of the common people, which deployed grotesque bodily imagery in a profane, often obscene, rebellion against the political, theological, and moral suffocation of official society and mocked the ultimate reality of death with fearless humor (Bakhtin, *Rabelais*; Berrong; Stephens, *Giants* 23–52). Each of these totalizing interpretations of Rabelais's giants is problematic: the folkloric models, because of their scanty documentation and circular reasoning; Bahktin's interpretation, because, despite its fascinating and critically useful categories of the carnivalesque and the grotesque body, it relies on faulty historical assumptions. Both approaches accept without proof that Rabelais's tales and the "Gargantuan Chronicles" demonstrate the existence of a prehistoric folklore; both use that hypothetical tradition to interpret Rabelais, while ignoring or minimizing his deep involvement with the world of scholarship and elite culture.

The giants were in fact a long-standing preoccupation of scholarship. Whereas most twenty-first-century readers associate giants with children's fairy tales and cartoons, educated Christians of Rabelais's time had to consider them historical figures, since their existence was asserted in several books of the Old Testament, most famously in Genesis, which states that "giants were upon the earth in those days"—that is, before Noah's flood (6.4 [Douai-Rheims vers.]). The view of biblical giants as historical was not thoroughly disproved until the twentieth century. Revisions made to the article "Giant" in the 1911 *Encyclopaedia Britannica* warned readers that scientists had now proved that giants, understood as "special races distinct from mankind" or "tribes of altogether superhuman stature" had never existed (Stephens, *Giants* 2). Yet their appearance in the Bible did not exempt the giants from critical scrutiny, even before Rabelais's time. Ancient Jewish and Christian commentators, notably Saint Augustine, wondered about these creatures, who were presented as historical yet were so uncanny. The interest long outlived Rabelais: the most exhaustive treatises on biblical giants were written from the late sixteenth to the early eighteenth century (92–97).

There was a clear need for such scrutiny, since the Old Testament accounts of the giants, based on extremely ancient legends, raised a number of interpretive dilemmas. Weirdly, Genesis 6.4 implies that the giants were born from sexual intercourse between angels and women, "after the sons of God went in to the daughters of men, and they brought forth children." However, the "sons of God" being angels entailed two disturbing conclusions: first, that angels sinned and fell twice, once before the fall of Adam and Eve and long afterward, a suggestion that contradicted orthodox angelology; second, that giants were an unnatural hybrid race. This was an even more peculiar idea, since orthodox Christian angelology also denied that angels had bodies and the capacity to reproduce (Stephens, *Demon Lovers* 58–73).

Genesis 6.4 raised another disquieting problem, for its placement in the text suggested that the Flood was caused partially or even primarily by the sins of the giants and not only by the depravity of ordinary human beings. Indeed, the Pentateuch as a whole implied that the giants, both before and after the Flood, were unremittingly, perhaps even genetically, evil. That being so, one of God's crucial purposes for sending the Flood must have been the eradication of the giants. Yet when Moses sent scouts into the land of Canaan, long centuries after the Flood, they returned in terror, describing Canaanites so huge that the scouts felt like grasshoppers in comparison (Num. 13.34). How could the giants have repopulated so thoroughly if God intended the Flood to destroy them? After all, Genesis declared that only Noah and his family survived (7.12, 7.23). Moreover, one of Moses's principal opponents in the struggle for the Promised Land was Og, King of Bashan, who was even more confusingly described as one who "remained of the race of the giants" (Deut. 3.11). Later still, the future King David's opponent Goliath of Gath (1 Sam. 17.4), while not called a giant (e.g., Hebrew *Anakim* and *Rephaim*, Latin *gigantes*) was frighteningly huge.

These problems belonged to an even larger complex of mysteries, contradictions, and conundrums about the literal truth of the Bible's account of the earliest history, many of which concerned the Flood story (Allen). Where did the water come from that covered the highest mountains? Where did it go afterward? How large, exactly, was the ark? How many species did it embark, how could it store all their food, how could eight people manage the appalling sanitary challenges presented by the enormous menagerie? Saint Augustine attempted to resolve some of these problems but warned Christians not to waste their energy seeking detailed and precise answers. Between the fourteenth and the late seventeenth century, commentators progressively ignored Augustine's advice, raising problems of literal interpretation that were further complicated by increasing preoccupation with what we would now call scientific accuracy. Between 1665 and 1679, the Jesuit polymath Athanasius Kircher dedicated hundreds of huge folio pages to intricate scientific defenses of the Bible's accuracy on topics such as giants, Noah's ark, and the Tower of Babel (Allen 182–91; Godwin; Rowland; Findlen).

Thus the giants were a problem of interpretation for hundreds of years before and after Rabelais's time. Along with the rest of the Flood story, they constituted the single largest obstacle to acceptance of the Bible's historical accuracy. So was Rabelais's treatment of the giants, their genealogy, and their survival of the Flood a deliberate and irreverent parody of the Bible? Probably not (Duval, *Design of Rabelais's* Pantagruel 29–33). Rabelais's giants are certainly literary descendants of the biblical ones, yet that inheritance is not direct or uncomplicated, since it was mediated by a newer body of giant literature. Rabelais's giants recall quite precisely the stars of a narrative genre older than the "Gargantuan Chronicles," which emerged at the turn of the sixteenth century and went on to dominate a whole sector of historical writing for more than a hundred years. The consolidation of powerful nation-states and their bitter territorial rivalries in the time of Charles VIII, Louis XII, and Francis I inspired nationalistic strains of historiography, which defended rulers' claims to geographic territory and asserted the cultural superiority of their peoples, basing both kinds of pretensions on the evidence of newly discovered genealogies and chronicles. The royal ancestors described by these documents were supposed to be a race of giants who survived Noah's flood (Gen. 5–11). One can already see the similarity to Rabelais's assertions in the opening chapters of both *Pantagruel* and *Gargantua*—to wit, that his giants have "[connaissance certaine de leur] généalogie depuis l'arche de Noé jusqu'à l'âge présent!" (57; "certain knowledge of [their] genealogy, from Noah's Ark to the Present Age" [41]), with the implication that, if all rulers were required to produce such documentation, the world would be a better place. Rabelais was joking; these texts were not.

The giants of this patriotic historiography resembled those of Rabelais in another important way. Unlike the giants of the Old Testament, Greco-Roman mythology, and folklore, those described in the rediscovered genealogies were both profoundly good and deeply civilized. In fact, they had made the fundamental discoveries on which human culture and true religion depended. Noah himself was the first good giant. The ancient giants he sired after the Flood were the famous heroes of pagan antiquity, including Hercules, Isis, and Osiris. The good giants of this golden age prevailed for a long time after Noah, until races of evil giants emerged and plunged the world back into strife.

Modern readers are apt to ask themselves how anyone in Rabelais's time—the age of humanistic, philological inquiry by Erasmus, Guillaume Budé, and Rabelais himself—could have given serious consideration to such balderdash. Indeed, that is just Rabelais's point, but from an angle slightly different from ours: Rabelais understood how these new, pseudohistorical giant ancestors sprang from centuries of learned commentary on the Pentateuch. In view of the biblical giants' reputation for savagery and destructiveness, it was completely inappropriate that secular writers with pretensions to historiographic accuracy should invoke the biblical giants to exalt their patrons and their national history. The nationalistic writers were in fact attempting to solve the historical and theological problems raised by the giants; they hoped thereby to provide a firm *biblical* basis for the exaltation of their leaders' nobility and rights. What could be better propaganda for political legitimacy than a family pedigree and a national history vouchsafed by the Holy Bible? It was just this tangle of contradictory biblical evidence and quixotic motivations that made the nationalistic attempt to exploit the giants so appealing to the fancy of a Rabelais.

Although there were medieval precedents for fanciful nationalistic propaganda, such as Geoffrey of Monmouth's *History of the Kings of England* (1136), the watershed document, a collection of seventeen treatises, was published in 1498 by a retainer of Pope Alexander VI. Giovanni Nanni, or, as he styled himself, Annius of Viterbo (1432–1502), included in this remarkable miscellany a set of eleven newly discovered texts by renowned ancient authors, including a Babylonian, an Egyptian, a Persian, a Jew, and several Greeks and Romans, along with his own voluminous commentaries on them. Annius had forged all but one of the soi-disant ancient texts in his *Antiquities* (see Stephens, *Giants* 111–17, 339–43), relying on descriptions of lost works and occasional brief quotations preserved by authoritative ancient writers such as Pliny the Elder, Diodorus of Sicily, and Flavius Josephus.

Annius's dense and scholarly tome was built of short, terse texts surrounded by commentaries containing mountains of cross-references to practically every surviving ancient text his contemporaries esteemed. The format guided—indeed, almost forced—the reader to construct a coherent narrative by collating Annius's texts and commentaries with the Greek and Roman classics and the Bible. A careful, patient reader could assemble a unified history of world events, stretching from the antediluvian giants down to 1498, with special attention to the period between Noah and Alexander the Great. And what a strange tale it was: after the Flood, Noah, his sons, and their wives colonized Armenia and, so to speak, multiplied like rabbits. Thus, exactly one hundred years after the Flood, Noah and his clan sailed around the Mediterranean leaving new colonies everywhere they landed. The oldest and most illustrious colony was in Latium, stretching between Rome and—of course—Annius's own hometown of Viterbo. Some of Noah's more famous giant descendants, such as Hercules, were falsely claimed by the ancient Greeks as their own. Noah was particularly fond of his Etruscan offspring, settling on the Janiculum, naming it after himself (his other name was Janus), and founding a proto-Roman priesthood that foreshadowed the papacy. Yet Noah loved his other European children, even though he founded their civilizations somewhat later than the Etruscans'. Annius duly provided illustrious Noachian ancestors for the Gauls, the Teutons, and the Iberians, even substituting a detailed genealogy of Ferdinand and Isabella for his own account of Etruscan chronology, after their papal ambassador paid to publish his *Antiquities* (Stephens, *Giants* 98–138).

Scholars all around Europe immediately smelled a rat, and several denounced the collection as a fraud, scoffing at its audacious and naive rewriting of history. But it was immensely popular among the Latin-educated retainers of European princes, who adopted it as a basis for cultural and political propaganda. By the 1560s it was so infamous that one scholar felt obliged to refute its foundational document, the "Chaldaean History of Berosus," point by point in a substantial monograph, while others expressed dismay at its widespread influence among writers who should know better—and presumably did (Stephens, "When Pope Noah").

Annius's *Antiquities* were embraced most enthusiastically in France: of nineteen known editions by 1612, five were published in Paris by 1515. Such acceptance might seem paradoxical in view of the work's Italian, "Etruscan" bias and its genealogy of the Spanish monarchs. Yet because of their pseudoscholarly text and commentary format, the *Antiquities* were susceptible to having their distortion of history misrepresented in turn by uncooperative interpreters. This inherent vulnerability was enhanced by the three earliest Paris editions, which altogether omitted Annius's commentaries and printed only the brief rediscovered histories. These cut-down editions virtually erased Annius's Etruscans, since Annius performed his strongest cultural propaganda in his commentaries, and they implied a far more positive mythology of Celtic and Gallic France than he had given.

Far worse sabotage of the *Antiquities* was performed by Jean Lemaire de Belges, the *grand rhétoriqueur* poet, in his *Illustrations de Gaule et singularités de Troie* ("Illustrious History of Gaul and Singular Events Relating to Troy"), published between 1511 and 1513. Writing in French but adopting Annius's pose as scholarly commentator, Lemaire completely reforged the *Antiquities* by concealing their publication history, quoting Annius's commentaries only rarely, and treating them as unpublished manuscripts he had personally discovered. Lemaire's lively vernacular French eclipsed Annius's Latin labyrinth, making the reforged pseudohistories available to ladies and merchants, as it elegantly grafted the familiar myth of the Trojan refugee Francus's foundation of France (*Les singularités de Troie*) into the labored *Illustrations de Gaule*. The combination of myth and history, though far from seamless, dressed pro-French cultural propaganda in good prose storytelling, and so Lemaire's book was reprinted frequently until 1549. Moreover, Lemaire inspired imitators, who wrote prolifically until the 1620s, defending French claims to cultural and political hegemony (Stephens, *Giants* 139–84, 344–46).

The relevance of this literature will be clear to readers familiar with Rabelais's treatment of his protagonists in *Pantagruel* and the early chapters of *Gargantua.* These introductory passages present the Rabelaisian narrator, Alcofribas Nasier, as a learned but disorganized scholar, biased and patriotic, compiling a pseudohistorical encomium aimed at promoting his patron's hegemonic claims. Rabelais appears to have asked himself what joyful narrative mayhem could be created by crossing the *Illustrations de Gaule* with the "Gargantuan Chronicles" or, rather, by rewriting and continuing the chronicles as if he were Jean Lemaire, or even Annius (Rabelais was likely familiar with the *Antiquities*, at least at second hand, through Lemaire's quotations and through scholarly gossip). Rabelais's amusement at Lemaire's achievement is intimated in chapter 30 of *Pantagruel,* where the tutor Epistemon recalls seeing "Maître Jean Lemaire qui contrefaisait le pape . . . et il faisait baiser ses pieds à tous le pauvres rois et papes de ce monde" (490–91; "Master John Lemaire impersonating the Pope" with the jesters of Louis XII and Francis I as his cardinals "and making all the poor popes and kings of the underworld kiss his feet" [269]). While this chapter also evokes the antipapal pamphlets of Lemaire, its panoramic rewriting of history accords well with the pseudohistorical *Illustrations de Gaule.*

The combination of gigantology and the narratorial pose as tendentious, addled, scholarly rewriter of history provides some of the richest moments in the novels. Like Annius and Lemaire, Alcofribas builds "ces contes si véridiques" (497; "this most authentic tale" [273]) around a genealogy of the giants (see Stephens, *Giants*, plate 13), which is simultaneously a genealogy of his patron. (The idea may have been partly inspired by the earliest Gargantuan chronicle, which promised a genealogy of Gargantua but failed to deliver it.) At the same time, Pantagruel's pedigree as giant overlaps with the genealogy of Christ, providing a playfully serious complement (*serio ludens*) to the historiographic tomfoolery: recounting the giant's genealogy inaugurates an evangelical "redemptive design" in which the giant serves as a type or avatar of the Savior (Duval, *Design of Rabelais's* Pantagruel 14–40). Taking further cues from Annius's and Lemaire's naive rewritings of biblical history, Alcofribas provides new explanations for the origin of the giants, their connection to wine (like that of Noah-Janus), and their survival of the Flood (Rabelais's rewriting of rabbinical commentaries on Og is as audacious as Annius's claim that Noah was a giant, which it counters). Rabelais's hyperbole slyly alludes to the vexed question of discrepancies between Matthew's and Luke's versions of Christ's genealogy, which Annius claimed to have solved in his *Antiquities* (Stephens, *Giants* 127–38, 162–71). Yet Pantagruel's genealogy is not an irreverent parody of the Bible (Duval, *Design of Rabelais's* Pantagruel 29–33); rather it evokes the biblical pretensions of the pseudohistorians, who provided Old Testament genealogies of Pope Alexander VI and Cesare Borgia (as Annius did) or Charlemagne (as Lemaire did).

The radical novelty of Rabelais's giants, even with respect to the pseudohistorians, is revealed by Thaumaste's reactions on first meeting Pantagruel: "Thaumaste tressaillit de peur, le voyant si grand et si gros" ("Thaumaste quite started with fear when he saw how tall and stout Pantagruel was"). But on second thought the English scholar interpreted the giant's stature allegorically: "Il est bien vrai, comme le dit Platon, prince des philosophes, que si l'image de la science et de la sagesse était corporelle et rendue visible aux yeux des hommes, elle exciterait l'admiration de tout le monde" (415; "How true is the saying of Plato, Prince of Philosophers, that if the image of science and learning were corporal and visible to the eyes of men, it would arouse admiration from the whole world" [230]). Thaumaste's double take expresses the essence of Rabelais's giants: their inheritance from the evil monsters of pagan antiquity and folklore, the depraved hominids of the Old Testament, the redefined giants of the pseudohistorians, and the playful grotesques of the "Gargantuan Chronicles," and their evolution into humanistic incarnations of magnanimity, rectitude, wisdom, learning, and evangelical piety. Much of this process was inductive, as Rabelais uncovered the logic of his own fictional creatures and their world. Although they began life as a kind of compendium or mishmash of all the giant lore known to Rabelais's time, the compound was unstable and began falling apart after about chapter 10 of *Gargantua.* Thereafter, the treatment of themes relating to giants loses its scholarly pretensions and thereby ceases to be a source of parodic mischief. Indeed, after the climactic battle of *Gargantua,* chapter 49, Rabelais's treatment of his protagonists *as* giants all but disappears, except for occasional brief glimpses, such as Pantagruel's killing of the whale in *The Fourth Book* (984–89; 521–24). Yet even in such a brief reprise, the close thematic connection among giants, exaggerated erudition, and exaltation of the narrator's patron is maintained, despite the loss of the pretense of political urgency that animated the exordiums of both *Pantagruel* and *Gargantua*.

If Rabelais and good giants have become closely associated, cultural history also had a hand in the process. After Lemaire, the redefined, good giant race of pseudohistory had almost no career and certainly was never taken seriously outside that arena. Instead, the nature of biblical giants, their origin, their survival of the Flood, and the evidence of their existence to be gleaned from fossils (the giant bones of mastodons, etc.) preoccupied scholars, because they continued to stimulate questions about the historicity of the Bible and its relevance to the emerging rationalistic picture of the world. The last great attempt to understand the giants historically in relation to both the Bible and pagan antiquity may have been in Giambattista Vico's *New Science* (1744). Like Rabelais and the biblical tradition, Vico portrayed giants originating from the depravity of normal-sized human beings and degenerating into savagery; but he differed by suggesting that, as the giants slowly rediscovered through natural means the religious principles that God had revealed to their earliest ancestors, their stature shrank accordingly (112–15). Thus Vico conclusively redefined virtue and normality through the allegory of everyday human stature. Meanwhile, the process of scientific inquiry gradually worked its way toward early-twentieth-century demonstrations that giants were physically impossible, except as relatively infrequent endocrinological aberrations.

An interesting way of beginning student discussion might be simply to ask students whether they consider giants as historical or mythical. They might be asked what they think of advertisements for books and postings on the Internet that claim the giants of Genesis 6.4 built the pyramids, for instance (have students search for "biblical giants"). To understand the process that led from the Bible to Rabelais, students might also be encouraged—with appropriate precautions—to explore giants in popular Internet sources such as *Wikipedia*. To students wishing to investigate firsthand the learned context of Rabelais's giants, an instructor might suggest the following texts: Genesis, chapters 5–11; Ovid, *The Metamorphoses,* book 1; Saint Augustine, *The City of God,* book 15, chapter 20, to book 16, chapter 11; Annius and Lemaire (texts in Stephens, *Giants* 111–27, 156–60); the eighteenth-century biblical commentator Augustin Calmet (in Stephens, *Giants* 92–97); Vico, *New Science* (112–15); and the article "Giant" in the 1911 *Encyclopaedia Britannica.*

Rabelais and Feminism

Elisabeth Hodges

To pair Rabelais with feminism may at first glance seem an impossible task. It is far easier for teachers of early modern texts to retreat into a text's pleasure rather than face students' and their own reactions to the inherent misogyny of outrageous episodes like Panurge's proposal to rebuild the walls of Paris by replacing stones with women's genitalia. Yet to consider the place of women in art, society, and literature and how cultural products represent women prompts us to ask questions about fundamental relations among sex, discourses of power, fiction, and the human experience. The continued relevance of this theoretical nexus is visible in the passionate response to a recent polemic unleashed by the publication of Mireille Huchon's *Louise Labé: Une créature de papier* ("A Paper Creation"), in which the argument is made that Louise Labé, one of the greatest female poets of the French Renaissance, was little more than a literary confection cooked up by a group of male poets playing a who's who by using a fictional feminine pseudonym.[1] To be sure, polemics like the one surrounding Huchon's excision of Labé from literary history have revived interest in the effects of the female subject's erasure from literary history. The critical dismay at seeing perhaps the greatest poet to write about erotic desire from the perspective of an explicitly articulated female subject position leave the stage of literary history, I believe, testifies more to our own attachment to the subject—and to all that is bound up in this weighty signifier: identity, gender, the specificity of voice, artistic genius, and the location or site of that genius. This essay attempts to trace the significance of another such erasure—namely, the paradoxical representation of women in Rabelais. Generally speaking, it is easy to associate works like *Pantagruel* with the absence of female subjects.

Like the hero's own birth at the cost of his mother's life, the Rabelaisian world largely represents the human in terms of an unnatural lineage constituted through the male line and through a reversal whereby the son's text of 1532, *Pantagruel*, produces the story of the hero's father, *Gargantua* (1534).[2] To be sure, these are texts about a family of giants that propose images of humanity modeled on an outrageous scale that is literally gargantuan, larger than life. Just as the story of the hero's childhood and adventures are portrayed as excessive, so are the contours of the fictional worlds in which the story takes place unnatural. The texts that make up the Pantagruel series feature an imaginary world in which mothers die as sons are born and female characters find themselves swiftly expedited to other realms, such as that of death. Paradoxically, the women who appear in Rabelais's texts are so radically othered, either through their difference or their absence, that their brief moments of textual presence appear to depend almost entirely on an irredeemable emptiness, which marks the representation of life as contingent on maternal sacrifice. Rabelais thus marks the genesis of his literary oeuvre with an originary and artificial void, an absence rarely if ever referred to in successive volumes. If figured, it only disappears into the texture of Panurge's anxiety about being cuckolded.

Masculine genealogy has been said to function as the centralizing force of fictional genesis in Rabelais's work, as many scholars have remarked (e.g., Freccero, *Father Figures*; Rigolot, "Rabelais").[3] The absence of female characters in the giant's tale through whom natural generation might take place produces an effect that is worth pause and close study. While women fall outside the immediate range of what one might understand as Rabelais's diegetic world, they occupy places located in the extradiegetic contours of the fictional landscape in what Foucault referred to as heterotopias. By *heterotopia* I mean spaces that, although linked to the disposition of places in the real world, nonetheless maintain a distinct difference from the real. In Rabelais's topography, women are to be found in these contingencies, in the space of death or of speculation (the Sybilline prophecy in the *Tiers livre*), or utopic nonspaces (the Abbey of Thélème at the end of *Gargantua*). Like the reversed genealogy when the narrator, Alcofribas, turns from the son's tale to the father's, the spatial contours of Rabelais's fiction follow a similarly elliptical or inverted logic, juxtaposing incompatible links between real and imagined places.[4] One might characterize the representation of women in Rabelais as largely measured in terms of their lack, difference, and deferral, but the broader fictional enterprise of his work is organized along the lines of a series of elliptical narratives that seamlessly intermingle what would otherwise be entirely incompatible subjects, bringing together, in a unique potpourri, evangelism with obscenity and popular traditions like farce with classical epic (Defaux, *Marot*; Rigolot, *Langages*).

If we accept that women's place in Rabelais is largely elsewhere, marked or defined as a figure of lack or of difference, feminism and psychoanalysis have taught us to read such absence as productive despite what at first appears as an inescapable violence done to the representation of women, to the female body, and to the female subject (Cixous, "Rire"; Irigaray, *Ce sexe*). I'm not advocating blithely adding these texts to a course on Rabelais with little or no attention to historical specificity, yet reading these texts attentively alongside early modern fiction in which the representation of women troubles may well help students understand the extent to which representation codes and affects perception. To understand in broad terms the effects of language on the representation of gender provides students with a theoretical optic through which to think about the politics of poetics. Despite what some might consider an anachronistic pairing—namely, to have students read these foundational feminist texts alongside early modern fiction—reading Hélène Cixous and Luce Irigaray gives us an excellent vantage point from which to think through the effects of women's difference and the place of women in literary representations.

To consider how language reveals the traces of social practice enables today's students to ascertain both how women are written in literature and, what is perhaps more significant, how they are written out of it. To be sure, the historical conditions that produce women's difference and their absence from the canons of early modern literary and aesthetic achievement are facts that cannot be disputed, nor can the radical ambivalence with which women were represented (Jones). To examine the conditions that produce these effects provides access to a world that, even though alien in the vastness of its social difference for today's readers, may give them a critical apparatus for investigating similar phenomena in contemporary life and art and to raise awareness of the politics of literary criticism as an important aspect of teaching and learning at a critical distance.

Instead of attempting to square episodes like the idyllic cohabitation of women and men imagined in the Abbey of Thélème with the disturbing violence of Panurge's urban planning in *Pantagruel*, chapter 15, I propose that as we teach Rabelais, we examine closely what is produced from this lack and how students can be brought to think about the productive status of women's absence in early modern fiction. Absence is the obvious site from which to undertake a feminist reading of Rabelais. More problematic, and of particular interest to me, is how to comprehend the vexed presence of women in *Pantagruel*, a question that is more difficult to grapple with than the relative sheltering of women in a space of absence or difference. How might we understand the representation of women in Rabelais if it is only to serve the purpose of eventually excising women from the text into the gravitational pull of difference? How might we account for the violence done to those women who remain in the largely masculine world of the giant prince and his companions?

Pantagruel, chapter 15, is situated between two chapters that position Panurge as the prince's impossible double and most beloved friend, as an excessive and comical counterexample to Pantagruel's superior character, breeding, and education. The narrative of Panurge's escape from the hands of the Turks (ch. 14)—what in essence allows for his eventual encounter with the giant while on the road to Paris—like many other episodes in the text emerges as a product of narrative strategies of deferral that continually truncate an erratic textual logic underpinning the hero's encounters with the partially roasted Panurge and the explanation of how their paths came to cross. While the epic narrative is generally mobilized by a series of peripatetic *errances* through which the young prince learns from the book of the world while traveling through it, the Paris episodes (chs. 7–24) provide us with extended accounts of his experiences vis-à-vis education, courtship, and civility in a space that anchors the travelers to the limits of the city. The Renaissance city was understood as the site of a tripartite identity: as *urbs*, *civitas*, and *polis*, as pointing simultaneously to architectural space, to the notion of community in which social relations take place, and to the space of politics (Hodges). This coalescence of architecture, community, and politics functioned symbolically to make the city the seat of a nascent national consciousness at a time when cities like Paris and Lyon had nearly doubled in population, thus offering a location for the development of a new cosmopolitan identity.

More somber forms of identity were often linked to the cosmopolitanism commonly associated with the Renaissance city, but *Pantagruel*, chapter 15, veers radically away from a notion of presence predicated on a sense of national belonging. While the letter from Gargantua to his son (ch. 8) laying out the groundwork for a humanist education is among the more serious chapters in this series, the presence of Panurge, the literal embodiment of the text's hermeneutic excess, colors the Paris episodes with play and pleasure. By *pleasure*, I point not to the giant's or to Panurge's anticipated success with the opposite sex but rather to a concomitant form of pleasure, that of narrating the experience of and anxieties surrounding desire. The libidinal desires of the subject, as Lawrence Kritzman has shown, are an essential component of representing the human in Renaissance fiction. The key, I believe, to understanding Panurge's fantasy of the walls in *Pantagruel*, chapter 15, is to consider it less as an indictment against a presence (women's bodies) than as a retreat, into the space of narrative play, from the anxieties bound up with the vagaries of desire.

As the chapter begins, the protagonists walk in the city and reflect on the dilapidated ramparts of Paris:

> A leur retour, Panurge considéroit les murailles de la ville de Paris et en irrision dist à Pantagruel: "Voyez-cy ces belles murailles. O que fortes sont et bien en poinct pour garder les oysons en mue! Par ma barbe, elles sont compétement meschantes pour une telle ville comme ceste-cy, car une vache avecques un pet en abbatroit plus de six brasses." (276)

> On their return, Panurge considered the walls of Paris, and said to Pantagruel in derision: "Oh how strong they are! They're just the thing for keeping goslings in a coop. By my beard, they are poor defences for a city like this. Why a cow could knock down more than twelve foot of them with a single fart." (218)

The image of the city here bears little relation to conventional notions of urban space. Paris, as read through Panurge's discourse, is rendered the equivalent of a chicken coop, so poorly constructed that the walls can barely contain its inhabitants. Panurge denatures the urban space by replacing citizens with goslings and an imaginary enemy with bovine gas. The seamless integration of elements from the natural realm displaced into the built environment playfully puts the human elsewhere. The wall's feeble structure, while a product of human endeavor, is nonetheless subject to another hostile force, namely Panurge's critique of their insufficiency. Yet from the start, the trickster's critique is undermined by the absurd premises it advances. Like the fart from the cow, his words function as a foul assault on urban architecture. Indeed, they appear as a form of counter-discourse to Pantagruel's observation about urban fortification, which considers the example of Spartans whose virtue (understood as *virtutis*, or masculine force, as Hope Glidden notes in her excellent analysis of this chapter) sustains community better than any known material construction (276). By linking more conventional associations of urban semiotics with *civitas*, the abstract qualities that bind people together in a community, Pantagruel, like his off-kilter companion, privileges a concept of the city as quite literally a civic body, a space embodied in flesh and bone. Pantagruel's is based on a classical exemplar; Panurge's, on its comical inversion.

Bodies, like the textual corpus itself, are continually subjected to truncation, interruption, and expansion in Rabelais's fiction. The book's endless seriality and abrupt volumetric expansions, as when the narrator, Alcofribas, enters Pantagruel's gigantic physique, constitute a key quality of the work—namely, its ability to turn in on itself, to broaden perspectives, and to shift radically from place to place. Concerned about the vulnerability of the city's ramparts, Panurge offers what he thinks to be a more efficient (an economically inexpensive) means to reconstruct the walls:

> Je vois que les callibistrys des femmes de ce pays sont à meilleur marché que les pierres. D'iceulx fauldroit bastir les murailles, en les arrengeant par bonne symméterye d'architecture et mettant les plus grans au premiers rancz, et puis, en taluant à doz d'asne, arranger les moyens et finablement les petitz, puis faire une beau petit entrelardement, à poinctes de diamans comme la grosse tour de Bourges, de tant de bracquemars enroiddys qui habitent par les braguettes claustrales. Quel Diable defferoit telles murailles? (277)

> I notice that in this country the thing-o'-my-bobs of the ladies are cheaper than the stone. The walls ought to be built of them, arranged in good architectural symmetry with the biggest in front; and then sloping downwards, like the back of an ass. The middle-sized ones should be arranged next, and the little ones last of all. This done, there must be a fine little interlacing of them, in diamond points, as in the great tower of Bourges, with an equal number of stiff what-d'you-call-'ems, such as dwell in the claustral codpieces. What devil would be able to overthrow walls like that? (219)

This passage shuts down even the most intrepid and eager reader. Its comic absurdity is clear, but how do we square the implications of Panurge's urban planning with a conscientious reading that considers the effects of such a violent proposition on the representation of women? In effect, there are no women here, only dismembered parts, riven from whole bodies, from a totality that would have reminded us of their once human existence. Considered by Panurge to be of such paltry economical value, these abundant parts would serve a far better function if reassembled into essentially another body—namely, a new wall to enclose the city, a space, which both companions infer, equivalent to a literal embodiment of *civitas*. Yet this embodied wall is in fact a space of infinite multiplication, of female genitals symmetrically lodged in Panurge's bawdy encomium to architectural perfection that literally incorporates female difference into an edifice designed in his perverse fantasy to protect and defend the people of Paris.

One could easily make the argument, as many scholars have, that Panurge's obscene proposition points to a long-standing tradition of misogyny in representations of women in literature and art. There are nonetheless other stakes here that are worth pause. It is not only female pudenda enlisted in the would-be urban planner's scheme but male members as well, which Panurge proposes to couple with the other material of his wall to avoid any fissures or gaps. What begins as a fundamental lack, an insufficiency, shifts to a distorted fantasy of what Glidden has elegantly phrased as an "allegorical copulation in a landscape of courtly love and religiosity" (51). To this observation I would add that what may also be discerned is a critique that levels the distinction of virtue as a purely masculine attribute. Sexual difference is eliminated through the coupling of male and female members; their difference disintegrates in an activity that emulates sexual pleasure while also constituting the new embodied Parisian ramparts. Though much of the text's narrative force is predicated on exclusively masculine genealogies, here we see an important fissure in that system. The coupling of male and female parts, while it emulates the act of procreation, nonetheless participates in production, both textual and material in form. The complementary presence of male and female strength bound together symmetrically reveals not only Panurge's consistently outrageous perspective but also a playfully demented fascination with pleasure, heterosexual sex, and the body.

In many ways, the structure proposed by Panurge reflects a more generalized corporeal fragmentation (corps and corpus) present throughout Rabelais's text. Indeed, the uncomfortable coupling of dismembered male and female genitals lasts but a moment, as Panurge's attention shifts to another issue—namely, how to preserve his newfangled walls from the excrement of flies, which is the only perceived weakness in their otherwise impenetrable (and yet entirely penetrable) nature (277). Panurge recounts an interpolated fable in which an earnest lion caring for its wound presses a fox into service to help cleanse and salve what the lion perceives as an old woman's wound (her genitalia). The logic of this narrative shift from the walls of Paris to the animal realm is predicated on the evocative image of the wound, of a breach in the flesh that is not necessarily singular, as Irigaray reminds us, but can be read, like the giant's mouth, as opening onto another world, one characterized by an unfamiliar interiority. The sameness of the lion's and the old woman's wounds and the cat's naive assignment to the fox represents a desire to relate. This projection of one wound on the other and of practices of care that, although clearly intended for an outrageously comic effect (the fox inadvertently stimulates the old woman with his tail while diligently cleaning her wound, causing such a ruckus that she begins to fart), produces another uncomfortable pairing in the text between the animals and the old woman. The old woman, the lion, and the fox literally struggle to fill the terrifying emptiness they discover in her wound. To be sure, this representation of endless interiority speaks to an anxiety about the function of the female body and of bodies in general. Yet one could also say that Panurge's proposition brings together two discrete fantasies that deal with difference. In the case of the walls of Paris, Panurge incorporates the symbolic freight of women and men's sexual difference in a newly engendered image of civic virtue. In the fable, the dissimilarity disappears in the action of care, as a possible way out of the anxiety generated when one is confronted with what the text figures as the bewildering image of sexual difference.

The "walls of Paris" episode, understandably one of the more difficult chapters to teach because of the subject matter and the inherent violence of Panurge's proposition, may be read more broadly as an extended commentary on the relations between space and subjects, self and others, that complicate what is otherwise a textbook case of early modern misogyny. For Rabelais, the subjects in question are mapped on the bodies of giants and err to and from the outer reaches of known and unknown worlds, but the difficulty of becoming a subject remains the same. In becoming a subject, we inevitably measure our difference and sameness to others and look to the internal and external marks in language and on the body that distinguish individuals from one another as a way of ascertaining our discrete sense of self. To confront the ways in which forms of difference (gender, sex, or subjectivity) were understood and represented in fiction provides teachers a powerful opportunity to attune students to the inherent power of words and language.

Much of the work of feminist scholarship in the twentieth century has sensitized us to the issue of women's absence and to their representation as a phenomenon of lack. But women's presence, equally vexed, also provides literary critics with productive terrain. By framing a discussion of Rabelais with the works of feminists like Cixous, Irigaray, and also Judith Butler, we work in and around the language of sexual difference and get our students to think in terms of the ideological freight bound up in signifiers and processes of signification. To consider the how and the effects of representation on textual and sexual economies does more than reveal our attachment to the subject. It also points to a keen desire to imagine and understand the subject as embodied and gendered, as a sexed subject whose sameness or difference from ourselves allows us to begin to define human experience.

NOTES

[1] In addition to Huchon's book, see other responses to this polemic, including Marc Fumaroli's review of Huchon's book in *Le monde des livres*, 11 May 2006, and reactions in the press to both Fumaroli and Huchon, especially by Madeleine Lazard (Huchon's colleague and author of the Labé biography *Louise Labé, lyonnaise*), collected on the Web site of SIEFAR (Société Internationale pour l'Étude des Femmes de l'Ancien Régime).

[2] Carla Freccero, in *Father Figures*, seeks to dismantle the effects of this patriarchal lineage both in Rabelais's work and in literary criticism surrounding it. See also Freccero's "Damning Haughty Dames" and "'Instance'" (on the "haughty dame" episode). For a different yet equally fascinating analysis of the structure of *Pantagruel*, see Duval, *Design of Rabelais's* Pantagruel.

[3] This essay focuses on *Pantagruel*, but there is excellent work on the treatment of women in the *Tiers livre*: Florence Weinberg's "Written on the Leaves" and Cathy Schiffer's "Contextual Misogyny." For more on misogyny and the *querelle des femmes* in Rabelais, see Glidden; Goumarre.

[4] For an excellent analysis of space and place in Rabelais, see Conley, ch. 4. See also Hampton's reading of the garden as it relates to early modern notions of identity (*Literature*).

Queer Rabelais?

Carla Freccero

Gender and sexuality have long been a concern of Rabelais criticism. In its own time, Rabelais's work was associated with the *querelle des femmes*, a literary quarrel on the merits of women first begun in the French Middle Ages. The *querelle*, and Rabelais's place in it, centered on the debates about marriage in *The Third Book*, where Panurge consults a variety of experts on whether or not to marry. Here, as numerous scholars have noted, there appears a veritable catalog of misogynist arguments concerning women and their noxious effects on men.

But it was the episode of the haughty lady of Paris that attracted the attention of feminist criticism in the 1980s, in the form of imagined female responses to the text. In 1982, Wayne Booth confronted the problem of the relation between Rabelaisian humor and feminism. He recounts a moment in the past when he read aloud to his wife the story of how Panurge takes revenge on a Parisian noblewoman who rejects his advances by causing all the male dogs of Paris to urinate on her. Whereas he "was transported with delighted laughter" (68), his memory of his wife's response gives him pause in the present:

> But now, reading passages like that, . . . I draw back and start thinking rather than laughing, taking a different kind of pleasure with a somewhat diminished text. And neither Rabelais nor Bakhtin can be given the credit for vexing me out of laughter and into thought: it is feminist criticism that has done it. (68)

His conclusion is that "Rabelais's work is unjust to women not simply in superficial ways that the traditions have claimed but, to some degree, in its fundamental imaginative act" (66). Booth's response to the woman question in Rabelais, then, exemplifies a particular approach to gender studies in literature: it asks about the relation between representation and social actuality, treating the literary text as a reflection of social relations in the world.

Poststructuralist and psychoanalytic feminist criticism shifted the focus of analysis from the representation of women in a given text to the relationality of sexual difference in representation, from the social category of gender to its functioning as a sign in a signifying network. *Woman* is not a term used in isolation but a marker of difference relationally positioned in binary opposition to the term *man*. Instead of taking for granted that the literary text reflects, in mimetic fashion, social relations of gender, postructuralist analyses sought to understand the meaning of the textual inscription of the figure of woman. Further, psychoanalytic understandings of the symbolic role of sexual difference encouraged attention to the role of fantasy and desire in representations of gender and sexuality. So, for example, if one attends carefully both to characterizations of

Panurge, as a man, and to the function of woman in the chapters immediately following the degradation of the Parisian noblewoman, a more complex picture emerges.

In these chapters (21–24), which have, as their source, an Italian short story by Masuccio Salernitano, the question of woman's subjectivity is both raised and articulated. On the one hand, the episode of the haughty lady of Paris represents the female voice in direct dialogue with Panurge and leaves room in that dialogue for difference, especially the difference of interpretation that arises as a result, in part, of the gender of each speaker. On the other hand, the episode of the ring (*Pantagruel*, ch. 24) both thematizes woman as resistive inscription in the text and critiques efforts to force it to yield its meaning to masculine acts of reading. Finally, the episode suggests that woman, as sign, functions as a relay for the masculine unconscious and thus that woman per se is, as Luce Irigaray has argued (*This Sex*), nowhere to be found in the economy of masculine signification.

The lady whom Pantagruel abandoned when he left Paris on hearing of his father's death sends him a message, an inscribed diamond ring accompanied by a blank letter. In a gesture resembling his way of marking, by proxy, the Parisian noblewoman, Panurge tries all manner of decoding techniques to force the letter to yield letters. The message, ultimately decoded, is found instead in the materiality of the ring and its inscription. The false diamond and the phrase, "lamah hazabthani" (described as Hebrew in the text), must be translated (from matter to meaning on the one hand and, on the other, from one language and linguistic context to another) into "Dy, amant faulx, pourquoy me as tu laissée?," itself an untranslatable phrase insofar as translation must forgo the double meaning of the "diamant faulx" ("false diamond") conveyed by the French decoding (446; 247). The resistive inscription that is the woman's message signifies, but the materiality of the signifier refuses to yield itself in full.

Lamah hazabthani is also the phrase Jesus speaks to his father on the cross, and thus it is, for Pantagruel, an unconscious echo of his own situation of having lost his father, who has been, as the text puts it, "translated" to the country of fairies (442; 245). Pantagruel, like the lady, was abandoned by someone he loves. For her, it is he; for him, it is his father. She therefore occupies his place in relation to the lost object of love. In the encounter with difference, what Pantagruel finds is an identification. While readers might wish to point to this moment as further evidence of Rabelais's erasure of women, the text seems to have anticipated just that perception, for the identification with and erasure of the woman the episode performs occurs around the question of loss, erasure, or—better yet—"translation."[1] It also destabilizes the boundaries of sexual difference by scripting a cross-gender identification.

Recent work in the history of gender and sexuality has also helped early modern scholars better understand Renaissance gender (masculine and feminine), its relation to sexuality and sexual desire, and its similarities with and differences from modern Western regimes of gender and sexuality.[2] Instead of assuming the heterosexuality of such representations, queer theory, inspired by poststructuralist feminist approaches to gender and sexuality, denaturalizes them by querying the presumed heteronormativity of critical readings of the text, focusing on what is non- or antinormative in a given figuration. Thus, for example, if Pantagruel is understood to represent a particular masculine ideal of filial piety, along the lines of Vergil's Aeneas, Panurge could be seen to figure a perversion of that norm, which in turn conditions the reading of the episode of the lady of Paris in terms other than the defeat of femininity by a hegemonic masculine agent.[3] Indeed, to understand femininity as a figuration is also to understand masculinity differently and, in Rabelais, to understand how masculine homosociality and male friendship work in the world of his text.[4]

One episode in particular illustrates some of the insights that queer rereadings of Rabelais can provide, informed by studies of masculine friendship from antiquity through early modernity. This is the episode that describes Gargantua's emblem in *Gargantua*, chapter 8:

> Pour son image avoit, en une platine d'or pesant soixante et huyt marcs, une figure d'esmail compétent, en laquelle estoit pourtraict un corps humain ayant deux testes, l'une virée vers l'aultre, quatre bras, quatre piedz et deux culz, telz que dict Platon *in Symposio* avoir esté l'humaine nature à son commencement mystic, et autour estoit escript en lettres Ioniques: AGAPH OU ZHTEI TA EAUTHS. (88, 90)

> As his hat medallion, he had a fine piece of enamelled work set in gold plate weighing a hundred and thirty-six ounces, on which was displayed a human body with two heads turned toward one another, four feet and two rumps—the form, according to Plato in his *Symposium*, of man's nature in its mystical beginnings; and around it was written in Ionian script: Charity seeketh not her own. (56)

Gargantua's image is a device or *impresa*, a picture with an accompanying motto, a polyvalent symbol expressing an individual's personal philosophy. Some scholars have read the image as an exemplary case of Renaissance syncretism, with classical imagery assimilated by Christian doctrine, the reconciliation of eros (in the imagistic rendering of Rabelais's expression, "faire la beste à deux dos") and agape (as described by the quotation from Saint Paul), opposed notions synthesized into a harmonious, if humorous, symbol of the spirit of evangelical humanism.[5] To cite just one example of such a reading:

> The grotesque androgyne of Plato's Aristophanes is explicated by the Greek of Saint Paul: "Charity seeketh not her own." This medallion not only gives shape to the deepest of Rabelais's values; it also bears witness to the unity of wisdom which, for the Christian humanist, lies at the heart of ancient thought and scriptural revelation alike. (Greene, *Rabelais* 39)

The figure referred to as "androgyne" derives from a passage in Plato's *Symposium*, where Aristophanes describes mankind's sexual origin(s):

> First of all I must explain the real nature of man, and the change which it has undergone—for in the beginning we were nothing like we are now. For one thing, the race was divided into three; that is to say, besides the two sexes, male and female, which we have at present, there was a third which partook of the nature of both, and for which we still have a name, though the creature itself is forgotten. For though "hermaphrodite" is only used nowadays as a term of contempt, there really was a man-woman in those days, a being which was half male and half female . . . each of these beings was globular in shape, with rounded back and sides, four arms and four legs, and two faces, both the same, on a cylindrical neck, and one head, with one face one side and one the other, and four ears, and two lots of privates, and all the other parts to match.
> (Plato, *Collected Dialogues* 542 [189e–190a])

According to the syncretist interpretation, then, Rabelais is referring to the Aristophanic description of the "man-woman."

Marsilio Ficino, translator and interpreter of Plato for the sixteenth century, provides a Christianizing exegesis for the passage, likening it to the Fall:

> Summa vero nostre interpretationis erit huiusmodi. *Homines*, id est, hominum anime. *Quondam*, id est, quando a deo creantur. *Integre sunt*, duobus sunt exornate luminibus, ingenito et infuso. Ut ingenito equalia et inferiora, infuso superiora conspicerent. *Deo equare se voluerunt*. Ad unicum lumen ingenitum se reflexerunt. *Hinc divise sunt*. Splendorem infusum amiserunt, quando ad solum ingenitum sunt converse statimque in corpora cecidere. *Superbiores facte iterum dividentur*, id est, si naturali/nimium restitit quodammodo extinguetur. (Marcel 169)

> The gist of our interpretation will be this. "Men" (that is, the souls of men) "originally" (that is, when they were created by God), "were whole" and equipped with two lights, one natural, and the other supernatural; by the natural light they beheld inferior and co–equal things; and by the supernatural light, superior things. "They aspire to equal God"; they reverted to the natural light alone. Hereupon "they were divided," and lost their supernatural light, were reduced to natural light alone, and fell immediately into bodies. (Jayne 155)

Humankind's nostalgia, which draws each half together again, represents the soul's longing for reintegration with the divine light. Jerome Schwartz notes that Ficino interprets this myth through the words of Saint Paul, "For now we see through a glass, darkly; but then face to face" (1 Cor. 13.12 [King James Ver.]), thus possibly providing a subtext for the creature's position—the two heads ("l'une virée vers l'aultre") facing each other—and for a Neoplatonic synthesis of two concepts of love, eros becoming the mediator for agape ("Scatology" 271–72).

Ficino's reading, however, does not account for the fact that it is Aristophanes, not Socrates, who recounts the myth. The story is Babelian: it narrates the division of sexuality (its origin) as resulting from circular man's desire to displace the gods. Love, then, comes to be defined as the half creature's longing for its original, material wholeness. To Socrates's idealistic and mystifying definition of human eros as a mediating force in man's pursuit of transcendence (what we think of as Neoplatonic love) Aristophanes, the comic poet, opposes a wholly material explanation of human desire. He concludes, "And so all this to-do is a relic of that original state of ours, when we were whole, and now, when we are longing for and following after that primeval wholeness, we say we are in love" (Plato, *Collected Dialogues* 545 [193a]). The Rabelaisian passage, recalling in the specificity of its description Aristophanes's own humorous and minutely detailed portrait, highlights the physicality of the hermaphrodite rather than its (Ficinian) allegorical function, although it is not known whether Rabelais had access to the full text of the myth.[6]

Furthermore, Rabelais seems to emblematize the circular man's implied narcissism by turning his creature's heads inward so that the figure contemplates itself. This inward-turning posture, in turn, contradicts the Pauline motto, which stresses an essentially God- or other-oriented notion of love. The problem of the ironic twist in the creature's heads can be resolved, in Schwartz's view, by examining Renaissance interpretations of the androgyne provided by Eusebius and Leone Ebreo ("Scatology" 273). The turning of the heads to face each other might then represent the postlapsarian androgyne who struggles, through coition and marriage, to regain primeval wholeness. In this case Rabelais is both exercising his comic skills in the reference to heterosexual coitus and making the theological point that Christian marriage attempts to reestablish a harmonious union lost to humanity. These interpretations undoubtedly inhere in any late-Christian reading of Gargantua's medallion, but there are also elements of the discourse that militate against the integration of the medallion into such a scheme.

One text standing between Plato and Rabelais is Ovid's *Metamorphoses*, with its tale of the origin of the hermaphrodite. Hermaphroditus, according to Alcithoe's story in book 4, is a boy, and the story of his transformation provides a basis for the evil reputation of the fountain Salmacis (11.315–88).[7] A water nymph, whose name the fountain bears, sees Hermaphroditus and desires him. He rejects her, whereupon she waits, hidden, until he has stripped and is bathing in the pool, at which point she dives in, praying to the gods that they might never be separated:

> velut, si quis conducat cortice ramos,
> crescendo iungi pariterque adolescere cernit,

sic ubi conplexu coierunt membra tenaci,
nec duo sunt et forma duplex, nec femina dici
nec puer ut possit, neutrumque et utrumque videntur.
(11.375–79)

as when a twig is grafted
On parent stock, both knit, mature together,
So these two joined in close embrace, no longer
Two beings, and no longer man and woman,
But neither, and yet both. (93 [Humphries])

Although the two are ostensibly joined, Salmacis disappears, and it is Hermaphroditus whose consciousness governs the new creature (11.380–86). In Ovid's account, then, hermaphroditism is the reduction of an essentially masculine nature; the tale is also a playful fable about the origin of a certain kind of (nonnormative) male effeminacy, a man gendered feminine. The myth has interesting parallels with the account in book 3 of Narcissus and Echo in that both youths are strikingly beautiful, virginal, and desired by water nymphs who lose their identities and leave the youths trapped in enamored or horrified self-contemplation. The suggestive connections between these myths, and the loss of feminine identity incurred by the merging of masculine and feminine, might queer our sense of the gendering of the figure in Rabelais. Certainly, Ovid's myth of Hermaphroditus casts a more than skeptical shadow across attempts to view the merger as a positive symbol of the union of two sexes. Medieval Latin versions of the moralized Ovid interpret the hermaphrodite as a symbol of lust and concupiscence, emphasizing its material and physical aspects over the more spiritualized connotations of the term *androgyne*.[8]

Although the argument that the figure is an androgyne (or man-woman) apparently resolves the enigma of the device on the linguistic level, the passage actively resists the heterosexual interpretation such a (heteronormative) reading assumes. The words—for example, *testes* and *culz* ("rumps")—emphasize the androcentricity of the image rather than the merging of two opposite-sexed beings. The couple *virée vers*, alliteratively overdetermined as a reference to the distortion of the Platonic subtext, also stresses morphemic masculinity, *virée* containing *vir*, the Latin word for man. In *La sottie sans souci* ("The Carefree Sotie"), Ida Nelson creates a typology for what she calls the "registre homosexuel" ("homosexual register"), a linguistic code present in the wordplays, paradoxes, and puns of farcical poems and plays called *sotties*, performed or recited during carnival in medieval and Renaissance France.[9] She notes, for example, that the use of the word *virer* for turning is relatively rare, and its root, *vire*, also carries the meanings of "leg," "arrow," and "stick" (see Godefroy 536). Such linguistic networks of slang, in a text known for its wordplay, punning, and erotic double entendres, are suggestive, reinforcing the potential homoeroticism of Gargantua's emblematic image.[10]

Finally, Rabelais's text describes one figure, not two. If sexual difference is being asserted, it is in a context of sameness, further emphasized by the lack of features distinguishing one body from the other. The description proceeds by doubling or, inversely, halving a single entity. In a later Renaissance text, the language of doubling and halving becomes explicitly linked to the bond between men, which suggests that Rabelais's figure may indeed point to a more widespread Renaissance thematics. Michel de Montaigne describes the relationship between himself and Étienne de la Boétie:

> Le secret que j'ay juré ne deceller à nul autre, je le puis, sans parjure, communiquer à celuy qui n'est pas autre: c'est moy. C'est un assez grand miracle de se doubler; et n'en cognoissent pas la hauteur, ceux qui parlent de se tripler. . . . [E]t les plaisirs mesmes qui s'offrent à moy, au lieu de me consoler, me redoublent le regret de sa perte. Nous estions à moitié de tout; il me semble que je luy desrobe sa part. . . . J'estois desjà si fait et accoustumé à estre deuxiesme par tout, qu'il me semble n'estre plus qu'à demy. (*Essais*)
>
> The secret I have sworn to reveal to no other man, I can impart without perjury to the one who is not another man: he is myself. It is a great enough miracle to be doubled and those who talk of tripling themselves do not realize the loftiness of the thing. . . . And the very pleasures that come my way, instead of consoling me, redouble my grief for his loss. We went halves in everything; it seems to me that I am robbing him of his share. . . . I was already so formed and accustomed to being a second self everywhere that only half of me seems to be alive now.
>
> (*Complete Essays* [Frame] 142, 143)

Rather than an androgynous reconciliation of erotic differences, the figure portrayed on Gargantua's medallion, like Montaigne's description, presents a doubly powerful image of erotic sameness (G. Ferguson 206–07).

It is precisely that image of sameness—one man doubled or one man halved—that Rabelais could have found in Aristophanes, whose text is not confined to the portrayal of the androgyne or hermaphrodite but also describes the appearance of all three original genders and sexual orientations:

> Men who are slices of the male are followers of the male, and show their masculinity throughout their boyhood by the way they make friends with men, and the delight they take in lying beside them and being taken in their arms. And these are the most hopeful of the nation's youth, for theirs is the most virile constitution.
>
> (Plato, *Collected Dialogues* 544 [191–92e])

All the sexes—male, female, and hermaphrodite—were circular people or double beings, and all were divided in half. This explains the genesis of homosexuality and in turn gives rise to the possibility that Rabelais's comment on the double-headed being, "telz que dict Platon, *in Symposio*, avoir esté l'humaine nature à son commencement mystic" ("according to Plato in his *Symposium*, of man's nature in its mystical beginnings"), refers to the doubly masculine being. Rabelais's omission of the sexual organs included in Aristophanes's portrayal ("two lots of privates") in an otherwise physically detailed description (itself miming Aristophanes's painstaking catalog of parts) marks the ambiguity of Rabelais's suggestive image in a historical context where homoeroticism would be normatively condemned.

Montaigne's essay on friendship also points to another vital yet relatively unexplored component of Rabelais's text. Montaigne's narrated encounter with La Boétie in "De l'amitié" ("Of Friendship") provides an explicit clarification for Pantagruel's mysterious reaction to the trickster figure of the book, Panurge:

> Si on me presse de dire pourquoy je l'aymois, je sens que cela ne se peut exprimer, qu'en respondant: Par ce que c'estoit luy; par ce que c'estoit moy. . . . Et à nostre premiere rencontre, qui fut par hazard en une grande feste et compagnie de ville, nous nous trouvasmes si prins, si cognus, si obligez entre nous, que rien des lors ne nous fut si proche que l'un à l'autre. (*Essais*)

> If you press me to tell why I loved him, I feel that this cannot be expressed, except by answering: Because it was he, because it was I. . . . And at our first meeting, which by chance came at a great feast and gathering in the city, we found ourselves so taken with each other, so well acquainted, so bound together, that from that time on nothing was so close to us as each other. (*Complete Essays* [Frame] 139)

Pantagruel, on encountering Panurge in *Pantagruel*, chapter 9—"Comment Pantagruel trouva Panurge, lequel il ayma toute sa vie" (356; "How Pantagruel found Panurge, whom he loved all his life" [196])—testifies similarly to the great bond of love that is immediately established between them:

> Car, par ma foy, je vous ay jà prins en amour si grande, que, si vous condescendez à mon vouloir, vous ne bougerez jamais de ma compaignie, et vous et moy ferons ung nouveau pair d'amytié, telle que feut entre Enée et Achates. (362)

> I've taken such a liking to [you], I swear, that if I have my way you'll never stir from my side. Indeed you and I will make such another pair of friends as Aeneas and Achates. (201)

Both Rabelais and Montaigne cite the *Symposium* in their texts on love. While the Socratic discourse ultimately places spirit over body, the *Symposium* remains a playful and solemn celebration of masculine eros and, as such, cannot be completely assimilated in a heteronormative culture such as that of early modern France or our own. Montaigne rejects, at a certain point, the question of classical eroticism by commenting, "Et cet'autre licence Grecque est justement abhorrée par nos mœurs" (*Essais*; "And that other, licentious Greek love is justly abhorred by our morality" [138]), while continuing to describe friendship in physical terms that liken it to Rabelais's hermaphrodite:

> En l'amitié dequoy je parle, elles se meslent et confondent l'une en autre, d'un melange si universel, qu'elles effacent et ne retrouvent plus la couture qui les a jointes. . . . Nos ames ont charrié si uniement ensemble, elles se sont considerées d'une si ardente affection, et de pareille affection descouvertes jusques au fin fond des entrailles l'une à autre. . . . (*Essais*)[11]

> In the friendship I speak of, our souls mingle and blend with each other so completely that they efface the seam that joined them, and cannot find it again. . . . Our souls pulled together in such unison, they regarded each other with such ardent affection, and with a little affection revealed themselves to each other to the very depths of our hearts. . . . (139, 140)

In Rabelais's text the erotic connotations are tempered by the quotation from 1 Corinthians 13.4–5: "Charity . . . seeketh not her own." The motto ironically underscores the specularity of the figure that, in looking at an image of the other, contemplates itself. This hermaphroditic self is an other, its other a self. The Pauline statement thus mitigates the heterodox eroticism of the figure's masculine self-contemplation by introducing the notion of spiritual or brotherly love, man's love for that which is other in himself, or God (Rahner and Vorgrimler 65). Paul's "Charity . . . seeketh not her own" in the Rabelaisian passage repeats, in spiritual terms, the depiction of difference incorporated into sameness in the hermaphrodite. The relation of otherness defined by the text would then be one of man to God, or man to himself through or in God.

It is perhaps impossible to know whether Gargantua's emblem promotes or condemns this figure of masculine self-love, whether the emphasis is on the narcissism of the image or the seamless union of two in one. But the suspension of heteronormative assumptions about the image of the hermaphrodite in Rabelais allows its queer potential to emerge, a potential that finds echoes and reverberations elsewhere in his books, in the representations of male friendship between Pantagruel and Panurge, and in other early modern discourses about masculinity and male friendship in sixteenth-century French literature.

NOTES

1 For a detailed reading of these episodes, see Freccero, "Damning Haughty Dames" and "'Instance.'"

2 See Bray; LaGuardia, *Intertextual Masculinity*; G. Ferguson; Reeser; and Schachter.

[3] Gérard Defaux's reading of Panurge describes him as queer, though not in homoerotic terms (*Pantagruel*).

[4] See Eve Kosofsky Sedgwick's study of masculine homosociality.

[5] Screech, "Emblems"; Carpenter. Schwartz remarks, "The medallion may then be interpreted as a fusion of two apparently irreconcilable opposites: sexual love and Pauline charity. Here again a Renaissance writer chooses the Androgyne theme as the vehicle for the synthesis of contraries, reconciling fleshly *eros* and Pauline *agape*. What greater expression of Renaissance optimism than this?" ("Aspects" 125).

[6] Gary Ferguson discusses the transmission of the Aristophanic fable in the French Renaissance (246–52).

[7] For examples of the positive symbolic value accorded the androgyne, see Eliade, esp. 103–17; also Jung. Reeser discusses the valorized use of the androgyne in French Renaissance texts. Examples of hermaphroditism as a derogatory concept can be found in Plato, Ovid, Dante, and D'Aubigné, as well as in more modern contexts, such as Foucault. G. Ferguson also examines the use of the hermaphrodite to indicate ambiguous and nonnormative gender and sexuality.

[8] See Giovanni di Garlandia; Berchiori; Virgilio. Delcourt writes, "L'androgyne occupe les deux pôles du sacré. Pur concept, pure vision de l'esprit, elle apparaît chargée des plus hautes valeurs. Actualisée en un être de chair et de sang, elle est une monstruosité, et rien de plus" (68; "The androgyne occupies the two poles of the sacred. As pure concept, pure spiritual vision, it appears to be invested with the highest values. Actualized in a flesh-and-blood creature, it is a monstrosity, and nothing more" [my trans.]), while Eliade says, "if a child showed at birth any signs of hermaphroditism, it was killed by its own parents. In other words, the actual, anatomical hermaphrodite was considered an aberration. . . . Only the ritual androgyne provided a model, because it implied not an augmentation of anatomical organs but, symbolically, the union of the magicoreligious powers belonging to both sexes" (100).

[9] While some of the patterns she discerns are suggestive and plausible, at least in Rabelais, she acknowledges the risk involved in assigning homosexual connotations to a vocabulary "qui n'était jamais enregistré directement comme possédant ce sens" (38; "to which such a meaning was never directly attributed").

[10] See, for example, in Nelson, the lexical entry "Teste Verte ou Teste Creuse ou Teste Ligière," where the proximity of the words *teste* and *verte* or *vert* may be seen to constitute a homosexual word game (169). Nelson also suggests that the reference to thirst in the name *Pantagruel* carries homosexual connotations. For a study of wordplay in the Middle Ages, particularly homophonic wordplay, see Dragonetti.

[11] See the extensive discussion of this question in G. Ferguson and in Schachter.

Masculinity and the Question of Gender

Lawrence D. Kritzman

The relationship between men and women is central to the understanding of Rabelais's narrative. Whether in Panurge's quest to find a faithful wife or in the allegorical tension between Fastilent and carnival, gender relations more often than not are depicted as excessive and even at times threatening the very nature of the social order. To speak of gender in Rabelais, and masculinity in particular, one must inquire how gender reflects the anxiety associated with sexuality.

Analyzing Rabelais on questions of gender is an activity most appealing to college-age students. They are sometimes put off by the multiplicity of intertextual references, difficult vocabulary, and historical allusions. What is striking, however, are the ways in which Rabelais's narratives appeal to contemporary questions concerning gender and the relationship between the sexes as they are represented in a Renaissance text. Most certainly the instructor must introduce students to various historical issues such as the *querelle des femmes* and the question of marriage and religion by assigning an essay or two of the work of Joan Kelly or Michael Screech (*Rabelais* [1979]). One cannot expect even advanced undergraduate students of French to master these subjects on their own. But while maintaining the importance of history, the instructor can help students see how the text foregrounds and appropriates various topoi that transcend time and space and are relevant today: patriarchy, the relation between gender and sexuality, masculinity and the fear of women, gender indeterminacy, the relation between the penis (the biological) and the phallus (the symbolic), the connection between sexuality and abjection, and the debate about what is considered to be unnatural activity.

Some colleagues fear that students cannot engage in gender studies without a substantial knowledge of the research in that field. They believe that in order "to do" gender one must apply models that are foreign to the text, that one must submit Rabelais's work to the imperialistic authority of a particular approach to gender. Unfortunately this strategy weakens a student's ability to see how Rabelais's text represents and performs theories of gender.

At the beginning of the course, I ask students to keep a diary and locate and analyze relevant passages in the text that reveal something about gender. I require them to use the sixteenth-century dictionaries of Randle Cotgrave and of Edmond Huguet in order to understand the words in their historical context. Very early on, students discover that in the first two books, *Gargantua* and *Pantagruel*, the nexus of social organization is centered on the paternal figure. They are asked to read an essay by Jacques Le Goff that elucidates the social relationship between vassal and serf inherited from the Middle Ages. They write a short paper on how father-son relations are structured, metaphorically speaking, according to the feudal model. In their analyses students discover how Gargantua plays the role of chief vassal to his father in exploits such as war; he thereby assumes what we refer to today as the symbolic logic of the name of the father.

In keeping their diaries, students see how gender and sexuality intersect in the relationship between Gargantua and Pantagruel. Pantagruel, the son, has specific duties, which are articulated in the letter he receives from Gargantua, his father. To ensure the future of the family lineage, the son must execute his manly function through seminal propagation: "In the course of our transitory life, [man must] perpetuate its name and its seed, which is done by lineage sprung from us in lawful marriage" (*Complete Works* 158–59). In this context, the family becomes the locus for the perpetuation of civilization; it is the son's appropriation of patriarchal "law" that allows life to continue beyond death. Conceived as a duty in the institution of the family, the practice of male sexuality in the institution of marriage is less a question of intimacy than a vehicle for reinforcing the normativity of the social order. Without the ability to perpetuate the species and maintain the family name, the masculinity of the paterfamilias is put into question.

While compiling their diaries, students discover in the first two books the disproportionate amount of space reserved to depict male-male relations. The limited number of entries in their diaries concerning women suggests that women have little or no importance. Depicted as either mother or whore, the female figure is either a receptacle to maintain family lineage or a mere object of pleasure. The mother in particular is subject to extinction. In *Gargantua*, for example, Badebec dies when she gives birth to Pantagruel. Gargamelle, the first mother in the family geneology, disappears from the narrative just as Gargantua is born. Ironically, Rabelais's subsequent narratives ascribe importance to the mother, since without one the family lineage may be put into jeopardy. In keeping their diaries and paying particular attention to vocabulary, students discover that in the Rabelaisian universe woman are often depicted as abject beings capable of soiling the purity of the world. (Here the instructor might introduce a short essay from Julia Kristeva's *Powers of Horror* on the misogynistic concept of abjection in representing women in Western culture.) As opposed to women, monks are represented as physically depraved beings subject to behavior so perverse that the mere passage of a chaste female creates a phobic reaction functioning as a defense against the fear of engulfment:

> Veu que en certains convents de ce monde est en usance que, si femme aulcune y entre (j'entends des preudes et publicques), on nettoye la place par laquelle elles ont passé. (266)

> Seeing that in certain monasteries of this world, it is a practice, that if any women enters (I mean of the decent modest ones) they scour the place where she passed. (*Complete Works* 116)

Students observe how the dynamic of abjection functions in gender relations as male subjects project it onto women; this practice reveals the male subject's desire for separation and the need to remain pure.

Students react to Rabelais's paradoxes and ambiguities with both astonishment and consternation. They ask, How do we interpret this double talk? I use Gargantua's codpiece as a strategy to introduce the encomium as a genre and how it may raise questions of gender. Masculinity's other emerges in the encomium of Gargantua's codpiece; it is depicted as a decorative object lacking in authenticity. Rabelais foregrounds the description of the codpiece to examine the tension between seeming and being as a means to interrogate Gargantua's virility. At first, students accept the encomium of the giant's codpiece, inasmuch as the outside serves as a metaphor of the full inside:

> Pour la braguette feurent levees seize aulnes un quartier d'icelluy mesmes drap et fut la forme d'icelle comme d'un arc boutant, bien estachée joyeusement à deux belles boucles d'or que prenoient deux crochetz d'esmail, en un chascun desquelz estoit enchassée une grosse esmeraugde de la grosseur d'une pomme d'orange. (86)
>
> For the codpiece were taken up sixteen and a quarter ells of this same cloth. And the form of it was like a flying buttress, most merrily fastened with two beautiful gold buckles, caught up by two enamel hooks, in each of which was set a big emerald the size of an orange.
> (*Complete Works* 22–23)

Students question this hyperbole and jokingly ask whether the outside of the codpiece may not camouflage an emptiness within. They are surprised to learn that, instead of being a sign of virility, the emeralds that festoon the codpiece are a sign of impotence. The excessive ornamentation also suggests a certain degree of femininity. The inflated discourse used to describe the codpiece paradoxically functions as the sign of an imperfect masculinity lacking in fertility.

The Thélème episode in *Gargantua* provides another example of paradox that raises questions about gender and sexuality. Thélème depicts a utopian society inhabited by persons of both sexes, but the constraints imposed by this community rob them of their sexuality. The abbey, represented as an antimonastery and constructed in the shape of a hexagon, symbolizes earthly perfection. Built as a counterexample to traditional monasteries, this New Age abbey becomes a community where the emphasis is on sharing.

The abbey that Friar John founds is based on an antimonastic community that in part defines it by what it is not. Gone are the enormous walls that sequester the monks from women and the outside world; gone too are the misogynistic attitudes that the monks expressed toward women, treating them as abject beings. Those allowed to enter Thélème must be persons of noble birth and elegance.

Just as students observe that Thélème is defined by what it is not, they also discover in the episode that it says more about the role of sexuality by what it does not say. The women who are allowed entry into Thélème, like the men, must live in chastity, for in that community fleshly desires are sacrificed for those of the spirit. The spiritual and the corporeal are compartmentalized, and the corporeal is erased. In the world of Thélème, goodness and beauty can go hand in hand only if every trace of libidinal desire is erased. Students often ask whether the inhabitants of Thélème are really human without the tension associated with sexuality. They sometimes suggest that time has stopped in the spiritual world of Thélème, because the desire motivating sexuality can be realized only in the fluctuating rhythms of temporality. The exclusion of carnal desire from the world of Thélème, where the boundaries of inside and outside are carefully drawn, constitutes a form of violence, since it obliterates sexual desire. Devoid of sexuality, the Thelemites cannot be humanized until marriage and procreation occur. By analyzing this rhetoric of exclusion of carnal desire, students arrive at the conclusion that the utopian abbey whose motto is "Do as you will" represents a series of paradoxes that undercut the freedom for which it exists. The I of the individual Thelemites can come into being only through a set of norms that originate neither with the self nor from the other.

Thélème's idealized relationship between men and women can exist only if references to the body are eradicated. Paradoxically a utopic space (literally a nonplace), Thélème is grounded in a world free of conflict and impurity. The exclusion of sexuality from this society enforces borders that separate the potential impurity of the body from the purity incarnated in the nonplace of the spiritual.

The marriage question is foregrounded in *The Third Book*, where Panurge's indecisiveness reveals his lack of self-knowledge. His constant and immoderate fear puts into doubt his masculinity. Panurge no longer dons his codpiece, choosing instead a shroudlike garment, which suggests that he symbolically passes from the world of activity to the paralytic domain of death (see Kritzman, *Rhetoric*).

Panurge's quest to find a faithful wife reveals the anxiety of a male subject who wishes to find a mother for his child and become the mediator of his mortality. Wanting to be the "[batisseur] de pierre vives" (563; "[builder] of living stones"), Panurge must be certain that he will not be subject to female deception. Throughout the book, students witness his angry frustration in and fear of becoming a victim of cuckoldry. The various divinations and consultations that he takes part in result from a fluctuation between his desire to marry and his dread of the consequences. The marriage question for him represents his quest to control reality and the need to domesticate female desire. In short, sexuality for Panurge is always already a problem. If women are luridly sexual beings, he can defend himself only by engaging in regressive behavior.

In the Rondibilis episode, women are protean victims of uncontrolled jouissance. By consulting with the physican Rondibilis, Panurge becomes aware of the Platonic topos found in the *Timaeus*, *animal avidum generandi* (the female's animal-like hunger for generation). Women engage not in the quest for perfection, as the male species does, but in a self-gratifying narcissism, because of their inherent inability to control the sexual drive. Female sexuality, depicted as hidden and subject to excessive fluidity, is a constant threat. Rabelais's text suggests here that an image is in some sense forbidden to women because of their protean nature. The female figure is represented as physiologically flawed, as an unnatural scar. Women therefore become equated with the monstrous.

The prologue to *The Fourth Book* proposes moderation as the golden mean while at the same time drawing our attention to the ever-surfacing fear of excess and uncontrollable appetite. Through close readings and working once again with dictionaries of the period, we discover that the signs of the text lie in the symbolic order of language. Rabelais aims at substituting evenness and health for the excesses of Antiphysie. The prologue to *The Fourth Book* tells of the loss of a *coingnée* (a play on words between "hatchet" and "phallus"). This fable prefigures many of the appetitive crises that emerge in *The Fourth Book*. Couillatris loses his wooden *coignée*. When Jupiter sends his messenger Mercury, god of thieves, to present Couillatris with three axes to choose from, made of wood, silver, and gold, Couillatris chooses the one he lost. Jupiter rewards him for his honesty by giving him all three axes and accordingly demonstrates how tempered desire produces gold.

At another point in the prologue, however, Priapus, the phallic god, speaks and plays on the semantic ambiguity of *coignée*. Most striking in this context is that the figure of sexual conjunction represents an ideality, similar to the androgenic model, based on sexual harmony and the plenitude realized through the joining of opposing elements. The inversion of the hatchet into the helve suggests the heterosexual couple's access to harmony. The text thus suggests a model regulating desire: the conjoining of male and female bodies becomes a way of conceiving sexuality as a means to construct the social imaginary. This modality of acting in the world produces the corporeal knowledge that establishes harmony.

The Chicanous episode in *The Fourth Book* represents a cultural practice whose signification in terms of gender can be understood only in the context of popular culture and carnival behavior. To see how Rabelais uses the charivari as a metaphor of the relationship between the sexes, students are assigned a chapter from Mikhail Bakhtin's *Rabelais and His World*. They discover that this practice is associated with carnival and allowed male bonding for those who believed that a marriage was questionable. Men engaged in such activity, known as a ritual called "riding the stag," as a form of punishment—women were placed on horseback backward—for a wife accused of abusing her husband.

The anxiety associated with being a man is revealed in the Chicanous episode, where Rabelais stages the charivari of the pre-Lenten period. Reinforcing the social function of homoerotic bonding, these man engage in bacchic practices to affirm their masculinity. Students analyze how Rabelais appropriates this cultural intertext and discover how the representation of the misogynistic behavior of these men comes from fear. The display of aggression in vilification makes it seem unlikely that an autonomous male subject would ever cede power to a female other.

The Chitterling episode in *The Fourth Book* reveals hermeneutic confusion regarding gender and sexuality. Described by Xenophon as both "double and deceitful," the Chitterlings are a phallic figure that is female both in its grammatical and referential context (see Kritzman, "Représenter"). These sexually hybrid figures are both sausage and serpent. Looking like phalli, they are literally tripe sausages or intestines. Half their body is alimentary in nature; the other half, according to biblical and mythological references, takes the form of the seductive serpent of Eve and the satyr Priapus. This sexual temptation leads to a paradise lost. The Chitterlings are paradoxically human and inhuman, male and female, living and dead matter simultaneously. Beyond that, the priapic associations of these phallic figures are amplified by the given name of their queen, which, according to the "Brief Declaration," signifies in Hebrew "male member" (1147; *Complete Works* 601).

The synecdoche constituting the body image of the Chitterlings confounds any attempt to establish coherence. The identity selected from both sexes lacks gender specificity. The image suggests a bisexuality in which gender and sex intermingle.

In the episode, the Chitterlings march on Pantagruel, believing that he and his men are the monster Fastilent and his allies. Although warriors and the enemies of Fastilent, the Chitterlings are unable to control their emotions and so engage in strategies more temperate than war. Indeed, it is a woman who leads them. The paradox here is that according to French Salic law "women and effeminate men were not able to lead" (Reeser 179). In other words, this anatomical entity may act as a trope for the penis, but we know full well that it cannot represent a man, since it cannot assume leadership. Though metonymically related to the male body, it lacks the power of the paternal phallus. The Chitterlings therefore become an example of failed masculinity.

The feminization of the male member here may suggest Plato's belief that Eros is a woman. It also reflects the Platonic desire for men to assume the sexuality of both men and women. Since women are easily disposed of, men can survive without them. Like the nymph Ora, the queen of the Chitterlings, Nipleseth, bears the profile of a penis and yet has the ability to become pregnant and reproduce. Priapus, depicted as an edible piece of meat, is also made of intestinal matter, which undermines the delight of erotism, tarnishing it with abject fecal matter.

In the battle between Pantagruel and his men and the Chitterlings, it appears at first that the Chitterlings will win. Blinded by their desire, they display excessive courage. The confrontation between them and Gymnaste is revelatory. In battle these phallic figures are threatened, at least symbolically, with castration, for Pantagruel snaps the Chitterlings over his knee. The masculinity of these overly anxious figures is questioned. In a way their emasculation allows for the victory of those soldiers whose gender identity is not in doubt. One might even say that the Chitterlings can be seen as castrated not because they lack a penis but because they become dispossessed of phallic potency. Even if the silhouette of Nipseleth resembles a penis, it doesn't necessarily produce male behavior. In short, Rabelais's text suggests that anatomy is not destiny.

The question of male pregnancy is raised also in the episodes recounting the visit to the Island of Tapinois. The narrator describes the ruler of this island, Fastilent (Quaremeprenant), as an unnatural creature whose grotesque nature appears to be as much a question of his anatomy as it is one produced by his gender: "Voylà, dist Pantagruel, une estrange et monstrueuse membreure d'home, si home le doibs nommer" (978; " 'That,' said Pantagruel, 'is a strange and monstrous figure of a man, if man I am to call him' " [*Complete Works* 507]). Having a tiny brain, Fastilent embodies the Lenten period, which is perceived as gloomy and pleasureless. He is an austere monster, a tonsured demigiant who symbolizes infertility and engages in unproductive activity. As the narrative progresses, students learn that Fastilent does not like to attend weddings and disapproves of sexual reproduction. In analyzing vocabulary through use of dictionaries of the period, students come to realize that he represents unnatural sexual desires and thereby is an offspring of Antiphysie. To be sure, he is depicted as a "great lanterner" (440). In the sixteenth century, as Samuel Kinser suggests, *lanterner* is "a slang word for the penis" (113). The word therefore takes on a pejorative meaning.

Fastilent engages in unnatural sexual practices, one evidence of which is anal syphilis (113). Defilement becomes the libidinal source of negativity that produces a language at the borders of what may be conceived of as unnatural bodily activities. Guy Demerson suggests that Fastilent's half tonsure indicates loss of hair as a consequence of syphilis (964). Hair, the thing most accessible to the eye, is the focus of stigma. The text draws a parallel between the physical body and the psyche. Beyond that Rabelais makes Fastilent a questionable male. (" 'That,' said Pantagruel, 'is a strange and monstrous figure of a man, if man I am to call him. You put me in mind of the shape and features of Amodunt and Discord' " [*Complete Works* 507]).

The Lanterners are those who engage in perverse sexual practices. The sacrifice of family life for same-sex bonding can only spell the destruction of the species. In short, the monster is represented as homosexual, and to be homosexual is to threaten the survival of civilization itself.

One discovers in Rabelais's strategies of representation what can be explicitly seen in terms of gender. As grotesque as he is, Fastilent occupies a place from which Rabelais elaborates an image of the body resulting from unnatural activity. In rendering the body "strange and monstrous," Rabelais relegates the unnatural to a devalued social space. Fastilent is one of a series of male pregnancies in *The Fourth Book*. These births are the result of sexual practices associated with anality, "eating wind," and foods that produce flatulence and gastric discomfort (Berry, *Charm* 142–62). Birthing through the anal sphincter produces an end result (pardon the pun) that is dead matter. Fastilent engages in copulative behavior that becomes an imitation of the original. For Fastilent, being and being like are the same thing.

In Rabelais's narrative, projective identification challenges the so-called stability of gender identity. The tropological configurations in the representation of the Chitterlings and Quaremeprenant enable the emergence of a referent that sets in motion a way to conceive of gender otherwise. Ironically, Rabelais's text appears to defend the priority of patriarchy yet at the same time challenges masculinity as it is expressed in the male responsibility for the propagation of the species. On the one hand, Gargantua returns from the dead and imposes his will on Pantagruel to marry so that his lineage may continue. On the other hand, one finds throughout *The Fourth Book* many references to castration when sexual enjoyment cannot be achieved in a normative manner. In Rabelais's text, we observe what Jacques Lacan often refers to as surplus enjoyment, since the monstrous stillbirths found in *The Fourth Book* suggest the renunciation of bodily pleasure in favor of verbal acrobatics.

Students arrive at the conclusion that Rabelais's monsters, represented through incessant hyperbole, signal a refusal to adhere to traditional codes of what constitutes masculinity. Panurge and many of the monstrous characters in *The Fourth Book* are possessed by a negativity that produces either inaction or abject birth. If for Rabelais the normal trajectory of sexuality is realized in the covenant of marriage, then the failure to reproduce constitutes a form of perversion in the etymological meaning of that word ("going off track"). This deviation from the path leading to the goal of productive copulation undermines the preferred default of sexuality achieved through Christian *caritas* and posits it otherwise.

SPECIFIC EPISODES

On Becoming Human: *Gargantua*, Chapter 13

Virginia Krause

> Arbores fortasse nascuntur, licet aut steriles aut agresti foetu; equi nascuntur, licet inutiles, at homines, mihi crede, non nascuntur, sed finguntur.
>
> —Erasmus

> Trees may well be born trees, even when they bear no fruit; horses are born horses, even when they prove to be of no use; but, believe me, human beings are not born human, they only become so.

The following approach to teaching *Gargantua* offers a guided close reading of chapter 13 as part of an introduction to humanism in Rabelais's work. It should be noted at the outset that for the early modern period, the term *humanism* is something of an anachronism. As a substantive, it dates back only to nineteenth-century Germany, when it was forged to refer to the early modern zeal for classical antiquity and associated values. Today, it is used even more broadly, to designate the elevation of humanity posited as a supreme value. In the light of the long history of the idea of humanism, it is important to situate the early modern humanist project in its own context, beginning with its emergence in fourteenth-century Italy. Then, one spoke not of humanism (substantive), and very rarely of humanists, but rather of a curriculum known as the *studia humanitatis*, which placed new emphasis on the study of ancient languages, rhetoric, literature, and history.[1] In France, new institutions were created in defense of these ideals. Humanists such as Guillaume Budé lobbied for the creation of a kind of *mécénat* ("patronage") outside the university system over which presided the Faculty of Theology of the University of Paris, a frequent object of Rabelaisian satire for being too wedded to the old learning (Scholasticism) and resistant to evangelism. Francis I proved receptive to these ideas. He dreamed of founding a *collège royal* of international standing, inviting Erasmus to stand at its head. Who better to preside over this institution than Erasmus, the international figurehead for the humanist project? When Erasmus refused, the project was scaled back, taking the more modest form of a corps of *lecteurs royaux* in 1530 (the origin of the Collège de France). Francis I also pursued his cultural politics through policies and initiatives related to the book—through his politics of print, for instance, and through building the collections of the royal library at Blois, placing Budé at its head in 1522 and moving it to Fontainebleau in 1544. Indeed, the most tangible traces of the activities of the humanists are the books they produced: a proliferation of texts they glossed, translated, and printed, often based on the manuscripts they unearthed and edited.[2]

The broad contours of the historical context of Renaissance humanism should be provided, but students approaching Rabelais's humanism for the first time might benefit from a less common—and perhaps more fundamental—angle emphasizing the *human* in humanism. What is at stake in the humanist engagement with the notion of the human? More precisely, what role did literature play in the humanizing mission of humanists? In this essay, I propose an approach to presenting key literary components of the humanist project through close study of chapter 13. My reading should encourage students to probe Rabelais's vertiginous layering of text and gloss, should uncover a sustained reflection on the humanist practice of literature and on the limits of the human. This approach allows the instructor to introduce and examine concepts that may appear dry and obscure when presented in a lecture format while exploring the idea of the human with high stakes for the Renaissance as well as for us today.

Setting up the discussion of the beginning of *Gargantua*, I ask students to think about what is antithetical to the human: the nonhuman, antihuman, or inhuman. Modern philosophy and even science fiction offer analogies of nightmarish dehumanizing mechanisms (from fascism to cyborgs) as well as problematizations of human exceptionalism—challenging the boundaries dividing human beings from animals or from machines, for example. After positing this broad framework, I evoke three classic examples of Renaissance humanists' probing the limits of the human, giving students three quotations and commenting on them together.

In the first place, Giovanni Pico della Mirandola's famous manifesto from the *Oratio de hominis dignitate* illustrates the indeterminacy of the human, which can either reach toward the divine or fall back toward the animalistic:

> Nous ne t'avons assigné ô Adam, ni une place déterminée, ni une figure propre, ni un héritage particulier, afin que tu aies et possèdes, selon tes vœux et décision, toujours la place, toujours la figure, toujours les biens par toi élus. Toutes les autres créatures ont une nature définie contenue

> entre les lois par nous prescrites; toi seul, sauf de toute entrave, suivant ton libre arbitre auquel je t'ai remis, tu te fixeras ta nature. Je t'ai placé au centre de l'univers, afin que tu regardes avec d'autant plus d'aisance à l'entour de toi tout ce qui est au monde. Je ne t'ai fait ni céleste, ni terrestre, ni mortel, ni immortel; d'après ton vouloir et pour ton propre honneur, modeleur et sculpteur de toi-même, imprime-toi la forme que tu préfères. Tu pourras dégénérer en animal, être de l'ordre inférieur; tu pourras selon la décision de ton esprit te régénérer en créature divine, être de l'ordre supérieur. (Trans. and qtd. in Schmidt 143)

> We have given to thee, Adam, no fixed seat, no form of thy very own, no gift peculiarly thine, that thou mayest feel as thine own, have as thine own, possess as thine own the seat, the form, the gifts which thou thyself shalt desire. A limited nature in other creatures is confined within the laws written down by us. In conformity with thy free judgment, in whose hands I have placed thee, thou art confined by no bounds; and though wilt fix limits of nature for thyself. I have placed thee at the center of the world, that from there thou mayest more conveniently look around and see whatsoever is in the world. Neither heavenly nor earthly, neither mortal nor immortal have We made thee. Thou, like a judge appointed for being honorable art the molder and maker of thyself; thou mayest sculpt thyself into whatever shape though dost prefer. Thou canst grow downward into the lower natures which are brutes. Thou canst again grow upward from thy soul's reason into the higher natures which are divine.
> (Pico della Mirandolla 4–5)

Montaigne's "Apologie de Raymond Sebond" ("Apology for Raymond Sebond") offers a second example of a refusal to resolve the human question:

> La presomption est nostre maladie naturelle et originelle. La plus calamiteuse et fraile de toutes les creatures, c'est l'homme, et quant et quant la plus orgueilleuse. Elle se sent et se void logée icy, parmy la bourbe et le fient du monde, attachée et clouée à la pire, plus morte et croupie partie de l'univers, au dernier estage du logis et le plus esloigné de la voute celeste, avec les animaux de la pire condition des trois; et se va plantant par imagination au dessus du cercle de la Lune et ramenant le ciel soubs ses pieds. C'est par la vanité de cette mesme imagination qu'il s'egale à Dieu, qu'il s'attribue les conditions divines, qu'il se trie soy mesme et separe de la presse des autres creatures, taille les parts aux animaux ses confreres et compaignons, et leur distribue telle portion de facultez et de forces que bon luy semble. (*Essais*)

> Presumption is our natural and original malady. The most vulnerable and frail of all creatures is man, and at the same time, the most arrogant. He

> feels and sees himself lodged here, amid the mire and dung of the world, nailed and riveted to the worst, the deadest, and the most stagnant part of the universe, on the lowest story of the house and the farthest from the vault of heaven, with the animals of the worst condition of the three; and in his imagination, he goes planting himself above the circle of the moon, and bringing the sky down beneath his feet. It is by the vanity of this same imagination that he equals himself to God, attributes to himself divine characteristics, picks himself out and separates himself from the horde of other creatures, carves out their shares to his fellows and companions the animals, and distributes among them such portions of faculties and powers as he sees fit. (*Complete Essays* [Frame] 330–31)

Montaigne mounts a devastating critique of human "presumption": the arrogance we demonstrate in attempting to set ourselves apart from animals when, for the essayist, our true place is among the animals rather than above them.

Finally, with a quote from Erasmus's *De pueris instituendis* illustrating the fundamental idea that humans are not *born* but rather *made*, the scene is set for *Gargantua*:

> Arbores fortasse nascuntur, licet aut steriles aut agresti foetu; equi nascuntur, licet inutiles, at homines, mihi crede, non nascuntur, sed finguntur. (*Declamatio* 389)

> Trees may well be born trees, even when they bear no fruit; horses are born horses, even when they prove to be of no use; but, believe me, human beings are not born human, they only become so. (my trans.)

Rabelais composed his first two literary works—*Pantagruel* (1532) and *Gargantua* (1534)—in the immediate wake of Erasmus's *De pueris instituendis*, first published in 1529 and translated into French in 1537. The first chapters of *Gargantua* echo with the Erasmian notion of becoming human. According to Erasmus, human beings become human only if this endeavor is undertaken with the utmost seriousness and with the proper (literary) means. The stated purpose of Erasmus's treatise is to urge a new father to begin the literary education of his son at an early age. It further captures a fundamental thread in humanist thought—one that has slipped out of the critical vocabulary in use today, which tends to emphasize the place Renaissance humanism reserved for high erudition at the cost of eclipsing the early humanists' dream of fashioning what they called human beings. To fully grasp this dimension of the humanist, students must be encouraged to take full measure of this nonessentializing conception of the human. They must also be invited to look beyond our modern assumptions about the human, inevitably influenced by the social sciences, with their focus on behavior and properties. Humanist thought ultimately reached beyond a framework based on a would-be human substance or any stable and defining human attributes. In this sense, it is appropriate to speak not of a human being but of a human becoming.

In preparing students to read the beginning of *Gargantua*, I suggest using the quotation from Erasmus as a kind of master key, asking students to think about the following questions as they read: How does the Erasmian axiom that human beings are made and not born inform chapters 11–13 of *Gargantua*? What role does literary culture play in the process of becoming human in chapter 13?

Becoming Human

The first twelve chapters of *Gargantua* relate the genealogy, birth, and early childhood of the hero. True to Erasmian principles, the young hero leads a distinctly nonhuman existence before his education. The beginning of chapter 11, for instance, suggests that he resembles a rather rudimentary machine. He is engaged in the basic operations of the consumption of resources:

> celluy temps passa comme les petitz enfans du pays: c'est assavoir à boyre, manger et dormir; à manger, dormir et boyre; à dormir, boyre et manger. (102)
>
> he spent that time in the same manner as the other little children of that country: that is to say in drinking, eating, and sleeping; in eating, sleeping, and drinking; in sleeping, drinking, and eating. (59)

Not to forget the production of waste, the inevitable next stage following these primary operations:

> Il pissoit sus ses souliers, il chyoit en sa chemise, il se mouschoyt à ses manches, il mourvoit dedans sa soupe. (102)
>
> He pissed in his shoes, shat in his shirt, wiped his nose on his sleeve, sniveled into his soup. (62)

By suggesting his affinity with the household dogs, chapter 11 further conveys the nonhuman existence of the young hero. Far from exercising dominion over the animal kingdom (Gen. 1.26), Gargantua enjoys a reciprocal relationship with these small dogs. He eats with them out of the same bowl, and they exchange gestures of dog friendliness:

> Les petitz chiens de son pere mangeoient en son escuelle. Luy de mesmes mangeoit avecques eux: il leurs mordoit les aureilles. Ilz luy graphinoient le nez. Il leurs souffloit au cul. Ilz luy leschoient les badigoinces. (104–05)

> His father's little dogs ate out of his dish, and he ate with them. He bit their ears and they scratched his nose; he blew at their rumps and they licked his lips. (63)

The phrasing used emphasizes the reciprocity of their exchange through adverbs "luy de mesmes" and through the repetition of the construction "Ilz luy / Il leur," creating a rather endearing but distinctly nonhuman portrait of the young hero.

Finally, with Gargantua's acquisition of language in chapter 12, a sense of expectation and even suspense is created: has the hero now crossed the threshold separating animals and human beings? Indeed, language is a common criterion used for distinguishing human beings from animals, one singled out by a long philosophical tradition pitting man against animal. Although he cried out "à boyre, à boyre!" when he was born, this is the first time Gargantua displays a genuine ability to use language, as chapter 12 relates how he praised his hobbyhorses as though they were actual stallions in his stable. In case the reader has somehow overlooked that this chapter relates the hero's acquisition of language, the steward who serves as witness brings the point home:

> —Cor Dieu (dist le maistre d'hostel) nous avons trouvé un *causeur*. Monsieur le *jaseur*, Dieu vous guard de mal, tant vous avez la *bouche fraische*. (110; emphasis mine)
>
> "Bless my soul!" exclaimed the steward, "we've struck a *talker*. God keep you from harm, my *chatty* fellow, for you've got *a ready tongue*." (65; emphasis mine)

The burlesque equivalent of eloquence, such chattiness draws attention. However, his acquisition of language does not signal a qualitative break with the order of machines and the kingdom of animals. His antics amuse his father's guests, but they are not heralded as the first sign of genuine humanity.

The young hero fully embarks on the adventure of becoming human only in chapter 13, titled "Comment Grandgousier congneut l'esperit merveilleux de Gargantua à l'invention d'un torchecul" ("How Grandgousier Realized Gargantua's Marvellous Intelligence, by His Invention of an Arse-Wipe"). True to Erasmian principles, the decisive factor is not a given attribute (language, for instance) but rather a humanizing practice. Gargantua displays a remarkable aptitude for literary studies, albeit through the scatological avenue he has chosen. We must not let this chapter's lower bodily theme distract us from its higher meanings, since as Jeff Persels and Russell Ganim point out, Rabelais "has the vexing habit of mixing an *altior sensus* with the quest for a perfect asswipe" ("Scatology" xvi).

At stake in this chapter is the foundational opposition between cleanliness and filth. How does this opposition inform Rabelais's notion of the human? On the one hand, the young hero is "nect" (110; "clean" [66]) and thus seemingly closer to being civilized. On the other hand, cleaner and ostensibly more civilized, he is also significantly more invested in the lower bodily functions. Although this chapter heralds the beginning of cleanliness and control over bodily functions, as the hero is now officially toilet trained, this would-be praise for civilized cleanliness turns into a hymn to excrement (see Persels and Ganim, "Scatology"; Persels in this volume). The reader is thus left wondering if it is indeed cleanliness that makes one civilized (Erasmian civility) or if instead we are not most defined by a compulsion to pollute and produce waste, thereby laying claim to our environment (a hypothesis advanced most recently by Michel Serres). Cleanliness thus constitutes something of an impasse in resolving the human question in *Gargantua*. Literary study, in contrast, emerges as an unambiguously humanizing agent in the young hero's existence.

Students can now be guided to discover beneath the wildly scatological theme in this chapter a surprisingly coherent subtext derived from the five parts of classical rhetoric: *inventio* (finding a subject); *dispositio* (arrangement of the parts into a whole); *elocutio* (style or, more specifically, ornamentation); *memoria* (everything that serves to aid memory and, in particular, the ability to stock away in one's memory classical texts arranged by places); and, finally, *actio* (delivery), sometimes used interchangeably with pronunciation by humanists. Because elementary classes in schools of the time were devoted to grammar and rhetoric, the five parts of classical rhetoric were quite simply the nuts and bolts of Renaissance literary studies. Any person in sixteenth-century France having received a formal education would have been able to rattle them off in order.

Unexpected as this may be, chapter 13 rehearses the five parts of classical rhetoric in order, beginning with the chapter's title, which announces the first part of rhetoric, *inventio*, the all-important first part of any literary enterprise: finding a subject ("Comment Grandgousier congneut l'esperit merveilleux de Gargantua à *l'invention* d'un torchecul" ["How Grandgousier Realized Gargantua's Marvellous Intelligence, by His *Invention* of an Arse-Wipe"). Through rehearsing the five parts of rhetoric, Rabelais is conducting a playful metacommentary on literary studies even as he reflects on its place in the process of becoming human. To a modern ear, this emphasis on rhetoric may seem far indeed from the essence of literature. For Renaissance humanists, however, there was no clear distinction between rhetoric and poetics or, for that matter, between an art of discourse and what we would call literature.

Once the young hero has found a topic, he proceeds through the next four parts in their classical order. After an initial introduction in indirect discourse, this chapter consists solely of dialogue between father and son. Following Gargantua's announcement that he has found the perfect instrument, his father asks, "What is it?" Significantly, the young hero refuses to simply reveal the *fin mot de l'histoire* ("the truth of the matter"). Instead, he tells his father that he will tell him in due time.[3] By refusing to reveal the conclusion to his search prematurely, Gargantua insists on a proper *dispositio*: a well-structured narrative. The ordering of discourse is emphasized through the series of objects with which the young hero experiments: "une foys d'un cachelet de velours de une damoiselle" ("Once I wiped myself on a lady's velvet mask"); "Une aultre foys d'un chapron d'ycelles" ("Another time on one of their hoods"); "une aultre foys d'un cachecoul" ("Another time on a lady's neckerchief"); "une aultre foys des aureilletes" (110; "another time on some ear-flaps" [66]), followed by another series of experiments, each introduced by "puis" (112; "then" [67–68]). Rabelais emphasizes the order of Gargantua's discourse through this insistent use of sequential adverbs. By making such a conspicuous use of adverbs at this point in the chapter, Rabelais makes it clear that he is not only telling a story but also commenting on the act of ordering the parts of a narrative.

After this metacommentary on *dispositio*, Rabelais proceeds to the third part of rhetoric: *elocutio*. Having demonstrated his mastery of arrangement in prose narrative, the young hero utters two perfect octosyllabic rhyming verses, rhyme being perhaps the quintessential form of ornamentation for the period: "Tousjours laisse aux couillons esmorche / Qui son hord cul de papier torche" (112; "Who his foul bum with paper wipes / Will on his ballocks leave some chips" [67]). To his father's surprise ("tu rimes desja?" [112]), he proceeds to quote Clément Marot, the great master of rhyme, from "La petite épistre au roi":

> Ouy dea (respondit Gargantua) mon roy, je rime tant et plus et en rimant souvent m'enrime. (112)

> "Oh yes, my lord king," replied Gargantua. "I can rhyme that much and more, and when I rhyme I often catch the rheum." (67)[4]

This homage to Marot is followed first by an epigram and then by a rondeau, two genres closely associated with Marot's generation of poets. The importance accorded to verse in this chapter may be ironic, given Rabelais's place as the author of a masterpiece of prose fiction. His burlesque elevation of verse nevertheless echoes the privileged role accorded to poetry by humanists, for whom poetry had a special magic that eluded prose. The *Deffense et illustration de la langue française* ("The Defense and Illustration of the French Language"), for instance, was addressed to the future French poet, since Joachim du Bellay assumed that the Parnassian summit could be reached only through poetry (*Deffence*).

Lest we forget that we are in fact being led through the five parts of rhetoric, Rabelais's young hero then reveals that he did not compose the rondeau or the epigram himself. Rather he memorized these variations on Marotic topoi, after hearing them recited by an anonymous lady, thereby displaying his mastery of *memoria*:

> Par la mer de, je ne les ay faict mie. Mais, les oyant reciter à dame grand que voyez cy, les ay retenu en la gibbesiere de memoire. (114)

> I did not invent a line of it. I heard that fine lady over there reciting it and I kept it in the bag of my memory. (69)

As for the fifth part of rhetoric, *actio*, the young Gargantua delivers his material in a lively fashion that captivates his audience. That everything but the initial paragraph is presented as dialogue accentuates his delivery. His father's interruptions expressing interest or admiration confirm that the performance is enthralling.[5]

In the process of rehearsing the five parts of classical rhetoric, the young hero proceeds from prose to Marotic verse and, thus implicitly, to *imitatio* while proving that he is not just another sophist able to manipulate rhetoric, for he marries his rhetorical prowess with solid reasoning, as his father declares on hearing his young son's deductive reasoning. "O (dist Grandgousier) que tu as bons sens" (144; "Oh [. . .] what a good head you've got" [68]), Grandgousier exclaims, for his son has just uttered a perfect syllogism (from the Greek "reasoning"). The classic example of this three-part operation in deductive reasoning is, "All men are mortal (major premise); Socrates is a man (minor premise); therefore Socrates is mortal" (conclusion), which Gargantua recasts:

> Il n'est, dist Gargantua, poinct besoing torcher cul, sinon qu'il y ayt ordure. Ordure n'y peut estre si on n'a chié: chier doncques nous fault davant que le cul torcher. (114)
>
> "There's no need to wipe your bottom unless it's mucky," said Gargantua. "It can't be mucky if you haven't shat; we have to shit, therefore, before we wipe our arses." (68)

For humanists, literary studies rested on a firm rhetorical foundation, an art of discourse, a *techne*. Yet, crucially, beyond this emphasis on technique, something more elusive was at stake, something that could best be described as a mystique charged with crystallizing the meaning of the human.

The Literary Animal

When Gargantua finally unveils the perfect instrument for the task at hand, Rabelais allegorizes on the place of literature in becoming human. With considerable buildup—it is fully appropriate to speak of suspense (see Cave, *Préhistoires* 129–41)—the conclusion to Gargantua's search is revealed at the very end of chapter 13. The best ass wipe turns out to be a downy gosling. As Gargantua proceeds to describe this experience, we discover a densely packed allegory for becoming human resonating with the Erasmian notion of the human as well as with Pico's "human dignity," but with a conceptual richness that is Rabelais's own:

> Mais concluent, je dys et maintiens qu'il n'y a tel torchecul que d'un oyzon bien dumeté, pourveu qu'on luy tienne la teste entre les jambes. Et m'en croyez sus mon honneur, car vous sentez au trou du cul une volupté mirificque, tant par la doulceur d'icelluy dumet que par la chaleur temperée de l'oizon, laquelle facilement est communicquée au boyau culier et aultres intestines, jusques à venir à la region du cueur et du cerveau. Et ne pensez que la beatitude des Heroes et semidieux qui sont par les champs Elysiens soit en leur Asphodele, ou Ambrosie ou Nectar, comme disent ces vieilles ycy. Elle est (scelon mon opinion) en ce qu'ilz se torchent le cul d'un oyzon. Et telle est l'opinion de maistre Jehan d'Escosse. (116)

> But to conclude, I say and maintain that there is no arse-wipe like a well-downed goose, if you hold her neck between your legs. You must take my word for it, you really must. You get a miraculous sensation in your arse-hole, both from the softness of the down and from the temperate heat of the goose herself; and this is easily communicated to the bum-gut and the rest of the intestines, from which it reaches the heart and the brain. Do not imagine that the felicity of the heroes and demigods in the Elysian Fields arises from the asphodel, their ambrosia, or their nectar, as those ancients say. It comes, in my opinion, from their wiping their arses with the neck of a goose, and that is the opinion of Master Duns Scotus too. (69)

After this conclusion, Grandgousier is "beside himself with admiration" (69) for this proof of his son's "hault sens et merveilleux entendement" (116; "fine sense and marvellous understanding" [69]). Based on the literary aptitude Gargantua has just demonstrated, Grandgousier decides it is time for his son to begin his formal education.

Rabelais's literary ass wipe, a tribute to Erasmian humanism, is indeed a tour de force worthy of admiration. It evokes the traditional tripartite order of beings (animal, human, divine), situating the human once again not firmly in the middle but rather as a potential, a reaching toward. It is thus what allows us to reach toward the divine (demigods in the Elysian Fields) while simultaneously exercising burlesque dominion over the animals (the gosling made to serve as ass wipe). In contrast to the preliterary Gargantua, who shared a meal and reciprocal gestures of affection with little dogs, the hero now imposes his will on this representative of the animal kingdom: Gargantua firmly holds the gosling's head between his legs, a parody of the Old Testament definition of the human based on dominion over animals. Rabelais further suggests a line drawn between the animal and the human insofar as the dominated animal in question is a downy biped serving the pleasure and utility of man, also known as "the featherless biped" according to Plato's famous definition, even more famously mocked by Diogenes who deposited a plucked chicken in front of Plato's school, proclaiming, "Here is Plato's man." This burlesque parody of man's domination over the animals brings to a close Rabelais's Erasmian reflections on the humanizing mission of literary studies. From this point, students can be invited to explore the importance of the body for Rabelais's understanding of the human. (Note that the gosling is described as the best possible instrument because the softness and heat cause a sensation that rises up from the anus through the intestines and then into the heart and brain: this is not the top-down movement of human reason and will exercising dominion over the body.) Students may also be invited to reflect on the humanist understanding of the responsibility of literature. What makes literature so well suited to crystallizing a certain understanding of the human? What traces has the humanist grand narrative left on, for instance, the place of literature in the humanities today? Is literature still charged with a humanizing mission?

This guided close reading of chapter 13 was designed with two objectives in mind: presenting basic literary notions in Renaissance France; exploring the function of literature in the humanist grand narrative of human becoming.

NOTES

[1] See Duval's definition of *humanism* in Zegura, *Rabelais Encyclopedia* 120–22.

[2] For a broad survey of the humanist tradition from the sixteenth through the twentieth century, see W. Ferguson. For a nuanced account of the projects and institutions of early French humanists, see Gadoffre. On the professional applications of humanism (often neglected by scholars), see Boutcher. Clément directs our attention back to early humanists' fundamental understanding of the human as the fruit of the acquisition of the humanities (*Cynisme* 67).

[3] "—J'ay (respondit Gargantua) par longue et curieuse experience, inventé un moyen de me torcher le cul: le plus seigneurial, le plus excellent, le plus expedient que jamais feut veu.—Quel? dict Grandgousier.—Comme vous le raconteray (dist Gargantua) presentement" (110; "'By long and curious experiments,' replied Gargantua. 'I have invented a method of wiping my arse which is the most lordly, the most excellent, and the most convenient that was ever seen.' 'What's that?' asked Grandgousier. 'I shall tell you in a moment,' said Gargantua" [66]).

[4] The first two verses of Marot's "Petite epistre au roy" read: "En m`esbatant je faiz Rondeau en rime, / Et en rimant bien souvent je m'enirme" (*Œuvres poétiques* 87).

[5] "En voulez vous d'adventaige?—Ouy dea, respondit Grandgousier" (114;"'Would you like any more of this?' 'Yes, indeed,' replied Grandgousier" [69]); "Mais (dist Gargantua), voulez vous payer un bussart de vin Breton si je vous foys quinault en ce propos?—Ouy vrayement, dist Grandgousier" ("'But,' said Gargantua, 'will you pay me a puncheon of Breton wine if I catch you out on the subject?' 'Yes, I will,' said Grandgousier'" [68]).

The Predicament of Peace in *Gargantua*

Marcus Keller

The experience of war and the conditions of peace are often a timely topic for the undergraduate classroom, and few literary texts lend themselves as well as *Gargantua* to explore it in all its complexity. How should a community respond to arbitrary aggression? Is it possible to wage a just war? How can one establish and maintain peace with a defeated enemy? These are some of the questions I like to investigate with my students through an attentive reading of the Picrocholine war, the satirical account of war and peace that makes up roughly the second half of *Gargantua* (chs. 25–51). In my experience, teaching this text is as entertaining as it is challenging, because its complexity requires us to be selective—especially if the time in the classroom is limited. As Michael Screech rightly observes, "the Picrocholine War is like a rope, made up of many strands, which form a single whole but never merge completely" (*Rabelais* [1979] 173).

In this essay, I suggest a sequence that foregrounds the absurdity of war and the challenges of maintaining peace, putting less stress on the anticlerical satire and criticism of monastic life that Rabelais weaves into his narration of Picrochole's attack on Grandgousier and his people. The sequence, which can be taught in two to three sessions, deliberately focuses on select chapters rather than on the story as a whole, which alternates periods of war and episodes of relative peace.[1] This strategy allows students to examine critically the origins of the conflict between the cake bakers and the shepherds, to explore their kings' diametrically opposed approaches to war, and to probe the limits of those approaches. Students analyze Gargantua and Frère Jean as members of a generation of pragmatist leaders whose victory over Picrochole is compromised by their unbridled violence and called into question by the problematic vision of a peaceful society they create in the end, the community of the Abbey of Thélème. In *Gargantua*, war leaves no hero untainted and reveals above all that peace is not only precarious but also a predicament, posing complicated questions and requiring difficult choices.

To begin the discussion about war and peace in *Gargantua*, I ask students to scrutinize the origins of the conflict in chapter 25 and to consider who is responsible for it. Students tend to put the blame for the creation and escalation of the dispute on the Lernean cake bakers alone, since they pass through the land where the shepherds guard the vines, refuse to sell their products, and call the shepherds "jolis rouquins" (169; "crazy carrot-heads" [94]) and worse, to add insult to injury. Marquet humiliates and attacks Frogier, a "bien honnête homme" (171; "a distinguished young man" [94]). Finally, after the brawl, the shepherds pay market price for the desired cakes and add nuts and grapes to make up for their revenge.

When encouraged to take a closer look at the evolution of the conflict, however, students notice that, on the bakers' provocation, the shepherds are quick to retaliate. After being insulted, Frogier threatens economic sanctions and other vague reprisals. When Marquet tricks and whips him, Frogier calls him a murderer and throws a stick at the fleeing Marquet's head, almost killing him. With the assistance of fellow farmers, the shepherds attack the retreating cake bakers. Thus the escalation of violence can be attributed as much to the gentle yet forceful shepherds and farmers as to the uncooperative and provocative bakers.

If one considers that the Lerneans are under no obligation to sell their bread, the question of who is responsible for the conflict becomes even more difficult to answer. Frogier accuses the bakers of being dishonest neighbors and points out the economic interdependence of bakers and shepherds, even though, strictly speaking, shepherds do not produce the grain the bakers need. While the shepherds and farmers tend to Grandgousier's land, the enterprising bakers are manufacturers on their way to the city. The Lerneans' refusal to sell and their denigration of the shepherds as "croquants" ("boors") and "fainéants" (169; "lazy louts" [94]) indicate that they have become interested in other markets and sources of income.[2] I point out to the students that the shepherds assume they are entitled to purchase the cakes because of custom. I ask if the shepherds have a right to expect and ultimately force the bakers to sell them their products, especially if one considers that the shepherds' desire for cake could be argued to have triggered the controversy with the Lerneans, who are just passing by on their way to the city.

A careful evaluation of the initial conflict usually leads students to the insight that shepherds and bakers are equally responsible for the violent escalation of a chance encounter at what turns out to be the fateful "grand carrefour" (169; "great crossroad" [94]) of peace and war.[3] The idyll of Touraine, based on vague notions of good neighborliness and customary behavior, emerges as profoundly precarious in a world of changing economic and other interests. Peaceful cohabitation can quickly unravel if neighbors are pugnacious people with a tit-for-tat mentality.

The banal skirmish becomes a full-fledged war, because the Lerneans are ruled by a choleric despot. Under Picrochole, Rabelais's caricature of a belligerent tyrant, the dispute between the shepherds and the bakers grows fast out of proportion and turns into a grotesque and bloody war. To retrace the main characteristics of the Lernean king, I ask students to focus on chapters 26, 28, and 33 either in small groups or for a homework assignment. To begin the discussion, I explain that the tyrant's Greek name means "bitter bile," which in Rabelais's time was thought to be one of four humors triggering choleric behavior, treachery, and thirst for glory. I ask students to relate the significance of the name to Picrochole's impulsive, drastic actions. The name suggests that the king's behavior is solely the result of his character: there is no indication of previous experience, political ideals, or learning that might inform his decisions. Picrochole is Grandgousier's and Gargantua's opposite: he rushes to arms as soon as he hears about the shepherds' attack and sees the badly bruised Marquet, uncritically taking the visual evidence as irrefutable proof that what his people report is the truth. While still dining, he organizes an army of gigantic proportions, which he leads into a ruthless campaign against the quiet and peaceful people of Grandgousier "sans ordre ni organisation" (175; "in rash and disorderly fashion" [96]). Lacking any interest in the welfare of his people, the unreflecting king falls easy prey to his counselors, the *duc de Menuail* ("Duke of Chuckout"), *comte Spadassin* ("Earl of Swashbuckler"), and *capitaine Merdaille* (197; "Captain Dungby" [109]), whose claim to moral authority and political prudence is immediately undermined by their names and their obsession to become themselves rulers of foreign territories. Feeding Picrochole's unbridled megalomania, they propose an absurd plan for world conquest. Picrochole's few laconic comments and questions expose him further as a greedy and selfish tyrant who is preoccupied with his personal comfort. Finally, by responding to Ecephron, who wonders about the purpose of the huge military campaign, Picrochole himself reveals it as utterly pointless: "[la fin] sera . . . que nous pourrons nous reposer à notre aise quand nous serons rentrés" (203; "The end will be . . . that when we are back we shall rest at our ease" [112]). The Lernean king, already exhausted from just imagining his conquest of the world, wages a war for the sake of waging war, without any ideal or higher purpose. As commander in chief he ignores cautioning voices like Ecephron's and disregards warnings about the sinking morale of his disorganized troops. Notwithstanding all these flaws, Picrochole and his men wreak enormous havoc, until they are defeated by Gargantua.

Rabelais achieves great comic effect, despite the devastating results of Picrochole's regime, by limiting the tyrant's megalomaniac project of world conquest to a narrowly defined area of Touraine. I ask the students to note and reflect on the striking presence of topographical names, like the ford of Vède or the Abbey of Seuillé, that delimit the terrain of Picrochole's military campaign. Before long, they pick up on the hybrid, undefinable nature of the war between Picrochole and Grandgousier. Partly real, partly imagined, the military conflict between two peoples ruled by two kings is occasioned by a local skirmish and inscribed in an imperial master plan. Referring to Plato's *Republic*, Grandgousier thinks of the conflict as a civil war or "de troubles internes" (247; "sedition" [138]), even though he recognizes Picrochole as the king of Lerné and interprets his aggression as an attack on Grandgousier's domain and sovereignty. Shifting among the local, the national, and the global, the Picrocholine war conflates the qualities and dimensions of a civil war, an international conflict, and an imperial conquest. Rabelais transforms it into an absurd and cruel enterprise, an emblem of all wars, and in so doing suggests that all war is absurd.

With this critical understanding of Picrochole and the war he wages, the students are ready to shift the analytic focus to Grandgousier, Rabelais's model of an irenic prince. Split up in small groups for a compare-and-contrast exercise, they study chapters 28, 29, 32, and 46 to examine Grandgousier's approach to the conflict, which is diametrically opposed to Picrochole's. Grandgousier first wonders what the aggressor's motives are and asks God for advice and guidance. Considering the well-being of his subjects the highest priority, he insists that all options be exhausted before the decision to go to war is made. His swiftly convened council sends Ulrich Gallet to find out about Picrochole's grievances, and he calls Gargantua back from Paris to help avert the war. In his letter to Gargantua, he lays out a number of important principles that guide his action in the face of military menace. The contrast between this measured approach and Picrochole's impulsive behavior could not be starker.

Grandgousier is portrayed as a pious ruler, faithful to the Christian commands of clemency and generosity. He interprets Picrochole's erratic actions as a former friend's fall from divine grace:

> Dieu l'Éternel l'a abandonné à la gouverne de son libre arbitre et de sa raison privée. Sa conduite ne peut qu'être mauvaise si elle n'est continuellement éclairée par la grâce de Dieu. (187)
>
> God Almighty has abandoned him to the guidance of his own free will and understanding, which cannot but be evil unless it be continually prompted by divine grace. (103)

Rabelais opposes Grandgousier's devotion to Picrochole's superficial Christianity, which is displayed only on rare occasion. The trust in divine guidance and justice thus constitutes a fundamental difference between the two kings and their approaches to war.

Students also tend to observe the difference in age and physical strength between the two kings. Echoing a war-weary Charlemagne at the end of the *Song of Roland*, "vieux bonhomme Grandgousier" (183; "that good old man Grandgousier" [101]) bemoans the frailty of his body and dreads the heavy armor he must put on his shoulders, although he never actively takes part in the military conflict. Unlike Picrochole, he indulges in sensual pleasures and increasingly copious banquets after Gargantua's return (chs. 37–41), the defeat of Picrochole's scouts (chs. 45–46) and the final victory, "le festin le plus magnifique, le plus copieux et le plus délicieux que l'on ait vu depuis le temps du roi Assuérus" (265; "the most magnificent, the most sumptuous and delicious feast that had been seen since the days of King Ahasuerus" [149]). When Grandgousier is not organizing banquets or holding council, he is waiting and praying. Gargantua returns from the battlefield to find his father "dans son lit, [priant] Dieu pour leur salut et leur victoire" (241–42; "in bed, praying to God for their safety and victory" [135]). Whereas Picrochole is a man of direct action, Grandgousier relies on Gallet for his diplomatic efforts and on Gargantua and Frère Jean for the liberation of his people. Rabelais's irenic king is strikingly limited in his ability to translate words and ideals into action. Of an older generation, Grandgousier cannot prevent war in the face of a younger, ruthless tyrant. He is condemned to become the onlooker of an unavoidable and gruesome mass massacre; his principles, especially the wish to avoid bloodshed, are cruelly ineffective.

While Grandgousier tries to appease Picrochole through diplomacy and even bribery (ch. 32) but to no avail, Gargantua and his men counter Picrochole on the battlefield. In a text that seems carefully built on binary oppositions, the triangular constellation of the protagonists is striking. I invite students to reflect on the meaning of an opposition to Picrochole that is split between Grandgousier and Gargantua. If we take into account Frère Jean, Picrochole faces two formidable adversaries on the battlefield. Instructed and protected by Grandgousier, Gargantua and Frère Jean represent a younger generation that embraces his ideals and values but does not shy away from putting them into action. After all, it was Grandgousier who admonished his son that "vaines sont les études et inutile la volonté qui ne passent pas à exécution, grâce à la vertu, en temps opportun" (185; "study is vain and counsel useless unless at due season it is valorously applied and carried out" [103]). Besides the generational difference, Rabelais's split between Grandgousier's diplomatic efforts and Gargantua's violent attacks signifies a gap between irenic discourse and the military action that becomes necessary to respond to an aggressive enemy and that thus calls into question the validity of irenic discourse.

The difference between Picrochole and Grandgousier and their respective camps diminishes when one examines Gargantua and Frère Jean as war heroes. Their opposition to Picrochole proves effective because they share the tyrant's thirst for action. In chapters 36 and 44 we learn that Gargantua, who immediately follows his father's request to end his studies and apply his knowledge in the struggle against Picrochole, displays remarkable strategic skills. In tandem with Frère Jean, he offers a spectacle of raw physical violence. Gargantua destroys the castle of Vède and annihilates all its inhabitants after a cannonball attack. His desire for revenge echoes Frogier's: "La vendange vous coûtera cher!" (211; "You shall pay dearly for your vintage" [117]). Gargantua's initial misinterpretation of the cannonball as a grape pip and of other projectiles as horseflies lays only a thin comical veil on the ensuing carnage, which is narrated in gory detail:

> [Gargantua] abbatit à grands coups les tours et les fortifications et fit tout s'effondrer en ruine. De la sorte, tous ceux qui se trouvaient à l'intérieur furent écrasés et mis en pièces. (211)

> [Gargantua] threw down the towers and fortifications, laying it all level with the ground. In this way those inside were all crushed and smashed to pieces. (118)

The diluvial flood caused by the urination of his mare kills so many people that their corpses clog the nearby millstream. When Eudemon's horse gets stuck while crossing the stream and trampling over a human cadaver, Gargantua "du bout de son bâton, répandît le reste des tripes du vilain dans l'eau pendant que le cheval en question levait le pied" (213; "pushed the rest of the ruffian's guts down the water with his staff, while the horse pulled out his leg" [118]). Frère Jean's slaughter of two archers is described in similarly visceral terms. The use of medical terminology in this passage turns it into a parody of epic chivalric duels, but the graphic details of "l'énorme massacre" (241; "enormous slaughter" [134]) also reveal the monk's gratuitous brutality. When Frère Jean sees Picrochole's men flee the battlefield, he

> descend de cheval et . . . avec son grand braquemart, il frappait sur ces fuyards à tour de bras, sans se ménager, sans épargner sa peine. Il en tua tant, en jeta tant à terre qu'il brisa son braquemart en deux. Alors il se dit en lui-même que c'était assez massacré et tué, que le reste devait en réchapper pour en porter la nouvelle. (241)

> dismounted from his horse . . . and struck at the fugitives with his stout short-sword, making great sweeps with his arm and neither stinting nor sparing; and so many did he kill and bring to the ground that his sword broke in two. Then he decided that he had killed and massacred enough, and that the rest should be left to escape and carry the news. (135)

Having been attacked first, both Gargantua and Frère Jean act in self-defense, but the scope and nature of their response annul Grandgousier's principle that "le résultat sera atteint avec la moindre effusion de sang possible" (187; "our measures will be carried out with the least possible bloodshed" [103]). That Grandgousier's lieutenants prevail because one is a giant and the other has a mysterious frock rendering him invulnerable further dims the glory of their heroic deeds. In keeping with *Gargantua*'s gigantism, both heroes have a grotesque amount of blood on their hands. Yet, the satirical depiction of the violence suggests, disquietingly, that the bloodshed would have been worse had regular mortals confronted each other.

When Picrochole flees the scene after a devastating defeat, Gargantua follows him for a while "en tuant et en massacrant" (257; "killing and massacring" [144]) before he returns to reestablish peace. Immediately reverting to Grandgousier's irenic principles, he gives examples of extraordinary largesse in dealing with his soldiers and Picrochole's conquered people. Yet Gargantua's words and deeds are overshadowed by his violence during the war. This discrepancy lends him the first tinge of ambiguity. I ask students to study his address to the vanquished (ch. 50) carefully and to evaluate the extended exemplum of Grandgousier's clemency and generosity toward Alpharbal, king of Canaria. Echoing the grotesque reciprocation of violence at the beginning of the Picrocholine war, Alpharbal's return of an absurd amount of gifts as signs of his gratitude and Grandgousier's desperate attempts to contain the ruinous gift exchange expose as fiction both the Canarian king and the idea that clemency pays. Moreover, the exemplum demonstrates that clemency is not innocent but a calculated effort to humble and oblige the enemy to gratitude.

Gargantua is the first to recognize that Grandgousier's irenic principles might not be entirely realistic. Proclaiming that "la faiblesse de pardonner aux méchantes gens, leur offre l'occasion de plus facilement commettre de nouveaux méfaits" (263; "too feeble and spineless readiness to pardon malefactors is the cause of their lightly doing wrong again" [148]), he keeps Marquet and Picrochole's advisers as prisoners. In a position more imperious than generous, he stipulates that Ponocrates be the de facto governor of Picrochole's state as long as Picrochole's son is deemed unfit to rule. Finally, he declares Marquet "la source et la cause initiale de cette guerre" (265; "the origin and fomentor of this war" [148]), clearing his own subjects of any responsibility, as it is the victor's right. Well aware that he rules over a people still rancorous, Gargantua has a sizable escort accompany those whom he releases from captivity, so that they are not molested by the peasants. Even though, for the time being, the danger of warfare has vanished with Picrochole, the people's inclination to quarrel and retaliate has not. Fearing further uprisings, Gargantua even establishes a garrison in a newly built fort near La Roche-Clermault.

Thus at the end of the war there are already signs that the people have not changed despite their enormous suffering. It remains uncertain how long the reestablished peace will hold and if it will be more than another interwar period. We never learn what the reaction of the released prisoners is, if they become good neighbors again, and how they take to their new life under Ponocrates's rule. For a final discussion about the representation of war and peace in *Gargantua*, I point out to students that the narration does not return to the initial idyll of Touraine but moves on to the utopian Abbey of Thélème, where

> les gens libres, bien nés, bein éduqués, vivant en bonne société, ont naturellement instinct, un aiguillon qu'ils appellent honneur et qui les pousse toujours à agir vertueusement et les éloigne du vice. (285)

> people who are free, well-born, well-bred, and easy in honest company have a natural spur and instinct which drives them to virtuous deeds and deflects them from vice. (159)

Students quickly realize that the harmony of Thélème is as deceptive as that of a day during vintage season in Touraine, because it is built on the exclusion of pugnacious people like the shepherds and the cake bakers and of abusive rulers like Picrochole.

The peace of Thélème, relying on the utopian negation of any desire of distinction or will of domination, points most of all to the fact that peace in *Gargantua* remains a difficult, unresolved question. At the beginning, it is nothing more than a fragile state of nonwar that a virtuous king like Grandgousier cannot preserve because his irenic principles and discourses fail in the face of a ruthless enemy. Gargantua's military action reestablishes peace, but it is a peace secured only by the presence of a military escort and garrison—a meager result, if one considers the bloodshed that was required to achieve it.

Mixing the local and the global, the comic and the tragic, the parodic and the satirical, Rabelais casts the Picrocholine war as a horrid and dehumanizing enterprise that leaves no hero untainted and shows the limits of the noblest ideals. Through his artful narration he conveys the absurdity of war and reveals peace as profoundly precarious. Tightly interwoven with war, peace in *Gargantua* is an exception and calls for new ideas and strategies to realize and sustain it. Rabelais leaves it up to us and our students to find them.

NOTES

[1] For a reading of the Picrocholine war that focuses on the blending of war and peace and on the combination of genres (epic, colloquy, utopia), see Hampton, *Literature* 66–108.

[2] See Zegura and Tetel for an interpretation of the Picrocholine war as a series of perverted exchanges in an evolving economy (72–80).

[3] In his analysis of chapter 25, Rigolot, for whom the Picrocholine war is above all a fight "sur le terrain du langage" (*Langages* 130; "on the territory of language"), reaches a similar conclusion if for different reasons: "la question n'était pas de nous faire prendre parti dans cette rixe . . . on ne saurait mépriser des insultes aussi savoureuses" (132; "the point here is not to make us side with somebody in this brawl . . . it is impossible not to savor such juicy insults").

Teaching Gargantua's Letter to Pantagruel

Cynthia Skenazi

My teaching of Gargantua's letter to Pantagruel takes place in undergraduate, upper-division, middle-size classes on irony in sixteenth-century literature. I also offer an in-depth version of this course as a graduate seminar. My students read *Pantagruel* in conjunction with works by Desiderius Erasmus, Clément Marot, Marguerite of Navarre, Joachim du Bellay, and Michel de Montaigne. Both classes are taught in French and include a discussion of definitions of irony from antiquity to the twenty-first century. Gargantua's letter to Pantagruel provides a fruitful way of addressing some of the course's major concerns: How do we know a text is ironic? To what extent is irony a question of intention (on the part of the author) or of interpretation (on the part of the reader)? This letter has generated divergent reactions. It was hailed as a manifesto of humanism by scholars such as Lucien Febvre (*Problème* 183), and it has been presented as representative of Rabelais's intellectual, pedagogical, and religious ideals in numerous anthologies of French literature. For other critics, in contrast, chapter 8 of *Pantagruel* raises questions about education instead of offering a normative program of learning (Huchon, *Œuvres* 1268–69; Gray, *Rabelais et le comique* 157–67). Such readings not only stress the ambiguity of Rabelais's text, they also suggest that the criteria for defining humanism have changed over time and according to their interpreters. The tone of the chapter is at the heart of the debate: should Gargantua's advice to his son be taken seriously or with tongue in cheek? Is the letter a pastiche of Ciceronian epistolary style, or should its eloquence be taken seriously? My course capitalizes on the ludic and polemical potential of these ambivalences and on the linguistic game opened up by this process.

To view this chapter without a glance at its historical background would be to place a severe limitation on its meaning. By and large, Gargantua's letter belongs to the humanist culture of Francis I's time, with its emphasis on education and personal meditation of the Bible, read in the original text, but it popularizes these views in a vernacular language. Likewise, the inclusion of Greek and Hebrew in Pantagruel's course curriculum echoed royal propaganda, because these languages were beginning to be taught in Paris, at the Collège des Lecteurs Royaux ("College of Royal Readers"), founded in 1530 (the battle for making Greek and the Bible accessible was actually far from won). Other aspects of the letter would also have appeared familiar to Rabelais's fellow humanists: Gargantua's enthusiasm for knowledge, his blessing of a child born out of wedlock, his wish of immortality through his son, his observation that moral integrity, faith, and sound learning should be used well—if not used well, they lead to the downfall of the soul. Even the ways of conveying these ideas—a father's letter of advice, the description of a course curriculum—were hardly original. Gargantua's use of clichés reinforces this impression of déjà vu. We find, for example, the contrast between a dark and ignorant Middle Ages, on the one hand, and, on the other, the advent of an era of intellectual and spiritual renewal, a contrast that was a commonplace in humanist propaganda. Among other references that epitomize the recent enlightenment are the invention of the printing press, the growing number of libraries, and, less peaceful, the progress of artillery.

What is unusual, however, is the way in which this chapter lends itself to interpretations both serious and playful of such progress. In his enthusiasm for the new learning, Gargantua envisions a world in which everyone is equally erudite, regardless of social and gender distinctions. It is hard not to smile at his placing of women and girls after male criminals:

> Je voy les brigans, les boureaulx, les avanturiers, les palefreniers de maintenant, plus doctes que les docteurs et prescheurs de mon temps. Que diray-je? Les femmes et les filles ont aspiré à ceste louange et manne céleste de bonne doctrine. (247)

> I find robbers, hangmen, freebooters, and grooms nowadays more learned than the doctors and preachers were in my time. Why, the very women aspire to the glory and reach out for the celestial manna of sound learning. (194–95)

Other observations, such as Gargantua's praise of the erudition of his son's former tutors, also strike an ironic note, since the previous chapters insist on the negative aspects of Pantagruel's grand tour of the French universities: the young giant took great care not to spend too much time studying "de peur que la veue luy diminuast" ("for fear of spoiling his sight"); if he didn't make any scholarly progress, in contrast, "sçavoit fort bien danser et jouer à la paulme" (234; he became "very good at dancing and tennis" [183]).

Gargantua's description of his son's course curriculum, the aspect of the chapter that invariably attracts the students' attention, is inscribed in the world of imagination. One cannot expect students to be familiar with every aspect of the distant past; I therefore assign them Edwin M. Duval's comments on this chapter (Duval, *Design of Rabelais's* Pantagruel 43–51). Before starting the discussion, students understand that the curriculum list should be read as an ironic and polemical revision of the obsolete medieval system that was still in place. For his first degree, the bachelor of arts, a student was required to master the seven liberal arts, which consisted of three language arts, the trivium (grammar, rhetoric, dialectic), and four quantitative arts, the quadrivium (arithmetic, music, geometry, astronomy). Having left the faculty of arts, the student could then enter one of three faculties: law, medicine, theology, given in the order of their prestige. Gargantua's program represents a move away from such a Scholastic arrangement. Instead of grammar, Pantagruel is encouraged to learn Latin, Greek, Hebrew, Chaldean, and Arabic. These changes reflect the humanists' excitement of having access to texts from the ancients. Hebrew and Chaldean would allow Pantagruel to read the Old Testament in the original version, and Arabic would allow him to study medical texts. The study of dialectic, part of the existing requirements, is replaced by philology and history, which are both at the center of the humanists' interests.

The satire of the useless knowledge that forms the major aspect of the daily classroom is obvious in other aspects of Gargantua's pedagogical views as well: rhetoric is no longer an art of argumentation but focuses on the acquisition of a perfect style through imitation. Similar revisions appear in the arts that form the quadrivium. The brief mention of the quadrivium in the description of Pantagruel's course curriculum suggests that Gargantua considers this part less important than the language arts. Indeed, the giant gave his son the basic notions of the quadrivium during Pantagruel's childhood. Gargantua proceeds to a similar revision of the curriculum that was in effect in the faculties of law, medicine, and theology: he rejects the gothic conception of law with its useless emphasis on glosses; in medicine, he emphasizes the study of anatomy and privileges observation over the memorization of obsolete books by ancient authors that was then required; in theology, he focuses on personal and daily meditations of the Bible read in the original language and on leading a Christian life (Duval, *Design of Rabelais's* Pantagruel 43–51).

Despite these innovative ideas, students invariably find Pantagruel's encyclopedic course curriculum overwhelming; even a giant with unusual intellectual capacities, they observe, would be forced to study continuously. Whereas the previous chapters stressed Pantagruel's waste of time during his grand tour of the universities, Gargantua's educational program allows Pantagruel no free time. Course requirements in the twenty-first century are much lighter than they were in Rabelais's day, but even so Gargantua is obviously exaggerating: Pantagruel is asked to be fully acquainted with every aspect of nature (surprisingly, the letter does not ask him to travel): he should know the fish of every sea, river, or spring,

> tous les oyseaulx de l'air, tous les arbres, arbustes et fructices des forestz, toutes les herbes de la terre, tous les métaulx cachez au ventre des abysmes, les pierreries de tout Orient et Midy. (248)

> all the birds of the air, all the trees, shrubs, and bushes of the forest, all the herbs of the field, all the metals deep in the bowels of the earth, the precious stones of the whole East and the South. (195)

In addition, he is asked to go to all three faculties of law, medicine, and theology rather than to only one of them, as was the norm in Rabelais's time. Gargantua's educational program ends with a wish that strikes another ironic note: the giant writes to Pantagruel, "Somme, que je voy un abysme de science" (248; "let me find you a veritable abyss of science" [195]). As stressed in *Gargantua*'s "Advice to Readers", "le rire est le propre de l'homme" (37; "laughter is man's proper lot" [36]), and Rabelais fully exploits this remark in his fictional world.

Despite the scope of Pantagruel's curriculum, students are quick to point out significant omissions: Pantagruel is not asked to learn any modern language, not even French. His studies focus exclusively on the training of the mind; nowhere does Gargantua mention physical education. The relevance of Pantagruel's courses is another matter of concern: as the most astute students notice, his education is bookish, to the extent that he would be better equipped for a life of scholarship than for kingship. Gargantua himself confirms the lack of relevance of such education: when Pantagruel has grown into a man, he states, he will have to leave his studies: "il te fauldra yssir de ceste tranquillité et repos d'estude: et apprendre la chevalerie, et les armes pour defendre ma maison, et nos amys secourir" (248; "you will have to leave this quiet and repose of study, to learn chivalry and warfare, to defend my house, and to help our friends" [195]). Finally, who could take seriously Gargantua's wish to have his son show how much he "profited" from his studies: "Et veux que de brief tu essaye combien tu as proffité, ce que tu ne pourras mieulx faire, que tenent conclusions en tout sçavoir publiquement envers tous et contre tous" (248; "I wish you shortly to show how much you have profited by your studies, which you cannot do better than by publicly defending a thesis in every art against all persons whatsoever" [196])? Could this playful parody of Pico della Mirandola's legendary erudition really be the proof (or the goal) of Pantagruel's education (Defaux, *Rabelais* 218)?

We then discuss the chapter's first and last paragraphs, whose ludic tone also resists the unconditional praise of knowledge that some critics have attributed to this text. Pantagruel's intellectual skills, taking on a concrete form, sharply contrast with his father's elegant style. At the opening of the chapter, the giant is said to have "l'entendement à double rebras et capacité de mémoire à la mesure de douze oyres et botes d'olif" (244; a "double-sized intelligence and a memory equal in capacity to the measure of twelve skins and twelve casks of oil" [192]), and again, at the end of the chapter, on receipt of Gargantua's letter, Pantagruel's enthusiasm for learning is such that "tel estoit son esperit entre les livres comme est le feu parmy les brandes, tant il l'avoit infatigable et strident" (249; "his spirit among the books was like fire among the heather, so indefatigable and ardent was it" [196]). It is hard to forget that the verb *profiter* ("to profit"), which characterizes Pantagruel's zealous learning in the first and last sentences of the chapter as well as in Gargantua's letter (244, 248–49; 192, 196), referred to his enjoyment of earthly pleasures in chapter 5 (Gray, *Rabelais et le comique* 158).

As we read the closing lines of the chapter, I point out that the letter was sent from Utopia (from the Greek "nowhere"). Thomas More never thought of his fictional island as a possible and viable society. His description rather offered an optic of seeing the various problems plaguing sixteenth-century England in a ludic and critical perspective. Irony provided a way of eluding a unified view and a dogmatic position. Likewise, Gargantua's pedagogical views echo sixteenth-century humanists' enthusiasm for learning, but the giant's course curriculum is presented as a utopian program of education: it is an intellectual construction whose practical application may not even be desirable. To ask whether this chapter expresses Rabelais's educational ideas or is only a playful game is a ludicrous question; one cannot favor one meaning over the other, as one leads to the other in a circular way.

Irony is a heuristic tool insofar as this letter confronts its readers with unresolved problems and different interpretations. Irony is a rhetorical way of avoiding a dogmatic and monolithic position on education and on what should be taught. The chapter therefore engages its audience in an exercise that is the exact opposite of the position of Pantagruel as passive recipient of knowledge: it stimulates the reader's participation, requiring analytic skills as well as imagination. In contrast, Gargantua's pedagogical program fosters in his son a properly docile attitude toward authority: for the giant, knowledge is something given, to be mastered, not questioned, and is transmitted uncritically. The instructor is in total control of Pantagruel's education. Pantagruel may not choose his courses or give his opinion on the matters under consideration. His education is based on exhaustive reading and memorization, but the process of appropriation is lacking. His father does not even allow him time to digest what he learns, to reissue it as his own personal discourse. The letter hardly raises the question of the practical transmission of knowledge from teacher to student; Gargantua briefly mentions that Pantagruel has his tutor, Epistemon, and that Pantagruel attends courses given at the university, but as any instructor knows, learning requires practice, challenge, encouragement, correction, and close monitoring. To what extent is such an autocratic conception of pedagogy vulnerable to the charge of nonproductiveness? In contrast, a discussion of *Pantagruel,* chapter 8, provides students with an opportunity to deliberate, argue, and exercise choices; it engages them in a collaborative learning experience.

A problem one often encounters when teaching older, foreign literature is its alleged lack of relevance. This problem is not encountered with Gargantua's letter to Pantagruel, which opens discussion to important pedagogical issues in general. Each period and each society has specific expectations concerning education. Which ones are ours? What should be the goals of a liberal education? Can education improve society, as Gargantua claims, and if so, how? Since Pantagruel is destined to be king, should future rulers undergo special training that prepares them for leadership, and what should such a program be? Engaging students in debate, addressing questions that are relevant to their lives is a way of tapping into their ability to make and defend their claims in a persuasive manner. In addition, arguing requires both listening closely to others and elaborating on one's views. Interestingly, this kind of dialogue and exchange is missing in Pantagruel's education.

Discussion of Gargantua's letter also raises questions concerning the overall design of Rabelais's *Pantagruel*. This issue has tantalized generations of critics: does each discussion constitute a separate entity, or is there an overarching structure to the book as a whole? (Gray [*Rabelais et le comique*] and Duval [*Design of Rabelais's* Pantagruel] respectively epitomize each of these positions.) Should integration be favored over fragmentation and interruption? Do the characters have coherent and consistent features from one episode to another? The answers are by no means straightforward; arguments can be made both in favor of and against continuity. On the one hand, Gargantua's pedagogical views are directly related to the previous chapters insofar as they represent a move away from the Scholastic education epitomized by Pantagruel's grand tour of the French universities (ch. 5), his encounter with the pretentious Limousin scholar (ch. 6), and the list of books from the library of Saint-Victor's (ch. 7). His scholarly and sterile erudition stands in sharp contrast to Panurge's practical mind in the next chapter (ch. 9). Panurge has been investigating the world around him instead of books; his knowledge comes from experience and includes the learning of modern languages, especially useful for travelers and traders (Cave, "Panurge"). Surprisingly, Pantagruel does not understand Panurge's Hebrew, Latin, and Greek, although these languages were part of the curriculum devised by his father in chapter 8. Furthermore, although he is ironically praised as a scholar during his debate at the Sorbonne (256; 202), he never uses his knowledge, except in the Baisecul-Humevesne controversy, which does not require any erudition (ch. 13).

The letter's elegant Ciceronian style, with its balanced periods and elevated tone, seems to contradict the thesis of continuity and integration. For French humanists of the early sixteenth century, eloquence was a crucial skill for men who hoped to advance in public life, and Cicero was the major model in this respect. Yet who could have anticipated such carefully crafted rhetoric after having read Gargantua's epitaph for his wife at the end of chapter 3 (227; 178)? One of the most attractive aspects of *Pantagruel*, chapter 8, is the way it joyfully challenges our traditional habits of thinking and our notion of coherence. Throughout this chapter, there is a feeling of liberation from conformism. Significantly, Gargantua's letter often emphasizes productivity. Such vitality is epitomized by the motif of seminal propagation and the repetition of the verb *to profit* (La Charité, "Gargantua's Letter").

Because exchange is at the heart of the epistolary genre, as we close our discussion I ask students to imagine Pantagruel's answer to his father. After all, pastiche is a recurrent Rabelaisian technique, and this exercise provides a good way to understand the aspects of the chapter to which the students have been sensitive. Furthermore, it allows them to explore the relationship between father and son from a creative perspective. Throughout this chapter, Gargantua appears as a loving and responsible father who expresses concern for the future of his son and gladly assumes his duty to educate him. The giant's wish to see in Pantagruel an improved image of himself is a legitimate one. If education reflects Gargantua's enthusiasm for learning, it is also intended to prepare Pantagruel for civic life. Gargantua takes care not to hurt his son's feelings by stressing that he only wants to encourage him in his determination to study; at the same time, he asserts the authority of age and experience. Writing Pantagruel's letter of response to Gargantua's requires an alert involvement that makes students producers of textual meanings rather than passive consumers of knowledge. Because writing and reading are complementary, this exercise illustrates that Gargantua's letter to Pantagruel is inconceivable outside the framework of imaginative literature.

Pantagruel, chapter 8, can be discussed in relation to many other texts, such as the description of Gargantua's education (*Gargantua*, chs. 23 and 24). Drawing parallels with Montaigne's "De l'institution des enfans" in the first book of his *Essays* (1.26; "Of the Education of Children" [*Complete Essays* (Frame) 145–77]) also familiarizes students with sixteenth-century French literature and culture. Gargantua's letter to Pantagruel can also be taught in courses whose focus is not only or primarily literature of sixteenth-century France: it can be included in classes on rhetoric, education, history, comparative literature, or anthropology.

Deciphering the Sibyl: *The Third Book*, Chapters 16–18

Floyd Gray

Since formalism and New Criticism have been consigned (temporarily at least) to oblivion by the advent of contemporary cultural studies, the most compelling way to introduce students to Rabelais's world would seem to be through its contexts. However, these contexts are so numerous and varied that a useful or meaningful selection is always difficult. An alternative might be a selective review of the history of the various ways in which his work has been read. To this end, I like to begin each class with a commentary on a quotation—with which I may or may not be in agreement—from, say, Charles Sainte-Beuve, V. L. Saulnier, François Rigolot, Edwin Duval, Gérard Defaux, or Michael Screech, a quotation I choose for its pertinence to the subject I intend to develop on a given day. This has proved to be a particularly successful pedagogical tactic for exploring various critical perspectives and promoting classroom discussion—not always an easy thing to achieve. In addition, students are made aware of the troubling fact that no particular reading ever exhausts all the readings that texts are capable of producing. A concurrent fact is that undecidability, viewed positively, is one of the factors that make works of literature forever new and readable.

The essential questions about Rabelais are how and for whom his work is written. Obviously he is both a promoter of laughter and a purveyor of "sustantificque mouelle" ("sustantific marrow"), but to what extent and in what proportion? Since comic and serious elements coincide and clash on every page of his work, one tending to deflate and discredit the other, the answer is all the more difficult—especially when the text refuses to choose, neither electing nor rejecting an approach. If, however, the reader privileges one over the other, the comic-serious bilingualism that makes Rabelais's writing Rabelaisian no longer obtains. Reading Rabelais then is not a simple matter of deciding what is serious and what is comic and, consequently, what is pertinent or superfluous. A meaningful reading entails both possibilities, the one in conjunction with the other. Students must be undecided which, if either, finally predominates or matters.

I find it useful to begin my reading of Rabelais by reminding students that words have a life and a meaning of their own. They say what they say, but they imply more or less than they say. Literature, after all, is a peculiar form of writing, and literary writing is always more than a transparent conveyor of thought. This elementary fact needs to be stressed, because students today are less likely to have had prior experience in dealing with words that work to contrive or conceal meaning. Content may reflect context and intent, but perception of their interrelation depends ultimately on the reader's own insights, interests, priorities, and prejudices. Thus I advise students that they are about to embark on a tortuous and perilous adventure, since at every word there is the danger of anachronistic interpretation and the consequent risk of misunderstanding. Reading Rabelais may be fun, but it's hard work as well. It is probably not realistic to expect students to move much beyond a grasp of what Rabelais's text actually says or seems to say, but there is no reason not to explore and test with them the advantages, disadvantages, techniques, and strategies of different approaches—literal, analogic, metaphoric, historical, structural, deconstructive, and so forth.

In most classroom situations there is not time for a whole work of Rabelais, so it can be economical yet effective to select one or two representative episodes. I have chosen here as a working example the three chapters that make up the "sibyl of Panzoust consultation" episode. While a partial and partisan reading of *The Third Book* and, more particularly, of these three chapters might result in readers' negative reaction to the vast repertory of antifeminist theses that form their core, a more literary, rhetorically oriented reading might lead to the conclusion that Rabelais's rehearsal of arguments for and against women is playful in intent. Today's readers may not be amused by these tired and traditional arguments, but there is reason to assume that Renaissance readers read them differently, more as comedy or satire than as social statement. Students should therefore exercise care in deciphering sixteenth-century norms of cultural expectations and political correctness.

Both the form and content of *The Third Book* contributed to the development of the novel. A brief review of the history of the medieval *roman* and, as a reactionary counterpart, of the emergence of antiromance, antifemale literatures in medieval comedy and fabliaux might be in order. This introduction could lead to a discussion of the respective roles of history and subject, content and context, in the ordering of Rabelais's fictional world. Literary history, for instance, tells us that the *querelle des femmes*, first brought to the fore by Abel Lefranc (*Rabelais*), is closely linked to the spread and originality of the novel in France. Thus, even during the heyday of heroic romances, the fabliau tradition continued to flourish, hostile and ironic toward women. The clash between these two distinct traditions accounts for much of the success and some of the complexity of *The Third Book*. Although it has not always been recognized that Rabelais's novel, much as Cervantes's *Don Quixote*, is in part an antinovel, a parody of medieval romances and a comic rewriting of the place men afforded women in courtly or Marian literature, this context would seem to be more useful than twenty-first-century cultural ideologies for an understanding of Rabelais's conceptual world in the realization of the *The Third Book*.

Critics concur that *The Third Book* is the most troublesome of Rabelais's four books to present and explain, because of its subject and the novelty of its structure. *Pantagruel* and *Gargantua* are organized along chronological lines, dealing with the story of the birth, genealogy, childhood, education, and deeds of their heroes. The narration is spatial as well, in that it follows them in their journey across contemporary France and far beyond, to mythical places such as the land of the Dipsodes and the world in Pantagruel's mouth. The fictional structure of *The Third Book* is radically different from that of *Pantagruel* and

Gargantua in that, instead of being strictly linear, it repeats a series of questions, answers, and opposing interpretations, monopolizing a space in which time and location are of no great importance.

The theme of giants, which gave thematic coherence, comic perspective, and narrative development to *Pantagruel* and *Gargantua*, is replaced in *The Third Book* by a search for an answer to the question of whether Panurge should marry and, if so, if cuckoldry would be his unavoidable fate. Recourse to different methods for predicting the future, including, eventually, the "sibyl of Panzoust" oracle, results in a repetitive and fragmented narration. Although Panurge is the central character throughout, his doubts and concerns are eclipsed by the intrusion of the technical languages and specialized knowledge of his successive consultants. Confronted by pages of dense and learned references to various ways of looking into the future, the reader might rightfully wonder at their relevance. At the close of the book, Panurge and the reader have not advanced a step toward an answer to the questions that began their search. Reduced to its fundamental structure and theme therefore, *The Third Book*, much like Paul Valéry's Achilles, appears "immobile à grands pas" (151 ["Le cimetière marin"]; "his giant stride immobile"). Even the antifeminist literature Rabelais gleefully exploits seems mostly redundant and derivative, collected for show rather than effect.

This being said, we might approach the "sibyl of Panzoust" episode through a backward glance at Diogenes's gratuitous tub thumping in the prologue of *The Third Book*. In many ways, his feverish activity prefigures Panurge's senseless quest for answers to his matrimonial doubts. Similarly, if we examine the subject matter and structure of the three main sections into which *The Third Book* is divided, successively the chapters on debtors and creditors, divinations and consultations, the plant called Pantagruélion, we are plunged into page after page of heavy, even ponderous prose with little thematic or narrative necessity. These separate sections may develop a number of cultural, philosophical, and satirical themes, but whatever continuity or interchange exists among them seems inconsequential. Throughout, the reader is confronted with masses of pointless erudition. Instead of recounting the tale of Panurge's quest simply and directly, *The Third Book* continues to roll its circular tub.

Taken as representative of the various interventions in *The Third Book*, the "sibyl of Panzoust" episode allows us to witness the integral play of comic and serious in Rabelais's writing. In order to demonstrate its basic ambivalence, one could begin with the word *sibyl*. Students may not know that sibyls are prophetic female characters in Greek and Latin literature and that the most famous of them is the Cumaean sibyl; they may not know that Rabelais's sibyl, according to Pantagruel, is the eleventh of that name.[1] But specific knowledge of the classical world is not enough, because Rabelais's sibyl is both classical and Rabelaisian, as the coupling of sibyl with Panzoust makes immediately apparent. Since Panzoust is the very French-sounding name of a locality near Chinon, it is remote in time, space, and resonance from the sacred groves of the sibyls of antiquity. Together, the noble sibyl and the phonetically humorous Panzoust exemplify something more than a classical or topological reference—namely, Rabelais's penchant for joining the serious with the comic, thereby giving each a new and different kind of relevance and resonance.

The three chapters that make up the "sibyl of Panzoust" episode provide eloquent examples of the convergence of antithetical strata of referential languages in Rabelais's writing.[2] Although there is much serious learning here, it is distorted and subverted by the contexts in which it occurs. The erudition adduced by Pantagruel and Epistemon to justify Panurge's visit to a sibyl is disqualified by the comedy of Panurge's matrimonial quest.

How might today's readers make sense of this and other elements of chapters 16–18? They could locate Panzoust on a map of the Chinon region (provided in most modern editions of *The Third Book*). That this place is so small and insignificant and practically unknown before Lefranc uncovered it suggests that for contemporary readers it did not contribute to Rabelais's realism. But even if it did, the name *Panzoust* is transformed by its association with the sibyls of antiquity. There is nothing inherently serious or comic about the words *sibyl* and *Panzoust*, but each is endowed with a measure of both in Rabelais's world. One can identify and gloss allusions and references to other books, people, and things at will (which has been done routinely by countless commentators), but this exercise tells us more about Rabelais's experiences and encyclopedic learning than the meaning they acquire in a new context.

Consider Pantagruel and Epistemon's concerted deferral in chapter 16 of Panurge's projected visit to the sibyl's cave. Their circumstantial deliberations afford a perfect example of the pronounced tendency of Rabelais's prose to wander and digress, protracting narrative progression and forestalling events or actions. Pantagruel's recommendation that Panurge confer with the sibyl is suspended momentarily by the introduction of a number of learned arguments for or against. Epistemon then gives copious reasons for not wanting to accompany Panurge in this visit. There are allusions to a Canidia, a Sagana, a pythoness, and a witch, together with references to the Law of Moses and Alexander the Great's victory over King Darius at the Battle of Arbela, the latter serving as a pretext for a long digression into Alexander's disappointment, because of the distance between Persia and Macedonia, at not being able to make his victory known quickly in his homeland, having refused the offer of a man from Sidon who claimed to have found a way to make the news known in less than five days. This is an example both of Pantagurel's circuitous way of encouraging Epistemon to take advantage of the present opportunity to visit the sibyl and of Rabelais's procrastination, giving his prose time and space to accumulate great quantities of extraneous erudition, a static material that in the end turns out to be much more charged with meaning than the activity of Panurge's quest.

Throughout this episode—indeed, throughout the whole work—Panurge and Pantagruel speak different languages. Panurge's is centered on the future; Pantagruel's is grounded in the past. This alternation of opposing discourses provides the substance and structure of their ensuing dialogue, here as well as in the other consultation episodes that make up *The Third Book*. Discursive logic and dynamic progression depend on the interchange of conflicting references and interpretations. Students should be asked how best to assess this admixture of erudition and experience, of book learning and practical application. The references and recommendations made by Pantagruel, who is cast as a paragon of wisdom and classical learning, seem pedantic as well as beside the point in relation to the immediacy of Panurge's quest for a definite and definitive answer to his matrimonial doubts. As a consequence, the giant's learned language takes on a decidedly comic twist.

In chapter 17, a reluctant Epistemon and hopeful Panurge arrive at the soothsayer's abode. At once, the gravity of their visit is abrogated by the comedy of the sibyl's appearance and Panurge's clumsy presentation of welcoming gifts. Whereas the sibyls of antiquity were located in legendary surroundings, Rabelais's is housed in a thatched cottage, poorly built, poorly furnished, and blackened from smoke. In addition, his sibyl is not a graceful figure but an old woman, ill-favored, ill-dressed, ill-nourished, runny-nosed, languid, and in the process of making a green cabbage soup with a rind of bacon and old broth from a soup bone (see Rabelais, *Complete Works* 305–06). Hardly a propitious scene for the performance of a solemn oracular prediction! Not unexpectedly, the consultation quickly degenerates into farce. All the classical, historical, biblical, "sustantificque mouelle" content comes tumbling down in the face of a contrasting context.

Attention should be drawn to the portrayal of the sibyl, not as a goddess but an old hag, though Epistemon persists in seeing her only through Homer's eyes, then to the long parodic description of her traditional trance and solemn oracular proceedings. In her garden, instead of the rustling leaves of the god's sacred oak, there is an old sycamore, which she shakes three times, and on eight leaves that fall from it she writes a few short verses. These she tosses to the wind for Panurge and Epistemon to track down. The text they manage to put together is doubly ambiguous: first, because ambiguity is the nature of oracular utterances; second, because the words are ordered by rhyme, their meaning is difficult to interpret:

T'esgoussera	Husk or shell
De renom.	She'll undo;
Engrossera.	Pregnant swell,
De toy non.	Not with you.
Te sugsera	Suck a spell
Le bon bout.	Your sweet tip;
T'escorchera,	Flay you well,
Mais non tout.	Save a strip.
(624)	(*Complete Works* 307)

In the last of the three chapters, Pantagruel and Panurge disagree as to the meaning of the sibyl's prophecy, Pantagruel reading it as unfavorable to Panurge's expectations and Panurge as favorable. The sibyl's words, able to be twisted and turned in either way, become a kind of minitext that Panurge and Pantagruel explicate.[3] Their dual reading affords an excellent example of comic interplay and serves also as a parody of the interpretive process itself. Reading the same words differently, Pantagruel with learned reference to classical antecedents, Panurge in comic anticipation of married life, they are emblematic of much of modern Rabelais criticism. Confronted with a text that is dense and complex from the play of "substantificque" and ludic discourses,[4] should we not attempt to reconcile one with the other, to realize finally that Rabelais, without both, would no longer be Rabelais?

Even with little knowledge and less interest in classical antiquity or sixteenth-century realities, students may come to appreciate that to read Rabelais is to learn a new language, to discover a radical, even revolutionary way of revisiting writing, transforming it into a vehicle of literary practice and thought. But what are they to make of Panurge's matrimonial uncertainties, which are of little interest to us today? Here, context can help: reference to sixteenth-century debates on marriage as a sacrament, to the proper situation of women in society, or to the role of rhetoric in ordering literary discourse. But is there more to these chapters? The sheer number of words suggests that there is. Consider the larger issue of the rights of divination (a question debated at the time) and the legality of clandestine marriages (also of contemporary concern). These issues afford options for teaching Rabelais from a historian's perspective, for presenting his work as a mirror of Renaissance society and culture. This approach could lead into a discussion of the seminal interpretations advanced by Lucien Febvre's *The Problem of Unbelief in the Sixteenth Century* or Mikhail Bakhtin's *Œuvre de François Rabelais et la culture populaire*. Since there are frequent reflections of sixteenth-century reality in Rabelais, there is no reason not to use them as reminders of historical occurrences.

A multiple approach has the advantage of being more comprehensive, allowing for a description not only of Rabelais's writing but also of the world in which Rabelais lived. Students should be told that Rabelais was a monk, became a doctor, fathered children, was censored by the Sorbonne, enjoyed the confidence and company of the great and powerful of his day. But to what extent can biography help us determine how his text reflects his religious and political positions or even the form his writing assumes? For example, are allusiveness and ambiguity the result of the fact that the times were dangerous and that heretical writing could lead to death at the stake?

Deciphering Rabelais requires caution and a blending of strategy with enthusiasm. Lessons learned from actual classroom experiences may help us teach his work as we think it should be read. But there is no sure method of presenting a text that continues to engage its readers in an unending, sometimes intense, intellectual dialogue. This ongoing dialogue is a sign of the richness and vitality of a work that after almost five centuries continues to amuse readers, arouse interest, and elude finality or closure. There would seem to be no last word, except, perhaps, the long anticipated word of the "Dive Bouteille." But even this word remains tentative, inasmuch as it only lurks on the horizon of a potentially inauthentic, final book.

NOTES

[1] As Screech solemnly notes, "Strictement parlant, il n'y avait que quatre Sibylles, à qui l'on ajoutait quelquefois six autres . . ." (Rabelais, *Tiers livre* [Screech] 124; "strictly speaking, there were only four sibyls, to which six others were sometimes added"). Sibyl is the name given by the Greeks and Romans to prophetesses inspired by some deity, usually Apollo. Collections of the several sibyls' prophecies were made and were known as the Sibylline Books. These were a gathering of oracular utterances in Greek hexameters from the time of Solon, said to have been brought from Greece to Cumae and from there to Rome. They were consulted in cases of great calamities, in order to learn how the displeasure of the gods might be averted in the future. That the sibyl's language was always appropriately sibylline allowed it to be interpreted in more ways than one.

[2] Commentators tend to mention this episode briefly, if at all, and then only to locate and explain learned and topographical references.

[3] See Glauser, *Fonctions* 118–20, for an analysis of how the explication of this minitext unfolds in accordance with the expansive requirements of Rabelaisian writing.

[4] Students who read French may consult a more detailed analysis of the interrelation of serious and ludic in Gray, *Rabelais et le comique*, esp. 179–86.

Modes of Transit: Domestication and Estrangement in *The Fourth Book*

Andrea Frisch

When reading Rabelais, students are often understandably frustrated at their inability to identify literary allusions and historical figures that have even specialists of sixteenth-century France scurrying for the footnotes. This frustration can be especially acute with respect to *The Fourth Book*, since it lacks a clear generic shape: whereas one can recognize something akin to a bildungsroman in *Gargantua* or *Pantagruel* and a comic quest in *The Third Book*, it is much more difficult to discern an organizing structural principle in *The Fourth Book*. (The staggering erudition required to argue for the book's possible design, as Edwin Duval has done [*Design of Rabelais's* Quart livre], is ample proof of this difficulty.) Unlike Rabelais's first three books, the fourth does not stay focused on a central figure whose progress (or lack thereof) one may track through the narrative. Moreover, the book's constantly shifting locales confront readers with a new setting every few chapters.

For all these reasons, *The Fourth Book* is often characterized as a travel narrative. Frank Lestringant calls the book a "fiction en archipel" ("archipelago fiction"), which privileges spatial over narrative logic ("Insulaire" 249). And yet there are long stretches in *The Fourth Book* where the spatial frame provided by the island-hopping journey all but disappears, as the characters tell stories set in other places (and other times). The book devotes as many pages to the interstices between the island visits that punctuate the *Thalamège*'s journey as it does to the crew's encounters with various exotic island (and sea) dwellers. Analogous to the *Thalamège* itself, the interstitial passages of *The Fourth Book* serve to tether one narrative event to another.

The purpose of this essay is to highlight the pedagogical potential of the narrative spaces between what one might call the experiential episodes. Inspired by Mikhail Bakhtin's analyses of the Rabelaisian "chronotope" ("Rabelaisian Chronotope" 167), I aim to track moments of transit-transition and thus to investigate the ties that bind one bit of the travel narrative to the next. Such an approach to Rabelais's book encourages students to become attentive to the ways in which material that is ostensibly extrinsic to the narrative of the voyage proper is brought into that narrative and to consider the functions of such insertions. This reading strategy allows for—but by no means requires—the relegation of obscure content to the background of the discussion. Ultimately it brings to the fore assumptions about what constitutes the main narrative itinerary, whose path Rabelais seems continuously to divert, and encourages recognition of the mutual dependence of the principles of continuity and discontinuity. It thus cultivates a reading practice that can readily be applied to other texts but that does not sacrifice sensitivity to historical specificity.

One of the best passages with which to initiate classroom discussion of the narrative interstices between the events of the voyage comes from chapters 33 and 34, which recount the dramatic defeat of a sea monster (a *physetère* or whale). While Panurge trembles in fear, sailors futilely hurl missles of every description at the oncoming animal, who has got close enough to spray his attackers. "Allors Pantagruel, considerant l'occasion et neycesité, desploye ses braz et monstre ce qu'il sçavoit faire" (984; "Then Pantagruel saw the urgency of the situation and put out all his strength" [522]). At this moment of high narrative tension, with Pantagruel about to slay the *physetère* and Panurge about to fall apart, the narrator interrupts his account of the action with four examples of nations known for their skill in archery: the Indians, the Franks, the Parthians, and the Scythians. Each example carries with it an anecdote about the people in question; as the series progresses, the relation between the anecdote and bowmanship becomes increasingly indirect (984, 986; 522–23). The interlude continues with an encomium to Pantagruel's prowess with darts and arrows that provides a textbook display of Erasmian copia (cf. Cave, *Cornucopian Text*), offering no less than six colorful variations on the phrase "Pantagruel was a very good archer" (986; 523). Only then, finally, do we return to the scene of the struggle between man and beast, where (one imagines) Pantagruel has been waiting in a state of suspended animation, his bow drawn taut: at last the tension is released, our hero's darts and arrows fly, the whale is destroyed, and the journey continues.

Although *The Third Book* remains the book of storytelling par excellence, embedded narration like that found in the episode of the *physetère* in fact makes up a significant portion of *The Fourth Book*. If the ship carries Pantagruel and his companions from island to island, the characters' tale-telling is often the vehicle by which the narrative advances (cf. Keller). There are several ways to approach this aspect of the book. According to Alice Fiola Berry, Rabelais's narrative proceeds by metalepsis or "transumption"—what she also calls "leaps in logic" ("'Isle Medamothi'" 1045)—a technique that ultimately betrays a "profound sense of transcendental homelessness" ("Mithologies" 476). Whereas this approach effectively calls off the search for meaningful links between episodes, Terence Cave's recent treatment of commonplaces in Rabelais invites readers to plumb their potential depths with the guidance of the full range of Renaissance rhetorical terminology. Cave invokes Thomas Greene's study of the modes of Renaissance *imitatio*, "ranging from respectful citation to antagonistic reaction or parodic distortion," and Antoine Compagnon's examination of the distinctions in Montaigne's *Essais* among *allégation*, *citation*, and *emprunt* ("borrowing") (Cave, "Thinking" 37; to this one could add Gérard Genette's *Palimpsestes*).

I believe that the best approach in the classroom is a modified version of Cave's program: instead of asking students straightaway to examine the construction of the narrative in terms of sixteenth-century rhetoric, one begins with a set of more general narratological questions. These can be addressed initially without extensive specialized knowledge of Rabelais's allusions; responding to them enlists the technique of close reading, which lends itself well to both class discussions and student presentations. What provokes the telling of a given story? What are some of the thematic relations between the content of a story and the experiential frame that surrounds it? What impact does a given story have on the characters? As students deepen their familiarity with the period, they should be able to modify and refine their responses without necessarily rejecting or invalidating their preliminary reading.

By way of example, I pose these questions with reference to three passages where storytelling among the characters in *The Fourth Book* assumes primacy over the representation of their experience en route to the oracle of the Holy Bottle. If Alcofribas's discourse on archery works primarily to heighten narrative tension, the episodes studied below show how embedded narratives can function as agents of both domestication and estrangement, two conceptual categories that will be immediately accessible to most students.

The span from chapter 10 to 15 of the *The Fourth Book* consists almost entirely of embedded narration that does not relay events of the voyage proper. At the level of the characters, this passage serves to domesticate the potentially exotic experience of the island of Chéli by interpreting it in relation to people and places with which Pantagruel and his crew are familiar. When Frère Jean explains why he has refrained from consorting with the maidens on the island of Chéli, where his companions have spent the day, he cites the negative example of someone who turns out to be one of Pantagruel's "meilleurs amis" (888; "best friends" [472]). When the friar praises Chelian cuisine, Epistémon is reminded of a hungry monk he encountered in Florence twenty years earlier, searching in vain for a rotisserie (890; 473). The discussion of monks' attraction to the kitchen is extended with a reading souvenir of Pantagruel's (892; for more examples of moments in which the characters' memories drive the narrative, see Smith, "Rabelais"). Finally, Panurge trumps Pantagruel's story with an anecdote from contemporary French history (892, 894; 474–75). The larger narrative thus moves from the experiential *hic et nunc* of an exotic locale, Chéli, back home to France by means of the exchange of stories among the characters—or what J. M. Cohen translates as "gossip" (475).

Of the five subsequent chapters devoted to the Chiquanous (12–16), four are cast as embedded narration. Unlike the inhabitants of Chéli, the Chiquanous do not invite Pantagruel and his companions to dine with them. Instead of exploring the island, then, the group initially bides their time on the ship, listening to stories about these strange people, who provoke their clients' enemies into beating them and then collect both a salary and legal damages. After a summary description offered by one of the group's interpreters—the first time we hear of the presence of these intermediaries, who give off an unmistakable, if muted, whiff of the exotic—the trickster Panurge gives a lengthy and detailed account of one Basché's strategy for getting rid of the Chiquanous sent by a friar intent on harassing him. Embedded in Panurge's story is another substantial tale, attributed to Basché himself, that establishes an analogy between Basché's servants and those of François Villon.

Throughout this part of the episode, which is significantly longer than any of *The Fourth Book*'s experiential passages, Pantagruel and his companions remain on the ship, silent and immobile. They speak up only at the very end of Panurge's tale, to comment on the moral of the story (in a discussion that briefly recalls those of the *devisants* ["discussants"] in Margucrite de Navarre's *Heptaméron*) before giving way to Frère Jean's announcement that he intends to verify what he's heard by going onto the island and seeing for himself (912; 486). The report of the friar's encounter with the Chiquanous is sketched in a few paragraphs, a minuscule island of experience afloat in a sea of stories. When the *récit* finally rejoins the *histoire* (to borrow Genette's terminology), the Chiquanous have been more or less domesticated, narratively speaking: Friar John's experience coincides with both his and the reader's prior knowledge, as it essentially reiterates what we have already heard from Panurge.

The several chapters (29–32) devoted to the anatomization of Quaresmeprenant by Pantagruel's companion Xenomanes add new levels of complexity to this line of analysis. The description paradoxically underlines the monster's strangeness by proposing a series of comparisons between his constituent parts and quotidian entities like bonnets, bagpipes, and biscuits. This passage is well known for its elaborate wordplay; the important point to make in this context, however, is that Quaresmeprenant is, in the end, represented as nothing more than a verbal performance by Xenomanes. The travelers never actually encounter this beast en route to the oracle of the Holy Bottle; the story told by one of the characters is the sole repository of the exotic, which is never encountered in the *hic et nunc* of the travel narrative.

But just how exotic is Quaresmeprenant? Students will likely assent to Samuel Kinser's observation that "bewilderment about the overall nature of Quaresmeprenant seems to augment rather than diminish with the addition of details" to Xenomanes's description (63). We should be careful, however, about attributing our own bewilderment to Pantagruel and his companions. At the beginning of chapter 29, it is noted that Pantagruel has already heard tell of Quaresemeprenant and would like to meet him. Xenomanes's resistance to this plan motivates his description of the monster; his portrait of Quaresmeprenant is expressly intended to discourage a stopover on the monster's island. One might legitimately suppose, then, that the portrait's extravagant incoherence is designed less to puzzle Pantagruel and his companions than to scare them off.

As Timothy Hampton notes, Xenomanes's exorbitant description produces "a kind of monster made out of words" ("Signs" 186). It bears pointing out, however, that the crew of the *Thalamège* seems to have no trouble interpreting this monstrous discourse. If Xenomanes's portrait of Quaresmeprenant profoundly estranges the reader, the characters in the book, for their part, exhibit a certain familiarity with this creature. Indeed, listening to Xenomanes, each of the companions seems to recognize Quaresmeprenant, albeit from his own perspective.

Frère Jean, ready for a fight when he hears that the monster is at war with the female Andouilles, announces at the end of the passage that he's found his man: "C'est mon home. C'est celuy que je cherche" (978; "That's my man. That's the fellow I'm after" [519]). Panurge quickly sizes up the danger the friar's plan would expose them to: "Combatre Quaresmeprenant . . . . [J]e ne suys pas si fol et hardy ensemble!" (966; "What, fight against Lent? . . . I'm not so crazy or so rash as that" [513]). And Pantagruel, ever the sage, is reminded of something he's read "parmy les Apologues antiques" (972; "in the ancient fables" [519]). The language of this scene is a far cry from the rhetoric of the exotic that one finds in contemporaneous travel literature, which emphasizes the impossibility of both description and interpretation (see, e.g., Cartier): Xenomanes, Frère Jean, Panurge, and Pantagruel integrate Quaresmeprenant into their own interpretive frameworks with the greatest of ease.

Unlike most nonfictional travel narratives, the account of the journey of the *Thalamège* frequently stages its own reception. These scenes of storytelling, these interstices between events, transport readers into the heart of Rabelais's fictional world. The dual nature of the Quaresmeprenant chapters, as agents of both domestication (for the characters) and estrangement (for readers), opens up a broader discussion of the contingencies that determine the status of both the domestic and the strange. The category of contingency, of course, brings back historical specificity, now inserted into a framework that can give students concrete strategies with which to tame—if never fully to domesticate—Rabelais's *Fourth Book*.

CLASSROOM CONTEXTS

Thawing the Frozen Words: The Importance of Aural and Visual Culture in Teaching Rabelais

Elizabeth Chesney Zegura

Despite the satiric verve and cornucopian richness of Rabelais's prose, teaching his mock epic can be a daunting task. Filled with lists, disjointed episodes, and non sequiturs, his works are among the most difficult in the French language; and notwithstanding the enthusiasm and critical insights that we as teachers bring to the classroom, hoping to make the Pantagrueline tales more accessible, it is not unusual to hear our best students admit that they simply "don't get" Rabelais. For them his words, like those of the shipwreck victims in *The Fourth Book*, are effectively frozen.

The key to "thawing" his text may well be embedded in *Gargantua,* where Rabelais proposes strategies for learning that breathe new life into the Utopian prince's education. Replacing the rote memorization of Scholastic pedagogy with games, group discussions, peer tutors, and field trips, the humanistic preceptor Ponocrates institutes a student-centered approach to teaching that awakens his pupil's "desir de estudier" (154; "desire to study" [my trans.]) The new tutor's pedagogical regimen, which incorporates interdisciplinary, dialogic, interactive, and multisensorial activities into the adolescent giant's curriculum, also provides useful resources for teaching Rabelais. In addition to poring over classical authors; visiting apothecaries, printers, and clock makers; and discussing the biological properties of food at mealtime, young Gargantua sings and plays the lute, spinet, or harp each evening after dinner; and on rainy days, he explores "l'art de paincture et sculpture" (164; "the arts of painting and sculpture" [92]).

Taking a cue from Rabelais, I will focus in this essay on the way Renaissance music and art can enhance our own students' interest in the Pantagrueline tales. References to music, composers, painting, and architecture figure prominently in *Gargantua* and *Pantagruel*, reminding us that the cultural backdrop from which Rabelais draws his inspiration is not just literary but visual and aural as well. Simply hearing the works of Josquin des Prez or glancing at woodcuts from early editions of Rabelais's chronicles can help communicate the flavor of his world to modern readers. Often, however, we gloss rapidly over these extraliterary cultural manifestations in our haste to tackle the text. Particularly in the twenty-first century, as we become increasingly removed from the sounds, images, and commonplaces of Rabelais's world and interact with computer-literate young people who learn best in multisensorial environments, integrating period music and art into classes on Renaissance literature can go a long way toward helping students visualize and hear his world.[1]

Exactly which songs and paintings fare best in the classroom is by no means set in stone. Typically I work with Michelangelo, Sandro Botticelli, Paolo Uccello, Hieronymus Bosch, Pieter Brueghel the Elder, and Clément Janequin, not because they influenced Rabelais directly but because their paintings and sculpture tie in particularly well with facets of the Gallic physician's work that I emphasize in class, ranging from the carnivalesque feasts preceding the giants' nativity to the grotesque netherworld of *The Fourth Book*.[2] Their masterworks also have the advantage of being well known, accessible, and iconographically rich, yielding a complex array of themes, images, and insights that converge synergistically with those of Rabelais.

To make the learning process student-centered, entrusting the responsibility for class discussions and presentations not to the professor but to individuals or small groups of young people seems most effective. This strategy allows students to come up on their own with parallels between Rabelais and his fellow artists and with insights about the Renaissance. The instructor may promote the success of the presentations in a number of ways: by pairing the suggested or required audiovisual materials with specific texts on the syllabus, by supplying bibliographies for background research, by linking the appropriate images and audio files to the course Web site, by giving direction to the in-class discussions when needed, and by having the entire class familiarize itself in advance with the song or painting to be discussed on any given day. What follows is a sketch of the ways these resources can supplement and flesh out Rabelais's text.

Of the artists mentioned above, only Michelangelo was active during the Gallic monk's heyday. Certainly the French humanist would have heard of the "divine Michelangelo," not only in the accounts of travelers returning from Italy but also in the writings of fellow literati such as Ariosto. During his own visits to Rome, he may have encountered examples of the Italian master's artwork, including the ceiling of the Sistine Chapel. Our goal in using Michelangelo's paintings and sculptures to elucidate the Pantagrueline tales is not to demonstrate a direct link between the two artists but to give students a specifically humanistic context for appreciating the multidimensionality of Rabelais's giants.

True, the woodcuts found in early editions of *Pantagruel* and *Gargantua* help us visualize the large Utopian princes in the context of their Gallic and Gothic heritage, as mischievous folkloric behemoths lumbering through the countryside. Similarly, the famous nineteenth-century illustrations of Gustave Doré, who portrayed the infants Pantagruel and Gargantua as curly-haired cherubs with chubby cheeks and massive appetites, communicate the joie de vivre and good-natured verve of Rabelais's oversized heroes as well as their striking dimensions.[3] One need only look at Doré's engraving of Pantagruel inhaling the milk of four thousand cows, or at his rendering of the baby prince with a cradle strapped to his back like a tortoise shell, to sense the playfulness informing the French Romantic illustrator's vision of the giant as a baby. By the same token, his portraits of Gargantua and Pantagruel in armor during battles, next to ordinary knights whom they dwarf, capture the impression of superhuman prowess that the giants embody in Rabelais's prose. While these illustrations of specific scenes in the Pantagrueline tales help us envision the Utopian giants as burlesque, fanciful, and physically intimidating figures who people imaginary Gallic forests, rereading Rabelais's chronicles against the backdrop of Italian Renaissance art adds a key dimension to our understanding of his larger-than-life heroes.

Commissioned as a memorial to Florentine freedom, the immense statue of David that now stands inside the gallery of the Accademia di Belle Arti in Florence is likely to baffle students seeking parallels with Pantagruel and Gargantua. When asked for a list of similarities, other than the sheer size of the figure, they may observe that the subject of the statue is biblical and the style elegantly classical, not buffoonish or Gallic like Rabelais's family of giants—or that, from a purely physiological standpoint, Goliath rather than David was the giant in the Old Testament narrative. Certainly the biblical hero, repeatedly described as a mere boy or youth (1 Sam. 17.33 [New Rev. Standard Vers.]), was far from a colossus in terms of physical size and strength; but if encouraged to brainstorm, students have little difficulty making the leap from literal to figurative giganticism. The biblical hero's skill, courage, and resourcefulness are prodigious. In his oversized statue of David, Michelangelo represents physically the humble shepherd's gigantic character traits and intelligence. Rabelais's strategy is similar: although the sheer size of his protagonists is both a source of comedy and a wellspring of the fantastic in his Pantagrueline chronicles, their enormous stature symbolizes their giant-sized intellects, a defining aspiration of the Renaissance man. Like the Gallic physician, who performed some of the first autopsies in France, Michelangelo glorifies the human body and mind in his sculpture, as evidenced by the detailed musculature, veins, and sinews of David and by his determined and astute gaze as he readies his slingshot. Students researching Michelangelo's life will discover that the artist counted Pico della Mirandola, well known for his *Oration on the Dignity of Man*, among his teachers (King 62). Other works of the Italian master, including sculptures of

Bacchus and of two wrestlers and a painting titled *The Holy Family*, may be used as a springboard for discussing humanistic tendencies shared by Michelangelo and Rabelais: their syncretic blend of Christian and classical elements, their fascination with Bacchic as well as Apollonian inspiration, and the tensions that inform their works.

Another Italian Renaissance master who initially seems to be radically different from Rabelais is Botticelli, whose paean to spring entitled *Primavera* emblematizes the classicizing tendencies, cult of beauty, focus on rebirth, and hermeticism that permeated humanistic art.[4] While *Gargantua* and *Pantagruel* showcase the theme of new beginnings from the outset, with the birth of the infant giants, Rabelais's penchant for the grotesque often appears diametrically at odds with Botticelli's graceful figures, idealized landscape, and aesthetic elegance. On the far right side of the painting, Zephyr pursues the gauze-clad Chloris, who either pursues or is transformed into Flora, the flower-covered goddess of spring, who in turn restores vibrant life and fecundity to the earth under the gaze of Venus. This scene brings to mind the graceful imagery and fluidity of Petrarch's love poetry, which Rabelais in general eschews or even parodies, but focusing on Botticelli's Three Graces in the left half of the painting provides a platform for discussing the courtyard at Thélème, which holds an alabaster fountain topped by "les Troys Graces" bearing horns of plenty (278). Possibly inspired by a fountain in the *Hypnerotomachia Poliphili*, where liquid spills out of the goddesses' breasts "like silver twist," Rabelais's Three Graces emit water not only from their breasts but also from their mouth, ears, eyes, and other bodily openings (ch. 55).[5]

If we ask students to compare the Charities of the Botticelli painting with those in Rabelais's text, the response will be mixed. On one hand, students may compare the celebration of fecundity and abundance figured by Flora in the Italian tableau with the cornucopia held by Rabelais's Graces, and the literal fluidity of the fountain with the impression of movement generated by Botticelli's dancing figures, in their flexed feet, their interlacing fingers, and the windblown folds of their garments. Symbolically and allegorically, the two artists use the Graces to celebrate similar ideals: not simply the beauty, joy, and charm of their original prototypes but also the reciprocity and cooperation implicit in their pose, which both Botticelli and Rabelais advocate for their respective societies.[6] On the other hand, students who focus in detail on the Gallic doctor's alabaster fountain will note a significant difference between the two portrayals of the Graces: the water emanating from the women's bodily openings lends Rabelais's statue a kinetic quality similar to that of Botticelli's figures, symbolizing the same renewal and inspiration represented in the painting, but it also heralds the openness of the Abbey of Thélème with burlesque anatomical touches that are distinctively Rabelaisian.[7]

If comparing Rabelais with Michelangelo and Botticelli both enhances our appreciation of the Renaissance and underscores the Gallic physician's humanistic idealism, matching his works with those of Uccello and Bosch alerts students to a different side of Rabelais's genius. Battle and disaster scenes in Rabelais and Uccello often appear uniformly chaotic to students, who typically remark on the flying and fragmented objects, massive numbers of faceless and dehumanized soldiers, shifting dimensions, and occasional foregrounding of animals or zoological images in both the Gallic doctor's prose and the Italian master's paintings. The fallen helmets, outstretched trumpets, broken lances, armored bodies, and magnificent steeds that vie for space in the claustrophobic panorama of Uccello's *Niccolò Mauruzi da Tolentino at the Battle of San Romano* completely overshadow the tiny knight who lies dead on the ground, providing us an effective visual referent for the disorder or chaos of the Picrocholine war.

In both these visions of war, the artists have depicted a country road and bucolic farmland in the narrative or pictorial background, creating a vivid contrast between the promise of a plentiful harvest, figured by the well-tended vegetation, and the copious death, destruction, and emptiness that are the fruit of war. We see this negative copia clearly in Rabelais's frantic catalog of the Lernean bakers' atrocities at the onset of the Picrocholine war (chapter 26):

> [S]ans ordre et mesure prindrent les champs les uns parmy les aultres, gastans et dissipans tout par où ilz passoient . . . emmenoient boeufz, vaches, thoreaux, veaulx, genisses, brebis, moutons, chevres et boucqs, poulles, chappons, poulletz, ysons, jards, oyes, porcs, truyes, guoretz. (174)
>
> They took the fields one amongst another, wasting and destroying everything wherever they passed . . . they drove away oxen and cows, bulls, calves, heifers, ewes, lambs, goats, kids, hens, capons, chickens, geese, ganders, goslings, hogs, swine, pigs, and the like. (96–97)

While few would dispute the disorder of Rabelais's macaronic prose masterwork, imposing the adjective *chaotic* on Uccello's rigidly geometrical paintings may seem unwarranted, given his fascination with graphical perspective, his experiments with foreshortening, and the minute calculations he used to determine vanishing points in his artwork. Yet in his analysis of *The Flood,* James Elkins points out that "perspective pictures are endemically inconsistent," in large measure because "every painter assembles parts that don't belong together" (171). Students may conclude that this calculated disorder, present in both Uccello and Rabelais, stems from the conviction that war is chaos and from their cultivation of a hybrid artistic style, often labeled the late Gothic, that favors an abundance of detail.

Any discussion of monsters and grotesque bodies in art must include a look at the Dutch master Hieronymus Bosch, whose idiosyncratic paintings provide an unusually good frame of reference for understanding and visualizing those passages in Rabelais that challenge our imagination. From a geographic, temporal, and cultural standpoint, studying Bosch reminds us that Rabelais represents a crossroads between the northern European and Italian Renaissance, drawing his inspiration from both Gothic and humanistic, Italian and Netherlandish sources, including Erasmus. Marginally less eccentric than his more famous paintings, Bosch's *Ship of Fools* can be used in conjunction with related Renaissance texts and woodcuts to contextualize Rabelais's treatment of fools and folly. Originally part of a triptych that probably included *The Allegory of Gluttony* and *Death and the Miser* as well, *The Ship of Fools* may seem to figure the foibles or follies of humankind in a fairly orthodox way, without the ambiguity that is Rabelais's hallmark. Yet asking students to comment on parallels between the Pantagrueline tales and Bosch's painting draws their attention not only to the representation of fools and folly in Rabelais and the Renaissance but also to a plethora of other shared themes, ranging from music and clerical malfeasance, implicit in the merrymaking of a lute-playing nun and the monk sitting across from her, to the search for wisdom and the allegorical journey of life, suggested by both the acquatic background and the tree of life or knowledge that serves as a mast for the boat.[8]

For pedagogical purposes, the most useful work of Bosch for students of Rabelais is probably the Dutch master's *Garden of Earthly Delights,* a triptych that displays Adam and Eve before the Fall in the left panel, an earthly paradise in the center panel, and an oneiric vision of hell in the right-hand panel. Overall, the work contains an almost surrealistic collage of ill-assorted and misshapen forms, phallic symbols, domestic and exotic animals, grotesque monsters, nudes and scatological images, and dismembered body parts that yield countless analogies to Rabelais. Like portions of the Gallic physician's text, such as the inventory of musical instruments, kitchen utensils, farm and construction tools, and mundane household objects informing his anatomy of Quaresmeprenant, the right-hand panel of the triptych in particular seems chaotic and nonsensical, as one might expect in a depiction of hell. A fiery pit at the top of the frame serves as a warning to sinners; but the gigantic ears that serve as a portal to the abyss, along with the hybrid tree-man whose torso resembles a broken eggshell and the bird man who is ingesting a sinner while seated on a high chair or toilet, remind us of Rabelais's equally playful, imaginative, and symbolically rich netherworlds — not just Epistemon's visit to hell but also the world inside Pantagruel's mouth, the gastroworld journey of *Pantagruel,* chapter 33, and the entire *Fourth Book*.

Particularly for those who consider Rabelais's prose inaccessible and nonsensical, studying this triptych, searching for parallels and contrasts between the two artists, and speculating about the symbolic and creative processes at work in both masterpieces can open students' eyes to the cultural backdrop against which Rabelais is writing and provide a frame of reference for understanding his grotesque images. The specific parallels between Rabelais and Bosch are too abundant to enumerate here: in addition to the scatological content and sexual allusions mentioned earlier, students may point out the world-upside-down motif in both works, the artists' fascination with anatomy and the grotesque body, their shared penchant for animal symbolism, their recurring verbal and pictorial allusions to music, the hybridity and polysemic nature of their images, or their idiosyncratic blend of realism, idealism, and fantasy. For example, the Dutch master's exotic animals in all three panels of the triptych, including a giraffe and an elephant on the left-hand side, provide an excellent springboard for the discussion of Rabelais's Medamothi, the Amaurotes' first port of call during their *Fourth Book* journey. In the marketplace of this island city, crew members marvel at the "divers tableaulx, diverses tapisseries, divers animalux, poissons, oizeaulx et aultres marchandises exotiques et peregrines" (854; "diverse pictures, pieces of tapestry, animals, fishes, birds, and other exotic and foreign merchandises" [454]), buying three unicorns and a tarand: these creatures, like those in Bosch's triptych, reflect the mixture of fantasy and reality in the responses of early modern artists to contemporary travel literature and the voyages of discovery. The left and center panels of Bosch's masterwork also bring to mind the utopian and paradisiac thrust of the Pantagrueline tales, implicit in both the Abbey of Thélème and the Amaurotes' geographic quest for the *Dive Bouteille* ("Holy Bottle"), while the dark background, violent images, and pierced bodies of the right-hand panel find corollaries in the strange battles, frightening landscapes, and close brushes with death that the crew experiences in Rabelais's phantasmagoric *Fourth Book.*

Even for Rabelais's most realistic vignettes, such as the feast leading up to Gargantua's birth and the confrontation between bakers and winemakers preceding the Picrocholine war, a look at Brueghel's paintings of village gatherings and harvests can make the French author's descriptions more vivid and accessible to modern students. Although the Dutch artist's *Peasant Wedding* features a banquet of bread, porridge, and wine far less sumptuous than the tripe on which Gargamelle dines, the food and drink are nevertheless abundant, figuring the spirit of renewal implicit in both weddings and childbirth. Students may point out the bagpipers to the left of the table, who also appear in Brueghel's festive *Peasant Dance* with its panorama of merry villagers cavorting in the town square, much as they do in *Gargantua*, chapter 4, where revelers dance outside to the sound of "doulces cornemuses" (70; "the sweet music of the bagpipes" [48]). To the left in Brueghel's tableau, we even glimpse a table of tipplers reminiscent of Rabelais's "bien ivres" (71; "drunkards" [48]). The Dutch master's artistic output also includes the painting *Children's Games*, which matches up well with *Gargantua,* chapter 12, providing an interesting pictorial corollary to the young giant's recreational pursuits; and Brueghel's *Hay Harvest* features a horse-drawn cart heavily laden with fruit that is on its way to market, much like the "dix ou douze charges de fouaces" (168; "ten or twelve loads of cakes" [94]), that the bakers of Lerné drive toward the city in chapter 25. Visualizing Rabelais's pastoral setting with the help of Brueghel's painting helps us appreciate the rustic, almost arcadian, atmosphere that the Lernean bakers shatter when they refuse to sell their cakes for a fair price to their "bons et amiables voisins" (174; "good and friendly neighbors" [97]), who in fact provided the corn for the dough. As a result, it also drives home Rabelais's contrast between the shepherds' prelapsarian economy and ethos, based on Golden Age principles of reciprocity and generosity, and the precapitalistic greed and self-interest of the bakers, who attempt to manipulate their community's food supply for personal gain.

Bridging high and low culture, the sacred and the secular, and the Italian as well as northern Renaissance, the parallels between Rabelais's text and the graphic and plastic arts of his era are extensive; and the same holds true for early modern art songs and musical settings. These similarities include programmatic elements such as battle noises and street cries, also represented by Rabelais; multiple voice lines, which echo the Gallic physician's polyphonic discourse; and the use of sacred and secular, learned and popular materials by individual composers—at times in a single piece of music, in a manner reminiscent of Rabelais. A famous practitioner of this musical syncretism is Josquin des Prez, the Franco-Flemish composer whom Rabelais mentions in *The Fourth Book*, whose compositions included parody masses or masses on popular songs such as the *Missa Fortuna desperata* and *Missa malheur me bat*. Alcofribas may be alluding to one of his pieces, "Faute d'argent" ("lack of money"), in his description of Panurge (*Pantagruel*, ch. 16). As *The Fourth Book*'s list of composers suggests, the musicians whom Rabelais knew or knew of, and those whose work can help thaw his text, spring from a variety of cultures and countries. Josquin was probably born near the border separating modern-day France from Belgium; but like many of his contemporaries, he practiced his art in Italy for many years, while other musicians cited by Rabelais were Spanish, French, Flemish, and Italian by birth—a useful fact for impressing on students the international flavor of the Renaissance and Rabelais's own inspiration.

I will limit my examples here to a few songs by Janequin included in *Les cris de Paris* (Janequin, Sermisy, and Milano; "The Cries of Paris"), which might be used in conjunction with many of the scenes discussed above. Beginning with *Gargantua*, chapter 25, which chronicles the skirmish between shepherds and bakers who are taking their wares to market, I like to begin the class with a note of levity by playing "Martin menoit son pourceau" ("Martin Was Leading His Hog") on band 14. While Rabelais's bakers are taking their cakes, rather than pigs, to market, this rather bawdy, earthy song by Janequin reinforces the sense of cooperation and biological renewal informing Brueghel's *Hay Harvest*, which figures as the productive obverse of the Lerneans' destructive antiharvest. In the song, a peasant named Martin is taking his pig to market with a young woman named Alix, presumably his wife, who begs him to stop and "faire le péché de l'un sur l'autre" ("commit the sin of one on top of the other")—a euphemism for sex reminiscent of Rabelais's "beste à deux doz" (66; "the two-backed beast" [46]). What ensues is comic and mildly off-color, but the amical problem solving (what to do with the pig) and spirit of give-and-take (Martin holds and pushes, while the pig, tied to Alix's leg, pulls) that color the song effectively portray market day as it should be: a celebration of the shared body of the community rather than a time of hostility and greed.

Even more evocatively, Janequin's "Voulez vous entendre les cris de Paris" ("Do You Want to Hear the Cries of Paris?") captures the market atmosphere present at the beginning of Rabelais's chronicle, where Rabelais's alter ego, Alcofribas, poses as a hawker of wares at the fair. Much as Alcofribas boasts that his book is "sans pair" ("peerless") and "incomparable" (320; 168), the various street vendors in Janequin's "Cris de Paris" sing the praises of their "moustarde, moustarde fine" ("mustard, fine mustard"), their "petits choux tous chaulx" ("piping hot little cakes"), and their "beaulx espinards" ("pretty spinach"). Their raucous, overlapping voices communicate the competitive spirit of the marketplace, as each tries to drown out the others. The song contains numerous thematic links to Rabelais, including references to "vin blanc, vin cleret, vin vermeil, à six deniers" ("white wine, claret, red wine, for six deniers"), which anticipate his focus on wine in *The Third Book* prologue. Like Alcofribas, the hawkers not only boast but attempt to engage prospective buyers with questions, exclamations, changing rhythms, varied syntax, and facetious asides. Students listening to the recording will remark on numerous differences between sixteenth-century pronunciation and that of Modern French.

Not only does the song help establish the marketplace atmosphere of the first prologue, but it also finds echoes in the netherworld episodes of *Pantagruel*, where the joyful hawking of the book's opening pages takes on negative connotations: inside Pantagruel's mouth, a poor cabbage planter earns a meager living by carrying his produce to a market in the city (ch. 32), while several powerful figures in Epistemon's hell are condemned to work as hawkers for all eternity. Pope Julius, for example, appears as a "crieur de petitz pastez" (486; "crier of little pies" [267]), Dido and Penthesilea sell mushrooms and cresses (488; 268), Xerxes "crioit la moustarde" (482; "was hawking mustard" [266]), and Geoffrey of the Long Tooth is a purveyor of matches. In real time, moreover, Panurge forces the defeated King Anarche to toil as a hawker of green sauce (494; 271–72), training him to perfect his cries and sing in the proper key. In these episodes, hearing Janequin's song adds sound, substance, and pathos to role reversals that might otherwise seem abstract: as a vulgar crier of mustard like one of the singers in the recording, the noble Xerxes is transformed into a supplicant who begs and haggles like a fishwife rather than commanding others; hearing Janequin's polyphony also helps us realize that Epistemon's hell, literally a world upside down, is as cacophonous as Dante's last circles.[9]

To be sure, following Ponocrates's pedagogy to the letter would require teaching strategies far more elaborate than those outlined here. Instead of looking, listening, and talking *about* Rabelais, Gargantua's tutor would likely turn the learning process into play, perhaps challenging students to prepare a Rabelaisian feast, act out the Utopian prince's games (*Gargantua*, ch. 22), or draw a sketch of Quaresmeprenant. For that matter, encouraging students to create original illustrations for *Gargantua and Pantagruel* or to compose an original piece of music inspired by Rabelais is an excellent means of integrating visual and aural culture in the classroom. For students with modest musical and artistic skills, however, fleshing out Rabelais's texts with the discussions of Renaissance painting, sculpture, and song can be an effective way of thawing his frozen words and of helping them hear and visualize his world.

NOTES

[1] Smell, taste, and touch are also important senses in Rabelais's world; but short of staging a collaborative Rabelaisian feast during the semester, thawing these other sensory stimuli lies outside the scope of this essay.

[2] Images of the paintings and sculptures discussed in this paper are accessible online at sites such as *Web Gallery of Art* (www.wga.hu/index1.html), *Wikipedia*, and *WebMuseum, Paris* (www.ibiblio.org/wm/paint/auth/).

[3] See *Gargantua Eating Together with His Father's Puppies* (bk. 1, ch. 11) and *Pantagruel, Son of Gargantua, Is Nourished by the Milk of 4,600 Cows* (bk. 2, ch. 4) in Doré 7, 41. For a sampling of illustrations by other artists, see "Rabelais," which features images by Albert Dubout (1932), André Derain (1943), Albert Robida (1890), Henrietta Schem (1937), Antoni Clavé (1955), Louis Jou (1951), Gen Paul (1921), Istvan Barta (1934). See also Margaret Harp, who focuses on the illustrations of Jean Chièze and Derain, underscoring how their images both highlight Rabelais's characterizations, themes, and wisdom and reflect the artistic protocols and sociopolitical concerns of their own cultures. Harp is preparing a much-needed volume on illustrated editions of Rabelais.

[4] For an online image of the painting, see *Wikipedia*.

[5] Colonna 45–46. In addition to pointing out the similarity between these two literary fountains in her *French Renaissance Fountains*, Naomi Miller suggests parallels between these texts and the fountain in Boccaccio's *Amorosa Visione*, where water "flowed and tumbled and was tossed from eyes and breasts and limbs" (28). Miller reminds us that "the image of the woman with precious fluids . . . streaming from her breasts reverts to antiquity" (77). Her survey of medieval and Renaissance fountains in France touches on the use of cornucopia for symbolic and decorative purposes, also evident in Rabelais.

[6] For an interpretation of Botticelli's *Primavera* that focuses on the artist's message of civic and intercity harmony and peace, see Guidoni. Whether or not each figure in Botticelli's painting stands for a specific Italian city, as Guidoni contends, arguably the painting as a whole with its cooperative circle of Graces and central focus on love (the figure of Venus) and rebirth (Flora) conveys an overall message of peace and harmony that also informs Rabelais's Abbey of Thélème.

[7] Rabelais is not the only writer or artist to create a fountain in which water flows from the breasts and other openings of the female body. What distinguishes his Three Graces is the copia of these water-bearing openings, which on one level symbolize the abundant harvest of enlightened young people at Frère Jean's Abbey of Thélème; but on another level, the sheer exaggeration of this sculptural tradition adds an element of ribaldry to the description, which Hémard emphasizes in his illustrations for the Clouzot edition.

[8] The painting is far richer on an iconographic level than it initially appears. For example, either a skull or an owl, symbolizing both death and wisdom, peers out from a bouquet in the tree, rendering the nature and goal of the voyage equivocal. The victuals, drinking vessels, and wine in the painting potentially represent either the sin of gluttony, Christian communion, or a revitalizing banquet akin to the one in Rabelais's *Fourth Book*, chapter 64.

[9] The music of Janequin can elucidate a variety of other scenes in Rabelais: songs such as "Les oiseaux" ("The Birds") and "La bataille" ("The Battle") feature onomatopoeic techniques that mimic the songs and chirping of birds in the first example and the sound of trumpets, battle cries, and gunfire in the second.

“And Now for Something Completely Different”? Approaching *Gargantua* through Monty Python

Gary Ferguson

“And now for something completely different.” The phrase is immediately recognizable to any fan of Monty Python. I often use it as a segue in a first class dedicated to Rabelais’s *Gargantua*, after a brief introduction of the principal details of the author’s life and works. The phrase serves both to give an intimation that something unusual is about to happen and to prepare for the linguistic shift to English for an eight-minute clip that I then show from *Monty Python and the Holy Grail* (1975). Starting at the moment when Arthur receives his commission to search for the Grail, the extract opens with a hybrid cartoon sequence depicting God’s appearance to the king from a cloud; this scene is followed by Arthur’s setting out with his knights, their arrival at the “French” castle, the verbal exchange with the sentry, the hapless attempt to take the castle by storm, and finally the construction of a giant wooden rabbit, which is taken inside the walls while Arthur and his knights look on from hiding.

When the film clip starts, there are inevitably expressions of surprise, after which the group settles down to enjoy the fun. Following the presentation, I begin by asking who has seen the film or knows Monty Python generally. Familiarity with the British comedians among students in my courses at a midsized state university is generally strong but not universal, especially in view of the fact that some of them are often international students coming principally from France, the francophone Caribbean, and Africa. These preliminary questions lead me to ask class members to describe what they found funny in the clip and why. From this discussion, a number of parallels can be set up with the Rabelaisian text, of which, in preparation, students have read the prologue and perhaps (depending on the length of the period) the first thirteen chapters, which deal with the hero’s birth and early youth.

First of all, then, much of the comedy in the *Holy Grail* sequence is linguistic in nature, driven by the fact that Arthur’s interlocutor inside the castle is supposed to be French. There is, at the most basic level, a certain fun being poked at England’s rival twin, whose representative here speaks English, self-consciously, with an “outrageous accent” (Cleese et al. 26). More substantially, there is the mock invective verging on nonsense: “Your mother was a hamster and your father smelled of elderberries.” The statements rely not at all on the usual repertoire of insult but on the incongruity of the utterly bizarre. Similarly, in the phrase “I fart in your general direction,” the effect comes not only, even not so much, from the initial verbal proposition as from the disjunction between this and the qualifying phrase that follows. The French knights’ verbal performance also involves various macaronic inventions, mixing English and French, such as the memorable “Fetchez la vache!” (26), an imperative that is a prelude to the catapulting of a cow and other live animals and foodstuffs as missiles from within the castle. The scene thus plays out a kind of school food fight that depends, in the context of the representation of a medieval siege, on a comedy of inversion, of a world upside down. Even viewers with little or no knowledge of French can appreciate that the expression "Fetchez la vache" generates humor through the contamination of French by English. On a slightly more informed level, it is possible to see that it does so using an English verb that itself verges on the colloquial and the archaic, a verb as removed from any Latin-Romance etymological filiation as one could possibly wish. The humor of the phrase is also increased for anyone who understands the linguistic deformation being operated and especially, perhaps, for someone who has struggled with French conjugations in a compulsory language course and on occasion resorted to a similar macaronic strategy in a hopeful attempt to communicate (or at least to diffuse desperation through laughter). Here and there, other languages are thrown into the mix, as when, in the context of his "taunting," the sentry affirms defiantly "You don't frighten us, English pig-dog" (26). "Pig-dog" is comically incongruous in English, but also a literal translation of the German insult *Schweinhund*.

As the linguistic comedy works on multiple levels, principally that of the absurd and of farce, yet also that of more educated—even erudite—allusion, so too does the comedy generated by the subject matter. To take the most obvious example, the large wooden rabbit is, in and of itself, laughable, because so ridiculous and incongruous. The joke is spun out further when it becomes clear that the author of the ruse has forgotten to tell his companions that they are to hide inside it and emerge at night to take the French by surprise, which leads to the suggestion of repeating the exercise with a giant wooden badger. The rabbit, expelled from within the castle by catapult, serves to close the episode when it comes crashing down on top of a bemused and heavily burdened page. Of course the farcical scenario is also a parody, and few students, even if they have never actually read the epics of Homer and Vergil, fail to recognize the deformation of the story of the Trojan horse. Beyond this general allusion, however, there are more precise ones, which reserve a particular pleasure for those familiar with the ancient poems. When the rabbit is examined by the perplexed group of "French" knights, for example, it provokes the following exchange: "Un cadeau.—What?—A present.—Ah, un cadeau.—Oui, oui, allons-y.—What?—Let's go" (text from the film but not in the screenplay). The whole confused dialogue is comic, with some of the interlocutors needing English translations of their own supposed language, but the topic is not gratuitous, and if there is a student in the class with a classical background, he or she may well be able to identify the famous Vergilian intertext: "timeo Danaos et dona ferentis" (*Aeneid* 2.49; "I fear the Greeks even when they bear gifts"). Similarly, knowledge of the Arthurian romance tradition, with its supernatural episodes and unexpected encounters, and, more particularly, of the legends of the Round Table and the Grail certainly enhances the viewer's enjoyment, but such knowledge is not necessary to find the sequence funny. The appreciation of other comic elements is equally heightened by cultural knowledge that may transcend national boundaries but that is not necessarily universal. Actors prancing in order to suggest knights riding on horseback operates a shift in symbolic register from high to low. When some of these same actors are glimpsed clapping together two halves of coconut shells, the parody becomes richer, making obvious fun of the low-budget effects that form the repertoire of many a school play or local "am dram" production. At the same time, the film is making its own low-budget status explicit and incorporating this self-reflexively into its comic procedures.

Shifting the class discussion to focus on *Gargantua*, I note how language is also central to Rabelais's comedy. One of the principal elements making the Rabelaisian text funny is its linguistic inventiveness, playfulness, verve, energy, and (to use a more technical rhetorical term) *copia*, its frequent coining of neologisms and irreverent macaronic mixings, especially of French and Latin. I also describe briefly at this point the two major approaches—exemplified by Michael Screech (*Rabelais* [1979]) and Mikhail Bakhtin (*Rabelais*)—that have historically characterized scholarship on Rabelais: on the one hand, the erudite, humanist, Evangelical Rabelais; on the other hand, the carnivalesque and grotesque Rabelais, comically focused on the lower body. Looking ahead a little, I note that we will be able to appreciate the widely divergent readings to which these two approaches have given rise when we come to the chapters on the hero's gestation and birth. Depending on the length of the class period, these chapters will be discussed either at our next meeting or, after a short break, in the second half of this first one. The approaches of Screech and Bakhtin are also fundamental to our discussion of the "Prologe de l'auteur" ("Author's Prologue"), however, to which we turn at this point.

The collective close reading through which I guide the class begins by noting the opening address to "Beuveurs" and "Verolez" (50; "boozers" and "poxy friends" [37]), which immediately raises the question of the seriousness or jocularity of the relationship being established between author and reader and thus of the nature of the text that the prologue serves to introduce. Next we consider the initial simile, taken from Alcibiades in Plato's *Symposium*, that likens Socrates to a Silenus box, named for its similarity with the foster father of Bacchus—a comparison grounded in an opposition between outside and inside, container and contained, between physical ugliness, ridiculousness, frivolity, drunkenness, and laughter and precious healing substances, sobriety, virtue, "entendement plus que humain," "divin sçavoir" (50; "superhuman understanding," "divine wisdom" [37]). At this point, students may well be anticipating the author's next question: "A quel propos . . . tend ce prélude et coup d'essay?" (50; "Now what . . . is the purpose of this preamble, of this preliminary flourish?" [37]). Famously, the simile turns out to be a double metaphor for the book *Gargantua* and other Rabelaisian productions, real and imaginary. The novel should be judged not by its cover or title but by the material discovered when it is opened and read. And if this material itself should appear to be no more serious than the title, then "pas demourer là ne fault, . . . ains à plus hault sens interpréter ce que par adventure cuidiez dict en gayeté de cueur" (52; "you must still not be deterred, . . . but must interpret in a more sublime sense what you may possibly have thought, at first, was uttered in mere light-heartedness" [38]). Most students will not have difficulty in seeing that Rabelais, or rather M. Alcofribas, as the author calls himself on the title page, is establishing a distinction between the literal, most obvious meaning of the text and a "higher," more serious, hidden one, which must be discovered through a process of allegorical reading. Subsequently, this argument is made yet more explicitly—and famously—through the simile of a dog gnawing a bone in order to extract the most nutritious part, the marrow, from inside. In the same way, readers are exhorted to be

> saiges pour fleurer, sentir et estimer ces beaulx livres de haulte gresse, légiers au prochaz et hardiz à la rencontre; puis par curieuse leçon et méditation fréquente, rompre l'os et sugcer la sustantificque mouelle. (52)

> wise in smelling out, sampling, and relishing these fine and most juicy books, which are easy to run down but hard to bring to bay. Then, by diligent reading and frequent meditation, you must break the bone and lick out the substantial marrow. (38)

When I ask students which of the two main critical approaches to the works of Rabelais the prologue seems to be endorsing at this point, they generally agree that it is the one that emphasizes the erudite, humanist, Evangelical writer, the one that privileges "deep" meaning over "surface" sign, or, in Scholastic terms, reemployed directly in the canine comparison, *medulla* ("marrow") over *integumentum* ("covering"). If no one else in the class raises the question, however, I now ask whether everyone is quite sure that this series of comparisons, and especially the last one, is entirely serious or whether, on the contrary, it might not be something of a joke. Does the author really want the reader to approach his book like a dog chewing a bone? Because the dog is the most philosophical animal, according to Plato? And what about that other brief (mostly overlooked) implied simile, that of uncorking a bottle of wine to drink ("Crochetastes-vous oncques bouteilles?" [52]), which calls forth the expletive "Caisgne!" (literally, a female dog), which in turn leads on to the philosophical hound? Is Rabelais not making fun of us? Finally, as if this weren't enough, in the very next paragraph, with no warning at all, the author seems to do a volte-face, a complete about-turn:

> Croiez-vous en vostre foy qu'oncques Homère, escrivent l'*Iliade* et *Odyssée*, pensast ès allégories lesquelles de luy ont calfreté Plutarche, Heraclides Ponticq, Eustatie, Phornute, et ce que d'iceulx Politian a desrobé?

> Si le croiez: vous n'approchez ne de pieds ne de mains à mon opinion, qui décrète icelles aussi peu avoir esté songées d'Homère que d'Ovide en ses *Métamorphoses* les sacremens de l'Évangile, lesquelz un Frère Lubin, vray croque-lardon, s'est efforcé démonstrer, si d'adventure il rencontroit gens aussi folz que luy, et (comme dict le proverbe) couvercle digne du chaudron. (52)

> But do you faithfully believe that Homer, in writing his *Iliad* and *Odyssey*, ever had in mind the allegories squeezed out of him by Plutarch, Heraclides Ponticus, Eustathius, and Phornutus, and which Politian afterwards stole from them in his turn? If you do, you are not within a hand's or a foot's length of my opinion. For I believe them to have been as little dreamed of by Homer as the Gospel mysteries were by Ovid in his *Metamorphoses*; a case which a certain Friar Lubin, a true bacon-picker, has actually tried to prove, in the hope that he may meet others as crazy as himself and—as the proverb says—a lid to fit his kettle. (38–39)

Here, contrary to the literal sense of the first part of the prologue, the author expresses his utter disdain for allegorizing readings of ancient texts—and not only those purposefully anachronistic ones proposed by later Christian interpreters, as exemplified by the *Métamorphoses moralisées*, but also those by classical writers, including certain ancient commentators of Homer. What is more, the author continues, badgeringly, why should we read his own joyously drunken tales in this way either? In these concluding paragraphs, resolutely anti-allegorical, eating and drinking figure prominently, and notably in an extended eulogy on wine that celebrates the figure of the author as a "bon gaultier et bon compaignon" ("good companion and fellow-boozer"), welcome in all "bonnes compaignies de Pantagruelistes" (54; "choice companies of Pantagruelists" [39]). At this point, then, the erudite, humanist, serious Rabelais seems to have been well and truly displaced by the joyous, irreverent, drunken, carnivalesque Rabelais.

The conclusion of the class discussion focuses on how we might understand the two seemingly contradictory attitudes toward reading and interpretation advocated by the author in his prologue. What I try to bring students to see is that it is possible, through a variety of intellectual maneuvers, to effect some kind of reconciliation between them. For example, one could decide to admit only interpretations that seem reasonable or unexaggerated, perhaps those judged to be intentional on the part of the author. Yet each of these conditions raises problems, for who is to judge what is reasonable and what not? And how can we be certain of what an author had in mind consciously as he or she wrote? Furthermore, even if we could be sure, is it not the case that a literary work can generate meanings that go beyond authorial intention? Such maneuvers also necessarily supplement the text of the prologue in order to subvert its jarringly contradictory structure; they smooth over its disjunction and paradoxically reduce it. Thus the two opposing models of reading and interpretation juxtaposed by Rabelais are better held in dynamic tension. The point is that, like Monty Python's film, the Rabelaisian text works simultaneously in both ways, not in one or the other. It is both sense and nonsense, clever and mad; indeed, ultimately, it breaks down any easy and clear-cut distinction between such binaries. *Toute proportion gardée*, of course. Because, despite being a fan of the films and televised series of Monty Python, I would not want students to leave the classroom considering that these works and those of Rabelais represented equally rich and significant imaginary productions, that they were somehow culturally equivalent. In this context, it has happened more than once that a student has asked if one might not make an apposite literary comparison between Rabelais and James Joyce, a question that offers the possibility of an interesting excursus on the points of similarity and difference between the two great novelists, one early modern, one modernist. Finally, I note that even Rabelais's evocation of wine and revelry is susceptible of being read in different registers. As we have seen, the prologue ends with this theme, but it is also present at the beginning of the text and at various moments throughout it. Plato's *Symposium* describes a drinking party, and it is in this context that Alcibiades speaks of Socrates and Silenus figures. Behind Silenus stands the famously double-natured Bacchus/Dionysus, god of the vine, associated with drunkenness and debauchery but also with the theater and with mystical ecstasy, one of the four Platonic furies—with "low" carnival revelry and "high" literary creation and divine inspiration. In the shadow of the Silenus figure, a Renaissance humanist like Erasmus could even situate, in a Judeo-Christian perspective, the prophets, the apostles, and Christ himself ("Sileni Alcibiadis," *Adages* 3.3.1)—Erasmus the celebrated author of the no less paradoxical *Praise of Folly*.

In conclusion to this introductory class, I encourage students to remain attentive to this question of interpretation throughout their reading of *Gargantua*, since the hermeneutic problem is central to Rabelais's work as a whole, being raised at certain key points very explicitly and self-consciously. This is the case in the prologue to *Gargantua*; it is equally the case in the final chapter of the novel, with its reuse of a poetic enigma by "Merlin the Prophet," a.k.a. Mellin de Saint-Gelais, describing, according to Gargantua, the persecution of true believers in Christ's gospel or, according to Frère Jean, who rejects "allégories et intelligences tant graves" ("allegorical and serious meanings"), nothing more than a tennis match "soubz obscures parolles" (292; "wrapped up in strange language" [163]).

In my experience of teaching Rabelais over a number of years, this lesson always works well—indeed, students often remember it and comment on it positively in their final evaluations of the course. Having begun their reading of the text beforehand, they have almost always found it difficult and perplexing, especially undergraduates. As a result, they often come to class with some sense of trepidation: this book is going to be much harder than anything they've read so far; they're going to be totally lost. Introducing Monty Python into the beginning of the class has the effect of dissipating a good deal of this tension and anxiety, as well as of preparing students to see Rabelais quite differently—as potentially much more fun than they had expected. It encourages them to be more daring in their reading and not so intimidated by a text that they know to be a "great literary masterpiece" and that is, unquestionably, extremely challenging. It is also true that not all students enjoy Monty Python. In each class, there are generally one or two who admit that they "just don't get it," who find it, perhaps, too zany or too vulgar. This reaction itself can be useful pedagogically and incorporated into the class discussion, since Rabelais himself is likely to provoke a similar response. Students tend to love him or to hate him; seldom does he leave his readers indifferent.

Rare Books and Web Pages: Using Internet Resources to Teach Rabelais

Karen James and Mary McKinley

M. Alcofribas, in the prologue to *Pantagruel*, reports that people suffering from toothache found relief by wrapping the Gargantuan chronicles in hot cloths and placing them on their jaws, directly on the spot that was hurting. This claim for the beneficial qualities of the book as a material object can also hold true in the classroom. Introducing today's students to Rabelais's books as his earliest readers knew them—tiny volumes in Gothic print with curious woodcut illustrations—makes those works more immediate and helps students bridge the cultural gap separating us from them. The early history of printed book production adds an important dimension to students' appreciation of Rabelais's works. The Douglas Gordon Collection at the University of Virginia's Albert and Shirley Small Special Collections Library allows us to give students hands-on experience with early, sometimes first, editions of Rabelais. A visit there, including an orientation to books and their production in sixteenth-century France, is now a regular feature of our courses on Renaissance literature.

We schedule that visit after students have had an introduction to Rabelais and have begun reading *Pantagruel* or *Gargantua* in their modern editions. We refer students in advance to three online glossaries of terms useful for describing books from the first century of printing:

"Petit glossaire du bibliophile." *Galaxidion.* Glossary of bibliographic terms in French

"ABC de bibliophilie." *Bibliopolis*. This Canadian site provides English equivalents for most of its entries.

Denis Muzerelle's "Vocabulaire codicologique: Répertoire méthodique des termes français relatifs aux manuscrits." *Institut de Recherche et d'Histoire des Textes* (CNRS). Terms pertaining to manuscripts, many of which are also used to describe printed books; extensive glossary with equivalents in English, Italian, and Spanish

In preparation for the library visit and a discussion of early printing, we ask students to look up the most basic terms in the online glossaries: *la feuille* ("sheet"), *le feuillet* ("leaf"), *la page* ("page"), *le cahier* ("gathering or quire"), *la signature* ("signature"), *les pontuseaux* ("chain lines"), *les vergeures* ("wire lines"), *le filigrane* ("watermark"), *les caractères* ("letters or type"), *la gravure sur bois* ("woodcut engraving"), and so on. Henri-Jean Martin and Roger Chartier's beautifully illustrated history of the French book contains several relevant and informative articles, especially Jeanne Veyrin-Forrer's detailed explanation of how books were made in the sixteenth century and Natalie Davis's account of book production in Lyon ("Monde").

With a little initial help, students tend to be positive about engaging the text in its original form. We urge them not to be afraid of touching the books and turning their pages—with extreme care and clean hands, of course. They respond with interest and even excitement as they do so, cautiously holding a page up to the light as they look for the chain lines and watermarks. They exclaim over the tiny 16mo format of the 1542 *Pantagruel* and *Gargantua*, and they give close inspection to the woodcuts. They take turns trying to decipher the Gothic typeface. It is always a pleasure to see their reactions when, for the first time, they realize that they are holding a book that a sixteenth-century reader held and read. Rabelais's world becomes more immediate. For some students the experience does not go beyond that hour in the Special Collections seminar room. Others, however, are hooked. They consult the Gordon catalog. They return to Special Collections on their own. They ask to do a term paper on a topic that will involve more contact with those old books.

Not everyone has access to a collection of French books from the sixteenth century. That was the case at the University of Virginia before the Gordon books arrived in 1986. Most college and university libraries, however, own some books from the early age of printing, and librarians are usually happy to introduce students to them. After the experience of holding and examining a rare book, virtual reality can lend support, helping to develop an awareness of early printing and the book trade that enriches our reading and discussions for the rest of the semester. Rabelais wrote during one media revolution, and we are teaching his works in the midst of another, so it seems appropriate to follow our visit to Special Collections with an orientation to digital versions of his books and related Internet resources, including those created from volumes housed in the University of Virginia Library.

Rabelais's books are an integral part of *The Renaissance in Print*, the digital archive of sixteenth-century French books in the Douglas Gordon Collection at the University of Virginia. Supported by grants from the Florence Gould Foundation and the National Endowment for the Humanities, *The Renaissance in Print* provides complete digital facsimiles of the books online in a network of reference materials that introduce the books and their authors to nonspecialist readers. This essay explores ways that the archive, as well as other digital resources pertaining to Rabelais, may be adapted for use in a variety of class settings.

To browse the catalog of the University of Virginia Library Gordon Collection, go to the online catalog, Virgo, at http://search.lib.virginia.edu. Type "Gordon" (without quotes) in the search box; select "Call Number" from the drop-down menu to the right, then click on the Search button. Narrow your results by clicking on one of the facets on the left side of the screen. To see Gordon titles published in a particular year, type "Gordon" (without quotes), space, and the year in the search box and follow the same procedure. The records for Gordon books include links to a digital copy, if one exists. To view the list of Gordon books currently available online in digital facsimiles, go to the home page of *The*

Renaissance in Print and click on "Index of Digitized Works" in the column on the right side of the page. The index (alphabetical by author) contains links to the digital copy of each work in its entirety.

The Douglas Gordon Collection in the University of Virginia Library includes nine sixteenth-century editions of Rabelais's works, including *Pantagruel* and the *Pantagrueline Prognostication* (Lyon: Francoys Juste, 1542), *Gargantua* (Lyon: Francoys Juste, 1542), *Le tiers livre* (Paris: Michel Fezandat, 1552), *Le quart livre* (Paris: Michel Fezandat, 1552), and *Le cinquiesme livre* (Lyon: n.p., 1565), all of which have been digitized for *The Renaissance in Print*. Along with Marliani's *Topographia antiquae Romae*, edited by Rabelais and published in Lyon by Sebastien Gryphe in 1534, the collection includes a unique copy of a 1552 Parisian pirated edition of the *Quart livre*, published by the fictitious printer Iehan Chabin, and the first edition of the collected *Œuvres* (1553).

The early Rabelais editions available in digital image format on *The Renaissance in Print* naturally display spelling and typographic conventions that are hurdles for the uninitiated. With a little preparation, however, those hurdles become teaching tools that allow students to interact with sixteenth-century editions, albeit in a virtual environment. The appearance of the sixteenth-century pages may at first be daunting, but students' general comfort with digital media allows them to grasp the qualities of the original book more easily than we anticipated. Students understand that they are looking at a faithful reproduction of the real thing, and the excitement of that encounter carries over into their reading and learning experience. Because they typically expect to have difficulty reading the original editions, they are often agreeably surprised to find that the challenge is manageable after a brief initial period of (dis)orientation. Once they become familiar with the typography and spelling of Middle French, they derive great satisfaction from being able to read the same pages that sixteenth-century readers did.

Even in short reading assignments, the experience of working with the book in its original format (or the digital representation of that format) gives students the sense of engaging in serious scholarship. They feel at least temporarily empowered to bypass their anthologies or paperback editions; at the same time they develop a new appreciation for those modern editions with their notes and glossaries and familiar spelling. Classes using the modern Garnier-Flammarion edition of *Pantagruel* may wish to compare the paperback edition with the original text on which it is based by consulting the digital facsimile of the 1542 edition (Lyon: François Juste) in the Gordon Collection.

From the beginning we have imagined an audience for *The Renaissance in Print* that includes both researchers and teachers. The site is a work in progress. Our first goal was to digitize a significant selection of the books and make them available on the Web. Our next goal was to provide information about the books and their authors, as well as suggestions for further reading, for students and other nonspecialists. Colleagues from the United States, Canada, and Europe have generously contributed to those pages, and the network of reference materials continues to grow. The pages for Rabelais provide introductory material about the author and his works, with links to the facsimiles of his books. We offer here a few ideas about how they might contribute to courses on early modern France.

The Rabelais section can be reached from the link to "Literary Works" on the main page of *The Renaissance in Print*. The brief introduction to Rabelais's life and works includes links at the top to digital facsimiles of the five books. Links at the bottom of the main Rabelais page take readers to additional material. "More about the Books: Rabelais in the Gordon Collection" presents each of the five digitized volumes as part of a brief survey of the printing history and reception of Rabelais's works in the sixteenth century, with references to the relevant entries in Stephen Rawles and Michael Screech's *New Rabelais Bibliography*. In the passage about *Gargantua*, a reference to the October 1534 "Affaire des Placards" includes a link to information about the Protestant Reformation and the later French wars of religion. Rabelais's efforts to soften or mask his satirical stance in the 1542 edition are mentioned, along with bibliographic information on this edition and its facsimile. The section on the *Tiers livre* includes a link to information about Marguerite de Navarre, to whom Rabelais dedicated his *Third Book*. Readers can move from the Rabelais pages to facsimiles of Marguerite's work, or open more than one of the books on screen at the same time. Those interested in the concept of laughter in the French Renaissance may wish to consult the digital facsimile of Laurent Joubert's *Traité du ris* (Paris: Chez Nicolas Chesneau, 1579).

A third set of materials—"François Rabelais: Further Reading and Internet Resources"—provides references to primary modern print editions in French and English and a sampling of secondary sources intended to reflect the many different scholarly approaches to Rabelais. This limited list points the way to further study for interested readers and students, as does a link to the extensive "Agrégation" bibliographies (2007) for Rabelais, available on the SFDES (Société Française d'Etudes du Seizième Siecle) Web site.

In the "Internet Resources" section, as in the "Further Reading" section, we have not attempted to provide an exhaustive list of external links. We have chosen instead to highlight a few related online resources that we believe will be of greatest interest and utility to teachers, students, and nonspecialists. Because most of the introductions and reference materials in *The Renaissance in Print* are in English, we have made an effort to point readers to other relevant sites in French. For Rabelais, these include the excellent background information and glossary in *Le portail de la Renaissance Française: Rabelais et la Renaissance*, by Jean-Yves Pouilloux and Rémi Morel (Renaissance-France.org). Their site provides a summary and brief commentary for each of Rabelais's books, along with background on religion and other aspects of life in Renaissance France (*la médecine, l'université, la musique, les amours,* and *les tavernes,* for example) and biographies of key figures, including Du Bellay, Erasmus, Francis I, and Calvin.

Students interested in learning more about Rabelais bibliography may also consult the expert *notices bibliographiques* for two editions—*Œuvres* (Lyon; 1564) and *Tiers livre* (Paris: Chrestien Wechel, 1546)—included in the resources of the *Bibliothèques virtuelles humanistes* (BVH). The digital editions available on the BVH site and *The Renaissance in Print* provide ample illustration of Guillaume Berthon's outline of material bibliography based on Rabelais's books: "Le livre comme objet: Eléments de bibliographie matérielle." Berthon explains in very accessible terms how the material aspects of early printed books—including printer, *privilège*, format, and typography—expand and enrich our comprehension of the text. The succinct article works well as an introductory reading and point of departure for class discussions of what the physical features of a book printed in sixteenth-century France can tell us about the work it presents.

"Rabelais à haute voix" is another Internet resource for teaching, providing a selection of digital audio recordings by François Bon of passages from each of the first four books by Rabelais. Bon's recordings from the *Quart livre* correspond to the 1552 edition of the text, the same that has been digitized for *The Renaissance in Print*. Instructors may wish to have students listen to the recordings while reading along on the corresponding pages in the Gordon copy of the 1552 *Quart livre*. (Tips for how to do this are included on the Internet Resources page.) Instructors with a good Internet connection in the classroom could incorporate this multimedia work in class, or it could be assigned as homework. In undergraduate classes that may not include a study of the *Quart livre*, a brief introduction to the *paroles gelees* ("frozen words") in chapter 55 may be sufficient to give students an appreciation of the direction Rabelais takes in his later books. Including this recorded episode as a reading and listening exercise can also serve as the basis for a discussion of how French was pronounced in the Renaissance.

One of the most frequently read passages by Rabelais in introductory literature and survey courses of early modern France is *Pantagruel*, chapter 8, the letter from Gargantua to his son evoking the ideal of humanist education. This relatively short text provides a good opportunity for students to encounter Rabelais in a virtual sixteenth-century edition. The chapter is available in a link ("dossier pédagogique"—"François Rabelais, PANTAGRUEL: Chapitre viii") from the main page for Rabelais in *The Renaissance in Print*. Connecting with the real book through its online facsimile can be all the more valuable in classes where this particular passage is read by itself, perhaps in an anthology. When using the digital facsimile of the 1542 *Pantagruel*, students are still reading an excerpt, but they do so in a way that recognizes and even highlights its original context. To facilitate the process, we have provided a transcription of the chapter from the 1542 edition in the Gordon Collection, with only slightly modernized spelling and typography. Key vocabulary words in the transcription are hyperlinked to definitions in both French and English. (French equivalents are derived primarily from definitions in Huguet's *Dictionnaire de la langue française du seizième siècle* and from Greimas and Keane's *Dictionnaire du moyen français: La Renaissance*. English equivalents are from Randle Cotgrave's 1611 *Dictionarie of the French and English Tongues*.) Thumbnail images for each page of the transcription take readers to larger images of the corresponding book pages. At the top of the transcription, students will find a link to tips in French for reading Rabelais in a sixteenth-century edition ("Quelques notes sur le moyen français pour guider votre lecture de Rabelais dans les éditions du seizième siècle"), provided by George Hoffmann. With some preparation and support, even undergraduate students encountering Rabelais for the first time in a French class can read and appreciate a short passage like this in the original Middle French, allowing them not only to appreciate the chapter itself but also to learn about printing and the French language in Rabelais's day.

In addition to the recommended Internet resources pertaining to Rabelais, we also direct our students to sites that offer helpful background information on the Renaissance and the French language in the sixteenth century:

Rémi Morel and Jean-Yves Pouilloux, "Le siècle de la Renaissance." *Le portail de la Renaissance Française.* Information on many aspects of life and culture in sixteenth-century France in addition to sections pertaining specifically to Rabelais and his works

Lyon à la Renaissance (Académie de Lyon). Historical maps and background on culture, politics, and religion in Renaissance Lyon

Marc Bizer. *La muse Renaissante* (Univ. of Texas). Historical background on Renaissance France and an introduction to key literary figures and movements; guests must log in, but access is open to all.

Marc Bizer. *Petit guide de la langue du XVI*[e] *siècle ("le moyen français")* (Univ. of Texas). Outlining the most important aspects of sixteenth-century French, this is a helpful reference to students reading early modern French texts for the first time.

Randle Cotgrave, *Dictionarie of the French and English Tongues.* Online searchable version by Greg Lindahl

What does the future hold for users of *The Renaissance in Print*? When we wrote this essay in 2008, there were digital galleries for about two hundred volumes available on the "Index of Digitized Works." We continue to add introductory reference materials for those books, which offer a window on sixteenth-century printing, literature, travel, architecture, social conventions, philosophy, devotion, and religious conflict. Metadata will allow users to search the digitized collection by key bibliographic features, such as printers' marks, ornamental letters, and dedicatees. The next phase of the project will focus on creating searchable electronic texts corresponding to the digital facsimiles. Those resources will enhance the use of *The Renaissance in Print* for both teaching and research, allowing us and our students to search multiple volumes in the Gordon Collection for topics and phrases related to Rabelais and his contemporaries. We are also pursuing avenues of collaboration with the *Bibliothèques virtuelles humanistes* of the CESR (Centre des Études Supérieures de la Renaissance), an impressive digital library project that shares goals and users with *The Renaissance in Print*. To begin with, high-resolution images of the Gordon copy of the rare 1552 Fézendat edition of the *Tiers livre* are being used by the BVH team to prepare a transcription and, subsequently, a searchable XML file of the text for inclusion in the resources of FORSE (Fonds Rabelais et Ses Sources en Ligne).

Web pages complement books in our classrooms: Internet sites that feature sixteenth-century pages allow us to bring old books to life for our students. The use of online digital resources seems particularly appropriate for studying the period when the printed book was young. The Internet lets us view a revolution in media culture that occurred five hundred years ago in the light of another one taking place today, one based on technology that was new and even daunting to many of us just twenty years ago. We hope that *The Renaissance in Print* will enable colleagues elsewhere to give their students an introduction to Rabelais in the context of France's golden age of printing.

Reading the Rabelaisian Storm: An Exercise in Student Motivation

John Parkin

Reading Rabelais is at once a testing and an exciting experience. The openness of his texts with their complex ambiguities and the virtual exclusion of any character's inner discourse gives readers huge initiatives to perform some major scenes using their own decisions about the figures' motives and thus the writer's intentions. Who can say what Baisecul and Humevesne are thinking as they plead before the judge Pantagruel? Is not a student better equipped than his tutor to respond to the *écolier limousin* ("Limousin scholar"), whose wastrelly lifestyle may be a not too distant parody of his own? Why not point up the generosity and endearing self-awareness of Janotus de Bragmardo at the expense of the obvious negative satires? These episodes are too rich in comic potential to be reduced to a set of verbal cadenzas overlaid on a simple theme. If committed but relatively uninitiated students are encouraged to read as they see fit, their fresh approaches can reveal nuances and emphases that set agendas have caused experienced readers to miss.

Accordingly, I have more than once undertaken the following experiment with groups of good (i.e., motivated) students. It involves a live, prepared reading of the storm episode of the *Quart livre* with roles assigned to each individual and some roles shared. To diminish the authority of the tutor and the students' deference to the tutor's voice, it is essential that this reading be done in a relaxed, nonacademic forum (e.g., an evening get-together, outside class time) and that the students read their sections in advance. This experiment never fails as an exercise in textual discovery, and sometimes it gives outstandingly good results by offering students the chance to break the pattern of formal tutoring and respond to the text individually and in a semiorthodox context—that is, in the university but on their own time and according to their own agenda. The exercise enables them to see Rabelais's work as a script, which they interpret on their own instead of being forced down a particular interpretative road by their teacher (What does our teacher want us to say?) or his favored critics (What has been said before by people who know so much more than we do?).

I regard chapters 18–24 from the *Quart livre* as the greatest comic climax in Rabelais's work. The key questions they enshrine—What is the role of Panurge? How does his performance at this point redefine his place in the company? How do serious elements such as Pantagruel's prayers affect the humor?—are ones that depend so much on individual responses and modes of presentation that a group performance of this kind will always revitalize the text. Though not recommendable at every point in a course, such an exercise promotes exactly the kind of reader initiative that I think Rabelais himself favored. Other sections lend themselves to this approach—for example, the banquet sequence of the

Picrocholine war, with its shifting tonalities and the central contrast of the sober monarch Grandgousier with the adorable vulgarian Frère Jean.

The first occasion on which I attempted the exercise remains in my memory as the best. The students were a final-year group, highly at ease with one another as well as obviously, and for me thankfully, sociable. I began the reading of chapter 18—the onset of the storm following the bad omen of the "neuf Orques chargées de moines" (920; "nine ships loaded with monks")—but passed the remainder to the other readers, including Panurge's collapse into panic following his vomit. It was important that both the narrative text (e.g., the description of Pantagruel's prayer at the start of chapter 19) be handed around among the students, and likewise the many babbled contributions of Panurge, lasting as they do up to Pantagruel's climactic shout of "Terre! Terre!" (938; "Land! Land!") three chapters later.

The wretch's descent into subhuman noise (and self-serving prayers) extends an obvious satiric agenda. However the litany of terror to which it gives rise grants Panurge a comical status that can transcend value judgments and turn him into a lovable clown rather than a contemptible fool. The tone of the performance cannot be predicted, nor can the response of an audience of students who may defy received opinion and identify with a character whom, after all, Pantagruel has declared that he loves at their first meeting. It is open for anyone to follow Pantagruel's lead, since the great humorists have repeatedly created heroes whom one adores despite oneself: Til Eulenspiegel, Falstaff, Captain Macheath, Molière's Dom Juan, Jacques le Fataliste, Becky Sharp, Henry Miller's own persona, J. P. Donleavy's Ginger Man—all these characters behave with a glamorous extravagance, be it in terms of crime, sexual immorality, cynicism, hedonism, or, at this point in Panurge's career, self-indulgent fear. One would not respect a real person who behaved in such a way, yet one can applaud a fool who defies normal respectability.

Interestingly Panurge was not booed and hissed by the audience. Much to my surprise and satisfaction, the group, quite uninhibited in their responses, overturned the procedures of a standard seminar by interrupting the reading, bashing on the piano that happened to be in the room, refusing to sit still or remain seated, and yet without ever bringing the reading to a halt. I was delighted to see the students go so far in what one might call the Bakhtinian spirit. Obviously the Panurgian script is the fulcrum of the humor: deprived of his Panurge's nonsense, the rage of Frère Jean and the piety of Pantagruel have nothing to offset them. Meanwhile any comic actor would love to have such a profuse set of lines to exploit.

The atmosphere changed immediately at the start of chapter 21, with Epistémon's similarly inappropriate disquisition on wills. This scholarly contribution, totally unrealistic in the context of a real storm, cuts into his companion's pathetic repetitions (chs. 18–21) of "zalas" ("Alas") and "je naye" ("I'm drowning"), but it led to immediate groans and verbal expostulations from the nonreaders. It is fascinating to speculate on the reasons for such a response. Perhaps the students were reacting against the scholarly readings of Rabelais, which any syllabus is bound to impose on them. Serious relief is a useful technique in humor (see Attardo 89), but on this occasion the "problème de légiste" ("jurisprudential issue") that Rabelais is posing (Huchon, *Œuvres* 1530) proved a deplorable failure. Alternatively one might say that Epistémon is here comparable with Panurge in his stupidity: who wants to hear of his scholarly reminiscences concerning Caesar and Hercules,[1] and who is impressed by his trite admonition that to write a will at such a moment is a waste of time, because it would never reach one's executors?

Pedantry on such a level is inappropriate to say the least, yet it is fascinating to see how Panurge matches Epistémon in kind by immediately listing sixteen cases of monuments set up by figures of antiquity to commemorate the death of a hero or a loved one. It is entirely a matter of choice how one reads the inventory. Is Panurge responding to Epistémon's scholarly mode and displaying the erudition of which we know him to be capable?[2] If so, where the terror that has made him so ridiculous? Or should the list, over which Rabelais took considerable care (see Huchon, *Œuvres* 1530), be read at the same pace and with the same emotion as those lines that both precede and follow it? If so, it will lose all its humanistic quality and amount to a satire of the author's own scholarship—something not unknown in Rabelais's work.[3]

Whatever our choice from the range of possibilities, Frère Jean brings us back to serious concerns with his outraged demand "Resvez tu? . . . Ayde ici, de part cinq cens mille et millions de charretées de Diables" (936; "are you raving? . . . Come here and help us, in the name of the five hundred thousand million cartloads of devils" [497])—again juicy material for whoever was lucky enough to hold the floor, though it might as easily have been "Resvez vous?" ("Are you both raving?"), given my group's hostile response to Pantagruel's erstwhile tutor. A satiric response to Frère Jean is equally legitimate. His blasphemies apart, he could also be seen as wasting his breath on futile imprecations instead of getting on with the job and ignoring his useless companion. By contrast, I have always seen him to be enjoying the scene—if one is going to die, one might as well die happy—and his drunken verbiage fitted well into the spirit of our evening. The final line of chapter 21 is particularly rich with its reference to the psalms, to the legend of Saint Nicholas (patron saint of shipwrecked mariners?), and with Rabelais's Erasmian sideswipe at Tempête, tutor extraordinary at the Collège de Montaigu.

Perhaps it was self-indulgent of me to keep the two most powerful interjections of Pantagruel to myself. These are the prayer "Seigneur Dieu, saulve nous! Nous perissons!" (936; "Lord God, save us. We are perishing" [498]) and the joyful cry of "Terre, terre" (beginning ch. 22; "Land, land"), but if these are not given the proper emphasis, bellowed in the second case, then the serious implications of the event could be lost in its comical subversion—as happens to a degree, I have always felt, in the altogether less successful sequence of the Andouilles war. But what of the final reckoning, when the spineless Panurge suddenly becomes the irritating busybody, interfering now that the danger is past and calling the key man of action, Frère Jean, an idler?

Again the satiric reading, cued in by Eusthenes, is all too easy: "Passato el pericolo, gabbato el santo" (950; "with danger past, the saint's forgotten")—petrified to the point of inertia, Panurge has proved inadequate, self-serving, and superstitious. But the company never condemn him, and a vigorous reading of his litanies of terror will surely make us regret the ending of the sequence, much as the arrival at the isle des Macraeons ("Island of the Macraeons") marks a strong reduction in Rabelais's comic pressure and, on my advice, the natural end of the reading performance. What follows leads to a magnificent tragic climax (with the giant's tears at the end of chapter 28), but in between we have a didactic section best read in private and from which the Panurge issue is excluded.

That issue defies resolution—hence the vitality of at least one aspect of Rabelais studies. No instructor has the right to tell a class how they must read their way through the comic complexities of Rabelais's antihero or how they should evaluate the mystery of his relationship with Pantagruel. If Pantagruel never calls Panurge to account for failing in his duty during the tempest, why should we? It is quite legitimate for us to sympathize with one who is a victim of his own human failings, even if our moral inclination is to condemn the person. In the murder in the *Quart livre*, chapter 8, where Panurge condemns the sheep traders to a death similar to that which will later threaten him, one can enjoy the black humor, even if, strange to relate, we hear Frère Jean cue in the Pauline response of "Mihi vindictam" (880; "vengeance is mine").

The tone of each performance will vary: some Panurges will earn mere contempt, others will prove appealing in their weakness. This variety has important literary implications. Just as an actor will take a character in a particular direction through his performance, so a reader will choose from the different strategies that Rabelais has facilitated in his text. Many scenes possess this latent variety. Were one, for instance, to stage Panurge's first appearance (a very difficult thing to handle with a student group, given his impossibly complex linguistic rigmarole), the reader would have to impose an attitude and a mood on the performance. Is Panurge to speak too quickly for the Pantagruelists to be able to understand languages in which they should be fully competent? Is he to approach them ingratiatingly, or will he exaggerate the effects of starvation and distress, a comical travesty of a war veteran who has never really been farther east than the Charenton bridge that he has just traversed? His behavior, interpreted allegorically by Terence Cave,[4] certainly defies all logic. One explains it through one's own choices concerning the state of mind that Rabelais conceals from us.

Similarly, the mentality of Thaumaste was long ago deciphered by Michael Screech ("Meaning"),[5] though only by dint of conjecture rather than textual evidence. One can make Thaumaste into an enemy figure bent on defeating Pantagruel on his own ground but outsmarted by his scoundrelly companion. One can also turn him into a comedian who participates in a ridiculous dumb show that mocks the audience for believing that a genuine dialogue is taking place. A further option would be to see Thaumaste as a genuine seeker after knowledge who fools himself into thinking that his problems have been resolved and is then taken off for a good-old booze-up once the farce is over. What would remain very difficult, alas, would be to actually stage or even read that farce through. The description is so dense with gesture that two expert mimes might well decide to leave the actual text alone and simply improvise a series of movements, some obscene, some inquiring, some incomprehensible. The task might prove to be beyond the ability of a student group.

A more approachable section might be the dinner party on Gargantua's return from Paris. The shift of tone from the giants' unambiguous satires of the monastic system to Frère Jean's superlative monologue in the latter part of chapter 39 is an object lesson in Rabelaisian mixing of styles, and a reading of the entire sequence would surely enliven the didacticism by setting it against the foul-mouthed boor who will yet prove a vital ally in the final defeat of their enemy. The jester figure plays his traditional role of inverting established norms (clean living and true learning) while securing his place through unquestioned loyalty.

The pattern is much less clear in Rabelais's other great meal—namely, the Sunday lunch party comprising chapters 30–36 of the *Tiers livre*. Quite apart from the issue of Panurge's obsession (is he "genuinely and disturbingly mad" or merely a quirky eccentric? [Screech, *Rabelais* 260 (1979)]), one wonders how the tone of a reading might change as the disquisitions move from the sober-minded Hippothadée (a theologian but a good one?), through the misogynistic Rondibilis (a doctor, like his creator), to the potentially maddening Trouillogan ("philosophe perfaict" [692; "perfect philosopher"], according to Pantagruel, but perhaps a word-spinning charlatan for his father). Each contribution is different, as is the dialogue to which it gives rise, while set in the middle is the splendid chapter 34, where the minor characters have their say,[6] cracking jokes and recounting anecdotes based on an identity that the reader alone supplies.

Drinking parties, parlor games, joke-telling sessions, and rambunctious fun have proved through the ages to be valued parts of student life. To combine the study of Rabelais with a projection of student customs and traditions will hopefully enliven the text while proving its relevance. I wish my readers every success with classes that use this approach and this material.

NOTES

[1] I feel that the tongue was in the cheek when Rabelais composed the title of this chapter, "Continuation de la tempeste, et brief discours sus testamens faictz sus mer" (934; "Continuation of the Storm, with a Brief Disquisition on Wills Written at Sea").

[2] One easily missed example of this quality can be seen in the peripatetic discussions in which Panurge is engaged with Pantagruel at the Hotel St. Denis just before their encounter with Thaumaste (*Pantagruel*, ch. 18).

[3] I have never accepted that the tutoring of either Pantagruel or Gargantua amounts to a travesty of humanist education, but in the material on color symbolism in *Gargantua*, chapter 9, or the fatuities of Her Trippa or even Trouillogan one can see how too much knowledge can obscure mother wit.

[4] "A paradigm of fallen nature, . . . Panurge is indeed a walking Babel" (*Cornucopian Text* 112–13).

[5] The argument is rehearsed in Screech's *Rabelais* [1979] 86–96, which sees that Thaumaste's "head is so chock full of high esoteric, conventional signs that he is quite unable to recognise the natural or congruous meanings of the coarse gestures made by Panurge in reply" (88): a worthwhile reading, but one that a different staging of their comical debate could render superfluous.

[6] The participants are Carpalim, Ponocrates, and Epistémon. The contribution of the second named (concerning sacramental confession to a woman) was originally assigned to Pantagruel.

Teaching through Student Performance: Rabelais and the Rassias Method

David LaGuardia

From its opening pages, it is clear that *Gargantua* is not a text meant to be read silently by someone sitting alone in a chair; rather, the work should be read out loud, perhaps on the street, in the middle of a festival or holiday celebration, when both the professional orator who is reading it and his audience are drunk or at least a bit buzzed on cheap wine. The opening apostrophe of the work's famous prologue seems to bear this out: "Beuveurs tresillustres et vous Verolez tresprecieux (car à vous non à aultres sont dediez mes escriptz)" (50; "Most noble boozers, and you my very esteemed and poxy friends—for to you and you alone are my writings dedicated" [37]). From the important academic perspective concerned with elucidating the humanist, classical, evangelical, and Erasmian elements of Rabelais's oeuvre, this claim may appear scandalous. Most specialists recognize, however, that the work is unavoidably oral and theatrical. As Mireille Huchon puts it, quite forcefully:

> [Il y a] une certaine manière de lire le texte, aujourd'hui perdue. La lecture à voix haute, lecture conviviale s'il en est, où peuvent s'échanger des signes de connivence entre auditeurs, où le public peut applaudir, grincer des dents, rire à gorge déployée, est alors [au seizième siècle] fréquente. Le texte de Rabelais est un texte à dire, comme en attestent de multiples marques d'oralité: apostrophe, prise à partie du public, rôle de premier plan donné au récitant, etc. (*Œuvres* ix–x)
>
> [There is] a certain way of reading the text that has been lost today. Reading aloud, which is a convivial mode of reading if ever there was one, during which the listeners may exchange signs of complicity, grind their teeth, and laugh their heads off, is common at that time [during the sixteenth century]. Rabelais's text is one that has to be said [or recited], as many marks of orality attest in the text itself: apostrophes, asides to the public, the primary role given to the voice reciting the text, et cetera. (my trans.)

Similarly, Paul J. Smith states:

> Le roman de Rabelais n'est pas uniquement destiné à la lecture individuelle, mais aussi à la lecture à haute voix devant un auditoire. . . . Ainsi, Alcofrybas n'est pas un narrateur "de papier" (comme dans les romans des siècles plus récents); il est, au contraire, un *persona*, un rôle à jouer par un récitant professionnel. ("Voix" 138)

> Rabelais's novel is destined not solely for individual reading but also for reading aloud before a public. . . . Hence, Alcofrybas is not a "paper" narrator (as in the novels of more recent centuries); he is, on the contrary, a *persona*, a role to be played by a professional reciter. (my trans.)

In teaching Rabelais, we are faced with the daunting task of explicating the writer's formidable intellectual universe for a generation of students who have come to consciousness in an age of instantaneous information that is digested like fast food, quickly and badly. If ever there was a writer for the slow-food movement, it's Rabelais. Fortunately, my task here is not to describe pedagogical techniques for helping students to understand Renaissance humanism and evangelism; rather, my goal is to describe the merits of getting students out of their seats and forcing them to reactivate by themselves, in the classroom, some of the theatrical and even histrionic aspects of the Rabelaisian text. These techniques allow the students to get much closer to the original experience of reading these works as it is described by Huchon and Smith, which at times was festive and even ecstatic. As part of the celebrations in which they had a well-defined purpose and usage, *Gargantua* and the other books were physically and intellectually "intoxicating." The goal of the exercises I suggest here is to get students to experience, in their own bodies and minds, what that intoxication felt like. This experience happens when Rabelais's work is performed by reading it aloud in different ways.

The Rassias method was developed by my colleague John Rassias as a means of teaching modern languages to American students. Since its beginnings, the method has been used in universities all around the United States; it has also been used to teach English in countries as diverse as China, Kuwait, and Mexico. After fifteen years of using the method in the classroom, I would say that its essential point is to get students to realize three things: that speaking a language is a corporeal activity, which means that students must use their tongues, their mouths, and even their entire bodies to express themselves in languages and cultural contexts that are not their own; that the experience of speaking another language requires the breaking down of material and conceptual boundaries; that specific techniques and exercises can be used to develop a person's body and mouth as means of communicating with others.

What does this mean for Rabelais? The first time I taught a ten-week seminar on *Gargantua* and *Pantagruel*, during the fall quarter at Dartmouth a few years ago, the students in the class spontaneously forced me to use some of the techniques that I have been employing ever since. After weeks of reading long passages from the works aloud, which meant that we often found ourselves rolling with laughter (reciting these texts accentuates their humor, often catching both the students and their professor off guard), my students arrived one day in class with a few bottles of wine, some dried sausages, and even a pound of lard, and begged me to allow them to recite their favorite passages while imbibing and eating dried, salted meat. This kind of activity is illegal on most campuses, hence I don't recommend it as a formal exercise; nevertheless, its transgressive aspects are entirely in tune with the rebellious character of Rabelais's work.

Asking students to read passages aloud while emphasizing the necessity that they do so dramatically is perhaps the most basic technique of the Rassias method that can be applied to teaching literature. There are also variations on this theme that work quite well. When students are called on to read, they often do so in a monotone, at which point I interrupt the reading and ask the student to imagine that he or she is a bad actor in a soap opera, and hence that the intonation of the reading should be exaggerated. "Imagine that you are a student at the school of bad acting," I say to the students, "and that you have to perform this scene in front of your classmates." Variations of intonation and their effect on meaning are vitally important to the oral performance of a text such as *Gargantua*. I illustrate what I mean by reading myself in this way, which makes the students laugh and hence lures them into the strange world of the text.

Another basic technique from the method asks students to work the muscles of their tongues in unfamiliar ways. This exercise, known as "backwards buildup," is intended for classes in which the students are having difficulties with the phonetics of Rabelais's text, even in its modernized versions. (It should be noted that we performed all of the exercises I am describing using Demerson's modernized version of the text. Performances of Rabelais's Middle French would perhaps be appropriate for PhD classes.) It choses a particularly difficult and emblematic sentence—"[il faut] rompre l'os, et sugcer la sustantificque mouelle" (52; "you must break the bone and lick out the substantial marrow" [38]) is a good one—and has students learn to repeat it by heart. The meaning of the chosen sentence is as important as its phonetic characteristics: this famous phrase highlights the essential problem that is allegorized in *Gargantua*, that of the movement of interpretation from the surface level of a text toward its "higher" meaning, which is one of the basic premises of the Platonic philosophy that Rabelais both parodies and reaffirms in the prologue. The image of the philosophical dog patiently breaking the bone of the text in order to suck on its nutritious marrow provides one with an unforgettable emblem of the manner in which readers have to approach Rabelais's work, which requires that one meditate upon the meaning of scenes, episodes, and fictional events that appear to be quite "grotesque" at first glance. This "higher meaning" should be explained clearly and simply to the students once they have gone through the process of memorizing and repeating this tongue-twisting sentence.

The exercise itself is quite simple. The chosen sentence is broken up into manageable units ("il faut / rompre l'os / et sugcer / la sustantificque mouelle"), which the students learn to pronounce in reverse order, beginning with the last section and adding the preceding sections until they are able to repeat the entire sentence by heart. In one of the fundamental techniques of the Rassias method, students are chosen at random to repeat the different sections and ultimately the entire sentence without looking at the text. This technique forces them to memorize a fundamental idea of *Gargantua*'s famous prologue, and the physical experience of learning to enunciate such a difficult sentence will hopefully enable them to remember the crucial image that it represents, which is at the heart of the writer's narrative enterprise. Their memorization and oral performance of this idea also prepare them for subsequent scenes and exercises.

Students are not the only ones required to perform when the Rassias method is used in class. The professor should physically illustrate, as often as possible, the meaning that the text is trying to get across. When I discuss the allegory of the patient dog, I invariably grab an object of some kind—a book, a pencil, a rolled up piece of paper—and sniff at it, bite it, chew it, and so on. I can picture a strict disciple of the Rassias method bringing a plastic bone or even an actual marrowbone and a cleaver into the classroom in order to demonstrate what Rabelais is talking about to a room full of people who may never have seen or tasted marrow in their lives. Alas, in our low fat and fat-free age, it's hard to imagine the students actually liking bone marrow as much as the author of "ces beaulx livres de haulte gresse" (52; "these fine and most juicy [literally 'high in fat'] books" [38]) apparently did.

A much more extended exercise involves the acting out of specific scenes from the different works. In the fall of 2007, I invited John Rassias to come to a class I was teaching on *Gargantua*, in the context of a survey of medieval and Renaissance literature in French, so that we could act out two famous scenes from the novel. The first was that of Gargantua's birth in chapter 6. A student was engaged as narrator to read the passage, while I played the role of Gargamelle, John that of Grandgousier, and four students acted as the four oxen who were trying to pull the baby out of his mother's womb through an impenetrable blockage of tripe. With the help of a few props—a Malibu Ken doll starring as the baby, a small pillow—the professor playing the mother in the throes of childbirth can illustrate the movement of the baby who enters his mother's vena cava, climbs along her diaphragm beneath her shoulder blades, and eventually pops out of his mother's left ear, screaming, "à boire, à boire, à boire!" (80). The sight of their professor pretending to be pregnant and giving birth to a thirsty baby out of his/her left ear has an interesting effect on the students. They rock with laughter, witnessing a performance that they will be called on to stage themselves. The extent and depth of this laughter, which reaches quite a surprising level in the classroom, is an indicator of the "intoxication" of which I spoke earlier. The near delirium that the performative reading of the text provokes is a fundamental part of experiencing this "carnivalesque" aspect of Rabelais's world. The Rassias method for putting on scenes in class engages the students in an initiatory experience that pushes them to the brink of a kind of bodily ecstasy, signaled by uncontrollable laughter, which is a metaphor for the "rapture" of the mind that was the goal of both Platonic philosophy and its Renaissance reactivations.

The second scene we acted out during that class session was the giant's morning routine under his "Sophist" preceptors in chapter 21, which we carried out as follows: John played Gargantua snoring away placidly in his "bed," which was the desk situated in front of the classroom, while I read the passage aloud for the students. When I reached the long catalog of verbs in the imperfect describing the diverse actions of the waking giant—"Puis fiantoit, pissoyt, rendoyt sa gorge, rottoit, pettoyt, baisloyt, crachoyt, toussoyt, sangloutoyt, esternuoit, etc." (140; "Then he shat, pissed, spewed, belched, farted, yawned, spat, coughed, hiccuped, sneezed, etc." [82])—John acted out each verb. Subsequently, we chose students to play all the roles in both the birth scene and the awakening routine, asking them to exaggerate the actions that the text describes and to invent their own dialogues as best they could without looking at the text. The deep engagement of the students, who are spectators to these scenes of reading, when they understand that their classmates are making fools of themselves in an archaic foreign language, helps to break down some of the formidable boundaries separating them from the text. At one memorable moment, one of the students who represented Gargantua getting out of bed in the morning actually spat on the floor when he heard the verb *cracher*, which made the class explode with laughter.

The performance of this scene can and should be complemented by the staging of its companion piece, the description of Gargantua's "humanist" education in chapter 23. The dramatization of both scenes opens the way for an explanation of the Renaissance emphasis on both physical and intellectual education, which required the individual interpretation and "digestion" of texts through their proper pronunciation and performance. The proper enunciation of texts is an integral part of the search for the higher meaning of works that was announced in the prologue and that also lay at the core of humanist education.[1] In the limited context of a survey course, one has little time to spend on any one text, which means that I had my students perform only the above-mentioned scenes. In a work as richly theatrical and farcical as Rabelais's, however, the possibilities for student performance are practically limitless. Students might be asked to imitate Panurge's merry pranks (*Pantagruel*, ch. 16), Alcofribas lost in the giant's mouth (ch. 32), Janotus de Bragmardo's harangue (*Gargantua*, ch. 19), the *débat par signes* between Panurge and Thaumaste (*Pantagruel*, chs. 18–19), or the stealing of the bells from Notre Dame de Paris (*Gargantua*, ch. 17), and so on.

The reader may be wondering about the pedagogical efficacy of this kind of exercise and what it accomplishes beyond providing entertainment for the class. The Rassias method engages the students physically in a five-hundred-year-old text in a particular and specific way that may be closer to the original usage and experience of the work than our own silent readings. In his apostrophes to his readers, Rabelais often insists that laughter is not only an appropriate reaction to what he writes, it is also an essential one.[2] I have asked many students who witnessed this kind of class what they learned from the experience, and all agreed that seeing a scene acted out made this difficult text more enjoyable and intelligible. It has been argued that Rabelais's goal was in part to provide vivid, memorable images of higher truths that would remain in the minds of his readers or listeners (Dagron). As Demerson remarks, the ridiculous scene of the giant being born from his mother's left ear parodies literalist, Scholastic thinking about the virgin birth of Jesus (Rabelais, *Œuvres* [Demerson] 80n17), which is an explanation that one has to give in class once the merriment provoked by the dramatic exercise has died down.

Like Gargantua under his "humanist" preceptors, the students who are called on to act out scenes from the diverse books are obliged to reproduce in their own bodies and partly in their own words the ideas that the text represents visually and theatrically. The literal, physical reproduction of Rabelais's "grotesque" images is the first stage in the process of metaphorically "digesting" the "higher truths" that the writer wanted to communicate. If, for example, Gargantua's parodic birth is overly physical, festive, scatological, and literal, the reader who recognizes the sacred code that it parodies realizes that Christ is the spiritual opposite of these elements, which are nonetheless celebrated in the laughter that is the consequence of the parody. Similarly, the hyperbole of Gargantua's divergent educations makes the reader realize that learning must be accomplished by means not of rote memorization and repetition in the absence of discipline but by means of reproducing in and as one's own body a certain physical practice of reading, which includes "[une] pronunciation competente à la matiere" (65; "a pronunciation befitting the matter" [87]), performed before an engaged and avid audience. The Rassias method transforms the classroom into a performance space in which the physical pleasure of the text literally intoxicates the students, initiating the process of assimilating the fundamental ideas of Rabelais's profoundly foreign world.

NOTES

[1] See Smith, "Voix" 35, on the importance of dramatic performance and oratory to Renaissance education.

[2] See Bakhtin's famous remarks on the importance of "paschal laughter" in *Rabelais and His World*.

Reconstructing Early Modern Folk Laughter through Creative Writing

James M. Palmer

If, as Rabelais declares, laughter is humankind's proper lot, then his reader must feed on his "delicate maggots" (39) and enjoy doing so. Students early in my comparative literature course, which in the past has examined early modern Western literature of the body in translation, rarely take much pleasure in Rabelais's metaphors, disjointed episodes, syntax, parodies, and paradoxes, and this inability translates into a lack of appreciation for his moralizing and intellectual shrewdness. Students do not understand how his verbal constructs are related to a now lost tradition of folk humor and the grotesque, and experience with my students proves Mikhail Bakhtin correct: "Rabelais is the most difficult classical author of world literature" (*Rabelais* 3).

Part of the challenge of teaching portions of Rabelais is developing in students a sense of what was and is humorous and why and how the body in particular was examined in early modern texts. To this end, I read a section with students from the "Building of the Walls of Paris" (*Pantagruel,* ch. 15) to introduce our author. This passage raises more than mere questions; it raises eyebrows. Questions inevitably follow: "Why would anyone write—much less read—such a text? Is this considered funny? Why use body parts to defend a city?" Students find the building of the walls to be disgusting, calling the episode "gross," a term that for them has the same semantic range initially as *grotesque*. But that is precisely why I introduce Rabelais with this particular reading and do so very early in the semester, and it is why I read it aloud to them. It helps me engage them through the shocking nature of that passage, and it illustrates for them a lost sense of humor that must be re-created. It also helps raise student awareness of how our author renounces many "deeply rooted demands of literary taste" (Bakhtin, *Rabelais* 3).

My laughter at the passages I read aloud degrades, to be sure, but it also materializes. When students find me chuckle at and appreciate such a passage, they want to know why I'm doing so, especially since they know me to be rather conservative (and medieval). To this end, I supplement the primary text with readings from Bakhtin's *Rabelais and His World* that emphasize the elements or criteria I later present to students on their written assignment. On the very day I introduce Rabelais, I examine with students passages from Bakhtin on the "walls of Paris" episode (312–15), and I send students home to read selections from *Gargantua and Pantagruel* along with other pages from Bakhtin. Especially helpful are pages 16–31, which examine speech patterns (of the marketplace, profanities, etc.) and essential principles of grotesque realism. Some contextualization of medieval laughter helps for this and other texts we read during the semester. Useful are pages 93–98 on feudal truth and how laughter was an external defensive form of truth. Helpful, too, are the first four pages on the images of the material bodily lower stratum from chapter 6, especially pages 370–71.

Re-creating an appreciation for folk humor, classroom conversations draw attention to the ways modern readers might reduce important images and metaphors that cause laughter to narrow themes. The case Bakhtin makes about narrowing the grotesque metaphor related to the walls of Paris to an issue of fecundity is appropriate here. To supplement classroom conversation and secondary reading, I use a hands-on creative writing assignment to help undergraduate students internalize and appreciate what Bakhtin calls a lost "tradition of folk humor" (3). Appreciating Rabelais better, students are more prepared for other authors on our syllabus, including Chaucer, Quevedo, Gower, Cervantes, Molière, and even Shakespeare, Donne, and Swift.

Asking students to think like Rabelais, the assignment requires them to write an episode that our narrator has not given, perhaps narrating one of the places he mentions that he will omit, such as

> how, at each of his [Pantagruel's] meals, he swigged off the milk of four thousand six hundred cows; and how all the saucepan makers of Saumer in Anjou, of Villedieu in Normandy, and of Bramont in Lorraine were employed in making him a saucepan to boil his soup in; and how they gave him this soup in a great drinking-trough. (179)

Similarly, students could write a chapter from one of the narrator's other books, such as *On the Dignity of Codpieces*, mentioned in *Gargantua*, chapter 8, and which we're told he could tell us "a good deal more about" (55). Their challenge as authors is to do just that: tell us more by narrating something missing.

Students are asked to contextualize their piece so that there is little disjuncture in narrative voice, control, and story line. Not distributed until the end of our second day of discussion, the assignment reads as follows:

> Using your knowledge of Rabelais's text and the elements I've listed below, write a four-to-five-page creative essay giving us an episode that our narrator might recite for us about Gargantua or Pantagruel. Keep things in the same voice, perspective, and narrative style you've encountered in your readings.

Because the time devoted to Rabelais in our course is short, we focus on specific aspects of his narrative technique and folk humor. The assignment goes on to give particular guidance:

> Along with situating your episode into the larger work as a whole, your goal is to (1) use the language of "the marketplace" or of the "lower bodily

sphere"; (2) use the various genres of the billingsgate (such as curses, oaths, popular blazons); (3) bring what is held high down low (such as a parody of the litany); (4) elicit laughter from readers, bringing them closer to the action and distancing the selection from traditional epic; and (5) expose some type of folly in thought through parody and sarcasm (or expose a character as morally blind).

Naturally, we're unable for this assignment to consider fully all elements of Rabelais's writing (the allusions to classical, medical, religious, and philosophical texts may receive less treatment), but the elements given on the assignment are stressed in our readings and discussions. Students are given a basic rubric, which I use to assess the features of their creative work, and it serves us in class as a springboard the rest of the week as we read and discuss more passages from *Gargantua and Pantagruel*. We note specific aspects of Rabelais's narratorial voice and compositional features so that students can both successfully mimic and internalize some of the basic elements of folk humor.

The rubric offers a scale from poor, average, above average, very good, to outstanding for each of the following criteria, and each gradation is valued at two-point increments such that outstanding is worth ten points, while poor is worth only two. Criterion 11, on the utilization of a central metaphor, earns bonus points but is otherwise not scored.

1. Authors *situate their selection in the work as a whole appropriately*, using transitions, intertextual references to other events, characters, and so on.
2. The selection is organized effectively, and the narration flows smoothly.
3. There are no errors in grammar, spelling, and punctuation, unless intended. All sentences are clear, unless purposefully unclear for effect.
4. Authors *elicit laughter* from readers, bringing them *close to the action* at hand and distancing the piece from traditional epic.
5. The selection uses the language *of the marketplace or of the lower bodily sphere.*
6. Authors aptly *reverse the status quo*—that is, the mighty thrust downward into the bowels.
7. What was *low is held in high regard, and what was high is brought down low*, as explained by Bakhtin in the passage we read and discussed in class.
8. Authors use sufficient physical descriptions to help the reader visualize a character or situation, as Rabelais does in his text.
9. The selection *exposes some type of folly in thought through parody* and sarcasm. Characters involved in this selection are *themselves morally blind*, and their follies are exposed through their descriptions or actions.
10. Narrators of the piece present the same Gargantua or Pantagruel we've encountered in Rabelais's text and tell their story from the point of view of the present looking back.
11. The selection utilizes a central metaphor—perhaps a medical one.

Clearly Bakhtin's work on Rabelais and carnival heavily influences our reading of the text and my selection of the features of folk humor that we examine, so I italicize those elements that are especially important for our class. The criteria given to students helps them internalize some of the aspects of Rabelais narrative technique. Aside from the assignment that has students write about episodes in places noted, such as on codpieces and the astounding things Pantagruel did while still in the cradle that are omitted by our narrator (178), the most fruitful area to explore that we read is in *Pantagruel*, chapter 16, on "Panurge's Characters and Qualities" (222). Panurge's twenty-six-pocket cloak offers students plenty of opportunity to explore and find new contents and create marvelous adventures.

One student began her story:

> Another compartment contained lacey handkerchiefs that had been submerged in the most noble of latrines. [Panurge] peddled these as Her Highness's very own fragranced handkerchiefs which had been used to wipe her most royal tears. Noblemen's wives readily purchased these pieces of cloth to grant themselves more entitlement. . . .

Although not all students imitate Rabelais's style entirely, most find a good place to insert an episode, and they generally do quite well with at least four of the five elements required of them.

Another location in chapter 16 useful for exploration is when readers are told, "In another pocket he had a collection of needles and thread, with which he performed a thousand little devilments. On one occasion . . ." (224). Students may utilize this line to begin their narrative, or they may give a title such as "Book 2, Chapter 16b: Panurge's Character and Qualities, and How He Became Known as a Creative Tailor." As long as students are contextualizing in a clear and deliberate way, I am able to see how they respond to the text's invitation for collaboration and expansion. The student who gave this particular title went on to narrate a banquet episode in which Panurge manages to mingle with the banqueters until one by one they leave to relieve themselves. Pilfering their clothes, he works feverishly to "scoop up the unsupervised breeches" to "set to work applying his own advice: . . . create an invisible barrier, thus preventing his victims from getting certain body parts into designated areas. . . ."

Other students find good places for insertion but may forget their narrative and historical perspective. One student wrote: "Panurge . . . conquered plagues known as the Brown Death, the Green Mud, and the Yellow Raunch. Such plagues are known today as Hepatitis A, B, and C." This slip of historical perspective and context by naming the modern disease costs students a few points here and there (see assessment criterion 10 on the rubric), especially if Walmart or an automobile makes its way into an episode somehow (and both have), but responding to these slips are helpful teaching moments. Some of the lower-scoring essays have passages that contextualize the beginning well but do not seem to have our narrator's voice.

Because creative writing is not the focus of the course and because Rabelais can indeed be difficult, the assignment is not weighted too heavily and I tend to be lenient on my grading. The point is for students to appreciate the humor they encounter. They tend to do well using the language of the marketplace or of the lower bodily sphere and at situating a selection. What poses challenges is working to reverse the status quo and maintaining the narrative's historical point of view and context.

This assignment does not make all students love Rabelais, but it does help them appreciate his narrative art more than before. Having a hand at creating the language of the marketplace and the lower bodily sphere, at reversing the status quo, and at using satire, they understand better why passages are humorous. Helping students reflect on the ways they, like Rabelais, can create "delicate maggots" that provide entertainment as well as "substantial marrow" brings joy and laughter to their peers and to the instructor.

An Allegorical Framework for Reading *Gargantua* in a Great-Books Class

Jerry Root

In the context of a great-books course, Rabelais's *Gargantua* may best be presented to students as an allegorical coming-of-age story.[1] It is clearly and literally a coming-of-age story as we follow the birth, youth, education, and maturation of the young giant. It is less clearly an allegory, but its stake in allegory and its allegorical dimensions permit students to see beyond its rough surface and link it with works such as Augustine's *Confessions*, the romances of Chrétien de Troyes, and Dante's *Divine Comedy*. As an allegory, the coming-of-age tale is the story not just of Gargantua, the individual, but also of the humanist ideal of the educated "noble gentleman" (154).[2] This allegorical bildungsroman has several dimensions. It is an allegory of how a proper education can transform a life. It is an allegory of a broader, historical coming of age, embodied in the shift from medieval to Renaissance modes of thought. It is finally a positive allegory of humanistic enlightenment where we move from individual and above all corporeal concerns in an upward direction to collective concerns of social justice and equity, and then to the utopian and more philosophical preoccupations of the Abbey of Thélème.[3] If we teach the book with these broader allegorical dimensions in mind, the surface difficulties of *Gargantua* do not necessarily disappear but they no longer obstruct students' general comprehension.

The prologue to *Gargantua* is an obvious invitation to allegorical interpretation and a guide for how the reader should interpret the body of the story.[4] Prologues like this should be familiar to students in a great-books course. Rabelais's prologue recalls those to Marie de France's *Lais*, Chrétien de Troye's romances, and Guillaume de Lorris's *Romance of the Rose*, and even the first canto of Dante's *Inferno*.[5] Like the prologue to *Gargantua*, these medieval predecessors all broadly invoke an ancient authority, acknowledge the surface obscurities of this world, hint at a deeper meaning beyond the confusing surface, and urge on the reader a studious and charitable attitude. These clear parallels serve as an excellent starting point for student papers, class discussions, or group work. A series of questions can stimulate students' exploration of *Gargantua* and their grasp of the tradition. What is the deeper meaning that the prologue promises? What is the relation between the "pleasant titles" on the surface and the "substantial marrow" contained within (37, 38)? What is the nature of the reader's "labour" of interpretation (38)? How do the specific answers to these questions about *Gargantua* relate back to and shift away from the prologues of medieval romances?

The prologue to *Gargantua* also obviously problematizes its invitation to allegorize. This problematization, coming through the thickly ironic tone, the self-undercutting references to drinking and laughing, the mocking allusion to far-fetched allegories of Homer and Ovid, will be new and difficult for the student coming to Rabelais from the otherwise familiar frame of medieval romance prologues. The newness and difficulty also provide excellent teaching opportunities. Instructors could begin with the simple exercise of comparing a romance prologue (Marie de France's would probably work best) with the prologue to *Gargantua* and identifying the shift in tone. Once students have identified an ironic tone and a valorization of laughter and entertainment, they can be pressed to explore how these constitute a shift from the medieval prologues and what this shift means for *Gargantua* and for the Renaissance or literary history more broadly. These questions and discussions should build in such a way as to prepare students to take on one of the more complicated challenges of the prologue. Why does Rabelais invite readers to interpret his tale allegorically, at the same time mocking the very idea of allegorical interpretation?

One way to answer or at least focus on this question is to plunge students into the cornucopia of corporality of the first chapters. In my experience, and to my surprise, these chapters (from the birth to the discovery of the best ass wipe) are some of the hardest for students to come to terms with. Their difficulty usually stems from Rabelais's very literal representation of the human body and its corporeal functions. The representation of the body nicely embodies the paradigm shift from a medieval transcendental universe to a Renaissance focus on the human and the secular. If the bodies belong to giants and their lack of control harks back to the medieval fabliaux, Rabelais's medical gaze and anatomical precision nonetheless announce the calm, very humanistic acceptance of the body of Michel de Montaigne.[6] One of the stickiest scatological scenes, when Gargamelle's fundament escapes, can serve as a kind of degree zero of literality and corporality. Gargamelle's nurses reach under her skirt, expecting the baby. Instead, they "[find] some rather ill-smelling excrescences" (52). Students want to dismiss this scene as disgusting. I insist that they ask why Rabelais would depict these nurses with their hands full of excrement. The answer, I believe, is that Rabelais takes the literal body seriously. In effect, he will not allow his readers to dismiss even the most unpleasant aspects of the body. By giving a doctor's account of digestion and defecation— defecation is a typical side effect of childbirth—Rabelais exemplifies a humanistic acceptance of the whole range of human experience.

The early chapters also clearly lend themselves to an allegorical interpretation that will make particular sense in a great-books context. Rabelais sets up the allegory of coming of age negatively and positively. Negatively the allegory requires a conversion and above all a purgation of the old, the bad, the sinful. Positively, the allegory is Platonic: it requires not conversion and purgation but the positive construction of a foundation on which one builds an edifice that helps us ascend to a higher plane. In both respects, chapters 1–13 represent Gargantua's unreformed youth. They resemble the preoccupation with the body and with the peccadillos of this world found in chapters 1–8 of Augustine's *Confessions*. In a more general way they resemble the youthful self-absorption of Chrétien de Troyes's heroes, Perceval and Yvain, and even the Inferno stage of Dante's portrait of himself as a groping, erring pilgrim.

The negative allegory is quite explicit and requires that we reread the birth scene. We must see as a purgation Gargamelle's fundament escaping just before Gargantua's birth. Rabelais is allegorizing biologically the need to get rid of the old to make way for the new. The corporeal version of this process is defecation. The negative allegory of biological purgation informs the less spectacular image of intellectual purgation that we see in Gargantua's education. Once certain that Gargantua's sophist education has not worked, Ponocrates brings in the doctor Theodore to administer a drug that will purge Gargantua's brain of all that Gargantua has learned (87). Likewise, the exclusions announced in the inscription of the Abbey of Thélème (ch. 54) recall the social purgation necessary for a new social order to be born (Marshall, "Allegory" 150; Screech, *Rabelais* [1979] 194–95). The purgation of excrement to make way for a new birth can also generally be seen as an image of the relation of medieval to Renaissance: one needs to get rid of the first to move to the second. The negative version of the allegory of coming of age requires a wiping away of the past, especially the sinful or erring past. Augustine's *Confessions* is the extreme example, where confessing the sins of the past is like a purgation of the past and its youthful follies. Augustine announces at the beginning of book 7 of the *Confessions*, "By now my adolescence, with all its shameful sins, was dead" (133). He clearly wants to purge and kill this shameful, sinful past. Although Rabelais equates excrement with sin, he does not embrace the negative allegory as fully as Augustine.[7] In other words, he is not quite willing to kill the body, to do away with excrement, or to equate the body with sin.

The positive allegory is more subtle. It allows Rabelais to shift away from an economy of purgation and above all of sin toward a more Platonic and humanist conception of the coming-of-age process. The positive allegory reminds us of Boethius and Plato, in which youth and the youthful preoccupation with the body is merely a stage of development. The great-books instructor would do well to follow Rabelais here and take students back to Plato's *Symposium*. Diotima, in her great speech to Socrates, indicates that the right way to approach a comprehension of beauty is to begin with love of one body, to move to love for the beauty of many bodies, to move from there to love of souls, and finally to move from practice to knowledge and then to an abstract contemplation of beauty (104). The key lesson of the Platonic ontology is that one does not leave behind, purge, or kill the body; one builds on it in stages appropriate to age and development. Rabelais's novel and hero follow this pattern as we move from the excrement of the birth scene to the incontinence of his youth ("But he shat himself every hour" [54]) to the meditation on cleaning his bottom (ch. 13) to the far more reformed regime that Ponocrates makes possible: "he got rid of his natural excrements" (89). Likewise with liquids, we go from Gargantua's pissing in his shoes (62) to his pissing on Paris from Notre-Dame (74) to his mare pissing a flood (117) to the elegantly controlled fountain of Thélème, "sprouting water from . . . breasts, mouths, ears, eyes, and other physical orifices" (155). This Platonic sublimation of the body is an important step from the Augustinian and medieval condemnation of the flesh. In this positive allegory of coming of age, excrement, urination, and the body have replaced sin as the sign of youthful folly. As the boy giant grows, the bodies and products of the body become less and less corporeal, more and more controlled. Unlike Augustine, Gargantua can grow out of his physical nature, reform and shape it into something appropriate to his stage of development.

The explicit chapters on education provide the tools for Gargantua to mount the "flight of steps" (Plato, *Symposium* 105) that lead beyond youthful foolishness and simplicity toward the refined and well-rounded qualities of the inhabitants of Thélème. In my experience, these chapters are easier than the first chapters for students to follow and understand. As a phase in the allegory of coming of age, they are reminiscent of the early chapters of Augustine's *Confessions* and his self-directed search for truth. Augustine's early and erroneous attempts to find the truth through literature (book 1), material things and the body (book 2), the theater (book 3), astrologers (book 4), and the Manichees (book 5) correspond structurally to the negative education that Gargantua's first tutors administer. The coming-of-age story seems to have a structural slot built into it for educational experiences that do not work. *Perceval* is a good example of a bildungsroman structure where the first educational lessons do not work as the protagonist hopes or lead where he thinks they will. Chrétien's *Yvain* gives us a more direct parallel. The first half of the romance constitutes a bad education that must be eliminated with a bout of madness in the forest and an ointment, very like doctor Theodore's purgation drug, that purges Yvain so he can start anew (331–32 [lines 2921–3005]).

The education chapters also construct a broader allegory than Gargantua's coming of age; they represent a historical coming of age, from medieval to Renaissance learning. In a great-books course, these chapters can generate a surprisingly dynamic discussion of the difference between the Middle Ages and the Renaissance. Students can easily make a list of items in Rabelais's vision of good and bad education. While the exercise is destined to favor the Renaissance, it is a good way to get students to take stock of what they know about each period and to see how Rabelais represents and embodies the transition between the two. This exercise is also helpful for getting students to see that Rabelais is having his protagonist perform his own coming of age. This performance comes into sharp focus in chapter 15, when Eudemon's eloquence is contrasted with Gargantua's "bellowing like a cow" (72). The early chapters emphasizing incontinence and potty talk correspond to youth. They also correspond to improper education. The implication is that an organized educational regime can bring the individual and society out of the Dark Ages. With education, even a fairly young boy like Eudemon can exhibit the qualities associated with a Renaissance education. The badly educated Gargantua and his tutors represent the Middle Ages; the well-educated Eudemon and his tutors represent the Renaissance. Through this juxtaposition students grasp Renaissance ideals quite concretely.

If Rabelais is using the education chapters as a broad historical allegory of shifting paradigms of knowledge, students in a great-books course should grasp the significance of the allegory. Vergil's *Aeneid* and Augustine's *Confessions* made similarly grandiose claims. Vergil refashions the epic tradition in the service of the Roman Empire, and Augustine does the same to show that the new empire one must serve is Christianity. Rabelais provides an elegant bookend to Augustine's *Confessions*. The church, at least the bad church of medieval corruption, is pushed aside, and secular education is pushed into a central spot. The new empire is education itself—or the well-fashioned person that it facilitates.

From the perspective of an allegory of coming of age, the Picrocholine war and the Abbey of Thélème can both be taught as performances or practical applications of this new educational regime. Each setting gives the protagonist the occasion to apply the knowledge and skills his Renaissance education has provided. If we teach these scenes by focusing on practical application of knowledge, the more elusive meaning of the scenes and even their historical and intertextual complexity can be bracketed. Students can focus concretely on creating a list of ways that Gargantua's new Renaissance education manifests itself in his conduct in the war or in his construction of the Abbey of Thélème. First, this exercise helps students recognize the importance of practical and applied knowledge in the Renaissance. Second, it allows them to use one part of the book to analyze another and thus deepens their overall engagement. Finally, they will see in both episodes how Rabelais's hero incarnates a significantly new set of qualities and virtues from the ones they know from earlier texts.

The war with Picrochole serves as a vehicle for the young Gargantua to grow up. The war is in fact reminiscent of the early chapters and Gargantua's youth, only in this case it is Picrochole who is playing and who is out of control, while Gargantua and above all Grandgousier give more appropriate examples of adult moderation and control. We see the contrast immediately when Picrochole reacts to the report of stolen cakes. He flies into a "furious rage" (96). His men take to the fields in a "disorderly fashion" (96). On Picrochole's side, "everyone was in disorder" (99). Even after the battle, the last pathetic image we have of Picrochole is when his horse stumbles and infuriates him so that he slays it (144). Picrochole's penchant for disorder is the adult version of the young Gargantua's excessive corporeality. Grandgousier's reaction to the report of the stolen cakes is an example of more appropriately adult conduct. Grandgousier prays to "God to moderate Picrochole's anger" and then "orders inquiries to made into this matter" (107). Gargantua is at first "alarmed" by the same report. But he follows his father's model and his preceptors' (Ponocrates and Gymnaste) advice. They send out men to "reconnoitre" the country "so that they might advance to La Roche-Clemault with plans formed in accordance with the actual situation" (113). The military coming of age seems to culminate later when Gymnaste asks Gargantua if they should pursue the enemy. Gargantua says no: "For according to true military practice you must never drive your enemy into the straits of despair" (132). He concludes his advice by observing that the enemy is "guided by luck, not by judgement" (133). The classically educated young prince is clearly getting the chance to apply what he has learned. This self-possession and self-control show that he has come a long way from the little boy who "snivelled" into his soup (62).

The war with Picrochole gives Rabelais a chance to show Gargantua in the process of applying the knowledge he has acquired from his new tutors. This practical application of knowledge and the attention we see to the "actual situation" show Gargantua and Grandgousier to be Renaissance men in the style of Machiavelli. Gargantua's insistence on making "plans formed in accordance with the actual situation" counters the pipe dreaming of Picrochole's advisers (109–13). Gargantua's attitude echoes *The Prince* directly: "But since my intention is to say something that will prove of practical use to the inquirer, I have thought it proper to represent things as they are in a real truth, rather than as they are imagined" (Machiavelli 50). Rabelais's intense attention to local geography seems also to echo Machiavelli's advice. The prince must obtain a "clear understanding of local geography" (48). This understanding will help him defend himself and will help him even to understand and read the landscape of places he does not know. Great-books students will contrast this specific attention to local geography with the metaphoric and generic landscape that they might have seen in the epic *Song of Roland*: "High are the hills and the valleys dark" (814). The war with Picrochole can serve as an excellent example of a fictionalized account of the real-world political awareness and advice of Machiavelli's *The Prince*.

If *The Prince* helps students understand the modernity of Rabelais in the context of the war with Picrochole, it has the opposite effect when it comes to the Abbey of Thélème. For, in the light of the practical advice of *The Prince*, Rabelais's utopian community can only seem abstract and ideal. This discrepancy opens up a space for the comparative discussion of Rabelais and Machiavelli. How is it that Rabelais's young prince can follow to the letter Machiavelli's advice on fighting a war but then go on to create a community that can only be thought of in the realm of the "imagined" rather than the "real" and "practical" (Machiavelli 50)? Ideally the discussion of this question will lead students to explore Machiavelli's rather negative image of people ("they are ungrateful, fickle, liars, and deceivers" [50]) and to compare this attitude with Rabelais's very positive image: "people who are free, well-born, well-bred . . . have a natural spur and instinct which drives them to virtuous deeds" (159). This comparison could be broadened to include Martin Luther's views of humankind and lead students to a dynamic discussion of the power of free will and the vision of these three important thinkers on the ability of individuals to effect change in the world and in themselves.

These contrasting views of human nature show why Rabelais needs to resort to allegory and Machiavelli does not. Machiavelli bases his attitude on an observation of the world as it is. Rabelais's utopian vision is not a reality; it is the wished-for result of a humanistic education. In the logic that I have sketched out here of an allegorical bildungsroman, the Abbey of Thélème is the culmination of the individual's and the culture's educational voyage. This end point cannot be described realistically. It is rather an "anamnesis," a Platonic model of the mind returning to its divine origin (Whitman 112). It is a goal of humanistic enlightenment, where a radically free will can exist only because it is checked by a proper education. In the terms of Plato, or Montaigne, we should all be able to aspire to the harmony this balance makes possible. Gargantua's journey from birth to the Abbey of Thélème was anchored in the real, physical, corporeal world. If not realistic, it was nonetheless focused on being in and moving through the real world. It was also clearly a spiritual and metaphoric journey, one of growing up physically, coming of age intellectually, socially, and spiritually. As such it resembles the journeys of Aeneas, Augustine, Boethius, romance heroes, and our students. This comparative and allegorical framework helps instructors place Rabelais's great book at the heart of the tradition that so informs it and opens the door for students to embrace its lessons.

NOTES

[1] In semester 1 we cover, roughly, Homer, Plato, Greek drama, Aristotle, Vergil, Ovid, the Gospels; in semester 2, Augustine, *Song of Roland,* Chrétien de Troyes, Marie de France, Aquinas, Chaucer, Luther, Machiavelli, Rabelais, *Lazarillo de Tormes*, Shakespeare.

[2] For a later and yet very similar version of an allegorical bildungsroman, see Spenser's *Fairy Queen*, and in particular the "Letter of the Authors" to Sir Walter Raleigh. Even more explicitly than Rabelais, Spenser acknowledges that his book is an allegory, designed "to fashion a gentleman or noble person" (625).

[3] Jon Whitman's description of "positive" allegory in the context of Boethius's *Consolation of Philosophy* informs my approach to *Gargantua* (112–19).

[4] For an in-depth reading of the prologue, see Marshall, "Worrying."

[5] Marie's prologue to the *Lais* is the most succinct of these. Like Rabelais, she acknowledges an ancient authority, the obscurity of ancient writings, the need to gloss and explain these obscure writings, and her own onerous role as a writer trying to move the tradition forward (see verses 1–48).

[6] See in particular where Montaigne talks about the size of his penis (*Complete Essays* [Screech] 317) and his bowel movements (388).

[7] Recall that Rabelais claims that monks "eat the world's excrement, that is to say, sins" (125–26). The link of excrement and sin should also bring to mind canto 18 of Dante's *Inferno*, where the flatterers' punishment includes being "plunged in excrement" (verse 113).

Comic Realism: Teaching *Gargantua and Pantagruel* in Comparative Contexts

Carl Fisher

. . . literature was the best plaything that had ever been invented to make fun of people.

—Gabriel García Márquez,
One Hundred Years of Solitude

The archetypal elements of comedy are easy to chart—plot, character, techniques—and the same can be said of realism, which creates mimetic representation and, depending on the period of production, a mirrorlike tableau of reality. In many ways, the cathartic (almost therapeutic) aspects of comic representation are not entirely dissonant with the circumstantial detail and extensive description of realism; through different techniques and with different anticipated reactions, both genres typically move toward a mean and support the status quo. By comparison, authors who intertwine comedy and realism create complex, playful, subversive texts. The comic realist perspective interrogates the world as it is and undermines our consciousness of it. Comic realism provides a narrative playing ground for readers to suspend disbelief, in the knowledge that the worlds they are reading are fictional microcosms, yet it has the ability to open their minds to critical reflection. Comic realism merges the sacred and the profane, the tangible and the fantastic, the physical and the philosophical, the traditional and the emergent, the real and the imagined, in an attempt to surprise readers into a re-cognition of their received realities.

Rabelais's *Gargantua and Pantagruel* fits this model, using insight and laughter as complementary factors, making fun and making funny, criticizing a world that tends not to tolerate criticism. All the authors discussed in this essay probably found in comic realism a strategy to tell uncomfortable truths and hide them behind the fool's grin, often at the risk of censorship and political persecution. Comic realism criticizes authority, social systems, belief structures, and individual behavior. It takes humanity in general as its source but usually is also specific to a time and place. What fascinates about comic realism is its dynamic narrative quality and the insightful commentary that entertain and educate long after the original contexts of production and reception. The same cannot always be said about realism, which is frequently static and primarily of historical interest, or comedy, which is often ephemeral. While the passage of time makes some texts opaque, students respond to comic realism from earlier periods precisely because it still seems contemporary. In teaching the concept of comic realism and how to situate it in world literature, I use *Gargantua and Pantagruel* as a primary text for a transhistorical examination that considers four other works as intertexts: Miguel de Cervantes's *Don Quixote*, Jonathan Swift's *Gulliver's*

Travels, Nikolai Gogol's *Dead Souls*, and Gabriel García Márquez's *One Hundred Years of Solitude*. Presenting the aesthetic techniques and sociohistorical contexts of other works that range across time and space highlights aspects of the Rabelaisian tradition.

A few comments on *Gargantua and Pantagruel* are in order, especially in the context of comic realism, because the text remains a challenge for student readers. The narrative freedom of the text requires explanation, especially as students typically look to understand literary methodology through reduction to genre and historical periodization. Grasping the concept of comic realism and the freedoms and constraints of a mixed genre allows them to make a whole out of what might seem disconnected: the episodic, the grotesque, the absurd, the violent; the myriad satiric targets; subplots or discourses about education, travel, and war; and interpolated games, inventive lists, and interruptions. I always emphasize that the playful and episodic quality of the text is not haphazard but designed to work in juxtaposition, similar to the picaresque, and that the whole adds up to a broad communal mirror and a thoroughgoing social critique, from the opening chapter on how giants are born to the disjointed "[f]anfreluches antidotées" (58; "corrective conundrums" [42]) of the second chapter; the many catalogs and lists, which can mix real texts with made-up titles (such as the books Pantagruel finds at the library at Saint Victor's abbey [*Pantagruel*, ch. 7]; or the interpolation by Bridoie [Bridlegoose] of Latin case law [*Tiers livre*, chs. 39–42]); or the pseudo-Socratic dialogues, particularly Panurge's various interrogations as he travels with Pantagruel. Rabelais was not the first to employ these techniques, of course; teaching *Gargantua and Pantagruel*, I situate the work in the tradition of Apuleius (*The Golden Ass*) and Petronius (*The Satyricon*), as well as explain Menippean satire and the mixture of seriousness and mockery, especially since the Rabelaisian narrator enjoys showing off his classical knowledge. Satire, as far back as we trace it, was always a mixed genre dedicated to exposing folly and discrediting dangerous behavior. François Rigolot, in this volume, emphasizes the Lucianic model of hybridity as essential for Rabelais and Renaissance humanism (e.g., in Erasmus's *Praise of Folly*) and shows how the hybrid text utilizes both a claim to the fecundity of nature and the right to dialogic ambiguity.

Mikhail Bakhtin, in *Rabelais and His World*, points out many of the structural elements of comic realism, and he describes Rabelais as a carnivalesque writer whose heteroglossic and multivocal narratives provide for transgressive representation. Bakhtin posits that the extraordinary force of Rabelaisian laughter comes from two sources: a deep-rooted, folkloric base, which links comedy to the primal complex of death, birth, fertility, and growth, and a recognition of the gross realities of life. Instead of shunning or escaping realism, the Rabelaisian text embraces it, warts and all. Rabelais's narrator compares his text to a silenus, a multivalent image that at once refers back to Bacchus, to an apothecary's box decorated with whimsical images "arbitrairement inventées pour inciter les gens à rire" (51; "lightheartedly invented for the purpose of mirth" [37]) but containing rare and precious medicines, and to Socrates, ugly but wise, a noble philosopher not afraid to pretend simplicity and devastate with irony in his dialogues. Inside the human silenus, like the Dionysian principle and Socratic wisdom, one finds

> un céleste et inappréciable ingrédient: une intelligence plus qu'humaine, une force d'âme prodigieuse, un invincible courage, une sobriété sans égale, une incontestable sérénité, une parfait fermeté, un incroyable détachement envers tout ce pour quoi les humains s'appliquent tant à veiller, courir, travailler, naviguer et guerroyer. (51)
>
> a heavenly and priceless drug: a superhuman understanding, miraculous virtue, invincible courage, unrivalled sobriety, unfailing contentment, perfect confidence, and an incredible contempt for all those things men so watch for, pursue, work for, sail after, and struggle for. (37)

In the first prologue, Rabelais also references the drunken, argumentative search for truth in Plato's *Symposium*, which suggests Rabelais's attempt to complicate a reader's reaction, to seek truths in unexpected places, and to promote intertextuality, which was groundbreaking and which inspires authors to the present day.

Rabelais's influence on world literature, directly and indirectly, validates an approach to *Gargantua and Pantagruel* that foregrounds the almost experimental quality of blending detailed description with a playful tone. Students may not initially be attuned to identifying comic realism, but they recognize it in much contemporary fiction (if they are readers) and in examples drawn from popular culture. The blended use of hyperbole, parody, irony, pastiche, slapstick, and farce characterizes everything from stereotypical sitcoms to late-night monologues to sharp political satire and typifes a wide swath of the American representational vernacular. When asked for contemporary examples of comic realism, many students mention recent television shows—*Seinfeld*, *The Office*, *Malcolm in the Middle*, *Arrested Development*, all of which have in common a narrative structure that incorporates a sense of the absurd, a flirtation with the grotesque, and the intermingling of traditional comic techniques. Every generation has its pop cultural touchstones, and student-generated classroom examples can provide a shorthand for seeing not only the comic-realistic axis but also the way in which the works are similar in technique yet infused with history. Students recognize what makes them laugh but do not always know why they identify and empathize with a comic work.

To take one model that has worked well in a discussion of Rabelais, I have concentrated on *Seinfeld*, which ran a final episode in 1998 ("The Finale," in which the main characters are jailed for being bad Samaritans, a satire on their self-serving lifestyles) but lives continually in syndication and is a show most students know but cannot always interpret. On the surface, the main characters are a group of friends who get themselves into situations that require intervention and resolution. The sitcom format is almost picaresque: in episode after episode, the characters never seem to learn from their mistakes. The key to the characterization is not the misadventures or the lack of change but the outsized egos the characters display in the face of a world that rarely validates their self-importance, a world in which authority always attacks individual desire. Their urbanity is both idealized and satirized. Students can almost always give examples from the show to discuss, even if they don't have an encyclopedic knowledge of its nine-year run. The characters' appetites are continually on display; George eats a pastrami sandwich while in bed with his girlfriend, or he gets caught taking an éclair from the garbage; Kramer is constantly raiding Jerry's refrigerator or gorging (with Newman) on Kenny Rogers chicken. Exaggeration is constant, in bragging or in bodily references (a petite woman has "man hands," and someone can spit a great distance in a parody of the Zapruder film of the Kennedy assassination). Consumerism is a running theme, as one might expect in a show set in the late 1980s and early 1990s, whether it is the continual product recognition or Elaine's work for the Peterman catalog or Jerry's purchasing a Cadillac for his parents. Corporations are monolithic and uncreative, from fashion companies to sports franchises to the media. Trusted figures, from the local dry cleaner to soup cooks to government officials, are hostile, uncaring, or corrupt. The main characters are taken advantage of by others and are manipulative among themselves.

The show and characters may not have all the qualities of Rabelaisian comedy—pointing out the constraints in commercial modern comedy in comparison with literary texts can be an enlightening exercise in the classroom—but in ten or twenty years what will remain viable in *Seinfeld*, after Kenny Rogers Roasters is remembered only on *Wikipedia*, are the ways in which the show recognizes human quirks and absurdities in its contemporary world and the comic techniques it uses to reveal them. The fallible body and sexual mores are consistent comic realist tropes, while ego, greed, ambition, intolerance, are timeless themes, as is the need to expose them.

Students are often surprised by both the modern relevance and the long history of comic realism. They come to recognize the combination of low and high, the nuanced complexity of literary representations, and the comic-realist mode across cultures. Given students' heightened visual sensitivity but attenuated critical perception—students are familiar with popular media, which do not encourage reflection—*Gargantua and Pantagruel* becomes a good starting point for a genre study of comic realism, illustrating both the techniques and the expectations of the literary paradigm: humorous, ribald, and blithe on the surface but intensely serious beneath the surface.

Rabelais may not have been the first comic realist, but he is a fulcrum for later examples of the genre. We move from *Gargantua and Pantagruel* to another extended text, *Don Quixote*. The sheer length of the comic realist novel can be turned to advantage. Comic realism literally knows no bounds; it refuses to be constrained. Both works have picaresque qualities: extensive travel segments that move the characters to many different locations, combine drifting with purpose, infuse intense activity with education, and engage local populations in carnivalesque episodes that allow freewheeling, unexpected, sometimes disorienting effects. Surprise provokes laughter but also moves toward recognition and blends emotional and empirical reactions. The plot and characters of *Don Quixote* owe much to Rabelais; so do Cervantes's grotesque realism and satiric intent. (Note: translation counts. I recently taught from the 1755 Tobias Smollett translation, because it seemed the closest in tone to the Spanish original. Smollett was himself a ribald satirist unafraid of representing grotesque reality and bodily functions.) In evoking both ridicule and sympathy for the main characters, the text follows the Rabelaisian project and the progression of Renaissance humanist ideals.

Quixote is an undernourished dreamer who lives not in reality but in a self-induced madness. His knight-errantry is not community-building but usually a danger to himself and others. *Don Quixote* represents the incongruity of the knight in the modern world—the dwindling of the chivalric code, the relegation of knights to an easily mocked mythology—and certainly critiques the romance tradition. Language itself enhances the misinterpretation of reality and leads to inappropriate associations ultimately recognized as madness (anticipating Locke's *Essay concerning Human Understanding* [1690] and its fictional parody, *Tristram Shandy* [1759–68], which owes an enormous debt to both Rabelais and Cervantes). Sancho Panza is Rabelaisian in his desire for comfort, companionship, and his predilection for excess, a plebian body craving sustenance and rejuvenation. Sancho also must maintain a home and appease his wife while harboring grandiose dreams of his own, particularly the idea of one day becoming governor of an island. The combination of realism and romance makes Sancho a sympathetic figure, just as Don Quixote's return to reason in the final chapters of the second book make the hero a figure of pathos. The relationship between Quixote and Sancho can be compared with that of Pantagruel and Panurge. The novel also presents the world of the marketplace, spans the social hierarchy, incorporates the actions and the voices of maids, servants, shepherds and goatherds, innkeepers, merchants, local government officials, petit nobility, and the spectacle that arises from their interaction.

Cervantes models his preface to the reader on Rabelais's prologue, from the opening invocation to the "[i]dle reader," calling his novel "an ugly child" in a nod to the silenus box, introducing a friend's voice that mocks the mindless "citation of authors" and attacks "idle books of chivalry," and ending with a hearty hope for the reader's health (33–39). Just as Rabelais negotiates the public world through the private act of reading, so too does Cervantes attempt to create a bond with the reader through signposted chapter headings, self-reflexive narrative intrusions, and repeated nods to reading processes and practices. Both texts have many scenes of farcical confusion and slapstick violence, pointing often to the absurdity of the human condition. As Henri Bergson says, the mechanical in the human is ridiculous: "rigidity is the comic, and laughter is its corrective" (21). Laughter at ridiculous ideas, unimaginative and joyless individuals, inhuman rituals, selfish behavior, and rigid social order characterizes comic realism.

Gulliver's Travels adapts the comic realist premises and techniques to an Enlightenment milieu, using the satiric potential while sharing the utopian-dystopian axis, which highlights and exemplifies the critique of human grandeur and self-importance. Unlike the knowing narrators created by Rabelais and Cervantes, Swift's narrator unwittingly reveals his inadequacies and lack of understanding of the world around him; in this way, he seems like a character that could have come from either of the earlier texts. In each of his travels Gulliver describes remarkable locales that contrast the British and European models of society (à la More's *Utopia*), and Swift utilizes his innocent narrator to integrate comic realist techniques. The Enlightenment perspective accelerates the departure of comic realism from folk culture, which Bakhtin points out in *Rabelais and His World* (34), but Swift maintains grotesque and fantastic elements. From Gulliver's first journey to the final episodes with the Yahoos, Swift makes Gulliver the butt of sexual humor. In Part 1, chapter 1, the repeated invocation of his benefactor, Master Bates, immediately marks Gulliver as being unaware of the implications of his words. Grotesque realism and the evocation of the lower bodily stratum, to use Bakhtin's words, find repeated representation in all the travels—for example, in how the Lilliputians must feed Gulliver and cart away his waste.

Gulliver in Lilliput resembles Gargantua also in the huge quantity of cloth needed to clothe him and in his ability to put out a fire with a stream of urine (cf. *Gargantua* 17). But where Gargantua's floodlike stream shows his as yet untamed ways—after all, Gargantua is in Paris to continue his education—Gulliver's shows his barbarism. What Gulliver imagines as heroic completely disgusts the empress, who refuses afterward to be near that besmirched wing of the court. When Gulliver is tiny among the giants in Brobdingnag in part 2, court ladies "often stripped [him] naked from Toe to Toe and lay [him] full-length in their bosoms" (95). Far from appreciating this intimacy, he complains about the smell of their giant bodies, about their moles and imperfections, and is particularly disgusted when they have no modesty about using the toilet in front of him. Gulliver himself craves privacy, and in a scene that echoes Sancho Panza, must find a way to discharge "the Necessities of Nature," as he says, "which another could not do for [him]" (73). In part 4, he is repeatedly assailed by the Yahoos. When they first see him, they "begin to discharge their Excrements on [his] Head" from the trees above, and he is "almost stifled with the Filth, which fell about [him] on every Side" (194). He is mortified when a female Yahoo is attracted to him sexually.

Swift's attitude toward the body has received a great deal of critical attention, with phrases such as "scatological imagination" and "excremental vision" (see Brown). In Swift studies, the Enlightenment context becomes a pigeonhole for understanding Swift: the rational mind's control versus the body's excesses. But, for Swift as for Rabelais, the key is in the balance. It is hard to overlook scenes containing the filthy, degenerate Yahoos (sometimes seen as Swift's true vision of humanity) or the images of rampant desire, yet they must be recognized as coming from Gulliver's point of view (and must be filtered through the eighteenth-century complaints of *Gulliver* as a low work and through the censorious judgments of Victorian gentility). The grotesque physical realities of *Gulliver's Travels* are only part of the text: perhaps a more important aspect of the Rabelaisian inheritance is the thorough criticism of the political world.

The utopian aspects of *Gargantua*—for example, the description of how the Thélémites live and their "Fais ce que voudras" (285; "Do what you will" [159]) philosophy—finds a distorted, dystopian mirror in Gulliver's adventures and in the descriptions of the various societies Gulliver visits. Each society, despite the narrator's original impressions, shows its dark underside. The Lilliputians go to war for an absurd reason: eggs have always been broken from the larger end, but when the emperor's son cuts his finger while breaking an egg, "the Emperor his Father, published an Edict, commanding all his subjects, upon great Penalties, to break the smaller End of their Eggs." This edict leads to rebellions in which "eleven Thousand Persons have, at several Times, suffered Death, rather than submitting to breaking their Eggs at the smaller End" (31). The controversy continues when the emperor of a neighboring country offers refuge to "Big-Endian Exiles," leading to a protracted and destructive war. The episode is reminiscent of the bakers' argument in *Gargantua*, chapter 25, which leads to the war with Picrochole. Here and throughout *Gulliver's Travels*, court counselors and toadies, described as inhabiting European courts, are similar to Picrochole's advisers. The Lilliputians see the giant Gulliver as a weapon, able through sheer size to disarm their enemy. The various ridiculous scientific visions of part 3, from floating islands to immortals, satirize contemporary ideas, and the genocidal Houyhnhnms in part 4, the horselike figures idealized by Gulliver, suggest the insight and prescience possible in comic realism.

At the center of comic realism is a sense of ethics. Even at its most cynical, it holds to certain values that may belong to their period but remain consistent across time. When Falstaff in *Henry IV* proclaims his antiheroic ideology, he is a comic realist hero. "What is a hero?" he asks. "A word. What is in the word honor? What is that honor? Air" (5.1.134–35). He values survival above all else, but the play shows, with the emergence of Prince Hal, that there are things worth fighting for, that there are principles that need to be validated as central to human society. Excess and cowardice may be funny, but they are not sustainable. Pleasure is not in and of itself negative, and celebration is an important part of being human, but sustained excess is destructive. Power may be used for good, but often it is shown to be corrupt.

Swift's message follows Rabelais. In part 2 of the *Travels*, sure that his hosts will admire Europe as a model, Gulliver pridefully describes everything from European politics to the justice system, including a joyous description of war and the use of gunpowder, which strikes horror in his listeners. The king's commentary mimics the wisdom of Gargantua's address to Picrochole's troops (*Pantagruel*, ch. 48). That the Brobdingnagians are peaceful Gulliver mocks as shortsighted. After hearing Gulliver's account of his homeland, the king concludes that human beings are "the most pernicious Race of little odious Vermin that Nature ever suffered to crawl upon the Surface of the Earth" (108). The satire may be sharper than Rabelais's, but the axis of constructive-destructive, utopian-dystopian, and community-individual is Rabelaisian. Although Quixote eventually realizes his madness, Gulliver never sees the insanity of own worldview, ending his days whinnying like a horse and cut off from his family and community.

The progressive adaptation of comic realism can be followed to the texts of Gogol. A number of his works make excellent comparative texts, not only the novel *Dead Souls* but also short stories such as "The Nose" and "The Overcoat." Bakhtin noted that Gogol and Rabelais were critically connected through popular culture and the use of vernacular language. In an essay on the relation between the two authors, he argues that Gogol is to the modern sense of the comic what Rabelais was for the Renaissance. He connects the authors, at least indirectly, through the Ukrainian tradition of popular festivals, and he writes that grotesque realism underlies much of Gogol's work. He compares *Dead Souls* with Rabelais's *Fourth Book*, claiming that Gogol creates "a merry, or carnivalesque, journey through the underworld, through the kingdom of death" ("Rabelais and Gogol" 32). It is through Chichikov's plan to buy and sell souls that we have the most honest if not the most direct representation of the serf economy. In the reactions of all those who hear of the plan, we get a reflection of social attitudes and of an unstable world. This variation on the Lucianic journey to the underworld is multidimensional and holds the possibility of renewal.

Gogol's "The Nose" stands out for the absurdity of the conceit, from Ivan Yakovlevich's confusion over finding a nose in a roll to his wife's assuredness that he cut it off shaving someone to his attempt to surreptitiously dispose of the nose. Also, Kovalyov's reaction to finding his nose missing, the way others react to his lack of a nose, and the ridiculousness of a nose desiring autonomy suggests a multiple displacement: physical loss, a body part's independent life, and the ultimate renewal or rejuvenation when the nose returns. As appalling as the assessor is in his egotism and self-centeredness, the nose is worse. Gogol's narrator tells the story as an incongruous, perhaps nonsensical, occurrence; yet while he says that sometimes these things happen, questions and ellipses undermine narrative stability and create a space for humor. As with the Rabelaisian text, it is left to the reader to fill in blanks and understand the story better than either the characters or the storyteller does.

"The Overcoat" also compares well with Rabelais. The clerk Akaky Akakievich at first seems to be a Bergsonian puppet, mechanistic and without any real joy in life, a copyist doomed to endless repetition, his one desire to have the comfort of the overcoat—human warmth and physical pleasure—and perhaps the respect that the coat would bring. When he finally achieves his goal, his vanity overcomes restraint, and he enters worlds both above and below him on the social scale that are foreign and dangerous. He drinks with his office mates, a carnivalesque world of rapid conversation and laughter to which he does not belong. He is victimized, first by robbers, then by an uncaring bureaucracy. The final episode of the story, the comic haunting of the city by the protagonist's ghost, bridges the world of the living and the dead, leaves the official and social realm uneasy, and shows the reader an unstable world mirrored in an unstable text.

Just as Cervantes, Swift, and Gogol form a tradition that can be followed chronologically with Rabelais as a touchstone, García Márquez's *One Hundred Years of Solitude* works well with *Gargantua and Pantagruel*. Magic realism utilizes caricature, farce, irony, hyperbole, ribaldry, and revelry; like comic realism it fits the model for authenticity and subversiveness that Bakhtin articulates. *One Hundred Years* attends to circumstantial realism but puts the ordinary details into extraordinary contexts. The narrative highlights innocence and decadence and criticizes destructive aspirations and depredations, with a fantastic quality that makes the reader always question the relation between official and authentic history. The novel strikingly incorporates carnivalesque conventions, from Gypsies to the spirit world, from the lower bodily stratum to the winding and unwinding of history. It bursts with life, whether it is José Arcadio's endless energy, Úrsula's multiple resurrections, Aureliano's thirty-two armed uprisings, Arcadio's gargantuan appetites, Rebeca's parents' bones, Remedios's levitation, or Melquíades's disappearances and reappearances—and this catalog only scratches the surface. Carnivals and marketplaces are literal and figurative; the cycle of life and death, ebb and flow, is a constant and a source of humor. Although José Arcadio Segundo complains about the fecundity of his animals—for example, yelling at them, "Cease Cows. . . . Cease, because life is short!" (273)—he revels in the plenty, riotously feasting and drinking, and sorrows in the loss when a plague-like rain kills all his livestock. Fittingly, García Márquez writes himself into the devolving years of his mythical city, Macondo—a utopian vision turned to apocalyptic disaster—and when he eventually leaves for a scholarship in Paris, it is with nothing but "two changes of clothing, a pair of shoes, and the complete works of Rabelais" (434). The reference is not coincidental, as García Márquez's attempt to contradict official history replicates Rabelais's opposition to official culture.

The texts discussed here work well together pedagogically. Shared themes include human nature, social engagement, representations of collective action, the significance of the historical moment, the utopian-dystopian axis, the intellect-materiality split, the interrelation of the popular and the elite, inventiveness and imagination, the misuses of education, and the purpose of narrative and the treatment of narrative form. These texts are so rich, so full and vibrant, that they fulfill what Erich Auerbach says in *Mimesis* about Rabelais—that he "invites the reader to deal directly with the world and its wealth of phenomenon" (276). The suspension of disbelief, as necessary for comic realism as it is for tragedy, absorbs the reader in the story but creates distance for reflection. Savage humor allows the discussion of serious topics with a disarming tone. Because the world remains corrupt, unethical, and violent, comic realism maintains currency. At the same time, the critique finds its balance in the celebratory, particularly in physical delight. Bodily functions are metaphors for what is natural and free, contravening the artificiality and accretions of civilization; their representation mocks oppressive forces in the public realm. The body is primal and contains memory and identity that no amount of civilizing force can fully control.

However, to say only that the texts share common themes and techniques elides a critical element of their connectedness. Comic realism engages disparate historical moments—sixteenth-century France, seventeenth-century Spain, eighteenth-century England, nineteenth-century Russia, twentieth-century Latin America—and draws structural and sociopolitical parallels. Why do the technical and aesthetic elements of comic realism endure? How does it continually change and adapt? If, as Bakhtin argues, Rabelais responds to the disintegration of the medieval world and the new instability ahead, the same could be said for Cervantes, Swift, Gogol, and García Márquez. Cervantes projects a modernity and the breakdown of traditional relationships; Swift tries to conceptualize the human side of the Enlightenment project and critiques the dark underside; Gogol sees a society moving from agrarian to urban, marked by upheaval; García Márquez channels the dislocations of a violent century. The ability to contextualize historically each work depends on an instructor's expertise, but recognizing the structural similarity across centuries is essential. All these writers engage their present and write alternative histories. They provide a new perspective on official history, a counternarrative that balances the private and personal with the social and public, that juxtaposes bodily functions, sexual and excremental, with scenes of governance and war. Most significant is that the comic realist text avoids sentimentality, which, like the nostalgia in *One Hundred Years of Solitude*, it imagines as destructive stagnation.

Finally, it is even possible to recognize Rabelais in postcolonial novels, which use mimicry and mockery to "write back" to empire. Some writers may make overt reference to Rabelais, but it is not necessary (and in many cases it would be inappropriate) to establish a direct connection. Rabelais is tied to the colonizing process by being part of the Western humanist tradition. In many postcolonial novels, the repressive forces of coloniality are juxtaposed with images of indigenous culture and tradition. To take one example, Amos Tutuola's *The Palm-Wine Drinkard* incorporates characterization and narrative detail that could come from *Gargantua and Pantagruel*. The novel combines the folkloric and the fantastic, the main character is a drinker of epic proportion, and his wife gives birth through a swollen thumb; the child at birth could talk "as if he was ten years of age," paralleling the birth of Gargantua (31). Essays in a recent critical book, *Cheeky Fictions: Laughter and the Postcolonial*, note the influence of Rabelais and carnivalesque narrative on postcolonial fiction, seeing comic realist techniques as a weapon in the arsenal in the struggle for autonomy and self-definition (Reichel and Stein). Texts by Alejo Carpentier, Salman Rushdie, V. S. Naipaul, and many others could be part of a course on comic realism.

Rabelais recognized, as García Márquez would write over four hundred years later, that "literature was the best plaything that had ever been invented to make fun of people" (417). Laughter has both destructive and productive possibilities, and the writers profiled here utilize both. Mockery reduces authority, transgressively rejects the monological, opens a window of opportunity for thought and perspective, and in subversion finds the potential for wholeness. From Renaissance humanism to Enlightenment satire to Russian absurdism to Latin American magic realism and even postcolonial examples, the elements of comic realism prove eminently adaptable.

"The Truth Is Out There": Rabelais in a Survey Course on Monsters

Kathleen Long

Although I teach the Rabelaisian corpus in many of my courses, from a freshman writing seminar to graduate seminars, for the purposes of this essay I focus on a broad-ranging survey, sometimes called a general education course, which I offer under the title Monsters A–X: Aristotle to the *X-Files*. This course, taught in English, is devised to attract a wide range of students from different disciplines and even different colleges (along with students from the College of Arts and Sciences, students from the College of Agriculture and Life Sciences take this course, as well as engineering students, industrial and labor relations students, etc.). The overt purpose of this course is to use popular culture to encourage literacy through reading original texts. To this end, the syllabus includes a number of texts that have been reinterpreted in films, musicals, or TV series: *Notre-Dame de Paris*, *The Phantom of the Opera*, *Dracula*, and even *Beowulf*. The course, developed over the past decade, is divided into themes and focuses on questions of race, gender, species, and—most recently—knowledge. The idea that we believe that certain creatures are monstrous—that is to say, frightening, terrible, worthy only of being destroyed—merely because of our imperfect knowledge, our own limitations, and therefore potentially our own monstrosity, was raised by Saint Augustine in his *City of God against the Pagans*, and it calls for the introduction of Rabelais, in particular *The Fourth Book*, into the course.

Many monster narratives are structured around a quest for knowledge: Pliny's *Natural History*, Mary Shelley's *Frankenstein*, even Bram Stoker's *Dracula*, can be read in this light. This quest is also linked to a geography of the monstrous that distorts spatial relations among various locations, particularly political units (states, regions, cultures, and even neighborhoods that house different social classes). The problematic nature of this quest is quite evident in the works of François Rabelais and in the sci-fi television series *The X-Files*. After putting the question of whether he should marry to every authority in France (and Europe) in the course of *The Third Book*, Panurge sets out with his companions to find the *Dive Bouteille* ("the Divine Bottle") in *The Fourth Book*. In the course of their travels, these characters come across monster after monster (or monstrous situation after monstrous situation), each of which bodes ominously for the chance of finding the truth that they seek. Quaresmeprenant (Lent) is incomprehensible as he is described (514–19); the frozen words (566–70), long since divorced from their context, hold no clear meaning but are subject to endless interpretation (by Rabelais scholars as well as by characters in the novel). Similarly, the FBI agents Mulder and Scully travel all over the United States, and eventually the world, to find the truth, which remains continually out of their grasp. The hapless agents rarely solve a case; instead, either the monster escapes ("El Mundo Gira"; "X-Cops"), is killed ("Jersey Devil"; "Detour"), or presents itself and solves the case itself ("Postmodern Prometheus"). Various episodes of *The X-Files* serve as meditations on the space of the monstrous (always out there, where the truth is) and on how narrative form itself mimics the monstrous and covers the truth. The strange monster narratives of *The X-Files* draw students in, slow them down (students realize that they don't really understand what is going on, and that they have to pay attention to nuances of language, lighting, characterization, and spatial-temporal play), and provide access to the even more complex texts of Rabelais. Similarly, the disjointed and then reconstructed group narrative of *Dracula* enjoins students to consider the importance of narrative voice, and of what is missing as well as what is reported, a lesson that they can then bring back to Rabelais. In the end, the epistemology of the monstrous, closely related to the more flexible, Pyrrhonian, form of skepticism (Popkin), binds all these texts together. The bewildered agents come no closer to the truth, trapped in interpretive processes that fold back on themselves instead of leading to some sort of reality or truth. This focus on interpretative processes also echoes the functioning of narrative in Rabelais's *Third Book*, where the manner in which the question is asked becomes more significant than the answer sought.

The most useful episodes of *The X-Files* for the purposes of approaching Rabelais are "The Jersey Devil," a modified wild-man narrative that places various levels of monstrosity in concentric circles around a center of supposedly normative society (but which is itself profoundly corrupted); "Field Trip," in which a giant hallucinogenic fungus causes people to see and hear only what they want to see and hear, in the attempt to cover the fact that they are being digested by the same fungus; "X-Cops," in which the monster is unreadable except as a manifestation of the subjective fears of whichever individual encounters it; "El Mundo Gira," which presents the monster as a creation of the narrative process; "The Postmodern Prometheus," in which various forms of monster narrative are manipulated or played with self-consciously, causing the text itself to be as fascinating as the subject matter. Each of these episodes enables students to consider how monster narratives offer a critical take on how we rationalize our subjective responses to the world around us. This combination of rationalizing discourse (or at least the forms of it) and irrational subject matter is omnipresent in Rabelais, for example in his discussion of Gargantua's birth:

> I doubt whether you will truly believe in this strange nativity [that is, by ear]. I don't care if you don't. But an honest man, a man of good sense, always believes what he is told and what he finds written down. Is this a violation of our law or our faith? Is it against reason or against Holy Scripture? For my part I find nothing written in the Holy Bible which contradicts

> it. If this had been the will of God, would you say that he could not have performed it? For goodness' sake do not obfuscate your brains with such an idle thought. For I say to you that to God nothing is impossible. If it had been His will women would have produced their children in that way, by the ear, for ever afterwards. (52–53)

The authorial persona repeats arguments that would be familiar to his readers, lulling them into complacency before returning to the problematic premise of birth through the ear. Similarly, characters in *The X-Files* often present paranormal phenomena in the discourse of anthropology or medical sciences, for example in "Bad Blood," when Mulder reviews many of the world's myths concerning vampires and Scully offers scientific explanations for vampiric behavior. The joke, made apparent at the end of the episode, is that the people they are investigating really are vampires.

The tenth chapter of *Gargantua* represents an extended example of rationalizing discourse used to justify a subjective interpretation, as the authorial persona expounds on his view that the color white signifies joy by citing authorities (Aristotle in particular), using logic (of sorts), rejecting different views, and citing biblical, classical, and pseudoscientific examples (59–61). The slippery quality of the language used reveals the fault lines of this rationality (Jeanneret, *Défi* and *Paroles*). After these few examples are discussed, students are encouraged to bring in their own examples of rationalization from the works of Rabelais—for example, Janotus de Bragmardo's dysfunctional logic and Picrochole's excessive war plans, while containing moments of logical discourse, clearly defy reason.

In this course, we focus on particular moments in *The X-Files*, in *Gargantua*, and in *The Fourth Book*, to see how evasive language or signs, and therefore knowledge, can be. "X-Cops," as a parody of a popular form, the reality TV show, which does not need a parody, already echoes Rabelais's use of popular forms of literature. The show plays a number of games with the form, to make viewers conscious of how they are being manipulated. The familiar theme song ("Bad boys, bad boys, what you gonna do, what you gonna do when they come for you?") starts us thinking that we know what will happen: a crime will occur, and someone will be arrested. But this is *The X-Files*, so we should expect the unexpected. The criminal is a monster that no one ever sees, except in the form of claw marks on a door, some pictures drawn by police artists, several highly marked dead bodies (with wounds or a broken neck), and physical symptoms of illness. Various characters describe how the monster looks to them, but it becomes clear over the course of the show that the monster takes on different forms for different people: it is a giant wasp for a police officer who was terrified by stories of a wasp-man as a child; Freddy Krueger for the woman who is the first to report an intruder in the time frame of the show (it turns out later that there were previous reports outside of this frame) and for the police artist who draws a portrait based on her description.

This description of the monster that proliferates into unreadable images is reminiscent of Xenomanes's description of Lent in *The Fourth Book*: the list of analogies makes it impossible to imagine what the creature looks like:

> His lobes are like a gimlet.
> His vermiform excrescences like a tennis-racket.
> His membranes like a monk's cowl.
> His funnel like a mason's hod.
> The vault of his cranium like a patchwork bonnet.
> His pineal gland like a bagpipe. (513)

To further complicate matters, Lent is never seen by any of the other characters in the book, and so the text stands in for the monster just as various marks, symptoms, and images stand in for the monsters in "X-Cops." The result is that Lent can be neither comprehended nor even imagined, as the language literally stands in the way of any possible interpretation. As the students read Rabelais in the same weeks that this episode is screened, they are encouraged to note details that evoke the same issues, draw up lists of various forms of signs found in both Rabelais and "X-Cops," and discuss how those signs operate. Generally, I do not hand out critical or theoretical material for students to read at this point (given their already significant reading load); concepts are presented either by *PowerPoint* summaries with additional explanations or by short handouts. Sometimes the literature students do these presentations; sometimes I present the background material.

The narration of the "X-Cops" episode is more complex than my summary here makes it seem, so I have students look at the episode in detail. To frame it in the reality show tradition, the first image on the screen is a caution that alludes to *Cops*: "The following is a special episode of *The X-Files*. Viewer discretion is advised." Scenes from the upcoming episode are briefly presented, as they would be in *Cops*, with a focus on arrests. The theme song from *Cops* is played. The illusion of reality is played with from the beginning. Actors playing cops speak in realistic dialogue (i.e., they use simple sentences, direct statements) but in a way that suggests it is scripted rather than natural speech. How should one read the imitation of realistic dialogue?

Language similarly takes on a life of its own in the chapter of *Gargantua* "The Drunkards' Conversation" (48). The proliferation of ways of talking about drinking distracts the reader from the topic at hand (particularly when the drunkards begin to speak in rhyme and imitate Scholastic discourse). The students trace how the use of language evolves in this chapter from direct, simple language to theological, literary, and philosophical discourses, from "Draw!—Pass it over!—Fill it up!" to "Waiters, you're good at transubstantiation, turn me from a non-drinker to a drinker" and "Argus had a hundred eyes to see by: a waiter needs a hundred hands, as many as Briareus, to pour out unwearyingly" and

"Natura abhorret vacuum. Nature abhors a vacuum" (49–51). Just as Rabelais stretches the realism of his narrative by means of excessive or discordant language, so in "X-Cops" the realism is broken with a police report, coming over the radio, not of a crime but of a monster. This interruption of normalcy mimics Rabelais's clever conjunction of geographical precision when he locates the giant's tomb in which the book of *Gargantua* was supposedly found, with the outsized nature of that tomb and its contents (42).

Other forms of linguistic disconnect link Rabelais's work to *The X-Files*. When the deputy arrives at the scene, he has a brief exchange with a woman speaking Spanish, a language he only partly understands and speaks in a broken fashion. There are various linguistic impasses in Rabelais's work: Janotus de Bragmardo's incoherent harangue ("Well now, *de parte Dei, date nobis clochas nostras*" [77–78]) and Pantagruel's first encounter with Panurge, in which Panurge begs for money in twelve different languages before trying French (196–201; see Demonet). In "X-Cops," what is known at first is based on miscommunication. We hear a cat meow (is this the monster?) and see large scratches on the door. As it turns out, these scratches are the sign left by the monster. The deputy goes around back, and we see the dutifully arranged signs of urban squalor: an old sink, old mattresses, trash. . . . But these signs indicate more the ability of the author or director to create the impression of reality than any underlying reality.

This emphasis on the unstable nature of signs is echoed by the insistence on the framing of the narrative, on the authorial or editorial interventions required to keep the narrative flowing. In this opening scene of "X-Cops," as the deputy is investigating the report of a monster, he walks around the corner, into the dark and out of the frame, then runs back into the frame screaming. At this point, the cameraman, following his escape, runs into a wall. The presence of the cameraman will be felt frequently thereafter, making us aware of the staging of the scenes. Rabelais also frequently interrupts the narrative to comment or elicit comment from his readers—for example, at the beginning of *The Fourth Book*, "God save you and keep you, good people. But where are you? I can't see you. Wait till I put on my spectacles. Ha! Ha! Fair and softly Lent goes by! Now I can see you" (439). Another example of such interruption appears in *Gargantua*, at the beginning of the Picrocholine war:

> For the priests, curates, preachers, physicians, surgeons, and apothecaries who went to visit, dress, heal, preach to, and admonish the sick all died of the infection. Yet these robbing and murdering devils never took any harm. What is the reason for that, gentlemen? Consider the problem, I beg of you. (97)

In the "X-Cops" episode, at no point does the audience see the monster, but when the deputy gets back into his squad car, it is overturned by what must be the monster. This opening sequence ends with the *X-Files* theme and the line "The truth is out there," which appears at the beginning of every *X-Files* episode. All this careful framing tells the viewer that the presentation of the narrative is as significant as, if not more significant than, the narrative itself. After the first few examples are pointed out to students, they are encouraged to find their own examples of framing techniques in both Rabelais and in "X-Cops." They are sometimes also encouraged to think back to other narratives they have read, and other episodes, for similar examples, since we work on Rabelais rather late in the semester.

For the rest of the evening, the cops run from one part of Los Angeles to another, in pursuit of the monster, moving from monster to monster in a way that touches on the random. This pursuit is reminiscent of the voyages of Panurge and his friends in *The Fourth Book*, as they travel from island to island looking for answers but only finding more questions. Mulder and Scully prove that they are FBI agents by producing their ID cards, which they are asked to do several times during the episode, as if their identity is questionable. The badge only works as a marker of identity for those who recognize and accept it. In a similar gesture of self-identification, any two of the Ennasin (a race of people) in *The Fourth Book* are linked by sexual or social relations described by means of analogies (e.g., two people name each other "eiderdown" and "mattress" [468–71]). The identities of these two are made coherent by the analogies given, but these analogies do not extend the connection beyond them, so that their identities are meaningless outside the context of their own personal and factitious relationship (see Randall, *Building*). That is to say, there is no system of identification that is universal to all the Ennasin.

In "X-Cops," the illusion of reality is repeatedly created but also repeatedly violated. The censorship of obscenities ("With all due respect, what the 'beep' are you talking about?") destroys the illusion that events are being presented live. When Scully urges Mulder to be careful what he says, because they are on live television, he replies, "I don't think so, Scully, that woman just said 'beep.' " The added complication is that Mulder emits the sound rather than the word *beep*. It is in this surreal context that the two go off to find "concrete proof of the paranormal." Mulder explains to the cameraman who is in his car that the paranormal is that which cannot be established by scientific means, suggesting the impossibility of finding concrete proof of it. This quest is analogous to Panurge's persistent desire to find concrete proof of a negative, that he will not be beaten, cuckolded, and robbed, which launches its own endless voyage in *The Fourth Book*.

The signs of monstrosity proliferate in "X-Cops," just as monsters as indecipherable signs proliferate in *The Fourth Book*. To the claw marks on the woman's door are added pictures of a werewolf, drawn some time ago, and the picture of Freddy Krueger drawn by the police artist. It seems that only the person being attacked by the monster can see the monster. Meanwhile, Mulder notices what look like bite marks on the deputy's hand and concludes that the man has been attacked by a werewolf. On examination by another doctor (Scully is also a doctor), it appears that these marks are stings, not bites. Scully cautions Mulder, "Together they look like a pattern, especially when we want them to." In other words, the only evidence we have about this monster is a number of signs that are disjunctive and unclear. The truth out there seems to be moving further and further away as we interpret the signs. In the meantime, the police artist, frightened by the talk of monsters, is found murdered, with a pink fingernail at the site. This fingernail belongs to a prostitute, Chantara Gomez, a fact that is evident from her matching pink wig. She saw her boyfriend, Chuco, killing the artist and tried to help. The cops seek Chuco in a stereotypical crack house straight out of *Cops*. But Chuco has been dead for at least several days. When the cops go back outside, Chantara is dead, killed exactly the way she said Chuco threatened to kill her. Each piece of information contradicts the preceding piece. The deputy saw the wasp-man again, not Chuco. Flattened bullets suggest that something was there. Finally, the deputy tells of childhood stories of a wasp-man with a mouth full of stingers that terrified him when he was young. Is all this occurring only in the deputy's head? Is he crazy, or driven by narrative to see what he is told to see (like everyone else)?

This proliferation of signs that point to an absent subject informs our discussion of the "frozen words" chapters in *The Fourth Book*. The scene begins with incomprehensible voices:

> "Can you hear something, comrades?" he asked. "I seem to hear people talking in the air. But I can't see anything. Listen." . . . Indeed, the more keenly we listened, the more clearly we made out voices, till in the end we could hear whole words. (566–67)

These voices exist detached from the people who emitted them. The explanation for them is at once concise and absurd:

> My lord, don't be afraid. This is the edge of the frozen sea, and at the beginning of last winter there was a great and bloody battle here between the Arimaspians and the Cloud-riders. The shouts of the men, the cries of the women, the slashing of the battle-axes, the clashing of the armour and harnesses, the neighing of the horses and all the other frightful noises of battle became frozen in the air. But just now, the rigours of winter being over and the good season coming on with its calm and mild weather, these noises are melting, and so you can hear them. (568)

Despite this explanation, the noises, separated from their original context, are indecipherable:

> Then he threw on the deck before us whole handfuls of frozen words, which looked like crystallized sweets of different colours. We saw some

> words gules, or gay quips, some vert, some azure, some sable, and some or. When we warmed them a little between our hands, they melted like snow, and we actually heard them, though we did not understand them, for they were in a barbarous language. (569)

The words melt together into gibberish:

> When they had all melted together, we heard: Hin, hin, hin, hin, his, tick, tock, crack, brededin, brededac, frr, frrr, frrrr, bou, bou, bou, bou, bou, bou, bou, bou, tracc, tracc, trr, trrr, trrrr, trrrrr, trrrrrr, on, on, on, on, on, ouououououou, Gog, Magog, and goodness knows what other barbarous sounds. (569)

While detective shows are all about reading signs and finding out the truth about a crime, both Rabelais and the creators of *The X-Files* suggest that the proliferation of signs leads only to a focus on the signs and away from any possible truth, in a sort of infinite regress that resembles the Derridean supplement. Translators are present in a number of *X-Files* episodes ("X-Cops" and "El Mundo Gira," for example) to mediate different languages, but they are rarely reliable mediators. Panurge translates himself until he is comprehensible to Pantagruel when they first meet, but with the frozen words no mediation is possible. Language and other signs, divorced from the context of their production, lose their meaning. Since the origin of the signs in "X-Cops" is never found, all that can be achieved is the imposition of a more or less arbitrary and factitious interpretation of these random, yet somehow connected, manifestations. This interpretation in turn is presented as the origin of the narrative. Both *The X-Files* and *The Fourth Book* speak to the unstable nature of signs and the creative potential of that instability.

Mulder comes to the conclusion that the monster appears to each person as the person's worst fear; it is entirely subjective. Shortly after this point, Mulder turns to the cameramen (who are off-camera) to explain that he is returning to check on the eyewitnesses of one of the murders. After this scene, more cameramen appear, as if to underscore that the viewer is subject to the same manipulation that the characters in the episode are experiencing. An assistant at an autopsy that Scully conducts proceeds to die almost instantaneously of hanta virus when Scully mentions the disease. Scully asserts, "It looks for all the world like it's the hanta virus, but it's not." If the only evidence available to us is misleading, how can we know what is happening?

Finally, the deputy goes back to the crack house and gets trapped in it. Mulder and Scully realize the potential danger, enter the house, find the cameramen hiding in the closet downstairs (so who is filming this scene?) and run upstairs to save the deputy. Daylight comes, and the monster, which has only appeared at night, disappears. Except that we never saw the monster. Did it ever exist? Only wounds and dead bodies signal that a monster was there. Scully concludes, "You didn't get the proof you wanted." Mulder responds, pointing to the camera, "It all depends on how they edit it."

This combination of surreal subject matter and realistic presentation (which suggests that we are being told some version of the truth) introduces students effectively to some of the epistemological problems that inform Rabelais's work. On an obvious level, the story of a family of giants evokes disbelief, even while the author insists in various ways on the signs of truth that his audience generally accepts: a precise location for the giant's grave (42), realistic (and yet hyperbolic) descriptions of battles ("He beat out the brains of some, broke the arms and legs of others, disjointed the neck-bones, demolished the kidneys, slit the noses, blackened the eyes, smashed the jaws, knocked the teeth down the throats, shattered the shoulder-blades, crushed the shins . . ." [99]), colloquial language. The insistence on breaking the narrative frame by addressing readers (e.g., in *Gargantua*, the question about God's presence when the village is massacred; the prologue to *The Fourth Book*). Questioning how something might happen makes readers conscious of the rhetorical manipulation underlying the storytelling, thus creating disbelief or doubt. The deployment of a range of rhetorical styles, from bad academic Latin (77–78) to complex humanist speeches, shows the range of situations in which manipulation might take place. In both Rabelaisian corpus and "X-Cops," we are warned that the illusion of truth created by a style of speech or way of framing the narrative is not the truth—though this illusion may be all that we have.

Signs are the necessary mediators of the world for us, in that we judge what has happened or what something is by the signs it leaves behind it or carries with it, but our attempts to interpret them and understand the world merely obscure the object we seek and take us further away from the truth. This gap between signifier and signified in both Rabelais's work and *The X-Files* opens up the opportunity to talk about poststructuralist notions of language (Saussure) and other forms of postmodern theory, such as the Derridean notion of the supplement (see Jeanneret, *Défi*, for the best discussion of the problem of the sign in Rabelais; and Cave, *Cornucopian Text*). Derrida's concept can be connected to Rabelais by means of the skeptical notion of infinite regress (Sextus Empiricus 2.9), in which one term is explained by another, which itself must be explained by yet another, and so on.

This more theoretical approach draws the literature students into the discussion but can be accessible as well to students majoring in the sciences, who will be able to identify scientific truths that are briefly presented in *The X-Files* (and also in Rabelais, although many of his sixteenth-century medical truths have since been discredited). The *X-Files* episodes about monsters generally present one scientific fact that suggests the truth-value of the episode, like Rabelais's mischievous tendency to cite imaginary sources alongside works that actually existed and his discussion of childbirth in which current medical understanding is mixed with ancient mythology (51–53). Of course, once a fact is presented in the *X-Files*, it is rapidly distorted and veers off into science fiction.

The obvious benefit of using material from *The X-Files* is that it draws students into the course. I find the television series more effective than other monster narratives in introducing Renaissance material, because it takes various levels of culture (popular and elite) and puts them under skeptical scrutiny, much as Rabelais did in his works. Most of the issues concerning Rabelais and *The X-Files* presented here are raised to the students in the form of questions, first about the series, then about the books. The level of sophistication of *The X-Files*, particularly in matters of epistemology and metanarrative, is far greater than that of most monster narratives and so makes a better introduction to monstrosity as it plays out in the Renaissance than most modern and postmodern works. In short, the series is fun but also makes students think and read more carefully, a necessary preparation for Rabelais.

NOTES ON CONTRIBUTORS

Tom Conley is Lowell Professor of Romance Languages and Visual and Environmental Studies at Harvard University. He is the author of *Film Hieroglyphs*, *The Graphic Unconscious*, *Cartographic Cinema*, *An Errant Eye*, and *The Self-Made-Map*.

Edwin M. Duval is professor of French at Yale University. He is the author of three books on the design of Rabelais's works. His current project is a book on relations among musical form, poetic form, and lyric genres in France from the mid-fourteenth to the end of the sixteenth century.

Gary Ferguson is professor of French at the University of Delaware. He is the editor of Anne de Marquets's *Sonets spirituels* and author of *Mirroring Belief: Marguerite de Navarre's Devotional Poetry* and *Queer (Re)Readings in the French Renaissance: Homosexuality, Gender, Culture*.

Carl Fisher is professor of comparative literature at California State University, Long Beach, where he is chair of the Department of Comparative World Literature and Classics. He has written on Defoe, Fielding, Sterne, Rousseau, Godwin, Hannah More, and the representation of pigs in the eighteenth century.

Carla Freccero is professor of literature, feminist studies, and the history of consciousness at the University of California, Santa Cruz. She is the author of *Father Figures: Genealogy and Narrative Structure in Rabelais*, *Popular Culture*, and *Queer/Early/Modern*.

Andrea Frisch teaches sixteenth- and seventeenth-century French literature at the University of Maryland, College Park. She is the author of *The Invention of the Eyewitness* and is writing a book about the influence of the wars of religion on literary aesthetics.

Kirsten A. Fudeman is assistant professor in the Department of French and Italian at the University of Pittsburgh. She is the author of *Vernacular Voices: Language and Identity in Medieval French Jewish Communities* and the coauthor, with Mark Aronoff, of *What Is Morphology?*

Floyd Gray is professor emeritus at the University of Michigan. He is the author of *Le style de Montaigne*, *Rabelais et l'écriture*, *Gender, Rhetoric, and Print Culture in French Renaissance Writing*, and *La renaissance des mots*.

Timothy Hampton teaches French and comparative literature at the University of California, Berkeley. He is the author of *Fictions of Embassy: Literature and Diplomacy in Early Modern Europe*.

Elisabeth Hodges is associate professor of French at Miami University. She is the author of *Urban Poetics in the French Renaissance* and is writing a book on the poetics of eccentricity in French Renaissance literature.

Karen James is director of *The Renaissance in Print* (Gordon Project) and a faculty member of the French department at the University of Virginia. She recently completed a bilingual edition of Pernette du Guillet's *Rymes*, in collaboration with Marta Rijn Finch.

Scott D. Juall is associate professor of French at the University of North Carolina, Wilmington. He is writing a book on ideology and imperialism in sixteenth-century French travel narratives.

Marcus Keller is associate professor at the University of Illinois, Urbana-Champaign where he teaches sixteenth- and seventeenth-century French literature and culture. He is the author of *Figurations of France: Literary Nation-Building in Times of Crisis, 1550–1650*.

Virginia Krause is associate professor of French studies at Brown University. She is the author of *Idle Pursuits: Literature and "Oisiveté" in the French Renaissance*. Her current research focuses on witchcraft in Renaissance France.

Lawrence D. Kritzman is John D. Willard Professor of French, Comparative Literature, and Oratory at Dartmouth and director of the Institute of French Cultural Studies. He is the author of *The Fabulous Imagination: On Montaigne's Essays* and the editor of *Columbia History of Twentieth-Century French Thought*.

David LaGuardia is professor of French and comparative literature at Dartmouth College. He is the author of *Intertextual Masculinity in French Renaissance Literature: Rabelais, Brantôme, and the Cent nouvelles nouvelles*. He is currently writing a book about memory and memorial writing in sixteenth-century France.

Kathleen Long is professor of French in the Department of Romance Studies at Cornell University. She is the editor of *Religious Differences in France, Past and Present* and the author of *Hermaphrodites in Renaissance France*.

Deborah N. Losse is dean of humanities in the College of Arts and Sciences at Arizona State University. She is the author of *Rhetoric at Play: Rabelais and Satirical Eulogy* and *Sampling the Book. Renaissance Prologues of the French Conteurs*.

Mary McKinley is Douglas Huntly Gordon Professor of French at the University of Virginia. She is the author of two books on Montaigne and coedited and contributed to *Critical Tales: New Studies of the* Heptameron *and Early Modern Culture*.

Jan Miernowski is a professor at the University of Wisconsin, Madison, and at the University of Warsaw. He is the author of *Signes dissimilaires: La quête des noms divins dans la poésie française de la Renaissance*, *Le Dieu Néant*, and *L'ontologie de la contradiction sceptique*.

John O'Brien is professor of French Renaissance literature at Royal Holloway, University of London. He is the author of *Anacreon Redivivus* and the coeditor of Remy Belleau's "Les odes d'Anacréon," *La "familia" de Montaigne*, and *Theory and the Early Modern*.

James M. Palmer is associate professor of English at Prairie View A&M University. He has written on medieval and Renaissance literature and medicine, pedagogy, and composition.

John Parkin is professor of French literary studies at Bristol University. He is the author of a book on humor in Marguerite de Navarre's *Heptaméron* and the coeditor of *French Humour* and *Laughter and Power*.

Jeff Persels is associate professor of French and director of European Studies at the University of South Carolina. He has written on Rabelais, Stefan Zweig, and Montaigne and coedited *Fecal Matters in Early Modern Literature and Art*.

Michael Randall is professor of French and comparative literature at Brandeis University. He is the author of *The Gargantuan Polity: On the Individual and the Community in the French Renaissance*.

Todd W. Reeser is associate professor of French at the University of Pittsburgh. He is the author of *Moderating Masculinity in Early Modern Culture* and *Masculinities in Theory*.

Richard Regosin is emeritus professor of French at the University of California, Irvine. He has written on d'Aubigné and Montaigne and is currently at work on a book on secrets and secrecy in French Renaissance literature.

Bernd Renner is professor of modern languages at Brooklyn College and of French at the Graduate Center, City University of New York. He is the author of *"Difficile est saturam non scribere": L'herméneutique de la satire rabelaisienne* and the editor of *"La satire dans tous ses états": Le "meslange satyricque" à la Renaissance française*.

François Rigolot is Meredith Howland Pyne Professor of French Literature at Princeton University. He is the author of *Les langages de Rabelais*, *Poétique et onomastique*, *Le texte de la Renaissance*, *Les métamorphoses de Montaigne*, and *L'erreur de la Renaissance*.

Jerry Root is associate professor of French and comparative literature at the University of Utah. He is the author of *"Space to Speke": The Confessional Subject in Medieval Literature* and is currently working on manuscript illuminations of the *Roman de la rose* and the Theophilus legend.

Cynthia Skenazi is professor of French and comparative literature at the University of California, Santa Barbara. She is the author of *Marie Gevers et la nature*, *Maurice Scève et la pensée chrétienne*, and *Le poète architecte en France: Constructions d'un imaginaire monarchique*.

Walter Stephens is Charles S. Singleton Professor of Italian at Johns Hopkins University. He is the author of *Giants in Those Days: Folklore, Ancient History, and Nationalism* and *Demon Lovers: Witchcraft, Sex, and the Crisis of Belief*.

Timothy J. Tomasik is associate professor of French at Valparaiso University (Indiana). His research focuses on the intersections between early modern literary works and culinary texts. He is the editor of *At the Table: Metaphorical and Material Cultures of Food in Medieval and Early Modern Europe*.

Valerie Worth-Stylianou is senior tutor and fellow of Trinity College, Oxford University. She is the author of *The Practice of Translation in Renaissance France*, *Confidential Strategies in French Tragic Drama*, and *Les traités d'obstétrique en langue française au seuil de la modernité*.

Elizabeth Chesney Zegura is associate professor at the University of Arizona, Tucson. She is the author of *The Countervoyage of Rabelais and Ariosto* and editor of *The Rabelais Encyclopedia* and is currently preparing a monograph on Marguerite de Navarre's *Heptaméron*.

SURVEY PARTICIPANTS

Robert April, *New York, New York*
Rohini Bannerjee, *Saint Mary's University*
Barbara Bowen, *Vanderbilt University*
Jean Braybrook, *Birkbeck College, London*
Leah Chang, *George Washington University*
Tom Conley, *Harvard University*
Thomas L. Cooksey, *Armstrong Atlantic State University*
Margery Crumpacker, *New York, New York*
Debashree Dattaray, *Jadavpur University*
Edwin M. Duval, *Yale University*
Gary Ferguson, *University of Delaware*
Carl Fisher, *California State University, Long Beach*
Carla Freccero, *University of California, Santa Cruz*
Andrea Frisch, *University of Maryland, College Park*
Edward J. Gallagher, *Wheaton College*
Floyd Gray, *University of Michigan (emeritus)*
Timothy Hampton, *University of California, Berkeley*
Bruce Hayes, *University of Kansas*
Elisabeth Hodges, *Miami University*
Chloé Hogg, *University of Pittsburgh*
Karen James, *University of Virginia*
Scott D. Juall, *University of North Carolina, Wilmington*
Neil Kenny, *University of Cambridge*
Virginia Krause, *Brown University*
Lawrence D. Kritzman, *Dartmouth College*
Eva Kushner, *University of Toronto*
David LaGuardia, *Dartmouth College*
Kathleen Long, *Cornell University*
Deborah N. Losse, *Arizona State University*
Eric MacPhail, *Indiana University, Bloomington*
Christopher Martin, *Boston University*
Eric Martone, *Kennedy High School*
Katherine Maynard, *Washington College*
Mary McKinley, *University of Virginia*
Jan Miernowski, *University of Wisconsin, Madison*
Peter Noble, *University of Reading*
John O'Brien, *Royal Holloway, University of London*
James M. Palmer, *Prairie View A&M University*
John Parkin, *University of Bristol*
Jeff Persels, *University of South Carolina*
Marina Peters-Newell, *University of New Mexico*
Laurie Postlewate, *Barnard College*
Anne Lake Prescott, *Barnard College, Columbia University*

Michael Randall, *Brandeis University*
Todd W. Reeser, *University of Pittsburgh*
Richard Regosin, *University of California, Irvine*
Bernd Renner, *Brooklyn College and the Graduate Center, CUNY*
François Rigolot, *Princeton University*
Jerry Root, *University of Utah*
Roy Rosenstein, *American University of Paris*
Nicolas Russell, *Smith College*
Marie Rutkoski, *Brooklyn College*
Martine Sauret, *University of Minnesota*
Cynthia Skenazi, *University of California, Santa Barbara*
William Spates, *Shorter College*
Timothy J. Tomasik, *Valparaiso University*
Ralph Vitello, *East Stroudsburg University of Pennsylvania*
Valerie Worth-Stylianou, *Trinity College, Oxford University*
Cathy Yandell, *Carleton College*
Elizabeth Chesney Zegura, *University of Arizona*

WORKS CITED

"ABC de bibliophilie." *Bibliopolis*. François Côté, Libraire, n.d. Web. 20 Oct. 2009.

The Advocate. Dir. Leslie Megahey. British Broadcasting Corporation, 1993. Film.

Albala, Kenneth. *Eating Right in the Renaissance*. Berkeley: U of California P, 2002. Print.

Allen, Don Cameron. *The Legend of Noah: Renaissance Rationalism in Art, Science, and Letters.* 1949. Urbana: U of Illinois P, 1963. Print.

Angenot, Marc. " 'L'intertextualité': Enquête sur l'émergence et la diffusion d'un champ notionnel." *Revue des sciences humaines* 89 (1983): 121–33. Print.

Apian, Pierre. *Cosmographia*. Antwerp, 1529. Print.

Arp, Robert, ed. South Park *and Philosophy: You Know, I Learned Something Today*. Malden: Blackwell, 2007. Print.

Attardo, Salvatore. *Humorous Texts: A Semantic and Pragmatic Analysis*. Berlin: De Gruyter, 2001. Print.

Auerbach, Erich. "The World in Pantagruel's Mouth." *Mimesis: The Representation of Reality in Western Literature*. Trans. Willard R. Trask. Princeton: Princeton UP, 1953. 262–84. Print.

Augustine. *The City of God.* Trans. Marcus Dods et al. New York: Random, 1950. Print.

———. *The City of God against the Pagans* (*De civitate dei*). Cambridge: Cambridge UP, 1998. Print.

———. *Commentaire de la première épître de S. Jean*. Ed. Aul Agnaëse. Paris: Cerf, 1984. Print.

———. *The Confessions*. Trans. R. S. Pine-Coffin. Harmondsworth: Penguin, 1983. Print.

———. *De doctrina christiana*. Trans. and ed. R. P. H. Green. Oxford: Clarendon, 1995. Print.

Ayres-Bennett, Wendy. *A History of the French Language through Texts*. London: Routledge, 1996. Print.

"Bad Blood." Writ. Vince Gilligan. Dir. Cliff Bole. *The X-Files*. Fox. 22 Feb. 1998. Television. Season 5, episode 12.

Bakhtin, Mikhail. *The Dialogic Imagination: Four Essays*. Ed. Michael Holquist. Trans. Holquist and Caryl Emerson. Austin: U of Texas P, 1981. Print.

———. "Discourse in the Novel." Bakhtin, *Dialogic Imagination* 259–422.

———. "Forms of Time and the Chronotope in the Novel." Bakhtin, *Dialogic Imagination* 84–258.

———. *L'œuvre de François Rabelais et la culture populaire au Moyen Âge et sous la Renaissance*. Trans. Andrée Robel. Paris: Gallimard, 1970. Print.

———. "Rabelais and Gogol: Verbal Art and Popular Humor." Trans. Michael O'Toole. *Australian Journal of Cultural Studies* 3.1 (1985): 29–39. Print.

———. *Rabelais and His World*. Trans. Hélène Iswolsky. Bloomington: Indiana UP, 1984. Print.

———. "The Rabelaisian Chronotope." Bakhtin, *Dialogic Imagination* 167–207.

Baldinger, Kurt. *Études autour de Rabelais*. Geneva: Droz, 1990. Print.

"The Battle of San Romano." *Wikipedia*. Wikimedia, 8 Jan. 2010. Web. 15 Mar. 2010.

Beaujour, Michel. *Le jeu de Rabelais*. Paris: L'Herne, 1969. Print.

Berchiori, Petro. "Ovidius Metamorphoseos Moralizatus." *Studii romanzi* 23 (1933): 87–132. Print.

Bergson, Henri. *Laughter: An Essay on the Meaning of the Comic*. Trans. Cloudesley Brereton and Fred Rothwell. New York: Macmillan, 1911. Print.

Berrong, Richard M. *Rabelais and Bakhtin: Popular Culture in* Gargantua *and* Pantagruel. 1986. Lincoln: U of Nebraska P, 2006. Print.

Berry, Alice Fiola. *The Charm of Catastrophe: A Study of Rabelais's* Quart livre. Chapel Hill: U of North Carolina P, 2000. Print.

———. " 'L'isle Medamothi': Rabelais's Itineraries of Anxiety (*Quart livre* 2–4)." *PMLA* 106.5 (1991): 1040–53. Print.

———. " 'Les mithologies pantagruelicques': Introduction to a Study of Rabelais's *Quart livre*." *PMLA* 92.3 (1977): 471–80. Print.

Berthon, Guillaume. "Le livre comme objet: Eléments de bibliographie matérielle." *Panurge*. Panurge.org, 23 Apr. 2007. Web. 20 Oct. 2009.

Bhabha, Homi K. *The Location of Culture*. London: Routledge, 1994. Print.

Bizer, Marc. *La muse Renaissante*. U of Texas, n.d. Web. 20 Oct. 2009.

———. *Petit guide de la langue du XVI*[e] *siècle ("le moyen français")*. U of Texas, 2000. Web. 20 Oct. 2009.

Bon, François. "Rabelais à haute voix." *Le tiers livre: Littérature et internet*. TiersLivre .net, 23 Feb. 2003–1 July 2008. Web. 20 Oct. 2009.

Bonnaffé, Jacques, narr. *Gargantua*. Paris: Thélème, 2002. CD.

Booth, Wayne. "Freedom of Interpretation: Bakhtin and the Challenge of Feminist Criticism." *Critical Inquiry* 9 (1982): 45–76. Print.

Bosch, Hieronymus. *Garden of Earthly Delights*. 1500–05. Oil-on-wood triptych. Prado, Madrid.

———. *Ship of Fools*. 1490–1500. Oil on wood. Louvre, Paris.

Botticelli, Sandro. *Primavera*. c. 1482. Tempera on panel. Uffizi Gallery, Florence.

Boutcher, Warren. "Vernacular Humanism in the Sixteenth Century." *The Cambridge Companion to Renaissance Humanism*. Ed. Jill Kraye. Cambridge: Cambridge UP, 1996. 189–202. Print.

Bowen, Barbara. *Enter Rabelais, Laughing*. Nashville: Vanderbilt UP, 1998. Print.

Brault, Gerard J. "Ung abysme de science." *Bibliothèque d'humanisme et renaissance* 28 (1966): 615–32. Print.

Braunrot, Bruno. *François Rabelais: A Reference Guide, 1550–1990*. New York: Hall, 1994. Print.

Bray, Alan. *The Friend*. Chicago: U of Chicago P, 2003. Print.

Broc, Numa. *La géographie de la Renaissance, 1420–1620*. Paris: Bibliothèque Nationale, 1980. Print.

Bromilow, Polly. "Inside Out: Female Bodies in Rabelais." *Forum for Modern Language Studies* 44 (2008): 27–39. Print.

Brown, Norman. *Life against Death: The Psychoanalytic Meaning of History*. Middletown: Wesleyan UP, 1959. Print.

Brueghel, Pieter, the Elder. *Children's Games*. 1560. Oil on panel. Kunsthistorisches Museum, Vienna.

———. *Hay Harvest*. 1565. Oil on wood. Lobkowicz Palace, Prague.

———. *Peasant Dance*. 1568. Oil on panel. Kunsthistorisches Museum, Vienna.

———. *Peasant Wedding*. 1567. Oil on panel. Kunsthistorisches Museum, Vienna.

Bruyérin-Champier, Jean. *L'alimentation de tous les peuples et de tous les temps jusqu'au XVIe siècle*. Trans. Sigurd Amundsen. Paris: Intermédiaire des Chercheurs et Curieux, 1988. Print.

———. *De re cibaria*. Lyon: Honoratum, 1560. Print.

Burke, Peter. "The Renaissance Dialogue." *Renaissance Studies* 3.1 (1989): 1–12. Print.

Calvin, John. *Concerning Scandals* [*De scandalis*]. Grand Rapids: Eerdmans, 1978. Print.

Camille, Michael. *Image on the Edge: The Margins of Medieval Art*. Cambridge: Harvard UP, 1992. Print.

Carpenter, Nan Cooke. "Rabelais and the Androgyne." *MLN* 68 (1953): 452–57. Print.

Carron, Jean-Claude, ed. *François Rabelais: Critical Assessments*. Baltimore: Johns Hopkins UP, 1995. Print.

Cartier, Jacques. *Bref récit et succincte narration de la navigation faite en MDXXXV et MDXXXVI, par le capitaine Jacques Cartier aux îles de Canada, Hochelaga, Saguenay et autres*. Ed. M. d'Avezac. Paris: Tross, 1863. Print.

Cave, Terence. *Cornucopia: Figures de l'abondance au XVIe siècle*. Trans. Ginette Morel. Paris: Macula, 1997. Print.

———. *The Cornucopian Text: Problems of Writing in the French Renaissance*. Oxford: Clarendon, 1979. Print.

———, ed. *François Rabelais:* Gargantua and Pantagruel. Everyman's Lib. New York: Knopf, 1994. Print.

———. "Panurge, Pathelin, and Other Polyglots." Ed. Jerry Nash and Barbara Bowen. *Lapidary Inscriptions: Renaissance Essays for Donald A. Stone Jr.* Lexington: French Forum, 1991. 171–82. Print.

———. *Pré-histoires: Textes troublés au seuil de la modernité*. Geneva: Droz, 1999. Print.

———. *Pré-histoires II: Langues étrangères et troubles économiques au XVIe siècle*. Geneva: Droz, 2001. Print.

———. "Thinking with Commonplaces: The Example of Rabelais." *(Re)Inventing the Past: Essays on French Early Modern Culture, Literature and Thought in Honour of Ann Moss*. Ed. Gary Ferguson and Catherine Hampton. Durham: U of Durham P, 2003. 35–49. Print.

———. "Travelers and Others: Cultural Connections in the Work of Rabelais." Carron 39–56.

Cave, Terence, Michel Jeanneret, and François Rigolot. "Sur la prétendue transparence de Rabelais: Réponse à Gérald Defaux." *Revue d'histoire littéraire de la France* 4 (1986): 709–16. Print.

Céard, Jean. *La nature et les prodiges: L'insolite au XVIe siècle.* 1977. Geneva: Droz, 1996. Print.

Céard, Jean, and Jean-Claude Margolin, eds. *Rabelais en son demi-millénaire*. Geneva: Droz, 1988. Print.

Cervantes, Miguel de. *The History and Adventure of the Renowned Don Quixote*. Trans. Tobias Smollett. New York: Modern Lib., 2001. Print.

Chaix, Gérald. *La Renaissance des années 1470 aux années 1560.* Paris: SEDES, 2004. Print.

Chastel, André. *La grottesque*. Paris: Le Promeneur, 1988. Print.

Chrétien de Troyes. *Arthurian Romances*. Trans. William W. Kibler. London: Penguin, 2004. Print.

Cixous, Hélène. "The Laugh of the Medusa." Trans. Keith Cohen and Paula Cohen. *Signs* 1.4 (1976): 875–93. Print.

———. "Le rire de la méduse." *L'arc* (1975): 39–45. Print.

Clark, Carol. *The Vulgar Rabelais*. Glasgow: Pressgang, 1983. Print.

Cleese, John, et al. Monty Python and the Holy Grail *Screenplay*. London: Methuen, 2002. Print.

Clément, Michèle. *Le cynisme à la Renaissance d'Erasme à Montaigne suivi de* Les epistres de Diogenes *(1546)*. Geneva: Droz, 2005. Print.

Cohen, Jeffrey Jerome. *Of Giants: Sex, Monsters, and the Middle Ages.* Minneapolis: U of Minnesota P, 1999. Print.

Colonna, Francesco. *Hypnerotomachia: The Strife of Love in a Dream.* 1592. New York: Da Capo, 1969. *Internet Archive*. Internet Archive, n.d. Web. 2 Nov. 2009.

Compagnon, Antoine. *La seconde main ou le travail de la citation*. Paris: Seuil, 1979. Print.

Conley, Tom. *The Self-Made Map: Cartographic Writing in Early Modern France*. Minneapolis: U of Minnesota P, 1996. Print.

Cotgrave, Randle. *Dictionarie of the French and English Tongues.* London: Islip, 1611. Greg Lindahl, n.d. Web. 20 Oct. 2009.

Cox, Virginia. *The Renaissance Dialogue: Literary Dialogue in Its Social and Political Contexts: Castiglione to Galileo.* Cambridge: Cambridge UP, 1992. Print.

Dagron, Tristan. "Silènes et statues platoniciennes, à propos du prologue du *Gargantua*." *Études rabelaisiennes* 33 (1998): 79–90. Print.

Dainville, François de. *Le langage des géographes.* Paris: Picard, 2002. Print.

Dante Alighieri. The Divine Comedy *of Dante Alighieri:* Inferno. Trans. Allen Mandelbaum. New York: Bantam, 1980. Print.

Davis, Natalie Zemon. "Le monde de l'imprimerie humaniste: Lyon." Martin and Chartier 255–77.

———. *The Return of Martin Guerre*. Cambridge: Harvard UP, 1983. Print.

———. *Society and Culture in Early Modern France*. Stanford: Stanford UP, 1986. Print.

Debailly, Pascal. "Juvénal en France au XVIe et au XVIIe siècle." *Littératures classiques* 24 (1995): 29–47. Print.

———. "Plaidoyer pour la satirologie." *XVIIe siècle* 205 (1999): 765–74. Print.

———. "La poétique de la satire classique en vers au XVIe siècle et au début du XVIIe." *L'information littéraire* 5 (1993): 20–25. Print.

———. "Le rire satirique." *Bibliothèque d'humanisme et renaissance* 56 (1994): 695–717. Print.

Defaux, Gérard. *Le curieux, le glorieux et la sagesse du monde dans la première moitié du XVIe siècle*. Lexington: French Forum, 1982. Print.

———. "D'un problème à l'autre: Herméneutique de l'*altior sensus* et *captatio lectoris* dans le prologue de *Gargantua*." *Revue d'histoire littéraire de la France* 85 (1985): 195–216. Print.

———. *Marot, Rabelais, Montaigne: L'écriture comme présence*. Paris: Champion-Slatkine, 1987. Print.

———. *Pantagruel et le sophistes: Contribution à l'histoire de l'humanisme chrétien au 16e siècle.* The Hague: Nijhoff, 1973. Print.

———. *Rabelais Agonistes. Du rieur au prophète: Études sur* Pantagruel, Gargantua, Le quart livre. Geneva: Droz, 1997. Print.

———. "Sur la prétendue pluralité du prologue de *Gargantua*." *Revue d'histoire littéraire de la France* 85 (1985): 716–22. Print.

Delcourt, Marie. *Hermaphrodite: Mythes et rites de la bisexualité dans l'antiquité classique*. Paris: P.G.F., 1958. Print.

Delumeau, Jean. *La civilisation de la Renaissance*. Paris: Arthaud, 1967. Print.

Demonet, Marie-Luce. *Les voix du signe: Nature et origine du langage à la Renaissance (1480–1580).* Paris: Champion, 1992. Print.

Derrida, Jacques. *De la grammatologie*. Paris: Minuit, 1967. Print.

Desan, Philippe. *L'imaginaire économique de la Renaissance*. Mont-de-Marsan: Interuniversitaires, 1993. Print.

Desroches, Rosny. "L'utopie: Evasion ou anticipation?" *France and North America: Utopias and Utopians*. Ed. Mathe Allain. Lafayette: Center for Louisiana Studies, 1978. 83–92. Print.

Desrosiers-Bonin, Diane. "Gargantuan Chronicles (*Chroniques gargantuines*)." Zegura, *Rabelais Encyclopedia* 94–95.

"Detour." Writ. Frank Spotnitz. Dir. Brett Dowler. *The X-Files*. Fox. 23 Nov. 1997. Television. Season 5, episode 4.

Diogenes Laertius. *The Lives and Opinions of Eminent Philosophers*. Trans. C. D. Yonge. Forgotten Books, 16 Mar. 2010. Web. 21 Dec. 2010.

Dixon, J. E., and J. L. Dawson. *Concordance des œuvres de Rabelais.* Geneva: Droz, 1992. Print.

Doré, Gustave. *Doré's Illustrations of Rabelais: A Selection of 252 Illustrations by Gustave Doré.* New York: Dover, 1978. Print.

Dragonetti, Roger. *La vie de la lettre au Moyen Âge: Le conte du Graal*. Paris: Seuil, 1980. Print.

Du Bellay, Joachim. *La deffence, et illustration de la langue françoyse*. 1549. Ed. J.-Ch. Monferran. Geneva: Droz, 2001. Print.

Du Cange, Charles du Fresne. *Glossaire françois, faisant suite au Glossarium mediæ et infimæ latinitatis, avec additions de mots anciens extraits des glossaires de La Curne de Sainte-Palaye, Roquefort, Raynouard, Burguy, Diez, etc.* Niort: L. Favre, 1879. Print.

Dupriez, Bernard. *Gradus, les procédés littéraires*. Paris: Union Générale, 1984. Print.

Duval, Edwin M. *The Design of Rabelais's* Pantagruel. New Haven: Yale UP, 1991. Print.

———. *The Design of Rabelais's* Quart livre *de* Pantagruel. Geneva: Droz, 1998. Print. Études rabelaisiennes 36.

———. *The Design of Rabelais's* Tiers livre *de* Pantagruel. Geneva: Droz, 1997. Print. Études rabelaisiennes 34.

———. "En quoi les œuvres de Rabelais sont-elles hybrides?" *Rabelais ou "Les adventures des gens curieulx."* Ed. Diane Desrosiers-Bonin. *Études rabelaisiennes*, forthcoming.

———. "History, Epic, and the Design of Rabelais's *Tiers livre*." Carron 121–32.

———. "Interpretation and the 'Doctrine Plus Absconce' of Rabelais' Prologue to *Gargantua*." *Études rabelaisiennes* 18 (1985): 1–17. Print.

———. "La messe, la cène, et le voyage sans fin du *Quart livre*." *Études rabelaisiennes* 21 (1988): 131–41. Print.

———. "Rabelais and French Renaissance Satire." *A Companion to Satire: Ancient and Modern*. Ed. Ruben Quintero. Malden: Blackwell, 2007. 70–85. Print.

Eco, Umberto. *The Open Work*. Cambridge: Harvard UP, 1989. Print.

Edson, Evelyn. *The World Map, 1300–1492: The Persistence of Tradition and Transformation*. Baltimore: Johns Hopkins UP, 2007. Print.

Eliade, Mircea. *Mephistopheles and the Androgyne*. Trans. J. M. Cohen. New York: Sheed, 1965. Print.

Elkins, James. "Precision, Misprecision, Misprision." *Critical Inquiry* 25 (1998): 169–80. Print.

Ensemble Clément Janequin. *Une fête chez Rabelais*. Motette, 1997. CD.

Erasmus, Desiderius. *The Adages of Erasmus*. Comp. William Barker. Toronto: U of Toronto P, 2001. Print.

———. *Declamatio de pueris statim ac liberaliter instituendis*. Ed. Jean-Claude Margolin. Geneva: Droz, 1966. Print.

———. *The Education of a Christian Prince*. Ed. Lisa Jardine. Trans. Neil M. Cheshire and Michael J. Heath. Cambridge: Cambridge UP, 1991. Print.

———. *Praise of Folly*. Trans. Betty Rice. London: Penguin, 1993. Print.

Estienne, Robert. *Dictionarium latinogallicum*. Paris: Imprimerie de R. Estienne, 1552. Print.

Faguet, Emile. *Seizième siècle*. Paris: Société française d'imprimerie et de librairie, 1898. Print.

Febvre, Lucien. *Life in Renaissance France*. Ed. and trans. Marian Rothstein. Cambridge: Harvard UP, 1977. Print.

———. *Le problème de l'incroyance au XVI*[e] *siècle: La religion de Rabelais*. 1942. Paris: Albin Michel, 1968. Print.

———. *The Problem of Unbelief in the Sixteenth Century: The Religion of Rabelais*. Trans. Beatrice Gottlieb. Cambridge: Harvard UP, 1982. Print.

Ferguson, Gary. *Queer (Re)Readings in the French Renaissance: Homosexuality, Gender, Culture*. Hampshire: Ashgate, 2008. Print.

Ferguson, Margaret W., Maureen Quilligan, and Nancy J. Vickers, eds. *Rewriting the Renaissance: The Discourses of Sexual Difference in Early Modern Europe*. Chicago: U of Chicago P, 1986. Print.

Ferguson, Wallace K. *The Renaissance in Historical Thought: Five Centuries of Interpretation.* Boston: Houghton, 1948. Print.

"Field Trip." Writ. John Shiban, Vince Gilligan, Frank Spotnitz. Dir. Kim Manners. *The X-Files*. Fox. 9 May 1999. Television. Season 6, episode 21.

"The Finale." *Seinfeld*. NBC. 14 May 1998. Television. Season 9, episode 23.

Findlen, Paula, ed. *Athanasius Kircher: The Last Man Who Knew Everything*. New York: Routledge, 2004. Print.

Fine, Oronce. *Nova Totius Gallia*. 1525. Jérôme de Gourmont, 1553. Print.

Flandrin, Jean-Louis, and Massimo Montanari, eds. *Histoire de l'alimentation*. Paris: Fayard, 1996. Print.

Folengo, Teofilo. *Baldo*. Trans. Ann E. Mullaney. 2 vols. Cambridge: Harvard UP, 2007–08. Print. I Tatti Renaissance Lib.

———. *Opus Merlini Cocaii*. . . . Tuscany, 1521. Print.

Forster, E. M. *The BBC Talks of E. M. Forster, 1929–1960*. Ed. Mary Lago, Linda K. Hughes, and Elizabeth MacLeod Walls. Columbia: U of Missouri P, 2008. Print.

Foucault, Michel. "Des espaces autres." *Architecture / Mouvement / Continuité* (1984): 46–49. Print.

Frame, Donald M. *François Rabelais: A Study*. New York: Harcourt, 1977. Print.

———. "Translator's Note." Rabelais, *Complete Works* xxv–xxvi.

Freccero, Carla. "Damning Haughty Dames: Panurge and the 'Haulte Dame de Paris.'" *Journal of Medieval and Renaissance Studies* 15 (1985): 57–67. Print.

———. *Father Figures: Genealogy and Narrative Structure in Rabelais*. Ithaca: Cornell UP, 1991. Print.

———. "Feminism, Rabelais, and the Hill/Thomas Hearings: Return to a Scene of Reading." Carron 73–83.

———. "The 'Instance' of the Letter: Woman in the Text of Rabelais." La Charité, *Rabelais's Incomparable Book* 45–55.

———. "The Other and the Same: The Image of the Hermaphrodite in Rabelais." Ferguson, Quilligan, and Vickers 145–58.

Fumaroli, Marc. "Louise Labé, une géniale imposture." *Le monde des livres* 11 May 2006: 7. Print.

Gadoffre, Gilbert. *La révolution culturelle dans la France des humanistes: Guillaume Budé et François Ier*. Geneva: Droz, 1997. Print.

Gaignebet, Claude. *À plus hault sens: L'ésotérisme spirituel et charnel de Rabelais*. Paris: Maisonneuve, 1986. Print.

García Márquez, Gabriel. *One Hundred Years of Solitude*. Trans. Gregory Rabassa. New York: Harper, 1998. Print.

Garden of the Earthly Delights. *Web Gallery of Art*. Web Gallery of Art, 2002. Web. 15 Mar. 2010.

Gardiner, Michael. "Bakhtin's Carnival: Utopia as Critique." *Bahktin, Carnival, and Other Subjects: Selected Papers from the Fifth International Bakhtin Conference*. Manchester: U of Manchester P, 1993. 20–47. Print.

Geiringer, Erich. "Cohen's Rabelais." *Medical History* 5.1 (1961): 77–82. Print.

Genette, Gérard. *Palimpsestes: La litterature au second degré*. Paris: Seuil, 1982. Print.

Geoffrey of Monmouth. *The History of the Kings of Britain*. Trans. Lewis Thorpe. 1966. Baltimore: Penguin, 1975. Print.

Geonget, Stéphan. *La notion de perplexité à la Renaissance*. Geneva: Droz, 2006. Print.

"Giant." *Encyclopaedia Britannica*. 11th ed. 1910–11. *Internet Archive*. Internet Archive, n.d. Web. 15 Mar. 2010.

Giovanni di Garlandia. *Integumenta Ovidii*. Ed. Fausto Ghisalberti. Messina-Milano: Principato, 1933. Print.

Girardi, Raffaele. *La società del dialogo: Retorica e ideologia nella letteratura conviviale del Cinquecento*. Bari: Adriatica, 1989. Print.

Glauser, Alfred. *Faux Rabelais: Ou, De l'inauthenticité du* Cinquième livre. Paris: Nizet, 1975. Print.

———. *Fonctions du nombre chez Rabelais*. Paris: Nizet, 1982. Print.

———. *Rabelais créateur*. Paris: Nizet, 1966. Print.

Glidden, Hope. "Rabelais, Panurge, and the Anti-courtly Body." *Études rabelaisiennes* 25 (1991): 35–60. Print.

Glucksmann, André. *Les maîtres penseurs*. Paris: Grasset, 1977. Print.

Godefroy, Frédéric. *Lexique de l'ancien français*. Paris: Champion, 1971. Print.

Godwin, Joscelyn. *Athanasius Kircher: A Renaissance Man and the Quest for Lost Knowledge*. London: Thames, 1979. Print.

Gogol, Nikolai. *Dead Souls*. Trans. Richard Pevear and Larissa Volokhonsky. New York: Vintage, 1997. Print.

———. *"The Diary of a Madman" and Other Stories*. Trans. Andrew MacAndrew. New York: New Amer. Lib., 1960. Print.

Goodwin, Barbara. "Taking Utopia Seriously." *The Politics of Utopia: A Study in Theory and Practice*. Ed. Goodwin and K. Taylor. London: Hutchinson, 1982. 3–30. Print.

Gougenheim, Georges. *Grammaire de la langue française du 16ᵉ siècle*. Paris: Picard, 1974. Print.

Goumarre, Pierre. "Rabelais: Misogynie et misogamy." *Littératures* 15 (1986): 59–92. Print.

Goyet, Francis, ed. *Traités de poétique et de rhétorique de la Renaissance*. Paris: Librairie Générale Française, 1990. Print.

Gray, Floyd. "Ambiguity and Point of View in the Prologue to *Gargantua*." *Romanic Review* 56 (1965): 57–62. Print.

———. *Gender, Rhetoric, and Print Culture in French Renaissance Writing*. Cambridge: Cambridge UP, 2000. Print.

———. *Rabelais et le comique du discontinu*. Paris: Champion, 1994. Print.

———. *Rabelais et l'écriture*. Paris: Nizet, 1974. Print.

———. "Rabelais' First Readers." La Charité, *Rabelais's Incomparable Book* 15–29.

———. "Structure and Meaning in the Prologue to the *Tiers livre*." *L'Esprit Créateur* 3.2 (1963): 57–62. Print.

Greene, Thomas M. *The Light in Troy: Imitation and Discovery in Renaissance Poetry*. New Haven: Yale UP, 1982. Print.

———. *Rabelais: A Study in Comic Courage*. Englewood Cliffs: Prentice, 1970. Print.

Greimas, Algirdas Julien, and Teresa Mary Keane. *Dictionnaire du moyen français: La Renaissance*. 1992. Paris: Larousse, 2001. Print.

Grève, Marcel de. *L'interprétation de Rabelais au XVI*[e] *siècle*. Geneva: Droz, 1961. Print. Études rabelaisiennes 3.

Grynaeus, Simon. *Novum orbis regionum*. Paris: Parvum, 1532. Print.

Guidoni, Enrico. La Primavera *di Botticelli: L'armonia tra le cittâ nell'Italia di Lorenzo il Magnifico*. Rome: Kappa, 2005. Print.

Hampton, Timothy. *Literature and Nation in the Sixteenth Century: Inventing Renaissance France*. Ithaca: Cornell UP, 2001. Print.

———. "Signs of Monstrosity: The Rhetoric of Description and the Limits of Allegory in Rabelais and Montaigne." *Monstrous Bodies / Political Monstrosities in Early Modern Europe*. Ed. Laura Lunger Knoppers and Joan B. Landes. Ithaca: Cornell UP, 2004. 179–99. Print.

Harley, J. Brian. *The New Nature of Maps*. Ed. Paul Laxton. Baltimore: Johns Hopkins UP, 2001. Print.

Harp, Margaret. "Twentieth-Century Illustrators' Interpretations of the Works of Rabelais." *Quidditas* 28 (2007): 107–30. Print.

Hartley, L. P. *The Go-Between*. Ed. Douglas Brooks-Davies. London: Penguin, 1997. Print.

Hayes, E. Bruce. "La farce hybride dans l'œuvre rabelaisienne: Les exemples de Thaumaste et de Dindenault." *L'hybridité des récits rabelaisiens*. Ed. Diane Desrosiers-Bonin. Geneva: Droz, forthcoming.

Heath, Michael J. *Rabelais*. Tempe: Medieval and Renaissance Texts and Studies, 1996. Print.

Heitsch, Dorothea, and Jean-François Vallée, eds. *Printed Voices: The Renaissance Culture of Dialogue*. Toronto: Toronto UP, 2004. Print.

Heller, Henry. "The Evangelism of Lefèvre d'Étaples: 1525." *Studies in the Renaissance* 19 (1972): 42–77. Print.

Hémard, Joseph, illus. *Gargantua et Pantagruel*. By François Rabelais. Ed. Henri Clouzot. Paris: Crès, 1922. Print.

Hempfer, Klaus W. *Poetik des Dialogs: Aktuelle Theorie und rinascimentales Selbstverständnis*. Stuttgart: Steiner, 2004. Print.

"Hibride." *Le Robert: Dictionnaire historique de la langue française*. Paris: Dictionnaires Le Robert, 1992. Print.

"Hieronymus Bosch." *Yale University Art Gallery*. Yale Univ. Art Gallery, n.d. Web. 31 Aug. 2008.

Hodges, Elisabeth. *Urban Poetics in the French Renaissance*. Aldershot: Ashgate, 2008. Print.

Hoffmann, George. " 'Neither One nor the Other and Both Together.' " *Études rabelaisiennes* 25 (1991): 79–90. Print.

Holquist, Michael. "Bakhtin and Rabelais: Theory as Praxis." *Boundary 2* 11.1–2 (1982–83): 5–19. Print.

Holt, Mack B. *The French Wars of Religion, 1562–1629*. London: Cambridge UP, 1995. Print.

Huchon, Mireille. *Le français de la Renaissance*. Paris: PUF, 1988. Print.

———. *Louise Labé: Une créature de papier*. Geneva: Droz, 2006. Print.

———, ed. *Œuvres complètes*. By François Rabelais. Paris: Gallimard, 1994. Print.

———. *Rabelais*. Paris: Gallinard, 2011. Print.

———. "Rabelais et les satires de la *Nef des Folz* de 1530." Renner, *Satire* 77–92.

———. *Rabelais grammarien: De l'histoire du texte aux problèmes d'authenticité*. Geneva: Droz, 1981. Print.

Hugo, Victor. *Les contemplations*. Vol. 2. 1858. Project Gutenberg, 29 Aug. 2009. Web. 8 Dec. 2010. E-book 29844.

Huguet, Edmond. *Dictionnaire de la langue française du seizième siècle*. Paris: Champion, 1944–67. Print.

Hyman, Mary, and Philip Hyman. "Imprimer la cuisine: Les livres de cuisine en France entre le XVe et le XIXe siècle." Flandrin and Montanari 643–55.

———. "Les livres de cuisine et le commerce des recettes en France aux XVe et XVIe siècles." *Du manuscrit à la table*. Ed. Carole Lambert. Paris: Champion-Slatkine, 1992. 59–68. Print.

———. "Les livres de cuisine imprimés en France: Du règne de Charles VIII à la fin de l'ancien régime." *Livres en bouches* 55–75.

Irigaray, Luce. *Ce sexe qui n'en est pas un*. Paris: Minuit, 1977. Print.

———. *This Sex Which Is Not One*. Trans. Catherine Porter and Carolyn Burke. Ithaca: Cornell UP, 1985. Print.

Isidore of Seville. *Etymologiarum libri xx*. Augsburg: Günther Zainer, 1472. Print.

Jacob, Christian. *The Sovereign Map: Theoretical Approaches in Cartography throughout History*. Ed. Ed Dahl. Trans. Tom Conley. Chicago: U of Chicago P, 2006. Print.

Janequin, Clément, Claudin de Sermisy, and Francesco da Milano. *Les cris de Paris: Chansons de Janequin et Sermisy*. Dir. Dominique Visse. 1982. Harmonia Mundi, 2002. CD.

Jauss, Hans Robert. *Aesthetic Experience and Literary Hermeneutics*. Trans. Michael Shaw. Minneapolis: U of Minnesota P, 1982. Print.

Jayne, Sears Reynolds. *Marsilio Ficino's Commentary on Plato's* Symposium. Columbia: U of Missouri P, 1944. Print.

Jeanneret, Michel. *Le défi des signes: Rabelais et la crise de l'interprétation à la Renaissance*. Orléans: Paradigme, 1994. Print.

———. *Des mets et des mots: Banquets et propos de table à la Renaissance*. Paris: Corti, 1987. Print.

———. "Parler en mangeant: Rabelais et la tradition symposiaque." *Études rabelaisiennes* 21 (1988): 275–81. Print.

———. "Les paroles dégelées (Rabelais, 'Quart livre,' 48–65)." *Littérature* 17 (1975): 14–30. Print.

———. *Perpetuum mobile: Métamorphose des corps et des œuvres, de Vinci à Montaigne*. Paris: Macula, 1997. Print.

———. "Polyphonie de Rabelais: Ambivalence, antithèse et ambiguïté." *Littérature* 55 (1984): 98–111. Print.

"The Jersey Devil." Writ. Chris Carter. Dir. Joe Napolitano. *The X-Files*. Fox. 8 Oct. 1993. Television. Season 1, episode 5.

Jones, Ann Rosalind. "Cluster on Early Modern Women." *PMLA* 109.2 (1994): 187–89. Print.

Jordan, Constance. *Renaissance Feminism: Literary Texts and Political Models*. Ithaca: Cornell UP, 1990. Print.

Jouanna, Arlette, Philippe Hamon, Dominique Biloghi, and Guy Le Thiec. *La France de la Renaissance: Histoire et dictionnarie*. Paris: Laffont, 2001. Print.

Jung, C. G. *Mysterium Coniunctionis: An Inquiry into the Separation and Synthesis of Psychic Opposites in Alchemy*. Trans. R. F. C. Hull. Princeton: Princeton UP, 1970. Print.

Keller, Abraham. *The Telling of Tales in Rabelais: Aspects of His Narrative Art*. Frankfurt am Main: Klostermann, 1963. Print.

Kelly, Joan. "Early Feminist Theory and the *Querelle des femmes*." *Signs* 8 (1982): 4–28. Print.

King, Ross. *Michelangelo and the Pope's Ceiling*. New York: Penguin, 2003. Print.

Kinser, Samuel. *Rabelais's Carnival: Text, Context, Metatext*. Berkeley: U of California P, 1990. Print.

Knecht, R. J. *Francis I*. Cambridge: Cambridge UP, 1982. Print.

Kristeva, Julia. "Bakhtine, le mot, le dialogue, et le roman." *Critique* 239 (1967): 438–65. Print.

———. *Étrangers à nous-mêmes*. Paris: Flammarion, 1988. Print.

———. *Powers of Horror: An Essay on Abjection*. Trans. Leon S. Roudiez. New York: Columbia UP, 1982. Print.

———. *Strangers to Ourselves*. Trans. Leon S. Roudiez. New York: Columbia UP, 1991. Print.

———. "Word, Dialogue, and Novel." *The Kristeva Reader*. Ed. Toril Moi. New York: Columbia UP, 1986. 34–61. Print.

Kritzman, Lawrence D. "Représenter le monstre dans *le Quart livre* de Rabelais." *Études rabelaisiennes* 33 (1998): 349–59. Print.

———. *The Rhetoric of Sexuality and the Literature of the French Renaissance*. Cambridge: Cambridge UP, 1991. Print.

Kushner, Eva. *Le dialogue à la Renaissance: Histoire et poétique*. Geneva: Droz, 2004. Print.

La Bruyère, Jean de. *Les caractères*. Ed. Robert Garapon. Paris: Garnier, 1962. Print.

———. *The Characters of Jean de la Bruyère*. Trans. Henri van Laun. London: Routledge, 1929. Print.

La Charité, Raymond C. "Gargantua's Letter and *Pantagruel* as Novel." *L'Esprit Créateur* 21.1 (1981): 26–39. Print.

———. "Lectures et lecteurs dans le prologue de *Gargantua*." *French Forum* 10 (1985): 261–70. Print.

———. "Rabelais and the Silenic Text: The Prologue to *Gargantua*." La Charité, *Rabelais's Incomparable Book* 72–86.

———, ed. *Rabelais's Incomparable Book*. Lexington: French Forum, 1986. Print.

———. *Recreation, Reflection, Re-creation: Perspectives on Rabelais's* Pantagruel. Lexington: French Forum, 1980. Print.

La Chesnaye, Nicolas de. *La nef de santé avec le gouvernail du corps humain et la condamnation des banquetz a la louenge de Diepte et sobriete et le traictie des passions de lame*. Paris: Antoine Vérard, 1507. N. pag. Print.

LaGuardia, David P. "Doctor Rabelais and the Medicine of Scatology." Persels and Ganim, *Fecal Matters* 24–37.

———. "French Renaissance Literature and the Problem of Theory: Alcofribas's Performance in the Prologue to *Gargantua*." *EMF: Studies in Early Modern France* 10 (2005): 5–38. Print.

———. *Intertextual Masculinity in French Renaissance Literature: Rabelais, Brantôme, and the* Cent nouvelles nouvelles. Hampshire: Ashgate, 2008. Print.

Langer, Ullrich. *Vertu du discours, discours de la vertu: Littérature et philosophie morale au XVIe siècle en France*. Geneva: Droz, 1999. Print.

Lanson, Gustave, and Paul Tuffrau. *Manuel d'histoire de la littérature française*. Paris: Hachette, 1938. Print.

Laqueur, Thomas. *Making Sex: Body and Gender from the Greeks to Freud*. Cambridge: Harvard UP, 1990. Print.

Lauvergnat-Gagnière, Christiane. *Lucien de Samosate et le lucianisme en France au XVIe siècle: Athéisme et polémique.* Geneva: Droz, 1988. Print.

Lavocat, Françoise. *La Syrinx au Bûcher: Pan et les satyres à la Renaissance et à l'âge baroque*. Geneva: Droz, 2005. Print.

Lazard, Madeleine. *Louise Labé, lyonnaise*. Paris: Fayard, 2004. Print.

Lefranc, Abel, ed. *Les grandes et inestimables cronicques du grant et énorme géant Gargantua.* Nogent-le-Rotrou: Champion, 1912. Print.

———. *Les navigations de Pantagruel: Étude sur la géographie rabelaisienne.* Paris: Leclerc, 1905. Print.

———. *Rabelais: Études sur* Gargantua, Pantaguel, *le* Tiers livre. Paris: Albin Michel, 1953. Print.

Le Goff, Jacques. *History and Memory*. Trans. Steven Rendall and Elizabeth Claman. New York: Columbia UP, 1992. Print.

Lemaire de Belges, Jean. *Œuvres de Jean Lemaire de Belges*. Ed. Jean Stecher. 4 vols. Louvain, 1882–91. Print.

Lenormant, Charles. *Rabelais et l'architecture de la Renaissance.* Paris: Grozet, 1840. Print.

Le Roy Ladurie, Emmanuel. *The Royal French State, 1460–1610.* Trans. Juliet Vale. Oxford: Blackwell, 1994. Print.

Lestringant, Frank. *L'atelier du cosmographe*. Paris: Albin Michel, 1991. Print.

———. "L'insulaire de Rabelais, ou la fiction en archipel (pour une lecture topographique du *Quart livre*)." *Rabelais en son demi-millénaire.* Ed. Jean Céard et Jean-Claude Margolin. Geneva: Droz, 1988. 249–74. Print. Études rabelaisiennes 21.

———. "Rabelais et le récit toponymique." *Écrire le monde à la Renaissance: Quinze études sur Rabelais, Postel, Bodin et la littérature géographique*. Caen: Paradigme, 1993. 109–27. Print.

Ligier, Hermann. *La politique de Rabelais*. Paris: Sandoz et Fischbacher, 1880. Print.

Livres en bouches: Cinq siècles d'art culinaire français. Paris: Hermann; Bibliothèque Nationale de France, 2001. Print.

Lucian. "How to Write History." Lucian, *Works* 6: 2–72.

———. *Les œuvres de Lucian de Samosate, philosophe excellent, non moins utiles que plaisantes . . . , repurgées de paroles impudiques et profanes qui sont reduites en propos plus honnestes, traduites du grec par Filbert Bretin, Aussonois*. Paris: Abel l'Angelier, 1581. Print.

———. *Opera, quae quidem extant, omnia. . . .* Ed. Jacobus Micyllus. Paris: Vascosabus, 1546. Print.

———. *The Works of Lucian in Eight Volumes*. Ed. and trans. A. M. Harmon, K. Kilburn, and M. D. Macleod. Cambridge: Harvard UP, 1913–67. Loeb Classical Lib.

Lyon à la Renaissance. Académie de Lyon, n.d. Web. 20 Oct. 2009.

Machiavelli, Niccolò. *The Prince*. Trans. George Bull. Introd. Anthony Grafton. London: Penguin, 2003. Print.

Magnus, Olaus. *Carta marina*. Venice, 1539. Print.

Marcel, Raymond, ed. and trans. *Marsile Ficin: Sur le banquet de Platon ou de l'amour*. Paris: Belles Lettres, 1956. Print.

Marguerite de Navarre. *L'Heptaméron*. Ed. Renja Salminen. Geneva: Droz, 1999. Print.

———. *The Heptameron*. Trans. Paul A. Chilton. Harmondsworth: Penguin, 2004. Print.

Marie de France. *Lais*. Trans. and introd. Robert Hanning and Joan Ferrante. Grand Rapids: Baker, 1978. Print.

Marin, Louis. *Utopics: Spatial Play*. Trans. Robert A. Vollrath. Atlantic Highlands: Humanities, 1984. Print.

———. *Utopiques: Jeux d'espaces*. Paris: Minuit, 1973. Print.

Marot, Clément. *Œuvres poétiques*. Paris: Classiques Garnier, 1996. Print.

Marsh, David. *The Quattrocento Dialogue: Classical Tradition and Humanist Innovation*. Cambridge: Harvard UP, 1980. Print.

Marshall, F. W. "The Allegory of Rabelais' *Gargantua*." *Australian Journal of French Studies* 24.2 (1987): 115–54. Print.

———. "Worrying the Bone Again: The Structure and Significance of the Prologue to *Gargantua*." *Australian Journal of French Studies* 24.1 (1987): 3–22. Print.

Martin, Henri-Jean, and Roger Chartier, eds. *Le livre conquérant: Du Moyen-Âge au milieu du XVIIe siècle*. Paris: Promodis, 1982. Print. Vol. 1 of *Histoire de l'édition française*. 4 vols.

Mayer, C.-A. *Lucien de Samosate et la Renaissance française*. Geneva: Slatkine, 1984. Print.

McFarlane, I. D. *A Literary History of France: Renaissance France, 1470–1589*. London: Ernest Benn; Tonbridge: Barnes and Noble, 1974. Print.

McKinley, Mary. "Bakhtin and the World of Rabelais Criticism." *Degré Second: Studies in French Literature* 2 (1987): 83–88. Print.

Michelangelo. *David*. Marble, 1504. Galleria dell'Accademia, Florence.

Miernowski, Jan. "Literature and Metaphysics: Rabelais and the Poetics of Misunderstanding." *Études rabelaisiennes* 35 (1998): 131–51. Print.

———. *Signes dissimilaires: La quête des noms divins dans la poésie française de la Renaissance*. Geneva: Droz, 1997. Print.

Milhe-Poutingon, Gérard. *François Rabelais, bilan critique*. Paris: Nathan U, 1996. Print.

Miller, Naomi. *French Renaissance Fountains*. New York: Garland, 1977. Print.

Montaigne, Michel de. *The Complete Essays*. Trans. Michael Screech. Harmondsworth: Penguin, 1993. Print.

———. *The Complete Essays of Montaigne*. Trans. Donald M. Frame. Stanford: Stanford UP, 1965 Print.

———. *Essais*. Ed. Pierre Villey and V.-L. Saulnier. *The Montaigne Project*. Division of the Humanities, U of Chicago, n.d. Web. 8 Dec. 2010.

Monty Python and the Holy Grail. Dir. Terry Gilliam and Terry Jones. EMI Films, 1975. Film.

More, Thomas. *Utopia*. Ed. George M. Logan and Robert M. Adams. Cambridge: Cambridge UP, 2002. Print.

"More Crap." *South Park*. Comedy Central. 10 Oct. 2007. Television. Season 11, episode 1109.

Morel, Rémi, and Jean-Yves Pouilloux. *Le portail de la Renaissance Française: Rabelais et la Renaissance*. Renaissance-France.org, n.d. Web. 20 Oct. 2009.

Morison, Samuel Eliot. *The European Discovery of America: The Northern Voyages*. New York: Oxford UP, 1971. Print.

"Mr. Hankey's Christmas Classics." *South Park*. Comedy Central. 1 Dec. 1999. Television. Season 3, episode 15.

"El Mundo Gira." Writ. John Shiban. Dir. Tucker Gates. *The X-Files*, Fox. 12 Jan. 1997. Television. Season 4, episode 11.

Muzerelle, Denis. "Vocabulaire codicologique: Répertoire méthodique des termes français relatifs aux manuscrits avec leurs équivalents en anglais, italien, espagnol." *Institut de Recherche et d'Histoire des Textes*. CNRS, 2003. Web. 20 Oct. 2009.

Nauert, Charles. "Humanism as Method: Roots of Conflict with the Scholastics." *Sixteenth Century Journal* 29.2 (1998): 427–38. Print.

Nelson, Ida. *La sottie sans souci: Essai d'interprétation homosexuelle*. Paris: Champion, 1977. Print.

Newberry Consort. *Villon to Rabelais: Sixteenth Century Music of the Streets, Theatres, and Courts*. Harmonia Mundi, 1999. CD.

Noiret, Philippe, et al., narr. *Gargantua*. Frémeaux, 2006. CD.

Nykrog, Per. "Thélème, Panurge et la dive bouteille." *Revue d'histoire littéraire de la France* 3 (1965): 385–97. Print.

O'Brien, John, ed. *The Cambridge Companion to Rabelais*. Cambridge: Cambridge UP, 2011. Print.

Origen. *Opera omnia. Patrologiae cursus completus: Series graeca*. Ed. J.-P. Migne. Vol. 11. Paris: Librairie orientaliste Paul Geuthner, 1938. Print.

Ovid. *Metamorphoses*. Vol. 1. Cambridge: Harvard UP, 1971. Print.

———. *Metamorphoses*. Trans. Rolfe Humphries. Bloomington: Indiana UP, 1972. Print.

Paris, Jean. *Rabelais au futur*. Paris: Seuil, 1970. Print.

Parkin, John. *Interpretations of Rabelais*. Lewiston: Mellen, 2002. Print.

———. "The Polygelastic Rabelais." *Études rabelaisiennes* 44 (2006): 47–62. Print.

Pelletier, Monique. *Cartographie de la France du monde de la Renaissance au siècle des lumières*. Paris: BNF, 2001. Print.

Pépin, Jean. *La tradition de l'allégorie: De Philon d'Alexandrie à Dante*. Paris: Études Augustiniennes, 1987. Print.

Persels, Jeff. "Bragueta Humanística; or, Humanism's Codpiece." *Sixteenth Century Journal* 28.1 (1997): 79–99. Print.

———. " 'Straitened in the Bowels'; or, Concerning the Rabelaisian Trope of Defecation." *Études rabelaisiennes* 31 (1994): 101–12. Print.

Persels, Jeff, and Russell Ganim, eds. *Fecal Matters in Early Modern Literature and Art: Studies in Scatology*. Aldershot: Ashgate, 2004. Print.

———. "Scatology, the Last Taboo." Persels and Ganim, *Fecal Matters* xiii–xxi.

"Petit glossaire du bibliophile." *Galaxidion*. Galaxidion: Le marché du livre ancien ou épuisé sur Internet, n.d. Web. 20 Oct. 2009.

Philostratus. *Life of Apollonius of Tyana*. Trans. F. C. Conybeare. Cambridge: Harvard UP, 2004. Print.

Pico della Mirandola, Giovanni. *On the Dignity of Man*. Trans. Charles Glenn Wallis, Paul J. W. Miller, and Douglas Carmichael. Indianapolis: Hackett, 1965. Print.

"Pieter Bruegel the Elder." *Wikipedia*. Wikimedia, 5 Mar. 2010. Web. 15 Mar. 2010.

Pinker, Steven. *The Stuff of Thought: Language as a Window into Human Nature*. London: Lane, 2007. Print.

Plato. *The Collected Dialogues, Including the Letters*. Trans. Hugh Tredennick et al. Ed. E. Hamilton and H. Cairns. Princeton: Princeton UP, 1961. Print.

———. *Symposium. Great Dialogues of Plato*. Trans. W. H. D. Rouse. New York: Mentor, 1984. 69–117. Print.

Plattard, Jean. *The Life of François Rabelais*. Trans. Louis P. Roche. New York: Knopf, 1931. Print.

———. *La vie de François Rabelais*. Paris: Boivin, 1932. Print.

Popkin, Richard. *The History of Scepticism from Erasmus to Spinoza*. Berkeley: U of California P, 1979. Print.

"The Postmodern Prometheus." Writ. and dir. Chris Carter. *The X-Files*. Fox. 30 Nov. 1997. Television. Season 5, episode 5.

Prescott, Anne Lake. *Imagining Rabelais in Renaissance England*. New Haven: Yale UP, 1998. Print.

"Primavera (painting)." *Wikipedia*. Wikimedia, 25 Feb. 2010. Web. 15 Mar. 2010.

Ptolemy, Claudius. *The Geography*. Trans. and ed. Edward Luther Stevenson. Introd. Joseph Fischer. New York: Dover, 1991. Print. Trans. of *Geographia*.

Pugliese, Olga Z. *Il discorso labirintico del dialogo rinascimentale*. Rome: Bulzoni, 1995. Print.

Pulci, Luigi. *Morgante: The Epic Adventures of Orlando and His Giant Friend Morgante.* Trans. Joseph Tusiani. Bloomington: Indiana UP, 1998. Print.

Queneau, Raymond. *Zazie dans le métro*. Paris: Gallimard, 1959. Print.

"Rabelais." *Magazine littéraire* 319 (1994): 17–64. Print.

Rabelais, François. *Les cinq livres*. Ed. Gérard Defaux, Jean Céard, and Michel Simonin. Paris: Librairie Générale Française, 1994. Print.

———. *The Complete Works of François Rabelais*. Trans. Donald M. Frame. Berkeley: U of California P, 1991. Print.

———. *Gargantua.* Trans. Andrew Brown. London: Hesperus, 2003. Print.

———. *Gargantua*. Ed. Ruth Calder et al. Geneva: Droz, 1970. Print. Textes Littéraires Français.

———. *Gargantua*. Ed. Gérard Defaux. Paris: Livre de Poche, 1994. Print.

———. *Gargantua*. Ed. Floyd Gray. Paris: Champion, 1995. Print.

———. *Gargantua and Pantagruel*. Trans. Jacques Le Clercq. New York: Random, 1936. Print.

———. *Gargantua and Pantagruel*. Trans. Burton Raffel. New York: Norton, 1990. Print.

———. *Gargantua and Pantagruel*. Trans. M. A. Screech. London: Penguin, 2006. Print.

———. *Gargantua and Pantagruel*. Trans. Thomas Urquhart and Pierre Le Motteux. London: Dent, 1929. Print.

———. *The Histories of Gargantua and Pantagruel*. Trans. J. M. Cohen. London: Penguin, 1955. Print.

———. *Œuvres*. Ed. Abel Lefranc, Robert Marichal, et al. 7 vols. Paris: Champion, 1912–65. Print.

———. *Œuvres complètes.* Ed. and trans. Guy Demerson. 1973. Paris: Seuil, 1995. Print.

———. *Œuvres complètes.* Ed. Mireille Huchon. With François Moreau. Paris: Gallimard, 1994. Print. Bibliothèque de la Pléiade.

———. *Œuvres complètes*. Ed. Pierre Jourda. 2 vols. 1962. Paris: Garnier, 1991. Print.

———. *Œuvres complètes de Maître François Rabelais*. Ed. Marcel Guilbaud. 5 vols. Paris: Nationale, 1957. Print.

———. *Pantagruel.* Trans. Andrew Brown. London: Hesperus, 2003. Print.

———. *Pantagruel.* Ed. Gérard Defaux. Paris: Livre de Poche, 1994. Print.

———. *Pantagruel.* Ed. Floyd Gray. Paris: Champion, 1997. Print.

———. *Pantagruel.* Ed. Verdun L. Saulnier. Geneva: Droz, 1964. Print.

———. *The Portable Rabelais*. Trans. Samuel Putnam. New York: Viking, 1946. Print.

———. *Quart livre*. Ed. Abel Lefranc. Geneva: Droz, 1955. Print.

———. *Quart livre*. Ed. Robert Marichal. Geneva: Droz, 1947. Print.

———. *Rabelais*. Trans. W. F. Smith. 1899. Cambridge: Cambridge UP, 1934. Print.

———. *Selections from* Gargantua and Pantagruel. Trans. Floyd Gray. New York: Crofts, 1966. Print.

———. *Le tiers livre*. Ed. Jean Céard. Paris: Hachette, 1995. Print.

———. *Le tiers livre*. Ed. M. A. Screech. 1964. Geneva: Droz, 1974. Print.

Rabelais and His World. CNDP. Films for the Humanities, 1994. Videocassette.

"Rabelais et la Renaissance." *Renaissance-France.org*. Renaissance France. org, 1995–2005. Web. 3 Nov. 2009.

Ragland-Sullivan, Ellie. *Rabelais and Panurge: A Psychological Approach to Literary Character*. Amsterdam: Rodopi, 1976. Print.

Rahner, K., and H. Vorgrimler. *Dictionary of Theology*. 2nd ed. New York: Crossroad, 1981. Print.

Randall, Michael. *Building Resemblance: Analogical Imagery in the Early French Renaissance*. Baltimore: Johns Hopkins UP, 1996. Print.

———. *The Gargantuan Polity: On the Individual and the Community in the French Renaissance*. Toronto: U of Toronto P, 2008. Print.

Rawles, Stephen, and Michael Screech. *A New Rabelais Bibliography: Editions of Rabelais before 1626*. Geneva: Droz, 1987. Print.

Reeser, Todd W. *Moderating Masculinity in Early Modern Culture*. Chapel Hill: U of North Carolina P, 2006. Print.

Regosin, Richard. "The Ins(ides) and Outs(ides) of Reading: Plural Discourse and the Question of Interpretation in Rabelais." La Charité, *Rabelais's Incomparable Book* 59–71.

———. "Opening Discourse." Carron 133–47.

Reichel, Susanne, and Mark Stein, eds. *Cheeky Fictions: Laughter and the Postcolonial*. Amsterdam: Rodopi, 2005. Print.

Rembrandt Harmensz van Rijn. *The Anatomy Lesson of Dr. Nicolaes Tulp*. 1632. Oil on canvas. Mauritshuis, The Hague.

Renner, Bernd. *Difficile est saturam non scribere: L'herméneutique de la satire rabelaisienne*. Geneva: Droz, 2007. Print. Études rabelaisiennes 45.

———. "From the 'Bien Yvres' to Messere Gaster: The Syncretism of Rabelaisian Banquets." *At the Table: Metaphorical and Material Cultures of Food in Medieval and Early Modern Europe*. Ed. Timothy J. Tomasik and Juliann M. Vitullo. Turnhout: Brepols, 2007. 167–85. Print.

———. " 'Ni l'un ni l'autre et tous les deux à la fois': Le paradoxe ménippéen inverse dans le *Tiers livre* de Rabelais." *Romanic Review* 47 (2006): 153–68. Print.

———. "Provocation et perplexité: Le double éloge paradoxal des dettes et de la rhétorique (*Tiers livre* II à V)." *Études rabelaisiennes* 50 (2010): 45–65. Print.

———, ed. *La satire dans tous ses états: Le "meslange satyricque" à la Renaissance française*. Geneva: Droz, 2009. Print.

The Return of Martin Guerre. Dir. Daniel Vigne. Fox Lorber Home Video, 1983. Film.

Rigolot, François. "Cratylisme et Pantagruelisme: Rabelais et le statut du signe." *Études rabelaisiennes* 13 (1976): 115–32. Print.

———. *L'erreur de la Renaissance. Perspectives littéraires*. Paris: Champion, 2002. Print.

———. *Les langages de Rabelais*. 1972. Geneva: Droz, 1996. Print.

———. *Poétique et onomastique*. Geneva: Droz, 1977. Print.

———. "Quand le géant se fait homme: Rabelais et la théorie de la *condescendance*." *Études rabelaisiennes* 29 (1993): 7–23. Print.

———. "Rabelais, Misogyny, and Christian Charity: Biblical Intertextuality and the Renaissance Crisis of Exemplarity." *PMLA* 109.2 (1995): 225–37. Print.

———. "The Three Temptations of Panurge: Women's Vilification and Christian Humanist Discourse." Carron 83–104.

Robinson, Christopher. *Lucian and His Influence in Europe*. London: Duckworth, 1979. Print.

Rodrigue, Michel, and Jean-Yves Mitton. *Les truculentes aventures de Rabelais*. Paris: Hors Collection, 2001. Print.

Rowland, Ingrid D. *The Ecstatic Journey: Athanasius Kircher in Baroque Rome.* Chicago: U of Chicago P, 2000. Print.

Sainéan, Lazare. *L'histoire naturelle et les branches connexes dans l'œuvre de Rabelais*. Paris: Champion, 1921. Print.

———. *La langue de Rabelais*. 2 vols. Paris: Boccard, 1922–23. Print.

Sainte-Beuve, Charles Augustin. *Les grands écrivains français, XVIe siècle*. Ed. Maurice Allem. Paris: Garnier, 1926. Print.

Salernitano, Masuccio. "Novella XLI." *Il novellino*. Ed. A. Mauro. Bari: Laterza, 1940. 322–28. Print.

Salmon, J. H. M. *Society in Crisis: France in the Sixteenth Century*. London: Methuen, 1975. Print.

Saussure, Ferdinand de. *Cours de linguistique générale*. Paris: Payot, 1980. Print.

Sawday, Jonathan. *The Body Emblazoned: Dissection and the Human Body in Renaissance Culture*. London: Routledge, 2006. Print.

Schachter, Marc D. *Voluntary Servitude and the Erotics of Friendship: From Classical Antiquity to Early Modern France*. Hampshire: Ashgate, 2008. Print.

Schiffer, Cathy. "Contextual Misogyny in the *Tiers livre*." *Chimères* 17.2 (1984): 53–67. Print.

Schmidt, Albert-Marie. *La poésie scientifique en France au seizième siècle*. Paris: Albin Michel, 1938. Print.

Schrader, Ludwig. *Panurge und Hermes*. Bonn: Romanisches Seminar der Universität Bonn, 1958. Print.

Schwartz, Jerome. "Aspects of Androgyny in the Renaissance." *Human Sexuality in the Middle Ages and the Renaissance*. Ed. D. Radcliff-Umstead. Pittsburgh: Center for Medieval and Renaissance Studies, 1978. 121–31. Print.

———. *Irony and Ideology in Rabelais: Structures of Subversion*. Cambridge: Cambridge UP, 1990. Print.

———. "Panurge's Impact on Pantagruel." *Romanic Review* 67.1 (1976): 1–8. Print.

———. "Scatology and Eschatology in Gargantua's Androgyne Device." *Études rabelaisiennes* 14 (1977): 265–75. Print.

Screech, Michael A. "Echoes of Augustine in Rabelais." *Augustine, the Harvest, and Theology (1300–1650): Essays Dedicated to Hiko Augustinus Oberman in Honor of His Sixtieth Birthday*. Ed. Kenneth Hogen. Leiden: Brill, 1990. 286–99. Print.

———. "Emblems and Colours: The Controversy over Gargantua's Colours and Devices (*Gargantua* 8, 9, 10)." *Mélanges d'histoire du XVIe siècle, offerts à Henri Meylan*. Lausanne: Bibliothèque Historique Vaudoise, 1970. 65–80. Print.

———. *Laughter at the Foot of the Cross*. London: Lane, 1997. Print.

———. "The Meaning of Thaumaste." *Bibliothèque d'humanisme et renaissance* 22 (1960): 62–72. Print.

——— "A Note on the Translation." Rabelais, *Gargantua and Pantagruel* [trans. Screech] xliv–xlvi.

———. *Rabelais*. Ithaca: Cornell UP, 1979. Print.

———. *Rabelais*. Trans. M. -A. Kisch. Paris: Gallimard, 2008. Print.

———. *Rabelais*. London: Duckworth, 1980. Print.

———. *The Rabelaisian Marriage: Aspects of Rabelais's Religion, Ethics, and Comic Philosophy*. London: Arnold, 1958. Trans. as *Rabelais et le mariage*. Trans. A. Bridge. Geneva: Droz, 1959. Print.

Sedgwick, Eve Kosofsky. *Between Men: English Literature and Male Homosocial Desire*. New York: Columbia UP, 1985. Print.

Serres, Michel. *Le mal propre: Polluer pour s'approprier*. Paris: Le Pommier, 2008. Print.

Sévigné, Marie de Rabutin-Chantal. *Lettres*. 2 vols. Paris: Gallimard, 1953–57. Print.

Sextus Empiricus. *Outlines of Pyrrhonism*. Trans. R. G. Bury. Cambridge: Harvard UP, 1976. Print.

Shakespeare, William. *The History of Henry IV (Part One)*. New York: Signet, 1965. Print.

"The Ship of Fools." *Wikipedia*. Wikimedia, 12 Mar. 2010. Web. 15 Mar. 2010.

Shrek. Dir. Andrew Adamson and Vicky Jenson. DreamWorks, 2001. Film.

Skarup, Povl. "Le physétère et l'Île Farouche de Rabelais." *Études rabelaisiennes* 6 (1965): 57–59. Print.

Smith, Paul. "Rabelais and the Art of Memory." *Rabelais in Context*. Ed. Barbara C. Bowen. Birmingham: Summa, 1993. 41–54. Print.

———. "Voix et geste chez Rabelais." *Literaturwissenschaftliches Jahrbuch im Auftrage des Görres-Gesellschaft* 33 (1992): 133–43. Print.

———. *Voyage et écriture: Étude sur le* Quart livre *de Rabelais*. Geneva: Droz, 1987. Print.

Snyder, Jon R. *Writing the Scene of Speaking: Theories of Dialogue in the Late Italian Renaissance*. Stanford: Stanford UP, 1989. Print.

Les songes drolatiques de Pantagruel. Introd. Michel Jeanneret. Geneva: Droz, 2004. Print.

The Song of Roland. Trans. and introd. Glyn Burgess. London: Penguin, 1990. Print.

Spenser, Edmund. *The Fairy Queen*. *The Norton Anthology of English Literature*. 7th ed. New York: Norton, 2000. 624–771. Print.

Stallybrass, Peter, and Allon White. *The Politics and Poetics of Transgression*. London: Metheun, 1986. Print.

Stapfer, Paul. *Rabelais: Sa personne, son génie, son œuvre*. Paris: Colin, 1889. Print.

Stephens, Walter. *Demon Lovers: Witchcraft, Sex, and the Crisis of Belief.* Chicago: U of Chicago P, 2002. Print.

———. *Giants in Those Days: Folklore, Ancient History, and Nationalism.* Lincoln: U of Nebraska P, 1989. Print.

———. "When Pope Noah Ruled the Etruscans: Annius of Viterbo and His Forged *Antiquities*." *Studia Humanitatis: Essays in Honor of Salvatore Camporeale*. Ed. Stephens. Spec. issue of *MLN* 119.1 supp. (2004): 201–23. Print.

Stewart, Susan. *On Longing: Narratives of the Miniature, the Gigantic, the Souvenir, the Collection*. 1984. Durham: Duke UP, 1993. Print.

Suidas. *Suidae Lexicon*. Ed. Immanuel Bekker. Berlin: Reimer, 1854. Print.

Swift, Jonathan. *Gulliver's Travels*. Ed. Robert Greenberg. 2nd ed. New York: Norton, 1970. Print.

Tetel, Marcel. *Études sur le comique de Rabelais*. Florence: Olschki, 1964. Print.

Tierney, Brian. *Rights, Laws and Infallibility in Medieval Thought*. Aldershot: Variorum, 1997. Print.

Tomasik, Timothy. "Textual Tastes: The Invention of Culinary Literature in Early Modern France." Diss. Harvard U, 2003. Print.

Tomkins, Jane P., ed. *Reader-Response Criticism: From Formalism to Post-structuralism*. Baltimore: Johns Hopkins UP, 1980. Print.

Tutuola, Amos. *The Palm-Wine Drinkard*. London: Faber, 1957. Print.

Uccello, Paolo. *Niccolò Mauruzi da Tolentino at the Battle of San Romano*. c. 1438–40. Tempura and oil on wood. Natl. Gallery, London.

Ullmann, Walter. *The Individual and Society in the Middle Ages*. Baltimore: Johns Hopkins UP, 1966. Print.

Valéry, Paul. *Poésies*. Paris: Gallimard, 1942. Print.

Venuti, Lawrence. "Translation, Community, Utopia." *The Translation Studies Reader*. Ed. Venuti. New York: Routledge, 2004. 482–502. Print.

Vergil. *Eclogues [and] Georgics [and] Aeneid 1–6*. Ed. G. P. Goold. Trans. H. R. Fairclough. Cambridge: Harvard UP, 1999. Print. Loeb Classical Lib.

Vesalius, Andreas. *De Humani Corporis Fabrica Libri Septem*. Brussels: Culture et Civilisation, 1964. Print.

Veyrin-Forrer, Jeanne. "Fabriquer un livre au XVIe siècle." Martin and Chartier 336–69.

Vico, Giambattista. *The New Science*. Trans. Thomas Goddard Bergin and Max Harold Fisch. 1948. Ithaca: Cornell UP, 1984. Print.

Virgilio, Johannus de. "Giovanni del Virgilio espositore delle *Metamorfosi*." *Allegorie librorum Ovidii Metamorphoseos*. Ed. Fausto Ghisalberti. *Giornale dantesco* 34.4 (1933): 43–107. Print.

Weinberg, Florence M. *The Wine and the Will: Rabelais's Bacchic Christianity*. Detroit: Wayne State UP, 1972. Print.

———. "Written on the Leaves: Rabelais and the Sibylline Tradition." *Renaissance Quarterly* 43.4 (1990): 709–30. Print.

Wey-Gómez, Nicolás. *The Tropics of Empire: Why Columbus Sailed South to the Indies*. Cambridge: MIT P, 2008. Print.

Whitman, Jon. *Allegory: The Dynamics of an Ancient and Medieval Technique*. Cambridge: Harvard UP, 1987. Print.

Williams, Wes. "'Being in the Middle': Translation, Transition, and the 'Early Modern.'" *Paragraph* 29.1 (2006): 27–39. Print.

Woodward, David, ed. *The History of Cartography 3: The European Renaissance*. Chicago: U of Chicago P, 2007. Print.

———. "Roger Bacon's Terrestrial Coordinate System." *Annals of the Association of American Geographers* 80.1 (1990): 109–22. Print.

Worth-Stylianou, Valerie. "Translations from Latin into French in the Renaissance." *The Classical Heritage in France*. Ed. Gerald Sandy. Leiden: Brill, 2002. 137–64. Print.

"X-Cops." Writ. Vince Gilligan. Dir. Michael W. Watkins. *The X-Files.* Fox. 20 Feb. 2000. Television. Season 7, episode 12.

Zaercher, Véronique. *Le dialogue rabelaisien. Le* Tiers livre *exemplaire*. Geneva: Droz, 2000. Print.

Zegura, Elizabeth Chesney, ed. *The Rabelais Encyclopedia*. Westport: Greenwood, 2004. Print.

———. "Toward a Feminist Reading of Rabelais." *Journal of Medieval and Renaissance Studies* 15.1 (1985); 124–34. Print.

Zegura, Elizabeth Chesney, and Marcel Tetel. *Rabelais Revisited*. New York: Twayne, 1993. Print.

INDEX

Modern Language Association of America

Approaches to Teaching World Literature

Achebe's Things Fall Apart. Ed. Bernth Lindfors. 1991.
Arthurian Tradition. Ed. Maureen Fries and Jeanie Watson. 1992.
Atwood's The Handmaid's Tale *and Other Works*. Ed. Sharon R. Wilson, Thomas B. Friedman, and Shannon Hengen. 1996.
Austen's Emma. Ed. Marcia McClintock Folsom. 2004.
Austen's Pride and Prejudice. Ed. Marcia McClintock Folsom. 1993.
Balzac's Old Goriot. Ed. Michal Peled Ginsburg. 2000.
Baudelaire's Flowers of Evil. Ed. Laurence M. Porter. 2000.
Beckett's Waiting for Godot. Ed. June Schlueter and Enoch Brater. 1991.
Beowulf. Ed. Jess B. Bessinger, Jr., and Robert F. Yeager. 1984.
Blake's Songs of Innocence and of Experience. Ed. Robert F. Gleckner and Mark L. Greenberg. 1989.
Boccaccio's Decameron. Ed. James H. McGregor. 2000.
British Women Poets of the Romantic Period. Ed. Stephen C. Behrendt and Harriet Kramer Linkin. 1997.
Charlotte Brontë's Jane Eyre. Ed. Diane Long Hoeveler and Beth Lau. 1993.
Emily Brontë's Wuthering Heights. Ed. Sue Lonoff and Terri A. Hasseler. 2006.
Byron's Poetry. Ed. Frederick W. Shilstone. 1991.
Camus's The Plague. Ed. Steven G. Kellman. 1985.
Writings of Bartolomé de Las Casas. Ed. Santa Arias and Eyda M. Merediz. 2008.
Cather's My Ántonia. Ed. Susan J. Rosowski. 1989.
Cervantes' Don Quixote. Ed. Richard Bjornson. 1984.
Chaucer's Canterbury Tales. Ed. Joseph Gibaldi. 1980.
Chaucer's Troilus and Criseyde *and the Shorter Poems*. Ed. Tison Pugh and Angela Jane Weisl. 2006.
Chopin's The Awakening. Ed. Bernard Koloski. 1988.
Coleridge's Poetry and Prose. Ed. Richard E. Matlak. 1991.
Collodi's Pinocchio *and Its Adaptations.* Ed. Michael Sherberg. 2006.
Conrad's "Heart of Darkness" and "The Secret Sharer." Ed. Hunt Hawkins and Brian W. Shaffer. 2002.
Dante's Divine Comedy. Ed. Carole Slade. 1982.
Defoe's Robinson Crusoe. Ed. Maximillian E. Novak and Carl Fisher. 2005.
DeLillo's White Noise. Ed. Tim Engles and John N. Duvall. 2006.
Dickens's Bleak House. Ed. John O. Jordan and Gordon Bigelow. 2009.
Dickens's David Copperfield. Ed. Richard J. Dunn. 1984.
Dickinson's Poetry. Ed. Robin Riley Fast and Christine Mack Gordon. 1989.
Narrative of the Life of Frederick Douglass. Ed. James C. Hall. 1999.
Duras's Ourika. Ed. Mary Ellen Birkett and Christopher Rivers. 2009.
Early Modern Spanish Drama. Ed. Laura R. Bass and Margaret R. Greer. 2006.

Eliot's Middlemarch. Ed. Kathleen Blake. 1990.
Eliot's Poetry and Plays. Ed. Jewel Spears Brooker. 1988.
Shorter Elizabethan Poetry. Ed. Patrick Cheney and Anne Lake Prescott. 2000.
Ellison's Invisible Man. Ed. Susan Resneck Parr and Pancho Savery. 1989.
English Renaissance Drama. Ed. Karen Bamford and Alexander Leggatt. 2002.
Works of Louise Erdrich. Ed. Gregg Sarris, Connie A. Jacobs, and James R. Giles. 2004.
Dramas of Euripides. Ed. Robin Mitchell-Boyask. 2002.
Faulkner's As I Lay Dying. Ed. Patrick O'Donnell and Lynda Zwinger. 2011.
Faulkner's The Sound and the Fury. Ed. Stephen Hahn and Arthur F. Kinney. 1996.
Fitzgerald's The Great Gatsby. Ed. Jackson R. Bryer and Nancy P. VanArsdale. 2009.
Flaubert's Madame Bovary. Ed. Laurence M. Porter and Eugene F. Gray. 1995.
García Márquez's One Hundred Years of Solitude. Ed. María Elena de Valdés and Mario J. Valdés. 1990.
Gilman's "The Yellow Wall-Paper" and Herland. Ed. Denise D. Knight and Cynthia J. Davis. 2003.
Goethe's Faust. Ed. Douglas J. McMillan. 1987.
Gothic Fiction: The British and American Traditions. Ed. Diane Long Hoeveler and Tamar Heller. 2003.
Poetry of John Gower. Ed. R. F. Yeager and Brian W. Gastle. 2011.
Grass's The Tin Drum. Ed. Monika Shafi. 2008.
H.D.'s Poetry and Prose. Ed. Annette Debo and Lara Vetter. 2011.
Hebrew Bible as Literature in Translation. Ed. Barry N. Olshen and Yael S. Feldman. 1989.
Homer's Iliad *and* Odyssey. Ed. Kostas Myrsiades. 1987.
Hurston's Their Eyes Were Watching God *and Other Works*. Ed. John Lowe. 2009.
Ibsen's A Doll House. Ed. Yvonne Shafer. 1985.
Henry James's Daisy Miller *and* The Turn of the Screw. Ed. Kimberly C. Reed and Peter G. Beidler. 2005.
Works of Samuel Johnson. Ed. David R. Anderson and Gwin J. Kolb. 1993.
Joyce's Ulysses. Ed. Kathleen McCormick and Erwin R. Steinberg. 1993.
Works of Sor Juana Inés de la Cruz. Ed. Emilie L. Bergmann and Stacey Schlau. 2007.
Kafka's Short Fiction. Ed. Richard T. Gray. 1995.
Keats's Poetry. Ed. Walter H. Evert and Jack W. Rhodes. 1991.
Kingston's The Woman Warrior. Ed. Shirley Geok-lin Lim. 1991.
Lafayette's The Princess of Clèves. Ed. Faith E. Beasley and Katharine Ann Jensen. 1998.
Works of D. H. Lawrence. Ed. M. Elizabeth Sargent and Garry Watson. 2001.
Lazarillo de Tormes *and the Picaresque Tradition*. Ed. Anne J. Cruz. 2009.
Lessing's The Golden Notebook. Ed. Carey Kaplan and Ellen Cronan Rose. 1989.
Mann's Death in Venice *and Other Short Fiction*. Ed. Jeffrey B. Berlin. 1992.
Marguerite de Navarre's Heptameron. Ed. Colette H. Winn. 2007.
Medieval English Drama. Ed. Richard K. Emmerson. 1990.

Melville's Moby-Dick. Ed. Martin Bickman. 1985.
Metaphysical Poets. Ed. Sidney Gottlieb. 1990.
Miller's Death of a Salesman. Ed. Matthew C. Roudané. 1995.
Milton's Paradise Lost. Ed. Galbraith M. Crump. 1986.
Milton's Shorter Poetry and Prose. Ed. Peter C. Herman. 2007.
Molière's Tartuffe *and Other Plays*. Ed. James F. Gaines and Michael S. Koppisch. 1995.
Momaday's The Way to Rainy Mountain. Ed. Kenneth M. Roemer. 1988.
Montaigne's Essays. Ed. Patrick Henry. 1994.
Novels of Toni Morrison. Ed. Nellie Y. McKay and Kathryn Earle. 1997.
Murasaki Shikibu's The Tale of Genji. Ed. Edward Kamens. 1993.
Nabokov's Lolita. Ed. Zoran Kuzmanovich and Galya Diment. 2008.
Works of Tim O'Brien. Ed. Alex Vernon and Catherine Calloway. 2010.
Works of Ovid and the Ovidian Tradition. Ed. Barbara Weiden Boyd and Cora Fox. 2010.
Poe's Prose and Poetry. Ed. Jeffrey Andrew Weinstock and Tony Magistrale. 2008.
Pope's Poetry. Ed. Wallace Jackson and R. Paul Yoder. 1993.
Proust's Fiction and Criticism. Ed. Elyane Dezon-Jones and Inge Crosman Wimmers. 2003.
Puig's Kiss of the Spider Woman. Ed. Daniel Balderston and Francine Masiello. 2007.
Pynchon's The Crying of Lot 49 *and Other Works.* Ed. Thomas H. Schaub. 2008.
Works of François Rabelais. Ed. Todd W. Reeser and Floyd Gray. 2011.
Novels of Samuel Richardson. Ed. Lisa Zunshine and Jocelyn Harris. 2006.
Rousseau's Confessions *and* Reveries of the Solitary Walker. Ed. John C. O'Neal and Ourida Mostefai. 2003.
Scott's Waverley Novels. Ed. Evan Gottlieb and Ian Duncan. 2009.
Shakespeare's Hamlet. Ed. Bernice W. Kliman. 2001.
Shakespeare's King Lear. Ed. Robert H. Ray. 1986.
Shakespeare's Othello. Ed. Peter Erickson and Maurice Hunt. 2005.
Shakespeare's Romeo and Juliet. Ed. Maurice Hunt. 2000.
Shakespeare's The Tempest *and Other Late Romances.* Ed. Maurice Hunt. 1992.
Shelley's Frankenstein. Ed. Stephen C. Behrendt. 1990.
Shelley's Poetry. Ed. Spencer Hall. 1990.
Sir Gawain and the Green Knight. Ed. Miriam Youngerman Miller and Jane Chance. 1986.
Song of Roland. Ed. William W. Kibler and Leslie Zarker Morgan. 2006.
Spenser's Faerie Queene. Ed. David Lee Miller and Alexander Dunlop. 1994.
Stendhal's The Red and the Black. Ed. Dean de la Motte and Stirling Haig. 1999.
Sterne's Tristram Shandy. Ed. Melvyn New. 1989.
Stowe's Uncle Tom's Cabin. Ed. Elizabeth Ammons and Susan Belasco. 2000.
Swift's Gulliver's Travels. Ed. Edward J. Rielly. 1988.
Teresa of Ávila and the Spanish Mystics. Ed. Alison Weber. 2009.
Thoreau's Walden *and Other Works*. Ed. Richard J. Schneider. 1996.

Tolstoy's Anna Karenina. Ed. Liza Knapp and Amy Mandelker. 2003.
Vergil's Aeneid. Ed. William S. Anderson and Lorina N. Quartarone. 2002.
Voltaire's Candide. Ed. Renée Waldinger. 1987.
Whitman's Leaves of Grass. Ed. Donald D. Kummings. 1990.
Wiesel's Night. Ed. Alan Rosen. 2007.
Works of Oscar Wilde. Ed. Philip E. Smith II. 2008.
Woolf's Mrs. Dalloway. Ed. Eileen Barrett and Ruth O. Saxton. 2009.
Woolf's To the Lighthouse. Ed. Beth Rigel Daugherty and Mary Beth Pringle. 2001.
Wordsworth's Poetry. Ed. Spencer Hall, with Jonathan Ramsey. 1986.
Wright's Native Son. Ed. James A. Miller. 1997.